MEETING OF MINDS

MEETING OF MINDS
INTELLECTUAL AND RELIGIOUS INTERACTION
IN EAST ASIAN TRADITIONS OF THOUGHT

Essays in Honor of Wing-tsit Chan
and
William Theodore de Bary

Edited by Irene Bloom and Joshua A. Fogel

COLUMBIA UNIVERSITY PRESS
New York

Columbia University Press
Publishers Since 1893
New York   Chichester, West Sussex
Copyright © 1997 Columbia University Press
All rights reserved

Library of Congress Cataloging-in-Publication Data

Meeting of minds: intellectual and religious interaction in East Asian traditions of thought: essays in honor of Wing-tsit Chan and William Theodore de Bary / edited by Irene Bloom and Joshua A. Fogel.
   p. cm.
   Includes bibliographical references and index.
   ISBN 0-231-10352-2 (alk. paper).
   1. Philosophy, Confucian.   2. Philosophy, Oriental.   3. East Asia — Religion.
I. Bloom, Irene.   II. Fogel, Joshua A., 1950–
B127.C65M44   1996
181—dc20   95–20957
                                         CIP

Casebound editions of Columbia University Press books are printed on permanent and
   durable acid-free paper.
Printed in the United States of America
c 10 9 8 7 6 5 4 3 2 1

CONTENTS

ACKNOWLEDGMENTS

This volume has had many benefactors. The editors would like particularly to thank three consummate scholars—Miwa Kai, Pei-yi Wu, and Philip Yampolsky—for their patience and help with correcting and smoothing translations and untangling all manner of textual knots. Samuel H. Yamashita offered expert guidance. Martin Amster provided invaluable help with research and with the preparation of the typescript and glossaries as well as with translation. Mariana Stiles supported our efforts in ways too numerous to detail and with a devotion to Professor Chan and Professor de Bary that all the contributors share.

IB and JAF

MEETING OF MINDS

INTRODUCTION

This volume is dedicated to Wing-tsit Chan and William Theodore de Bary in appreciation of their outstanding contributions to the study of East Asian thought and religion. It is certainly unusual to honor two scholars together in this way; it is even more unusual to find two scholars, both leaders and innovators in their field, whose working relationship over the course of almost half a century has been so close and productive. Each working in his own distinct style and mode, and also contributing to the work of the other, they have, out of their deep respect for one another and the remarkable complementarity of their efforts, given so much in turn to their students, colleagues, and the larger community of scholars. Together, they have both defined and immeasurably deepened the field of Neo-Confucian studies in the West, creating new scholarly resources and opening the way for future generations of scholars.

In the variety of endeavors in which Wing-tsit Chan and William Theodore de Bary collaborated over the course of many years, perhaps none has been more important than teaching. For many years, and until just two years before his death in August 1994, Professor Chan came to New York weekly to share with Professor de Bary instructional responsibility for a graduate seminar in Neo-Confucian thought at Columbia. Many of those whose contributions appear in this collection know, as beneficiaries, what an incomparable gift the association was — for us but also, quite obviously, for them as well. That work is now being continued by Professor de Bary with other collaborators; the fact that the wise and generous spirit of Professor Chan somehow seems to remain present suggests that great gifts are also long-lasting.

Different as their individual work has been, these two scholars also shared a great deal, including a commitment to encouraging broad communication and collaboration in the field of East Asian thought and religion and a recognition of the value of sustained working relationships with colleagues in Taiwan, Hong Kong, Korea, Japan, and, more recently, in the People's Republic of China. It is appropriate, and the editors are most grateful, that the contributors to this volume include two of the most distinguished Japanese scholars of Neo-Confucianism, Okada Takehiko and Minamoto Ryōen — for many years, honored colleagues and friends.

In addition to having cooperated in scholarly projects, practiced an interactive form of teaching, and maintained an international scholarly exchange, Wing-tsit Chan and Wm. Theodore de Bary have been visionaries in their own work, always mindful of the larger implications of the topics they addressed for contemporary East Asia and, more broadly, for the conduct of human life in "the wide house of the world." Theirs was a genuine and immensely productive "meeting of minds."

Mindful of their example, personal as well as scholarly, the contributors to this volume have examined some of the ways that "meetings of minds" have, over the course of centuries, contributed to the particular character of the larger East Asian tradition in which, amid all of the richness and diversity, certain common elements still seem to figure quite prominently. There can be little doubt that it is in the interactions between different traditions within cultures, as well as in cross-cultural encounter, that we discover some of the most fascinating dimensions in the history of thought and religion. Patterns of interaction within the East Asian culture area may be distinctive, however, for several reasons, including: (1) a conception of the nature of religious authority quite different from that found in Judaism, Christianity, Islam, or Hinduism; (2) the absence of a clear distinction between ecclesiastical and secular authority (between "church" and "state") or between religious and secular realms of experience; and (3) an enduring focus on the relation between knowledge and action and an often self-conscious concern with practical experience or practicality as the criterion for judging between correct or incorrect beliefs.

In the absence of an idea of revelation — of a revealed truth accessible either to a particular people or, potentially, through a dispersal of the religious message, to the entire human community — Confucians tended to see truth as something discovered within individual human minds and in the course of ordinary experience. Their concern was not with a message that had first to be accepted and then delivered to those who had yet to hear it but, rather, with a record of what the most worthy individuals of the past had thought and done and a reflection on what all human beings could be expected to do in the course of their own lives through fully realizing their own humanity. One might suggest that, with a historical record occupying the place that revealed truth occupied in the Western monotheistic traditions — and, in a different sense, in Hinduism as well — there was remarkable latitude for exchange and interaction among traditions. No doubt because of the centrality of individual and cultural experience, there seems to have been a persistent tendency among Confucians to base judgments concerning the acceptance or rejection of alternative ideas largely on assessments of how those ideas might be expected to condition or determine human experience or to affect the conduct of ordinary life. The essays that follow contain many examples of this concern for the practical implications of ideas and of resort to the test of experience rather than appeal to a more abstract notion of truth or to the sanction of a religious authority.

Here we have chosen to focus on interactions between the Confucian and Neo-Confucian traditions and other traditions of thought and religion at critical junctures in the history of China and Japan. One of the shared interests in these essays is how Confucianism interacted over time with other traditions — including Mohism, Taoism, Buddhism, and geomantic thought in China, and Buddhism, Shintō, nativist, and military thought in Japan — and how these interactions contributed to reconfigurations of the intellectual and religious landscape over time. Our examples are, of course, suggestive rather than exhaustive. Together, however, these essays provide a perspective on the dynamics of intellectual and religious encounter within the individual cultures of East Asia, including the range of responses within the Confucian tradition to challenges from "without," the ways in which culture and tradition were understood to be related, and the ways in which Confucian criticism of other traditions and appropriation from those traditions were often part of the same complex and mingled response. Intellectual and religious interactions with other traditions seem quite clearly to have contributed to the formation of the larger and more encompassing visions that emerged within the Confucian tradition at certain junctures and to the narrowing or focusing of the Confucian vision that occurred at others, yet it would be an oversimplification to suggest that the more encompassing visions necessarily issued from moments when Confucianism was in a more confident and expansive mode or that the narrowing or focusing of vision came about when it was in a more defensive posture.

Confucianism has often been represented by Western historians — and, more recently, under Marxist influence, by many Chinese historians — as fundamentally conservative. One of the most telling points to emerge from the essays in this collection is that a great deal of countervailing evidence, emerging in a variety of contexts, indicates the extraordinary openness of the tradition as it evolved in both China and Japan. No doubt one may observe in much of traditional Chinese thought a rhetorical tendency to invoke historical precedents and the established authority of the classics. It is not difficult to understand how this rhetorical tendency could be interpreted as revealing a retrospective cast of mind and, with it, a disinclination to accept new ideas or approaches to human problems. Such a retrospective cast of mind, reflecting a reverence for the achievements of the sages and worthies of antiquity and for the assembled resources of the culture, is no doubt a recognizable part of the Chinese tradition, as no less a Confucian than Hsün Tzu observed as early as the third century BCE. However, to assume that this retrospective tendency is incompatible with receptivity to change and the capacity for adaptation is at variance with a wealth of evidence presented in these essays.

Some authors discussing developments within the Chinese tradition suggest an inclination of Confucians and Neo-Confucians — Mencius and Chu Hsi being notable among them — to borrow at deeper levels and steadily to enlarge the Confucian vision. This is, of course, even more true of the Confucian tradition as it evolved alongside Buddhism, Shintō, and nativist thought in Japan. That there was a tendency from the beginning of the Tokugawa period to amalgamate Confucian and nativist elements of thought is the central point of Peter Nosco's essay; that *shingaku* (Ch. *hsin-hsüeh*), or the Neo-Confucian learning of the mind, was conducive to the modernization of Japan in cultivating a "spiritually independent mind-and-heart" and promoting cultural receptivity among the Japanese is a major theme of the essay by Minamoto Ryōen.

The idea of "visions," suggesting integrative apprehensions of reality, may be understood to imply religious modes of understanding and experience.

Taken as a whole, these essays support a tendency of recent scholarship that brings out the deeply religious dimensions of Confucian and Neo-Confucian thought and practice. What comes through here in particular is the tendency to openness and receptivity in Confucian religiosity rather than an impulse to narrowness, rigidity, or exclusivity.

Irene Bloom examines three interpretations of *jen*, or humaneness, in the thought of Confucius, Mencius, and Chu Hsi. Considering the interactive contexts in which these ideas took shape, she suggests that *jen* may be understood as an evolving vision of human and, ultimately, of cosmic relatedness. On this reading of Chu Hsi, his thought is characterized not only by openness and receptivity but by a philosophically significant, if unacknowledged, departure from Mencian premises. Rodney L. Taylor discusses Chu Hsi's attitudes toward the meditative practice of quiet-sitting, a practice inspired by Buddhism but, clearly, creatively adapted for Confucian purposes and toward the goal of more effective conduct of life in the world.

Patricia Ebrey surveys attitudes toward geomancy among some leading Sung Neo-Confucians, distinguishing between the essentially skeptical views of Ssu-ma Kuang, the Ch'eng brothers, and Chang Chiu-ch'eng, on the one hand, and the more religiously receptive view of Chu Hsi, on the other. Julia Ching examines Chu Hsi's responses to both philosophical and religious Taoism, concluding that Chu "turned primarily to Taoist philosophy and religion for expanding his understanding of the universe" and that "he used what he found, as data and material, to create something new—his own philosophical system, in which metaphysical ideas are dominant, and a place can be found for cosmology and metaphysics as well as for the philosophy of human nature and the practical doctrine of cultivation."

A great deal of work has been done in recent years on religious syncretism in China, especially during the Ming period. Chün-fang Yü's essay offers a new perspective on syncretism in the realm of popular religion by describing the cult of Kuan-yin in the Ming and early Ch'ing dynasties, examining the process of sinicization of this most revered of bodhisattvas, and raising the fascinating question of whether this sinicization represents a case of "the Confucianization of Buddhism." Attention is also devoted in this volume to syncretism as it presented itself in an earlier phase—in the twelfth century—as well as to what now appears to have been syncretism's closing chapter in the eighteenth century. The work of Koichi Shinohara, probing the interactions between the Southern Sung scholar-official Tseng K'ai and the Buddhist leader Ta-hui, opens up a new approach to the phenomenon of religious syncretism in the Southern Sung. Professor Shinohara suggests what he feels may have been the ultimate appeal of Buddhism to Sung Confucian scholars: a particular kind of freedom of spirit. Reflecting on eighteenth-century developments, and the "collapse of the unitary vision of Chinese religion" some six centuries later, Judith A. Berling sees the deepening repressiveness of the Manchu dynasty and the gradual but steady erosion of religious openness and freedom as one explanation for the failure of the integrative spirit and the loss of an attendant sense of cultural unity in Ch'ing China.

A different picture emerges in Japan, and it becomes possible, through attending to the differences in the Chinese and the Japanese experience, to gain a more adequate appreciation of the potential of ideas in history. Professor Minamoto's essay offers a new perspective on the reception of Japanese Neo-Confucianism in the early Tokugawa period, offering the perception that, amid all the diverse conceptual input from China, the common element in what was received in Japan, and that became crucial to the Japanese appropriation of Neo-Confucianism, was, again, *shingaku*, the learning of the mind. *Shingaku*, as Professor Minamoto understands it, "was the system of thought that in the early Tokugawa period advocated the unity of the Three Teachings." As he sees it, "The system of thought underlying the mind-and-heart made possible the coexistence of numerous schools of thought." "We cannot deny that *shingaku* gave to Japanese thought and culture an incomplete syncretism," he continues, "while by the same token creating, when supported by a transcendent force, the possibility for the unification of the diversity within the great richness of Japanese thought and culture." The problem that Professor Berling has identified as fundamental to China's early modern experience — the loss of a unitary cultural vision — takes on a larger significance in the light of Professor Minamoto's observation that in Japan, by contrast, "modernization proceeded smoothly not because Japan had a single, solitary culture, but because that culture was a unity amid diversity." Both the unity and the diversity were, in his view, in some sense attributable to the influence of Neo-Confucian *shingaku*.

Another dimension of the comparison between the Chinese and the Japanese experience becomes apparent in Peter Nosco's essay, especially when read in the light of Judith Berling's analysis of developments in eighteenth-century China. Whereas Professor Berling suggests that the eighteenth century in China witnessed the "collapse" of a unitary vision, Professor Nosco sees a parallel development in eighteenth-century Japan as no more than an anomalous lapse into an adversarial relationship between Confucian and nativist thinkers. This divisiveness, as he shows, was to be overcome in the late eighteenth and early nineteenth centuries through "the successful penetration of a host of eighteenth-century nativist assumptions into the broader scholarly discourse," a trend furthered especially by scholars associated with the Mito learning.

Okada Takehiko's essay, "Mastery and the Mind," is an exploration of East Asian views of the mind and of the intimate relation in the East Asian context between spiritual awareness and modes of praxis and a case study of creative interactions between Taoism, Buddhism, and Neo-Confucianism. Focusing particularly on the martial arts tradition in Japan and on the rise of *bushidō*, Professor Okada shows the subtle interplay of Neo-Confucianism and Zen Buddhism with older martial arts traditions. His vision is of an Eastern spirituality that is also practicality, with skill or "mastery" being a "method of the mind" and interioristic and quietistic tendencies being allied to practical effort (*jissenteki kufū*). This practicality, he suggests, is based on a naturalism (Ch. *tzu-jan chu-i*; Jap. *shizen shugi*) that reveals itself in "a uniquely tranquil passion that attempts a return to Nature."

The final essay in the volume, by Joshua Fogel, presents Japanese views of China in the late nineteenth and early twentieth centuries. In examining the travel account of the Confucian scholar Uno Tetsuto, he reflects on the kind of cognitive dissonance that may occur when vision and reality diverge. Uno's scholarly vision of a Confucian China was crowded and jostled by the harsh realities of ordinary life in the waning years of the Ch'ing dynasty. To him, the real, living Chinese people did not seem in any way to be the true lineal descendants of Confucius; in his estimation it was the Japanese who were more filial disciples of the sage. Writing on the eve of Confucianism's first full-scale confrontation with major detractors in China, Uno was pointing both to the tragedy of the disjunction between vision and reality in the birthplace of Confucianism and to the continuing and vital relevance of Confucian visions — over a long span of time and far beyond China's borders.

This is a book without conclusions — appropriately enough, since the subject is vast and the "meetings of minds" that have fascinated us continue to go on in new forms even today, with results that have yet to be determined. All the contributors to this volume are grateful for their contact with two great teachers whose lives and research have contributed so much to ongoing discussions of the Confucian and Neo-Confucian traditions in the twentieth century and even to the preservation of those traditions in vital form, in readiness for the twenty-first.

IB
JAF
June 1995

Chapter One

THREE VISIONS OF *JEN*

IRENE BLOOM

Jen, or humaneness, is part of the primary Confucian vision and with *li*, or ritual, is perhaps the most characteristic expression of Confucian ethical consciousness. As *li* encompasses the spheres that in other traditions might be distinguished as aesthetic versus practical and the realms of experience that might be contrasted as sacred versus secular, *jen*, similarly complex, involves both an ideal of human behavior and an insight into the human condition. As an ideal, *jen* expresses the characteristic Confucian concern with the moral possibilities involved in the human capacity for mutual responsiveness. As an insight, *jen* is the distinctively Confucian angle of vision on the psychological realities of being human. What human beings should become is always understood in relation to what they originally *are*, and, while ideas of human nature and visions of humaneness may change over time, ideal and reality are always recognized to be co-implicated. This, more than any other tendency, may define Confucian ethical thought, characterize it over time, and distinguish it from the orientations found in several other traditions: that it is so profoundly conditioned by the disposition to reflect on the connections between moral ideals and psychological realities.

Figuring into this co-implication of the ideal and the actual is a deep and abiding Confucian respect for human emotions. Again, like ritual, a structure of belief and practice that is constructed around the human emotions, *jen* is also concerned with the emotions and emotional control. This is a characteristic of *jen* that, while differently manifested, may be observed in virtually every major text of classical Confucianism and in the most central texts of the Neo-Confucian tradition as well. Even as views of the emotions change over time, and as the vision of *jen* evolves along with Confucian responses to the challenges of a changing life and of alternative philosophies, emotional control—involving both self-control and the potential to exert control over others—remains a constant feature of *jen*.

In exploring the relation between *jen* and the emotions, the focus here will be on the *Analects*, the *Mencius*, and Chu Hsi's "Jen shuo" (Discussion of Jen). Such a focus results not in a survey of this complex subject but merely in a sounding of three important visions of *jen*.[1] I suggest that, despite the continuity of concern with the emotions and the lack of surface ripples of disputatiousness to rile the seemingly calm philosophical waters, the changes in the concept of *jen* from Confucius to Mencius and from Mencius to Chu Hsi are greater than might initially appear. A considerable change occurs between the *jen* of Confucius—which is associated with fortitude, restraint, and self-discipline and the conviction that emotional control is morally crucial though psychologically difficult—and the *jen* of Mencius—which is associated with compassion, maturation, a sense of positive emotional energy, and a persuasion that sympathetic responsiveness to the needs of others is both morally fundamental and psychologically natural. Further, while Chu Hsi believed that by recording the words of Confucius and Mencius he was preserving their tradition for a later age, an enormous philosophical change has occurred between the *jen* of Mencius, with its psychological naturalism, and the *jen* of Chu Hsi, with its metaphysical grounding and associations with creativity, generativity, order, and the weight of the Neo-Confucian concept of *li*, or principle. An attempt to reduce these three complex visions to any particular set of determinants would be misguided, but in the conclusion I shall suggest how the differences between Mencius and Confucius and between Chu Hsi and Mencius may be more intelligible in the light of the intellectual interactions in which Mencius and Chu Hsi were involved in their own times.

Confucius on Jen

In one of his most influential articles, "Chinese and Western Interpretations of Jen (Humanity)" (1975), Wing-tsit Chan explores some of the major problems and issues in the interpretation of *jen*, pointing to certain differences between the Chinese understanding of *jen* and Western approaches to the concept in the most significant scholarly literature of the late nineteenth and early twentieth centuries. One of Professor Chan's observations has to do with a change he sees as having emerged in the thought of Confucius — in Confucius' innovative perspective on *jen* as both "a particular virtue, along with other particular virtues like wisdom, liberality, etc."[2] and as "a general virtue which is basic, universal, and the source of all specific virtues."[3] He explains,

> Until the time of Confucius, the Chinese had not developed a concept of the general virtue which is universal and fundamental from which all particular virtues ensue. But Confucius was propagating a comprehensive ethical doctrine which must have a basic virtue on which all particular virtues are rooted.[4]

Without reviewing Professor Chan's argument in detail, I assume the validity of his observation about the transformation of the concept of *jen* that appears to be under way in the *Analects* and the importance of the perception that *jen* was becoming the focus of a more coherent or encompassing ethical perspective.

What could explain such a transformation? One suggestion might be that it developed out of the confluence of several currents in Confucian thought: (1) an intuition that human beings are by nature fundamentally alike; (2) an understanding that ethical behavior involves a sense of mutuality or reciprocity; (3) a deepening sense of interiority; (4) an increasingly conscious and self-conscious insight into the motivation underlying human behavior. I would not argue that any one of these currents is so unambiguously clear as to overrun the more obvious alternatives. These four tendencies seem, in fact, to coexist in the *Analects* with others, a reflection, perhaps, of their incipience in Confucius' thought, of the irreducible complexity of that thought, and possibly also of divergent understandings of it on the part of the recorders.

For example, the idea of the fundamental similarity among human beings is supported by several passages, including Confucius' famous statement about human nature in 17:2,[5] though, as Takeuchi Teruo has observed, much of the discussion of *jen* in the *Analects* seems to revolve around an attitude aptly described as moral elitism.[6] Likewise, while a sense of reciprocity seems fundamental to the Confucian notion of *jen*, Confucius is consistent in emphasizing the importance of autonomous judgment and personal commit-

ment on the part of the morally serious individual. And while there is abun-
dant evidence in the *Analects* for a deepening sense of interiority, Confucius
reveals at many points a deep and abiding sense for the importance of "external" appearance and demeanor as both a sign and a determinant of "internal"
states.

My exploration will focus on the third and fourth of these tendencies —
what I have described, following Takeuchi, as a deepening sense of interiority
and an increasingly self-conscious concern with motivation.[7] In particular, I
would like to suggest that Confucius' insight into the motivation underlying
actions — one of the aspects of his personality and teaching that evidently most
compelled the respect of his disciples — profoundly conditions his concept of
jen. His concern with what Professor Chan describes as a "basic virtue" goes
beyond particular overt actions to include the capacity of individuals to be
aware of their own motivation and consciously to attend to the discipline of
their intentions and emotions.

Confucius' circumspection in discussing *jen* may have something to do
with this concern on his part with motivation. *Analects* 9:1 , surely one of the
most puzzling statements in the text, records that the Master seldom spoke of
"profit," "destiny," or *jen*. The fact that the reasons for this reticence are
nowhere specified, while the text actually contains numerous references to
jen, has intrigued commentators and inspired ongoing debate over the centuries.[8] This frequent recurrence of an idea about which Confucius "seldom
spoke" is plausibly, if only partially, explained by the fact that his disciples
questioned him so persistently about *jen*, undeterred and perhaps even im-
pelled by his spare, laconic responses to their inquiries.[9] They may have
become aware that *jen* was fundamental to his thinking about what it means
to be human. And Confucius, many of whose utterances seem to have been
conditioned by awareness or anticipation of their impact on his interlocutors,
may have been restrained by a certain kind of psychological insight from
allowing *jen* to become too accessible.

Pressed about whether a particular individual might be considered to
exemplify *jen*, Confucius usually reserved judgment, as if wary of allowing too
great a concession against the ideal.[10] Perhaps he sensed that to endorse the
nomination of a particular individual as an exemplar of *jen* might involve the
wrong kind of encouragement, possibly undermining the livelier realization
that *jen* involves ongoing effort and commitment over the course of a lifetime.[11] Definitions may provide resting places and may shelter limits, whereas
Confucius seems to envision *jen* as occupying an open moral space. He
emphasizes the undertaking of *jen* as the work of a lifetime, an endeavor
almost endless in its requirements. With Confucius, a lifetime begins to be an

intelligible unit, a span worthy of contemplation, particularly in the sense that the emotional control associated with *jen* is understood to involve a continuing project.[12]

When Confucius does speak of *jen*, he almost invariably does so in a cautionary rather than an expansive mode, associating it with self-restraint or self-control more than with sympathy or compassion. One sets one's will on *jen* (*chih yü jen*) (4:4) and applies one's strength to *jen* (*yung ch'i li yü jen*) (4:6). In response to Fan Ch'ih's question about *jen*, Confucius replies: "One who is *jen* is concerned first with what is difficult and only subsequently with success" (6:20). "Relinquishing arrogance, boasting, resentment, and covetousness" is acknowledged as "doing what is difficult," a necessary though not yet sufficient condition for behavior that might qualify as *jen* (14:2). Yen Yüan is told that "to control oneself and return to ritual propriety [*li*] is *jen*" (*k'o-chi fu-li wei jen*) (12:1).

Ssu-ma Niu, Confucius' interlocutor in *Analects* 12:3, is apparently perplexed on being told by Confucius that "the humane person is cautious in his speech" (*jen-che ch'i yen yeh jen*). Suspecting, perhaps, that caution in speech must be too minimal a requirement, and that Confucius may have been straining for the pun on *jen* (humaneness) and *jen* (chary of speech), he exclaims: "Cautious of speech! Is this what you mean by *jen*?" Confucius makes clear in his reply that "caution in speech" is not a definition of *jen* but a reminder of the difficulty involved in enacting it and of the danger entailed in allowing words to outpace actions: "When doing it is so difficult, how can one be without caution in speaking about it?"[13] Tseng-tzu's pun on *jen* (humaneness) and *jen* (a responsibility or burden) is more obvious; he is speaking in the pure Confucian idiom when he says: "The *shih* may not be without breadth and fortitude, for his burden is heavy and his way is long. *Jen* is the burden that he takes upon himself—is it not heavy? Only with death does his way end—is it not long?" (8:7).

Despite his reticence on the subject of *jen*, Confucius reveals enough of his own intuitions about it to make clear that it is an endeavor requiring perseverance and self-discipline and a responsibility that one must bear throughout the course of a lifetime. *Jen*, he seems to say, is a matter of the way we position ourselves, or the direction in which we are moving, a course determined by resolution, effort, and persistence. Interestingly, several statements about *jen* are cast in spatial terms. In 6:5 Yen Hui is remembered for having gone for "three months without his mind's departing (or being distanced) from *jen*" (*ch'i hsin san yüeh pu wei jen*).[14] In 7:29 Confucius asks, "Is *jen* far away? If I want *jen*, then *jen* arrives" (*jen yüan hu tsai; wo yü jen ssu jen chih i*).

Though translators have often been relatively free in rendering 6:28, sometimes introducing the notion of feeling or sentiment, Confucius does not
actually refer explicitly to feelings. Once again he relies on a spatial or
relational metaphor: "The ability to take what is near and grasp the analogy
can be called the direction of *jen*" (*neng chin ch'ü pi k'o wei jen chih fang yeh*).
While speaking about "grasping the analogy," he must surely be thinking of
human feelings, yet he does not mention the receptive qualities of sympathy,
empathy, and sensitivity to the needs of others — that is, qualities that draw the
individual out of himself and open him toward others. Rather, it seems clear
that he is thinking in terms of the moral commitment that derives from an
individual's own strength, resolution, and fortitude. *Jen* is at this point a matter
of a disciplined response, prompted less by something in the *other* than by the
cultivation of strength and emotional discipline within the self.

Confucius' response to Chung-kung's inquiry about *jen* includes what has
often been characterized as a "negative" statement of the "golden rule."[15] He
advises Chung-kung: "what you do not want for yourself, do not do to others"
(12:2). The fact that the statement takes a negative form may reflect a certain
psychological realism: to enjoin restraint from potentially harmful or hurtful
behaviors toward others is more practical than to demand positive responsiveness to their needs, an almost impossible assignment, even for the most
generously inclined. Given his intuition of a common human nature.[16] Confucius may have felt that human beings naturally have some awareness of
which behavior should be avoided because it might be injurious to others.
Even here he cannot have been unduly optimistic, however, because when
Tzu-kung invokes the same "golden rule," announcing his aspiration to follow
the urging of Confucius by not doing to others what he would not want done
to himself, the response is again cautionary: "Tz'u," the Master observes, "this
is not something to which you have attained" (5:11).[17]

A more positive approach to *jen* emerges in Confucius' response to Tzu-
chang's inquiry about *jen*, which earns the more forthcoming reply that one
who could carry out "the five" everywhere under Heaven could be considered
jen (17:6). Asked about "the five," he responds that they are respect, liberality,
fidelity, earnestness, and kindness (*kung, k'uan, hsin, min, hui*). He continues:
"If you are respectful, you will have no regret; if you are liberal, you will win
the multitude; if you are faithful, you will be trusted; if you are earnest, you
will be effective; if you are kind, you will be able to influence others."
Confucius seems confident that if an individual is able to practice these forms
of consideration such behavior must elicit positive responses from others, with
emotional self-control leading to control over others. Still, it is never his habit

to underestimate the difficulty of what is required to exert such control: "the five" constitute a fairly imposing prerequisite.

To take note of the difficulty that Confucius associated with the kinds of behavior associated with *jen* is not to imply that he was pessimistic about human moral capacity. The *Analects* is full of evidence that he was alive to the delights of learning, the pleasures of fellowship, the satisfaction of moral development, the joy of moral contentment as a grace to the simplest of lives.[18] Still, it would appear that *jen*, as he understood it, was not a particularly "warm" concept. Though it evidently involved the human need and capacity for interrelatedness, he seems to have associated it with strength, discipline, and the willingness to bear burdens, rather than with sensitivity, emotional responsiveness, or an effusion of fellow feeling.

In characterizing Confucius' view of *jen* Arthur Waley suggested that, of all the references to *jen* in the *Analects*, only two reflect a "tenderhearted" attitude, these being 12:22, in which Confucius answered Fan Ch'ih's question about *jen* by describing it as "loving people" (*ai jen*), and 17:21, in which he ruefully characterized the renegade disciple Tsai Wo as un-*jen* (*pu jen*) because he felt no compulsion to observe the three-year mourning for his parents.[19] Waley's observation seems valid; moreover, even in these two instances, with their overt invocation of emotion, the apparently "tenderhearted" attitude toward *jen*, is nonetheless also tough. Taken in context, Confucius' statement in 12:22 actually puts greater emphasis on the tough-minded art of "knowing people" than on the tenderhearted disposition of "loving people." Similarly, Tsai Wo's reluctance to devote himself fully to the practice of mourning seems to be regarded as a failure of dedication as much as want of a more "tenderhearted" filial sentiment. Mourning was a duty that, for Confucius, should be undertaken by a person out of a natural sense of reciprocity and gratitude to his parents for their nurturance of him during his own vulnerability in infancy. He assumes that failing to do what is prescribed by ritual (or doing what is proscribed by ritual) should make one feel uncomfortable or ill at ease. On ascertaining that Tsai Wo would "feel at ease" (*an*) with a shortened mourning period, the master knows that the disciple lacks the emotional discipline associated with *jen*.

In his work on the ancient meanings of the concept of *jen*, Takeuchi Teruo has pointed out that the oldest meanings of the concept of *jen*, as found in the *Shih-ching* (Classic of Poetry), have to do with external forms and appearances and with physical beauty. Professor Takeuchi suggests that this notion of *jen* was transmuted over time to refer to the internal beauty — or beauty of character — of the superior person. In parallel with this evolution there was an evolution of *jen* in its association with *jen* as a person or as a human being, and here the growth of associations included the notions of being humanlike, having human feelings, and feeling love. In his carefully documented opinion,

> These two senses (*jen* as virtue and *jen* as feeling) both entered into Confucius' discussions of *jen*, but there are many more passages in which Confucius spoke of *jen* as virtue. Moreover, Confucius thought of the virtue of *jen* as that which the *chün-tzu* should have. The *chün-tzu* represented manhood of the highest kind. By the time of Confucius the meaning of the term had become very broad, conveying the sense of a superior *shih* and an excellent man. The *jen* that was the beauty of character of the superior man naturally became the virtue that the *chün-tzu* had to have.[20]

The observations about *jen* offered here are, I believe, consistent with those of Professor Takeuchi; however, his "two senses" of *jen*, while distinguishable, may not, in the context of the *Analects*, be as discrete as might appear. Rather, it seems consistent with the evidence to argue that, for Confucius, *jen* is a virtue in two senses: (1) it is associated with a highly self-conscious awareness of one's own motivation and with emotional self-control; and (2) it is a form of emotional self-control so impressive that it carries with it the potential for control over the motivation and emotions of others. What might be added to Professor Takeuchi's characterization of the evolving sense of *jen* as implying "internal beauty of character" is that this beauty seems to be specifically identifiable with *emotional self-control*. And, in the sense that emotional self-control is understood to carry with it the potential for control over the emotions of others, the virtue of jen is connected with a concept of *te* (virtue) that has very ancient Chinese sources.

Mencius on Jen

Revering Confucius as he did, Mencius registered no disagreement with him either about *jen* or *hsing* (human nature), and perhaps felt none. Yet there are unmistakable differences in his approach to both *jen* and *hsing*. Mencius enlarges the primary Confucian vision of *jen*: his psychology is decidedly his own, as are his analogies and his tone. No one would say of him that he had the slightest reticence about speaking of *jen*: he speaks of it constantly, analyzes it, almost advertises it. He apparently cares little for *jen*'s connection with "caution in speech"[21] and is less inclined to think of it as a burden.[22] The homophone of *jen* that figures in his discussions is the more obvious and linguistically primitive one: *jen* as a human being.[23] "*Jen* is the human mind" (*jen jen hsin yeh*),[24] he says, and "*jen* is what it means to be human" (*jen yeh che jen yeh*).[25]

Like Confucius, Mencius recognizes the importance of the will (*chih*) and its role in setting priorities in an ordered and disciplined life,[26] yet he also has a discernibly different appreciation for the role of the emotions or affections in moral development. More directly or explicitly concerned with the emotions, which he understands to be shared by all human beings, and with the sense of mutuality that deepens among human beings through their awareness of shared emotions, Mencius seems to soften the Confucian emphasis on the difficulty of *jen*. The burden of *jen* is left behind or, at least, rests more lightly. *Jen* becomes more natural. The signs and promise of it are now discovered not only in the most resolute and dedicated among the moral elite but in everyone.

Even Kings Hui and Hsiang of Liang and King Hsüan of Ch'i, whom Mencius engages in the telling conversations recorded in Book 1, are encouraged to believe that humane government (*jen cheng*) is within their capacity. It is within their capacity precisely because *jen* itself is understood to derive from a personal endowment that is theirs to enlarge or extend. None of these rulers can plausibly be described as paragons of virtue, perhaps not even as serious aspirants, yet Mencius' argumentative strategy is to persuade them that they have within themselves all that is needed to carry out the behaviors associated with *jen*. It must have taken considerable moral confidence and conviction to put across the kinds of arguments that Mencius hurls at these tough-minded rulers, and it is striking that he approaches them not as a moral elite (a status they explicitly disclaim) but as human beings of ordinary human capacity (a status they are unable to disavow).

In his conversations with these rulers Mencius relies not on theoretical arguments or behavioral ideals but on anecdotal evidence deriving from the immediacies of their lives and experiences as rulers. Confronting these flawed rulers, who seem remarkably inclined to acknowledge their own weaknesses, he recognizes in them men who are anxious over losing wars, uneasy about leading lives of material indulgence amid a vast surrounding misery, perplexed about their responsibility for the dire suffering of the people, and, in at least one case, disquieted by the possibility of regicide. Again and again his strategy is, while accepting their frailty, to appeal to their ordinary humanity.

With King Hsüan of Ch'i, Mencius even goes so far as to interpret the king's impulse to spare an ox from being sacrificed (while ordering the substitution of the lamb, which, mercifully for the king, he did not see) as a sign of the king's "being unable to bear" (*pu jen*) the prospect of the animal's suffering.[27] Lest the king suffer undue disquiet over the widespread suspicion that, in fact, he was merely stingy, preferring to sacrifice a small animal rather than a large one, Mencius reassures him that his action revealed the "working of humaneness" (*jen-shu*).[28] Confucius, one suspects, might have been less generous, or perhaps less confident, in conveying his encouragement. Perhaps Mencius could be more confident because he was appealing not to the exceptional character of a morally superior man but to the humanity that the king undeniably shared with ordinary people. The move was, in effect, to emphasize and strengthen the connection between ideal and reality.

The phrase *pu-jen*, or unbearing (in the sense of "unable to bear to see the sufferings of others"), recurs in the passage in 2A:6, which contains Mencius' analysis of human nature. This most famous passage in the text begins with the affirmation "All human beings have a mind that cannot bear [to see the sufferings of] others." Mencius states that the *pu-jen jen chih hsin* (appropriately rendered in this context by James Legge as the "commiserating mind")[29] is shared by all human beings as a condition of their humanity:

> Here is why I say that all human beings have a mind that commiserates with others. Now,[30] if anyone were suddenly to see a child about to fall into a well, his mind would always be filled with alarm, distress, pity and compassion. That he would react accordingly is not because he would use the opportunity to ingratiate himself with the child's parents, nor because he would seek commendation from neighbors and friends, nor because he would hate the adverse reputation.

> From this it may be seen that one who lacks a mind that feels pity and compassion would not be human; one who lacks a mind that feels shame and aversion would not be human; one who lacks a mind that feels modesty and compliance would not be human; and one who lacks a mind that knows right and wrong would not be human.

> The mind's feeling of pity and compassion is the sprout of humaneness (*jen*); the mind's feeling of shame and aversion is the sprout of rightness; the mind's feeling of modesty and compliance is the sprout of propriety; and the mind's sense of right and wrong is the sprout of wisdom.[31]

Interestingly, the phrase *pu-jen* has a sense in the *Mencius* distinct from that found in the *Analects*. Whereas both instances of *pu-jen* in the *Analects* have to do with forbearance in the sense of a dutiful restraint,[32] Mencius characteristically uses the phrase to express an affective inability to bear the sight of the suffering of others or, as I. A. Richards so aptly put it, the "shuddering qualm"[33] experienced at the very prospect of their suffering. This "unbearing" or "commiserating" mind is taken by Mencius as a corollary of pity and compassion (*ts'e-yin*), a term that, again, has no place in the *Analects*,[34] but that has a seminal importance here, figuring as the "sprout" or "beginning" (*tuan*) of *jen*.[35] *Jen* has its origin, according to Mencius, in the *feeling* of pity and compassion; it is a development or a completion of an *affective* response to the suffering of others; it is naturally shared by everyone.

This view does not conflict with Confucius' idea of *jen*, though it does contrast with it in terms of the underlying psychology. While Confucius evidently hoped to encourage his disciples in the cultivation of *jen*, his encouragement was apparently conveyed more through his personal example and his interactions with them than through any expressed assurance that all human beings have an innate disposition for compassionate responsiveness to others that, in turn, reveals their potential for *jen*. Confucius' emphasis was on the strength and fortitude the morally noble person needed to cultivate and on the duties he was obliged to fulfill. And while his assurance that one has only to want *jen* for *jen* to arrive[36] may be taken to mean that the capacity of the noble person to cultivate his strength and to fulfill his duties was not in question, just how to overcome the difficulties involved in following Confucius' teachings must, to his struggling disciples, sometimes have been less than clear.[37]

Mencius is, by contrast, explicit in analyzing the source or origin of *jen*, identifying that source in shared affective responses common to *all* human beings. He tends to naturalize *jen*, insisting that the maturation of the "sprout" of pity and compassion into the behavior pattern known as *jen* is part of the normal course of development of human nature. And, by placing a clearer emphasis on affective responses and taking the human ability to recognize shared affective responses as a reliable guide to moral development, he apparently intends to heighten the sense of moral confidence surrounding the discussion of *jen*. Given Mencius' emphasis on the natural development of positive affective dispositions, which are found within every human being, *jen* begins to seem easier. As he says of the "four sprouts," they are reliably possessed by all human beings, and, when appropriately cultivated, they grow in a way that is at once natural and remarkable:

Human beings have these four sprouts just as they have four limbs. For one to have these four sprouts and yet to say of oneself that one is without them is to injure oneself, while to say that one's ruler is without them is to injure one's ruler. When we know how to enlarge and bring to fulfillment[38] these four sprouts that are within us, it will be like a fire beginning to burn or a spring finding an outlet. If we are able to bring them to fulfillment, they will be sufficient to enable us to protect "all within the four seas"; if we are not, they will be insufficient even to enable us to serve our parents.[39]

This famous passage illustrates the difference between Mencius and Confucius in their characteristic metaphors. Whereas Confucius was inclined to use spatial or directional metaphors, often suggesting a journey, Mencius was given to employing organic metaphors, such as plants, trees, and growing grain. The journey theme carries with it the concomitant notions of perseverance and endurance; the images are of a traveler through the world or along the stages of life's way. His course is difficult. Mencius' organic metaphors imply concomitant notions of enlargement, fulfillment, growth, and maturation; the images are of an individual who, being fully contextualized in nature, finds fulfillment within the natural process. His course may not be easy, but he has a lot of life's energies working within and for him. When Mencius speaks of the four "sprouts" or "beginnings" he evokes, at least indirectly, the positive energy of growing plants, the phonetic element in the character *tuan* depicting, according to one common etymology, a plant growing both above and below the surface of the ground. Other metaphors, such as the fire and the spring employed in 2A:6, are suggestive of a dynamic and growing energy: each rereading of that familiar passage must reevoke a vision of the faintly flickering flame beginning to burn brightly and the trickle of water bursting into a bubbling torrent.

The later books of the *Mencius* may reveal a certain defensiveness on Mencius' part. The challenge of Kao-tzu has already been prefigured in 2A:2, with a question from Kung-sun Ch'ou about Kao-tzu's ability to maintain an "unmoved mind"[40] and Mencius' insistence, in the midst of his description of the "vast, flowing *ch'i*," that Kao-tzu had never understood rightness, having made it something external.[41] Still, in 2A:6 there appear to be no challengers immediately on the scene as the passage culminates with its powerful images of the fire beginning to burn and the spring breaking through. The tone is one of confidence.

By contrast, 6A:6 acknowledges from beginning to end the shadowy presences of critics of the Mencian position who have evidently been pressing in on him and challenging both his optimism about human moral capacity and his natural egalitarianism.[42] When the "four sprouts" have a second coming in 6A:6, it is in the course of a discussion between Mencius and the disciple Kung-tu over some alternative views of human nature. Kung-tu, in reviewing various theories that evidently were current at the time, mentions three competing claims about the nature: (1) Kao-tzu's "narrowly biological"[43] view of the nature as neither good nor not-good; (2) the "strong environmentalist"[44] view that people's nature may become good or not-good depending on the circumstances of their lives (specifically, the quality of rule to which they are subjected); and (3) the "radically inegalitarian"[45] view that the nature of some is good, while the nature of others is not-good. It would appear that, while the subject of human nature had attracted considerable attention and a range of interpretations, Mencius may have been virtually alone in advancing the strongly affirmative and egalitarian position that the nature of every human being is potentially good;[46] at least, Kung-tu mentions no alternatives that resemble Mencius' view. As Mencius returns to his focus on the affective nature, he reaffirms that:

> As far as one's *ch'ing* is concerned, it is possible for one to become good; this is what I mean by the nature being good. If one does what is not good, that is not the fault of his *ts'ai* (capabilities).
>
> The mind of pity and compassion is possessed by all human beings. The mind of shame and aversion is possessed by all human beings. The mind of respect and reverence is possessed by all human beings. The mind that knows right and wrong is possessed by all human beings. The mind of pity and compassion is *jen* (humaneness); the mind of shame and aversion is rightness; the mind of respect and reverence is propriety; the sense of right and wrong is wisdom. Humaneness, rightness, ritual propriety, and wisdom are not infused in us from without. We definitely possess them. [To assume otherwise] is simply owing to a failure to think. Therefore it is said, "Seek and you will find them; let go and you will lose them." That some differ from others by as much as twice, or five times, or an incalculable order of magnitude, is because there are those who are unable fully to develop their capabilities.[47]

In this context Mencius does not use the word *tuan* ("sprout" or "beginning") that figured in his discussion of the nature in 2A:6, though he is even more explicit about the affective or emotional dispositions that characterize the natural human endowment. That the potential for goodness belongs to every human being is confirmed in his assertion that it derives from their *ch'ing*—from what is genuinely in them, or—as the term *ch'ing* may have come to be understood by Mencius' time—from the feelings or affections that everyone shares.[48] These genuine dispositions of human interiority, this affective capacity, must be fully developed (*chin*) to allow for the expression of the morally fulfilling behaviors of humaneness, rightness, ritual propriety, and wisdom. Yet such a process of development is seen by Mencius as wholly natural.

Mencius' powers of argument, and the depth of his conviction concerning the power of the human affections, are nowhere more clearly illustrated than in this passage. What is striking in 6A:6 is that he manages in this brief pronouncement to address all three competing claims about the nature. In response to Kao-tzu's argument that the nature is neither good nor not-good (i.e., that morality must be inculcated or imposed from the outside), Mencius asserts that the four powers of humaneness, rightness, propriety, and wisdom "are not infused in us from without." In response to the "strong environmentalist" claim that human beings are altogether creatures of circumstance, without any innate dispositions, he counters, "We definitely possess them. [To assume otherwise] is simply owing to a failure to think." In response to the "radical inegalitarian" position he asserts that the differences among people are *not* a matter of deficiencies in their *ch'ing* or their natural capacities (*ts'ai*) but derive from the fact that some are unable fully to develop these natural capacities (*pu neng chin ch'i ts'ai*).[49]

While this is, again, a position that does not conflict with Confucius' view of human nature, the nuance here is quite distinct. Confucius had affirmed in *Analects* 17:2 that human beings are "by nature close together, in practice diverging." He offered no further analysis of the original closeness, however, and when, in other contexts, he used the term *ts'ai* (used by Mencius to refer to the natural capacities or capabilities that human beings share), it was invariably in recognition of an individual's unusual or distinctive talents or abilities.[50] Mencius' claim that the failure of some to come up to others is owing to their inability to *develop* their natural capacities is consistently put forward alongside the essentially egalitarian claim that these morally significant *ts'ai* are originally possessed by everyone.

Here is the unstated yet significant difference between Mencius and Confucius on the subject of *jen*: by explicitly identifying the affective source of *jen* within the person, Mencius tends to naturalize and universalize the human capacity for *jen*. Because he understands *jen* more in terms of a positive psychological energy than in terms of self-discipline and restraint, he imbues it with a more vibrant coloration. This change in psychological perspective becomes the basis for his strong moral claims: having naturalized *jen* and reduced the difficulties associated with it, Mencius is able to argue that *jen* is within anyone's capacity. He goes well beyond this, however, making the far stronger claim that *jen* is conducive both to self-fulfillment and to positive responses from others.

Perhaps responding to claims of practical efficacy by Legalists and Mohists, Mencius remains unyielding in his insistence on the efficacy of *jen* in both the personal and the political spheres, where it is to be the motive and sustaining power behind humane government. *Jen* is no longer a burden, as it was in the *Analects*; it now is seen as the distinguishing characteristic of being human. And yet there is now, inevitably, the burden of explanation: how can *jen be* the human mind[51] and yet so often, demonstrably, not be the compelling human motive? Why is the human mind so often "lost"?[52] Water and fire reappear toward the close of Book 6A in a context quite different from that of 2A:6. Now the fire is the destructive fire of inhumanity (not-*jen*) that must be quelled by the power of *jen*:

> *Jen* overcomes not-*jen* just as water overcomes fire. Those today who prac-
> tice *jen* do it as if they were using a cup of water to put out the fire
> consuming a cartload of firewood, and then, when the flames are not
> extinguished, they say that water does not overcome fire. This is to make an
> enormous concession to what is not-*jen*, and in the end it must inevitably
> result in the destruction of *jen*.[53]

The challengers are evidently pressing in on Mencius, evoking from him a response in which his characteristic confidence is mingled with anxious concern. He knows the power of *jen*, and has argued so eloquently for it, yet he is forced to admit that *jen* can be damaged, even destroyed, if commitment to it is wanting. He follows this warning with another in which he once again evokes the image of the plant, likening the maturation of *jen* to the ripening of grain:

> The five kinds of grain are the most beautiful of all seeds. But if they are not
> ripe they are not even as good as the tares or weeds. Being *jen* depends
> entirely on enabling it to mature.[54]

Mencius's insistence on maturation is entirely consistent with views he has expressed earlier, and his confidence in the natural capacity of every human being for behavior that is *jen* seems undiminished. While he must continue to respond to skeptics who question his realism on the subject of *jen* — in other words, the possibility and the efficacy of this kind of emotional control — he does so with a clarity and an energy that suggest that, beyond being an argumentative strategy, *jen* is, for him, a vision that works within as well as without. The basis for his argument for *jen* is, in effect, a psychological one: it is bound up with the human capacity for psychological maturation.

Jen *in Chu Hsi's "Jen-shuo"*

By the twelfth century, when it came Chu Hsi's turn to rework the concept of *jen*, it had undergone a considerable evolution in the thought of intervening contributors to the tradition, including the Confucians of the Han and Neo-Confucians of the Northern Sung. Chu's "Jen-shuo," apparently a product of the early 1170s,[55] is comprehensive in its inspiration, alluding to the *I-ching* (Classic of Changes) and the *Hsiao-ching* (Classic of Filial Piety) as well as to the *Analects* and *Mencius* and drawing on the ideas of Ch'eng Hao and Ch'eng I, while criticizing the interpretations of their followers, Yang Shih (1053–1135) and Hsieh Liang-tso (1050–c.1120). One of the interesting aspects of the "Jen-shuo" is that it seems to have been painstakingly produced, almost in the manner of an negotiated settlement, out of exchanges and arguments that Chu Hsi had with his contemporaries, especially Chang Shih (1133–1180).[56]

Within Chu's brief essay *jen* is defined in metaphysical terms and defended in several distinct tonalities. In a positive mode Chu Hsi traces the metaphysical basis for *jen* to the mind of Heaven and Earth itself, discovering in it the cosmic source for the creativeness of the human mind. In a cautionary mode he voices the concern that to misperceive the nature of *jen*, as he believes Yang Shih and Hsieh Liang-tso had done, involves potentially serious consequences. Chu Hsi, like Mencius, displays considerable moral confidence at a theoretical level while revealing a certain anxiety at the practical level, though quite different perceptions underlie both his confidence and his concern.

Just as Mencius expressed no overt disagreement with Confucius on *jen* or *hsing* (human nature), Chu Hsi gives no sign in this essay that he has any disagreement with either of them on either subject. To the contrary, he defines his task to be that of recovering the concept of *jen* as it had been put forward in the teachings of the ancients and of reviving their commitment to practicing *jen* in ordinary life.[57]

At the same time Chu's understanding of *jen* differs from that of Confucius or Mencius in ways that are no less striking for being unstated. Confucius, with his thoroughly practical ethics and his stress on inner fortitude, had virtually nothing to say about a metaphysical basis for *jen*. Mencius, with his essentially psychological perspective, his commitment to the power of human sympathy, and his interest in the human capacity for communication, said scarcely more. By contrast, Chu Hsi opens his "Jen-shuo" with a quotation from one of the Ch'eng brothers: "The mind of Heaven and Earth is to produce things."[58]

Beginning with this expansive affirmation, Chu follows with an elaborate metaphysics of morals, asserting that *jen*, as the endowment of Heaven and Earth, is what connects human beings to the universe as a whole and allows them to participate in its purposes:

> In the production of man and things, they receive the mind of Heaven and Earth as their mind. Therefore, with reference to the character of the mind (*hsin chih te*), although it embraces and penetrates all and leaves nothing to be desired, nevertheless, one word will cover all of it, namely, *jen*. . . .
>
> The moral qualities (*te*) of the mind of Heaven and Earth are four: origination, flourishing, advantage, and firmness.[59] And the principle of origination unites and controls them all. In their operation they constitute the course of the four seasons, and the vital force of spring permeates all. Therefore in the mind of man there are also four moral qualities—namely, *jen*, rightness, propriety, and wisdom—and *jen* embraces them all. In their emanation and functioning they constitute the feeling of love, respect, correctness, and discrimination—and the feeling of commiseration pervades them all. Therefore in discussing the mind of Heaven and Earth it is said: "Great is *ch'ien*, the originator!"[60] and "Great is *k'un*, the originator!"[61] Both the substance and the function of the four moral qualities are thus fully implied without enumerating them.[62]

Already in these opening lines of the "Jen-shuo" Chu Hsi moves well beyond the Mencian argument about the human mind, with its relatively modest psychological claims about the plantlike "four sprouts" that, if cultivated, may be enhanced and developed into the four powers of humaneness, rightness, propriety, and wisdom. By invoking "the mind of Heaven and Earth" (*t'ien-ti chih hsin*), he places the discussion of *jen* in a universal or cosmic context; in introducing the idea of "the character of the mind" (*hsin chih te*), he designates a metaphysical source for the "four sprouts"; by asserting that *jen* embraces all the four moral qualities, he establishes it as the all-pervasive moral quality; and by analyzing the moral qualities in terms of substance and function (*t'i/yung*), he strengthens the notion of a substantial endowment prior to and more reliable than the emotional functions or expressions to which it gives rise.

To observe that Chu Hsi, in tracing *jen* to its source in the mind of Heaven and Earth, puts *jen* in a cosmic context is not to deny that Confucius or Mencius recognized that human beings are implicated in the life of the cosmos. Confucius could speak of Heaven as giving birth to the *te* that was in him,[63] while Mencius would affirm that by "fully developing one's mind, one knows one's nature, and in knowing one's nature, one knows Heaven."[64] Still, these statements might almost issue from moments of inspiration,[65] neither having a developed context, figuring into a sustained discussion or argument, or having an explicitly stated relation to *jen*. Later Confucians would go further, seeing parallels between human and cosmic processes. What distinguishes Chu Hsi's thought on *jen*, and particularly the discussion in the "Jen-shuo," is that here the metaphysical argument provides the groundwork for the entire ensuing discussion of *jen*. He continues:

> In discussing the excellence of the human mind, it is said, "*Jen* is the human mind."[66] Both the substance and the function of the four moral qualities (*ssu-te chih t'i-yung*) are thus fully presented without mentioning them. For *jen* as constituting the Way (Tao) consists of the fact that the mind of Heaven and Earth to produce things is present in everything. Before the feelings are aroused this substance is already existent in its completeness. After the feelings are aroused, its function is infinite. If we can truly embody and preserve it,[67] then we have in it the spring of all goodness and the root of all actions.[68]

In the foregoing passage, one of four in the "Jen-shuo" that directly recall the *Mencius*, the striking differences between the perspectives of Chu Hsi and Mencius become more apparent. In the first passage quoted above, Chu has introduced the idea of the "character of the mind," which is understood to be imprinted by Heaven and Earth, identified with substance, and implicated with generativity.[69] At this point, as strands from the *Mencius* and the *Mean* are being intertwined with the Neo-Confucian language of substance and function,[70] it becomes clear that, in saying that "*jen* is the human mind," Chu is not speaking, as Mencius had been, about the distinctive quality of the *fully developed* human mind, but of the mind as *originally endowed* by Heaven and Earth. The statement that "*jen* is the human mind" links Mencius and Chu Hsi; yet it also distinguishes them because, as invoked by Chu Hsi, it is no longer, as it was in the *Mencius*, a statement about maturation and about the humane capacity of the human mind after the "sprout" of "pity and commiseration" has been cultivated and developed. Here it is a statement about the "character of the mind" bestowed by Heaven and Earth at the outset, along with life itself.

> This is why in the teachings of the Confucian school, the student is always urged to exert anxious and unceasing effort in the pursuit of *jen*. In the teachings (of Confucius it is said), "Master oneself and return to propriety." This means that if we can overcome and eliminate selfishness and return to the Principle of Nature (*t'ien-li*), then the substance of this mind (that is, *jen*) will be present everywhere and its function will always be operative.
> . . . What mind is this? In Heaven and Earth it is the mind to produce things infinitely. In man it is the mind to love people gently and to benefit things. It includes the four virtues (of humanity, rightness, propriety, and wisdom) and penetrates the "four sprouts" (of the sense of commiseration, the sense of shame, the sense of deference and compliance, and the sense of right and wrong).[71]

It is noteworthy that Chu Hsi explains Confucius' famous statement about "mastering onself and returning to propriety" in *Analects* 12:1 as meaning to "overcome and eliminate selfishness and return to the Principle of Nature." Of course, the rites, or ritual propriety, for Confucius, represented an evolving human enterprise rather than a constant cosmic principle. Mencius nowhere suggests that the "four sprouts" are grounded in a constant cosmic principle such as *li*. Rather than cultivating the "four sprouts" as the agriculturalist tends emergent shoots, Chu Hsi advocates returning to what for Neo-Confucians of his school had become the most reliable of all realities, the source of life, the Principle of Nature (*t'ien-li*).

The term *t'ien-li* had not been part of the vocabulary of Confucius or Mencius. Even the term *li* itself occurs infrequently in the Mencian dialogues and invariably with the sense of an order created, rather than inherited, by human beings.[72] That this order is, in Mencius' view, created by human beings in a way consistent with their human nature is the basis for his insistence, contra Kao-tzu, that morality is not external to the nature. However, moral behavior is an achievement consonant with the natural tendency of human development rather than a return, through overcoming selfishness, to an originally complete and perfect endowment of principle that is present in the universe and in individual human beings from the outset. In tracing the origins of *jen* to the existence of *t'ien-li* as a substance "already existent in its completeness" in living beings, Chu Hsi offers an encouragement to humaneness that is less psychological than metaphysical. Whereas humaneness, for Mencius, involves a process of psychological development or maturation, for Chu Hsi, it is a matter of realization of one's originally perfect essential nature. It is, in other words, more a process of reclamation than of development.

About midway through the "Jen-shuo" there is a shift from the declarative mode to a conversational mode, as Chu Hsi responds to questions from the ever-present "someone" about the views of Master Ch'eng and the Ch'engs' followers. The questioner alludes to a statement (almost certainly Ch'eng I's) to the effect "that love is feeling, while *jen* is nature and that love should not be regarded as *jen*."[73] The questioner inquires whether Master Ch'eng had not been incorrect in denying that love is *jen*. Chu Hsi's reply is unambiguous:

> Not so. What Master Ch'eng criticized was the application of the term to the expression of love. What I maintain is that the term should be applied to the principle of love (*ai chih li*). For although the spheres of the feelings and the nature are different, their mutual penetration is like the blood system in which each part has its own relationship. When have they become sharply separated and been made to have nothing to do with each other? I was just now worrying about the students' reciting Master Ch'eng's words without inquiring into their meaning and thereby coming to talk about *jen* in isolation from love. I have therefore purposely talked about this to reveal the hidden meaning of Master Ch'eng's words, and you regard my ideas as different from his. Are you not mistaken?[74]

Chu's response to this question about the relation between the nature and the feelings, with its claim to be revealing the "hidden meaning" (*i-i*) of Master Ch'eng's words,[75] confirms that a subtle yet thoroughgoing transposition has occurred here. We may recall that Mencius' statement about the relation between the feelings and the nature was quite simple and essentially psychological: "As far as one's *ch'ing* is concerned, it is possible for one to become good; this is what I mean by the nature being good." Mencius seems to have had no intuition that feelings and nature pertain to "different spheres" (*ch'i fen-yü chih pu-t'ung*). One might say, in fact, that the habit of controlling one's feelings itself determines one's nature. Mencius even went so far in 6A: 6 as to say, "The mind of pity and commiseration is *jen*." (Interestingly, Legge, being well steeped in Chu Hsi's commentaries, was prompted to translate this simple statement into Neo-Confucian language, supplying the notion of principle (*li*) that is absent in the *Mencius*. In Legge's translation the statement becomes: "The feeling of commiseration *implies the principle of* benevolence." One wonders: could Mencius' omission of the word *li* have been inadvertent?)

When Chu Hsi explains Master Ch'eng's statement about the distinction between *jen* as the nature and *ai* as feeling by asserting that *jen* is the principle of love and that the spheres of the nature and feelings, while different, are interpenetrating, he assigns priority to principle as the source from which the emotional expression of love issues. The "four sprouts" are no longer "sprouts" or "germinations" in the sense that they were for Mencius—the affective promptings that, when nurtured, grow into moral powers. Rather, the "sprouts" have now become functions or expressions of the original endowment of principle. The order has been inverted: rather than *jen* developing from the "sprout" of commiseration, as in Mencius, commiseration now arises out of the endowment of *jen* that, as the substance of the mind (*hsin chih t'i*), is fully present from the beginning of life.[76] From another source we know that Chu Hsi disagreed with Chang Shih's suggestion that the term *principle of love* (*ai chih li*) was like *the beginning* (or "*sprout*") *of action* (*tung chih tuan*) or *the way of life* (*sheng chih tao*). Chu insisted that the word *principle* (*li*) is heavy (*chung*), whereas the word *beginning* or *sprout* (*tuan*) is light (*ch'ing*).[77] Not only does *principle* carry great metaphysical weight in this context, but it serves as a metaphysically secure stay or a support for the emotions.

Having defined *jen* as "the principle of love," Chu Hsi, prompted by another question, turns his attention to two alternative conceptions: the unity of all things and the self as the substance of *jen* (*wu yü wo wei i wei jen chih t'i*) and *jen* as the mind's possession of consciousness (*hsin yu chih-chüeh*). The former is an idea associated with Yang Shih, the latter a recurrent motif in the thought of Hsieh Liang-tso. Chu is critical of both views. In commenting on the view of *jen* as the unity of things and the self, he acknowledges that *jen* implies love for all but insists that "this is not the reality that makes *jen* a substance."[78] (He does not say, though it seems reasonable to assume, that the "reality" to which he refers is the metaphysical reality of principle, the sense of the unity of the self and all things being understood as a function of that substance. The *sense* of the unity of the self with all things is, in other words, an emotional apprehension of an underlying metaphysical reality.) Chu makes a similar argument against the notion of *jen* as the mind's possession of consciousness: "*Jen* includes wisdom, but that is not the actuality from which *jen* takes its name."[79] (Once again, the implication is that the "actuality" is principle, with wisdom or consciousness being its function.) For Chu Hsi, the metaphysical "reality" or "actuality" of principle must be understood as prior to the psychological "beginnings" or "sprouts" that are its expression.

The "Jen-shuo" closes with remarks on the behavioral consequences of misunderstanding the nature of *jen*. Chu warns that an effect of experiencing *jen* in terms of identification with others (*t'ung-t'i*) may be "to cause people to become vague, confused, and lacking in any effort to be vigilant, the impairment possibly reaching the point where one mistakes things for oneself." The effect of focusing on consciousness may be "to cause people to become anxious, fretful, and lacking in any quality of depth, the impairment sometimes reaching the point where one mistakes desire for principle."[80] The suggestion is that in the former case one loses a clear perspective on one's identity as a moral agent, while in the latter case one loses the power of moral discrimination and judgment. Chu Hsi likens one of these — following the analogy made famous by Mencius — to "forgetting," the other to "helping things grow."[81] He believes either extreme to be subversive of effective cultivation. His final comment is that to talk about *jen* in terms of consciousness "bears no resemblance to what has been revealed in the school of the Sage about the disposition of one who 'delights in mountains,'[82] and one who is 'able to hold on' [to what knowledge has allowed him to attain]."[83] He concludes: "It is to record their words that I have written the 'Jen-shuo.' "[84]

The words he has recorded, of course, are those of Confucius and Mencius, though in recording them he has turned them to quite a different effect. While he sees *jen* as a behavioral ideal, as had Confucius and Mencius, Chu Hsi approaches it in terms of his own insights into human nature and the emotions. Given his understanding of *hsing* as involving both a "nature ordained by *t'ien*" (*t'ien-ming chih hsing*), associated with principle, and a "physical nature" (*ch'i-chih chih hsing*), associated with material force (a distinction that neither Confucius nor Mencius had contemplated), Chu Hsi sees the effort of personal cultivation as involving a constant effort to refine the physical nature and to express more fully the "nature ordained by Heaven." As he urges in the "Jen-shuo," one must "eliminate selfishness and return to the Principle of Nature." At the close of the essay he is concerned with nurturing a temperament or a disposition (*ch'i-hsiang*) appropriate to such an effort of cultivation — the disposition of one who "delights in mountains" and of one who is "able to hold on" to his attainment — in other words, a calm and controlled disposition.

Only at the end of his essay, in discussing the consequences of *mis*understanding *jen*, does Chu Hsi reenter an explanatory sphere that might be described as psychological. Like Confucius and Mencius, Chu obviously has a profound concern with motivation. Like them, he understands motivation not simply in terms of the discrete motives underlying particular actions but as part of a complex pattern or disposition of the human personality. He is wary of the emotions, determined not to ignore their significance in human motivation, yet at the same time concerned to bring them under the control of a mind fully informed by principle. Whereas Mencius' anxiety is psychological, having to do with whether people will be sufficiently committed to *jen* to allow for its maturation, Chu Hsi's anxiety is fundamentally intellectual, having to do with whether people will understand its metaphysical basis. His underlying assumption throughout the essay seems to be that what subverts the practice of *jen* is misunderstanding its metaphysical status. He thinks that practice and, even more fundamentally, the temperament that determines practice, are governed by understanding. Those who understand their own endowment are more capable of achieving control over their emotions and desires, allowing the substance of their minds, which is *jen*, to be "present everywhere" and its function, which is love, to be "always operative."

Conclusions

Each of the concepts of *jen* discussed here is not just a view but part of a vision. Even if one possessed (as I do not) a wealth of evidence concerning the unstated motives of Confucius, Mencius, and Chu Hsi, it would be reductive and pointless to try to explain simply in terms of the challenges, the pressures, and the constraints that affected them how their complex visions came into being. Still, in light of the fact that these visions were created by thinkers who were deeply sensitive to their interactions with others, it may be helpful to consider the argumentative contexts in which they were working.

It is striking that Mencius' vision of *jen* was developed in a context in which he felt compelled to argue with contemporaries who, however much they may have differed on other issues, were alike in assigning scant value to human emotions. Mencius' vision seems to have come into focus in the course of arguments with latter-day Yangists, who were probably inclined to see the emotions as potentially detrimental to personal well-being and longevity,[85] and Mohists, who had minimal regard for the emotional life and room for only the most limited range of emotions in their narrowly pragmatic motivational scheme. Mencius' vision — involving compassion, maturation, and positive emotional energy—extended the original Confucian concern with the emotional life and moral motivation in such a way that *jen* came to include not only the hard-won emotional control of the *chün-tzu* but the natural emotional responsiveness of every human being. Because he was disputing with Yangists, known for a hedonistic individualism, Mencius may well have felt that it was incumbent on him to show that the practice of *jen* was, after all, good for the health. Because he was also contending with Mohists, known for a narrowly pragmatic consequentialism, he may have found it necessary to demonstrate that *jen*, as a complex behavioral pattern, actually worked. Through his notion of *jen* as the expression of the morally developed personality, Mencius was able to put forward a powerful argument in both cases, visualizing the individual who cultivates the capacity for *jen* as personally fulfilled, visibly healthy, and morally successful.

Just as the arguments going on in the background of the *Mencius* may be understood to figure into an understanding of Mencius' vision, so the arguments that figure in the background of the "Jen-shuo" have a similar relevance to Chu Hsi's. In the case of Chu Hsi, though the overt criticisms in his essay are directed at errant Confucians, the real adversaries are unquestionably Buddhists. Chu Hsi's adversarial relationship with Buddhists was complex, and it is a sign of his own youthful involvement with Buddhism, and a measure of the seriousness with which he continued to take it even in his maturity, that he was so deeply concerned about the effects Buddhism might have on its adherents. Even more disturbing for him was the fact that those who were not avowedly adherents of Buddhism might, in coming under its influence, lose their way. When toward the end of his essay Chu comes to speak in detail of the errors that worried him, it is evident that the most troubling were those likely to afflict Confucians who, being subject to Buddhist influence,[86] were impaired in their comprehension of what *jen* actually is. One common misconception might lead to adopting an essentially negative view of life in the world, which could mean insensitivity to the creative process and to the human role in that process. Another involved drifting beyond empathy toward a mental state in which subject-object dualisms tended to melt away. Still another entailed forgetting the stability associated with the substance of *jen*, confusing *jen* with the morally ambiguous function of consciousness. Both the text and the textual history of the "Jen-shuo" suggest that Chu Hsi believed that an individual's disposition (*ch'i-hsiang*) and motivation could be determined by his understanding of *jen*; much of what he said and wrote reflects his wariness of the potential of Buddhism to invade an individual personality, undermining the kind of metaphysical awareness that is essential both to personal stability and to moral motivation. In this, the intellectual understanding of *jen* became the central issue.

Where Chu Hsi differs most significantly from Mencius on the subject of *jen* may be seen in his departure from a mode of thinking that is primarily psychological for one that is heavily metaphysical. The larger investment in metaphysics is, of course, a feature of Ch'eng-Chu thought in general and not simply a feature of Chu's thought concerning *jen*. If the foregoing analysis is valid, however, Chu's vision of *jen* is distinct from Mencius' vision in that it involves not simply an elaboration of Mencius' thought—an enlargement of the Mencian conception with the addition of a metaphysical dimension—but, actually, an inversion of it. It is an inversion in the sense that, rather than seeing *jen* as evolving, through a process of maturation, out of the incipient "sprout" or "beginning" of commiseration, Chu believes all the "sprouts" to be grounded in the preexisting "character of the mind." "Sprouts," as he puts it, are light; principle is heavy; *jen* is now invested with the weight of principle.

Clearly, the Buddhist challenge faced by Chu Hsi was quite unlike the Yangist and Mohist challenges faced centuries earlier by Mencius. One of the differences was that, rather than undervaluing human emotions, Buddhism recognized the emotions as the central human problem. But, having problematized the emotions, Buddhism did not simply prescribe forms of religious discipline through which the emotions could be quieted or quelled; in the nondualist perspective of the high Mahayana tradition that developed in China, attention was drawn to the emotional life in such a way and to such an extent that the emotions came, paradoxically, to be revalidated. This was true above all in the Ch'an (or Zen) school where their discipline and deployment would become a kind of art form all its own.

The challenge for Neo-Confucians of the Sung, faithful to the Mencian vision, yet less sanguine than Mencius had been about the emotions, was to find ways both to order and control the emotions and to reaffirm them as fundamental to a life lived, not in emptiness and quietude, but within the family, the society, and "the wide house of the world." In describing *jen* as the "principle of love" (*ai chih li*), Chu Hsi seems to have been engaged in an effort to distinguish valid from invalid emotional expressions. In discovering in *jen* the "character of the mind" (*hsin chih te*), he expresses a belief that human moral propensities derive from cosmic processes and that the capacity of individuals for positive emotional expression and for emotional discipline originates in and requires a return to principle.[87]

Again, as with Confucius and Mencius, there is in Chu Hsi's thought a close connection between ideal and reality—here, between *jen* as a moral ideal and *jen* as the essential reality of the universe as a whole as well as of human nature. No longer an expression of moral potentiality understood solely in ethical or psychological terms, or even in purely human terms, Chu Hsi's *jen*, metaphysically secured, may be understood as a highly refined solution to the problem of emotional control in an environment in which Buddhism continued to pose a serious challenge. His vision — which involved identifying the humanity of the individual with the source of life and the sustaining power at the very heart of the universe — was, of course, something larger.

NOTES

1. Though I have not attempted to review it systematically here, the rich and extensive secondary literature on the evolution of the concept of *jen* and its transmutations in pre-Confucian, Confucian, and Neo-Confucian contexts is tapped selectively, inasmuch as this literature provides extremely valuable resources for such an exploration. This work has been done by such distinguished scholars as Wing-tsit Chan, Yamaguchi Satsujō, Takeuchi Teruo, and Shimotomai Akira. See especially Wing-tsit Chan, "The Evolution of the Confucian Concept *Jen*," *Philosophy East and West* (1995), 4:295–319, and "Chinese and Western Interpretations of Jen (Humanity)," *Journal of Chinese Philosophy* (1975), 2:107–29; Yamaguchi Satsujō, *Jin no kenkyū* (Studies of Jen) (Tokyo: Iwanami shoten, 1936); Takeuchi Teruo, *Jin no kogi no kenkyū* (Studies on the Ancient Meanings of Jen) (Tokyo: Meiji shoin, 1964); and Shimotomai Akira, *Jin no kenkyū* (Studies of Jen) (Tokyo: Daitō bunka daigaku Tōyō kenkyūjo, 1966). Other valuable contributions include Satō Hitoshi's essay, "Chu Hsi's 'Treatise on *Jen*,'" in Wing-tsit Chan, ed., *Chu Hsi and Neo-Confucianism*, 212–27 (Honolulu: University of Hawaii Press, 1986), and Wing-tsit Chan's "Chu Hsi's 'Jen-shuo' (Treatise on Humanity)," in his *Chu Hsi: New Studies*, 151–83 (Honolulu: University of Hawaii Press, 1989).

2. Chan, "Chinese and Western Interpretations of Jen (Humanity)," 107.

3. Ibid., 109.

4. Ibid., 107.

5. Confucius's spare statement in *Analects* 17:2 has it that human beings are "by nature close together, while diverging in practice."

6. Takeuchi, *Jin no kogi no kenkyū*, ch. 1 and p. 294. I do not mean to imply that there is any necessary tension between Confucius' recognition of the fundamental similarity among human beings and his moral elitism. It is enough to recognize that both parts of Confucius' statement in 17:2 carry their full weight: human beings are *both* "by nature close together" and "in practice diverging," the similarity and the divergence being equally significant.

7. Professor Takeuchi discusses the development of a sense of interiority — more specifically, a sense of an interior beauty of character — in ibid., especially pp. 77–80 and 292–94.

8. The passage is in some respects comparable to *Analects* 5:13, which has Tzu-kung reporting (depending on one's reading of the passage) on the difficulty of hearing from the Master on *hsing* (human nature) or *t'ien-tao* (the Way of Heaven). Philip J. Ivanhoe has written a thoughtful essay, entitled "Whose Confucius? Which *Analects*?" (unpublished), on the various interpretations over time of 5:13. *Analects* 9:1 has, in a sense, posed even greater challenges than 5:13, inasmuch as the *Analects* contains only two recorded references to *hsing* and only the lone reference in 5:13 itself to *t'ien-tao*, whereas Confucius is, in fact, recorded to have said many things about *jen*. For a discussion of some of the literature on 9:1, see Chan, "The Evolution of the Confucian Concept Jen,' 296–97.

9. Confucius is questioned on the subject of *jen* by Meng Wu (5:7), Fan Ch'ih (6:20), Tzu-kung (6:28), Yen Hui, Jan Jung (or Chung-kung) (12:2), Ssu-ma Niu (12:3), Tzu-chang (17:6), and even the reprobate disciple Tsai Wo (6:24).

10. Confucius' caution in recommending Tzu-lu in 5:7 is an example of this.

11. *Analects* 4:2 records Confucius as having said, "Those who are not *jen* cannot abide for long either in adversity or in prosperity. The humane find rest (or find peace) in humanity, while the wise find it advantageous." It seems quite clear, however, that *an jen* cannot mean "finding rest" or "finding peace" in the sense of a resting place beyond striving.

12. The consummate example here is, of course, *Analects* 2:4, which I am inclined to consider the world's shortest autobiography.

13. At several points *jen* is contrasted with glibness of speech, as if verbal agility almost amounts to a disqualification. See 1:3, 5:4, and 13:27.

14. See also 4:5, where Confucius speaks of not departing from *jen* (*wei jen*) for so long as the space of a meal.

15. Professor Chan has argued that the inclination of some Western scholars and missionaries to compare the Christian and Confucian formulations of the "golden rule" and to deprecate the latter for its apparent negativity involved a misunderstanding. He explains that Chinese commentators on the *Analects* have never taken the relevant statements about *jen* in the *Analects* to be negative and that the sense of *jen* found there is distinctly affirmative in the sense that its work is understood to involve the perfection of both self and society. See Chan, "Chinese and Western Interpretations of Jen (Humanity)," 120–24.

16. Confucius' statement in *Analects* 17:2 that human beings are "by nature close together, while diverging in practice," interestingly, also employs a spatial metaphor.

17. What Tzu-kung says, more literally, is "What I do not wish others to do to me, I also wish not to do to others." Does Confucius' comment pertain to Tzu-kung's actions or to his motivation?

18. *Analects* 7:16 is a particularly evocative expression of Confucius' capacity for moral joy.

19. *The Analects of Confucius*, trans. Arthur Waley, 27–28 (New York: Vintage [reprint of 1938 ed., published by George Allen and Unwin]).

20. Takeuchi, *Jin no kogi no kenkyū*, 294.

21. *Analects* 12:3.

22. *Analects* 8:7.

23. Takeuchi suggests that this association is already present in the background of Confucius' thought on *jen*, though, of course, Confucius does not draw attention to it or to the homophone.

24. *Mencius* 6A:11.

25. *Mencius* 7B:16. This statement is echoed in the *Mean* 20:5.

26. Compare *Analects* 2:4 and 4:4 and *Mencius* 2A:2.

27. *Mencius* 1A:7:8.

28. *Mencius* 1A:7:8. The term *jen-shu* is an intriguing one. Legge translates it as "an artifice of benevolence" (*The Chinese Classics*, vol. 2, p. 140). He is evidently following the interpretation of Chu Hsi, who understands it as *fa chih ch'iao*, an ingenious method, and, by implication, an action performed in full consciousness of its intended effect (*Ssu-shu chi-chu* [Collected Commentaries on the Four Books], commentary on *Mencius* 1A:7:8). However, since in the ensuing passage King Hsüan is made to admit that he himself had not grasped what was in his own mind (1A:7:9), it is difficult to avoid the impression that the "working" of humaneness was understood by Mencius to go beyond the purely conscious level.

29. *The Chinese Classics*, vol. 2, p. 201.

30. In 2A:6:2 Mencius recalls that the ancient kings had this "mind that cannot bear [to see the sufferings of others]." Here he affirms that people of the present also have it.

31. I am indebted to Richard John Lynn for help in translating this crucial passage. My translation is meant to be more literal than Lynn's more elegant one.

32. *Analects* 3:1 and 15:27. Mencius uses the phrase in this sense as well in 5B:1:1.

33. The phrase is used by I. A. Richards in his analysis of 2A:6 in *Mencius on the Mind* (London: Routledge and Kegan Paul, 1932), 19.

34. The character *ts'e*, meaning pity or commiseration, is not found in the *Analects*. The character *yin* occurs only in the sense of concealing or being hidden or obscure, not in the sense of pity or distress.

35. The "four sprouts" are clearly affective promptings, and when Mencius refers, literally, to *the mind* of pity and compassion, *the mind* of shame and dislike, etc., Legge (*The Chinese Classics*, vol. 2, p. 202) is certainly not incorrect in translating *hsin* as "feeling."

36. *Analects* 7:29.

37. Yen Hui's sense of being almost overwhelmed by the challenge of following the teachings of Confucius is expressed in *Analects* 9:10: "I look up to them and find them high; I try to penetrate them and find them firm; I look at them before me and suddenly they are behind. . . . I wish to give up but cannot do so; having exerted all my talent, it seems as if there is something standing up right before me, but though I wish to follow it, I find no way to do so."

38. The phrase is *k'uo erh ch'ung chih*, the word *ch'ung* being one used by Mo-tzu to speak of filling up an empty stomach or satisfying hunger. See Harvard-Yenching Institute Sinological Index Series, Supplement no. 21, *A Concordance to Mo Tzu*, 6/6/22 and 35/21/5.

39. *Mencius* 2A:6.

40. *Mencius* 2A:2:9.

41. *Mencius* 2A:2:15.

42. The suggestion here is not that Mencius was an egalitarian in the sense that he believed every person to be of equal worth or that he favored a society organized according to egalitarian principles. Rather, he was egalitarian in the sense that he believed that human beings share a common nature that is potentially good—always and in everyone. The distinction between "natural equality" and "evaluative equality" is effectively made by Donald Munro in *The Concept of Man in Early China* (Stanford: Stanford University Press, 1969), 1–22.

43. I have discussed this in another essay on Mencius entitled "Mencian Arguments on Human Nature (*Jen hsing*)," in *Philosophy East and West* (January 1994), 44(1). The basic line of argument is that Kao-tzu evidently believes that human beings share a similar nature, in that it determines their orientation toward survival, but that he fails to recognize that *hsing* also involves the disposition to moral responsiveness. Mencius does not reject Kao-tzu's view as entirely wrong, because of its recognition of primary biological needs, but only as too limited.

44. This is also discussed in "Mencian Arguments" (ibid.). The idea is that Mencius, while readily accepting the importance of environment (or "nurture") in human development, rejects the notion that environment is everything and that there are no natural human dispositions toward moral responsiveness.

45. I use the designation *radically inegalitarian* in its literal sense. Mencius rejects the idea that some human beings have an original endowment that is good, while others have an original endowment that is not-good. He does recognize that inequality results from the way that endowment is (or is not) developed.

46. After reviewing the alternative views, and then restating Mencius' view of the goodness of the nature, Kung-tu asks: "Then are *all* of them wrong?"

47. *Mencius* 6A:6:5–7.

48. A. C. Graham's view was that the word *ch'ing* cannot be definitely identified with the emotions in any pre-Han text. See his Appendix on *ch'ing* in "The Background of the Mencian Theory of Human Nature," *Tsing Hua Journal of Chinese Studies* (1967), 6(1,2); reprinted in *Chinese Philosophy & Philosophical Literature* (Singapore: Institute of East Asian Philosophies, 1986), 59–65. I am not prepared to differ on this point with so formidable an authority; however, it does seem clear enough that, whether or not Mencius identified the word *ch'ing* with the emotions, the "facts" (to use Graham's translation) to which he is referring seem to be "facts" of the emotional life.

49. *Mencius* 6A:6:7.

50. *Analects* 8:11, 8:20, 9:11, 11:8, and 13:2 (two occurrences).

51. *Mencius* 6A:11.

52. Ibid.

53. *Mencius* 6A:18.

54. Here *shu* is used transitively, in the phrase *shu chih*, meaning literally to "mature it" or "ripen it."

55. For a discussion of the dating of the text, see Chan, *Chu Hsi: New Studies*, 155–57.

56. For a discussion of Chu Hsi's interactions with Chang Shih concerning *jen* and the "Jen-shuo," see Chan, "Chu Hsi's 'Jen-shuo,'" 151–83.

57. Chu expresses this view with considerable vehemence in a letter to Lü Tsu-ch'ien in which he contrasts the clear explanations of the ancients with the "numerous superficial, abstruse, and wholly distorted corruptions on the part of later generations" and insists on the need, "when one has gained some understanding of the meaning of the term actually to occupy its space (*tsao ch'i ti-wei*)." See the Letter in Reply to Lü Po-kung in *Chu-tzu wen-chi* (Collection of Literary Works by Master Chu Hsi) (SPPY ed., under the title *Chu-tzu ta-ch'üan* [Great Collection of Literary Works by Master Chu Hsi]), 33:15b. A different translation of this portion of Chu's letter may be found in Chan, *Chu Hsi: New Studies*, 152.

58. The statement, which appears in *Wai-shu* (Outer Writings), 3:1a, is unattributed.

59. *Classic of Changes*, commentary on the *ch'ien* hexagram.

60. *Classic of Changes,* commentary on the *ch'ien* hexagram.

61. *Classic of Changes,* commentary on the *k'un* hexagram.

62. Translation adapted from Wing-tsit Chan, *A Source Book in Chinese Philosophy* (Princeton: Princeton University Press, 1963), 593–94.

63. *Analects* 7:22.

64. *Mencius* 7A:1.

65. Arthur Waley goes so far as to say that Confucius' statement in 7:22 may be considered among a category of statement that he characterizes as "pious formulae" (*The Analects of Confucius,* Introduction, 42), though it seems to me that such an interpretation would be almost impossible to verify.

66. Quoting *Mencius* 6A:11.

67. Professor Chan's translation reads, "If we can truly practice love and preserve it, then we have in it the spring of all virtues and the root of all good deeds." I believe that this translation anticipates and knowingly takes into account the reference further on in the text to *jen* as "the principle of love" (*ai chih li*). However as love (*ai*) has not yet been mentioned at this point, I prefer the more conservative, if less elegant, translation given here, assuming that what is truly to be embodied and preserved is the substance of *jen.*

68. Translation adapted from Chan, *Source Book in Chinese Philosophy,* 594.

69. Elsewhere Chu Hsi would explicitly follow the Ch'eng brothers in their association of *jen* with "seeds," once again emphasizing the creative capacity of the moral mind.

70. I do not mean to make any statement about the origin of this language, whether in Neo-Taoism or other sources, but only to point to its unquestionably important role in Neo-Confucian discourse.

71. Translation adapted from Chan, *Source Book in Chinese Philosophy,* 594–95.

72. There are just seven occurrences of the term *li* in the Mencius. Four of them are in 5B:1 in the passage that describes Confucius as the "complete concert" (*chi ta ch'eng*) and in which *li* is part of the compound *t'iao-li,* meaning regulated order. The implication of the passage is that the personality of Confucius is like a harmoniously ordered musical composition. Two more occurrences of *li* are found in 6A:7, where Mencius explains that what human minds have in common is a sense for *li* and *i,* order and rightness, and that it is order and rightness that "delight my mind." The final occurrence is in 7B:19, with the more unusual (and seemingly unrelated) meaning of "rely on."

73. This refers to *I-shu* (Written Legacy), 18:1a.

74. Translation from Chan, *Source Book in Chinese Philosophy,* 595.

75. I follow here Wing-tsit Chan's translation, but *i-i* might be more clearly translated as "forgotten meaning." I think the idea is that Chu Hsi takes his own explanation to be revealing Ch'eng I's actual idea, which has somehow become obscured because of misunderstandings. "Hidden meaning" should, of course, not be taken to imply any intention on Ch'eng I's part to shield or shroud his meaning in mystery.

76. In the *Chu-tzu yü-lei* (Classified Conversations of Master Chu Hsi) (Cheng-chung shu-chü 1970 reprint of the 1473 ed.), 25:3b–4a, in the course of discussing *Analects* 3:3, Chu Hsi speaks of *jen* as "the complete character of the original mind" (*pen-hsin chih ch'üan-te*).

77. Letter in Reply to Lü Po-kung, in *Chu-tzu wen-chi,* 33:12a–b.

78. "Jen-shuo," in *Chu-tzu wen-chi,* 67:21a.

79. Ibid.

80. "Jen-shuo," in *Chu-tzu wen-chi,* 67:21b.

81. *Mencius* 2A:2:16.
82. *Analects* 6:21.
83. *Analects* 15:32.
84. "Jen-shuo," in *Chu-tzu wen-chi*, 67:21b.
85. In "The Background of the Mencian Theory of Human Nature," A. C. Graham offered an illuminating perspective on Mencius' view of human nature by viewing it as a response to the challenge of the Yangist school, with its supposition of a human nature uninformed by any moral disposition. Following Graham's lead, I find it helpful to consider the possibility that Mencius' concept of *jen* can also be made more fully intelligible in the light of his arguments with both Yangists and Mohists.
86. In the course of analyzing the argumentative context in which Chu Hsi was working, Wing-tsit Chan suggests that Chu had three motives in writing his "Jen-shuo." The first, he says, was to correct the confused and mistaken theories that were prevalent among Chu's contemporaries. The second was "to show that the concept *jen* as love is based on the notion that the mind of Heaven and Earth is to produce things, and thereby prevent scholars from falling into the errors of emptiness and quiescence." The third was "to correct the erroneous theory that substance and function are two different things." (This third point perhaps requires some elaboration: Chu Hsi does, in fact, acknowledge that the nature and feelings, i.e., substance and function are different [*ch'i fen-yü chih pu-t'ung*], but he is concerned to clarify the "mutual penetration" between them [*ch'i mo-lo chih t'ung*]. In other words, substance and function are not to be viewed as distinct in the sense that they are separate.) Each of the three reasons adduced by Professor Chan involved an effort on Chu's part to correct a prevailing error concerning *jen*, and each of the errors is obviously traceable to Buddhism. See Chan, *Chu Hsi: New Studies*, 153.
87. Yamaguchi Satsujō and Wing-tsit Chan have argued that, while the key phrases of the "Jen-shuo" — "the character of the mind" and "the principle of love" — also occur in a Buddhist source, their occurrence there should not be taken as evidence that Chu Hsi borrowed them from that source or that he was inspired by Buddhism. (This issue turns, in part, on questions surrounding the contents of different editions of the *Ryūgan tekagami*. See Yamaguchi, *Jin no kenkyū*, 370–71, and Chan, "Chu Hsi's 'Jen-shuo,'" 157–58.) Assuming the validity of this judgment, there remains the related question of whether Chu Hsi, although perhaps not directly responsive to Buddhist influence in the sense that he might adopt Buddhist notions in elaborating his own view, may not have been responding to the challenge of Buddhism in more subtle ways. It is entirely conceivable, for example, that the Buddhist challenge may have contributed to Chu Hsi's sense that the metaphysical grounding of *jen* needed to be clarified and, in light of the wariness of the emotions that many Neo-Confucians shared with Buddhists, that the relation between the emotions and the nature had to be more fully defined.

GLOSSARY

ai   愛

ai chih li   愛之理

ai jen 愛人

an 安

an jen 安仁

Chan Wing-tsit 陳榮捷

Chang Shih 張栻

Ch'eng Hao 程顥

Ch'eng I 程頤

chi ta ch'eng 集大成

ch'i 氣

ch'i-chih chih hsing 氣質之性

ch'i fen-yü chih pu-t'ung 其分域之不同

ch'i-hsiang 氣象

ch'i hsin san yüeh pu wei jen 其心三月不違仁

Ch'i Hsüan wang (King Hsüan of Ch'i) 齊宣王

ch'i mo-lo chih t'ung 其脈絡之通

ch'ien 乾

chih 志

chih yü jen 志於仁

chin 盡

ch'ing ("what is genuinely in one," emotions) 情

ch'ing (light) 輕

Chu Hsi 朱熹

Chu-tzu ta-ch'üan 朱子大全

Chu-tzu wen-chi 朱子文集

Chu-tzu yü-lei 朱子語類

chün-tzu 君子

chung 重

Chung-kung 仲弓

ch'ung 充

fa chih ch'iao 法之巧

Fan Ch'ih 樊遲

Hsiao-ching 孝經

Hsieh Liang-tso 謝良佐

hsin 心

hsin chih te 心之德

hsin chih t'i 心之體

hsin yu chih-chüeh 心有知覺

hsing 性

I-ching 易經

i-i 遺意

I-shu 遺書

Jan Jung (or Chung-kung) 冉雍 （仲弓）

jen (chary of speech) 訒

jen (humaneness) 仁

jen (human being, person) 人

jen (responsibility, burden) 任

jen (seeds) 仁

jen-che ch'i yen yeh jen 仁者其言也訒

jen cheng 仁政

jen-shu 仁術

"Jen-shuo" 仁說

jen jen hsin yeh 仁人心也

jen yeh che jen yeh 仁也者人也

jen yüan hu tsai; wo yü jen ssu jen chih i 仁遠乎哉，我欲仁斯仁至矣

Jin no kenkyū 仁の研究

Jin no kogi no kenkyū 仁の古義の研究

Kao-tzu 告子

k'o-chi fu-li wei jen 克己復禮為仁

k'un 坤

kung, k'uan, hsin, min, hui 恭寬信敏惠

Kung-sun Ch'ou 公孫丑

Kung-tu 公都

k'uo erh ch'ung chih 擴而充之

li (principle) 理

li (ritual) 禮

Liang Hsiang wang (King Hsiang of Liang) 梁襄王

Liang Hui wang (King Hui of Liang) 梁惠王

Lü Tsu-ch'ien (Lü Po-kung) 呂祖謙 (呂伯恭)

Lun-yü　論語

Meng-tzu　孟子

Meng-wu　孟武

Mo-tzu　墨子

neng chin ch'ü pi k'o wei jen chih fang yeh　能近取譬可謂仁之方也

pen-hsin chih ch'üan-te　本心之全德

pu-jen (not able to bear)　不忍

pu jen (not humane)　不仁

pu-jen jen chih hsin　不忍人之心

pu-neng chin ch'i ts'ai　不能盡其才

Ryūgan tekagami　龍龕手鑑

Satō Hitoshi　佐藤仁

sheng chih tao　生之道

shih　士

Shih-ching　詩經

shu　熟

shu chih　熟之

Shimotomai Akira　下斗米晟

Ssu-ma Niu　司馬牛

Ssu-shu chi-chu　四書集註

ssu-te chih t'i-yung　四德之體用

ssu-tuan　四端

Takeuchi Teruo　竹內照夫

te　德

t'i/yung　體用

t'iao-li　條理

t'ien-li　天理

t'ien-ming chih hsing　天命之性

t'ien-tao　天道

t'ien-ti chih hsin　天地之心

Tsai Wo　宰我

ts'ai　才

tsao ch'i ti-wei　造其地位

ts'e　惻

ts'e-yin   惻隱

Tseng-tzu   曾子

tuan   端

tung chih tuan   動之端

t'ung-t'i   同體

Tzu-chang   子張

Tzu-kung   子貢

Tzu-lu   子路

Wai-shu   外書

wei jen   違仁

wu yü wo wei i wei jen chih t'i   物與我為一為仁之體

Yamaguchi Satsujō   山口察常

Yang Chu   楊朱

Yang Shih   楊時

Yen Hui   顏回

Yen Yüan   顏元

yin   隱

yung ch'i li yü jen   用其力於仁

Chapter Two

CHU HSI AND MEDITATION

RODNEY L. TAYLOR

Moral and spiritual cultivation for many Neo-Confucians involved the use of a form of meditation known as quiet-sitting (*ching-tso*; Jap. *seiza*).[1] The discussion of meditative practices by Confucians was widespread throughout much of the later history of Confucianism in China, Korea, and Japan, by both those who espoused the practice and those who opposed it. It was common for these later Confucians to refer to the teachings of quietude and the practice of quiet-sitting by the patriarchs of the Confucian learning of the Sung dynasty (960–1279), Chou Tun-i (1017–1073), Ch'eng I (1033–1107), Ch'eng Hao (1032–1085), and, in particular, Chu Hsi (1130–1200). Confucians who practiced meditation saw within it a fulfillment of the principles and procedures of moral and spiritual cultivation established by the patriarchs of the Sung learning. Those who opposed Confucian meditation saw a slippery slope of quietism that brought Confucian teaching and practice dangerously close to Buddhism.

Within Confucian discussions about moral and spiritual cultivation there was also debate on the question of the relationship between meditative practice and moral action. For some Confucians meditative practice gave rise to moral action; for others it was seen as a hindrance to the fulfillment of one's moral responsibilities. Throughout its history quiet-sitting has been anything but a quiet topic within the development of Confucian ideology and practice. Today it remains a salient element in the attempt by scholars to unravel the historical meanings of Confucian orthodoxy and its attending orthopraxy.

If we are to understand Confucian meditation fully, both in the perspective of those who practiced it and in the views of those who opposed it, it is imperative to understand its formative stage of development within the formation of Neo-Confucianism during the Sung dynasty. What role did meditation play for the patriarchs of the Sung Confucian learning? What use did Chu Hsi make of the practice himself and how did he incorporate it into his concept of learning? How did the Sung patriarchs and, in particular, Chu Hsi, avoid the stigma of association with Buddhism in the use of any form of contemplative practice?

Though extensive use was made of meditative practices and even broader discussion can be found by a wide spectrum of Confucians, very little scholarship examines the history and nature of Confucian meditative practices. It is noteworthy that the two scholars whom we are honoring in the publication of this volume have both written on the importance of quiet-sitting as a component of Neo-Confucian learning and moral cultivation. Wm. Theodore de Bary has discussed aspects of the practice as it relates to broader issues of Confucian learning and ideology.[2] W. T. Chan, in a pioneering study, has addressed questions of the role of quiet-sitting for Chu Hsi as well as the later Neo-Confucian tradition.[3] The present study builds on the work of both scholars. De Bary's discussion of the creation and establishment of Neo-Confucian ideology during the Sung period provides the intellectual context for Confucian meditative practice. Chan's work on quiet-sitting is a point of departure for closer study of the evolution of Chu Hsi's attitudes toward the practice as well as the examination of the role the practice played in Chu Hsi's full regimen of moral and spiritual cultivation.

A Half-Day of Quiet-Sitting . . .

In the discussion of meditative practice by later generations of Confucians, there is frequent reference to what is represented as Chu Hsi's rule for meditation and self-cultivation, "a half-day of quiet-sitting and a half-day of reading" (*pan-jih ching-tso; pan-jih tu-shu*). It is often presented as a motto for Chu Hsi's practice, one that Chu Hsi ostensibly had occasion to use frequently and advocate widely. As Wing-tsit Chan has pointed out, however, the importance of the phrase has been extended far beyond the context within which it occurs.[4] The phrase actually occurs only once in the writings of Chu Hsi. Recorded in the *Chu Tzu yü-lei* (Classified Conversations of Master Chu Hsi), it is advice given to only a single student, and only once to that student. The passage in which it occurs is the following:

> Kuo Te-yüan[5] came to say his farewell. Chu Hsi said: "In the course of a day it is best for a person to reduce his idle talk to but a sentence or two and the number of guests to but one or two. If one is in turmoil how is it possible to study successfully? On a day that is without affairs and free of concerns utilize a half-day of quiet-sitting and a half-day of reading. If this were to continue for a year or two then there would be no question but that one would progress."[6]

The phrase "a half-day of quiet-sitting and a half-day of reading" was picked up and used widely among later generations of Neo-Confucians, by both those who advocated quiet-sitting and those who opposed the practice. Those who advocated the practice saw in the phrase a rule for a daily regimen of meditative practice. Those who attacked the practice saw in the phrase advocacy of excessive meditation and a lack of concern for moral effort. Though the phrase is used only once,[7] its single occurrence does not permit us to conclude that one can dismiss or diminish the role of quiet-sitting for Chu Hsi. In fact, quite the contrary: Chu Hsi may have used this phrase only once, but he spoke a number of times on the practice of quiet-sitting in his writings. While he exercised caution in the advocacy of the practice and sought to ensure a balance of meditative practice with other forms of learning and self-cultivation, he saw quiet-sitting as a practice with a wide range of benefits including not only the strengthening of the process of learning but restoration of health and vitality, and even memory.[8]

Meditative practice was widespread in Chu Hsi's day; it was not something new or limited only to esoteric religious orders. Chu Hsi could look to both Taoist and Buddhist traditions for extensive experience and discussion of various forms of contemplative practice. He could look to his own tradition as well. The issue for Chu Hsi was not the acquisition of a new meditative practice, even within the context of Confucianism. His own early teachers taught meditation and strongly advocated its use. In other words, Chu Hsi did not have to be convinced of the benefits of meditation. Meditative practices were a given of the broader cultural milieu. In fact, one might suggest that there was a broad and general understanding of such practices, which in many respects took away the tradition-specific characteristics of meditation, creating a kind of melting-pot of contemplative practice. While specific schools still had their special forms of meditative practice and could argue that the practice could not be divorced from their teachings, at a more common level one could appreciate the similarities of general meditative practice. Such appreciation led to practice. The task for Chu Hsi was the intellectual incorporation of general meditative practices into his own formulations of the developing Confucian agenda.

Quiet-Sitting and the Young Chu Hsi

Though much is still not known of the origins of quiet-sitting as a form of contemplative practice within the Confucian tradition, in its earliest phases it is associated with several of the patriarchs of the Sung learning.[9] If not the actual practice of quiet-sitting, at least the teaching of quietude is dominant in Chou Tun-i, particularly in the form *chu-ching*, regarding quietude as fundamental. In turn, both Ch'eng I and Ch'eng Hao practiced and taught quiet-sitting, and their students Li Yen-p'ing (Li T'ung, 1093–1163) and Lo Ts'ung-yen (1072–1135) both became well known for their advocacy of the practice.

Chu Hsi learned quiet-sitting as a student of Li Yen-p'ing while he was still quite young. What Chu Hsi was taught suggests that Li Yen-p'ing regarded quiet-sitting not only as a means of calming the ordinary day-to-day perturbations of the mind, but as a method for reaching the innermost recesses of the mind as well. In the meditative vocabulary associated with both Li and Lo, the practice was said to have the capacity to deal not only with the *i-fa*, the manifest mind, but also the *wei-fa*, the unmanifest mind. The source of this often alluded to distinction was a passage from the *Chung-yung* (Doctrine of the Mean): "Before the feelings of pleasure, anger, sorrow and joy are aroused it is called equilibrium (*chung*, centrality, mean). When these feelings are aroused and each and all attain due measure and degree, it is called harmony."[10] The use of *wei-fa* and *i-fa* established a vocabulary for a distinction between unmanifest and manifest and the terms became a vehicle to explain and interpret the practice of quiet-sitting. Lo Ts'ung-yen used this passage as a basis for his discussion of the practice. "In quiet-sitting one is capable of seeing pleasure, anger, sorrow, and joy while they are yet unmanifest (*wei-fa*) and have not assumed material form."[11] Li Yen-p'ing echoed this same passage and suggested to Chu Hsi that through the practice of quiet-sitting he would come to see the Principle of Heaven within the unmanifest mind.[12] Such discussions, and in turn the instruction that Chu Hsi received from Li Yen-p'ing, emphasized the practice of quiet-sitting as a means of expressing the unmanifest mind.

Though Li Yen-p'ing's lasting influence on Chu Hsi may have been substantial, Chu Hsi's views of quiet-sitting developed and evolved in different ways. In what both Okada Takehiko and Conrad Schirokauer[13] see as a major turning point in the intellectual development of Chu Hsi, there is a turning away from Li Yen-p'ing with the gradual increase in influence of the teachings of Hu Hung (1106–1161) of the Hunan school. This influence has been studied in some detail, particularly by Schirokauer; the important point, however, is Chu Hsi's apparent change in attitude toward the teaching of quietude and quiet-sitting he had received from Li Yen-p'ing.

The basis of this change in attitude has been suggested in a poem by Chu Hsi and the response to it by Hu Hung. In 1159 Chu Hsi, annoyed because Hu Hsien had assumed office at an elderly age, composed a poem critical of the event. The last verses of the two quatrains read:

Holding firm to the recluse life, resting in the empty valley,
Wind and moonlight over a river demand my attention.

                 *   *   *

Entrust floating clouds to stretch and whirl calmly
Yet for ten thousand years the azure mountains are just azure.[14]

Hu Hung saw the poem and was critical of it, feeling that it was biased in favor of quietude and provided no basis for moral action. He wrote a poem in response, the last verse of which reads:

The hermit is partial to the azure mountain's beauty,
This is because the azure of the azure mountain never grows old.
The clouds come out of the mountains and rain in Heaven and Earth,
Having once been washed, the mountains are even more lovely.[15]

Okada interprets the difference between Chu Hsi and Hu Hung as expressed in these poems in the following way:

Unlike Li Yen-p'ing, Hu Hung felt that since the substance of the unmanifest, that is, the Principle of Heaven, can only be seen functioning in the manifest mind, unless one understands the "subtle beginnings" of the

Principle of Heaven in the manifest it is impossible to nourish and preserve the mind. He thought that in preserving and nourishing the substance of the unmanifest solely through quietude, one would sink into the uselessness of Zen learning. Accordingly his first priority was the understanding of the "subtle beginnings" and only afterwards were there preservation and nourishment of the unmanifest.[16]

Hu Hung and the Hunan school placed much greater emphasis on the manifest mind, remaining wary of discussions or practices that dwelt on the unmanifest mind. Hu An-kuo (1074–1138), the founder of the school, had said, "If you just apply yourself to the already aroused condition [i.e., the manifest], then there will be no waste of mental energy."[17] This tradition stood in contrast to the teachings of quietude and quiet-sitting of Li Yen-p'ing, which focused largely on the experience of the unmanifest itself. Chu Hsi's response to this challenge by Hu Hung seems to have been to shift his attention in learning away from the kind of quiet-sitting taught by Li Yen-p'ing. While Chu Hsi's own eventual position included attention to both the manifest and unmanifest components of the mind and continued to include the practice of quiet-sitting, there seems to be little doubt that Hu Hung was influential in moving Chu Hsi away from a form of teaching and practice dominated by concerns of quietude.

Hu Hung died in 1161. Chu Hsi never met him. The exchange of poems must have occurred sometime between 1159 and 1161. This exchange suggests that after the age of thirty Chu Hsi reassessed the role of quietude and quiet-sitting, and while they continued to play a role in his learning and self-cultivation, they did not play a major role. Instead they are subsumed in other forms of learning and self-cultivation, being carefully placed to respect the role they can play, but not placed so as to be susceptible to overemphasis and thus lead to a distortion of the Neo-Confucian learning as Chu Hsi came to understand it.

While both Okada and Schirokauer speak of the influence of Hu Hung on Chu Hsi, both are equally aware of the developing and evolving world view of Chu Hsi himself. Thus there is a sense in which Hu Hung may appear as an abrupt influence on Chu Hsi, but this must be put in the perspective of the development of Chu Hsi's own thought. There is also much here that has yet to be fully studied. One of the important elements yet to be fully understood is the role of Chang Shih (1133–1180), the principal source of Chu Hsi's knowledge of the Hunan school. He was the major disciple of Hu Hung but he was also a close friend of Chu Hsi. His relationship with Chu Hsi could have had a bearing on Chu Hsi's understanding of the Hunan school. It may be significant as well that once Chu Hsi criticized Hu Hung, Chang Shih put up little opposition and as a result the Hunan school ceased to exist as a separate school.[18]

What we can say is that both Li Yen-p'ing and Hu Hung played important roles as Chu Hsi developed and evolved his mature point of view. They both spoke to a common issue, that of learning and self-cultivation and its relation to mind. The issue of mind, while not the focus of this study,[19] remained an important foundation for Chu Hsi's attitude about quiet-sitting. The vocabulary of *wei-fa/i-fa* (unmanifest and manifest mind) was central to this concern. Li Yen-p'ing and Lo Ts'ung-yen both referred to quiet-sitting as a practice capable of experiencing the unmanifest mind, a state of tranquility before the arising of the feelings. For Chu Hsi, as we have seen, there were potential hazards involved in focusing too heavily on the mind in its tranquility and thus ignoring its active capacity in the world, the manifest mind. Part of the attraction of Hu Hung was to rescue the capacity of the mind for activity and participation in the world. But here too problems developed, as Schirokauer's study makes very clear.[20]

Hu Hung distinguished between mind and nature, identifying nature with the state before the feelings arise and mind with the state after the feelings arise. This was unacceptable in Chu Hsi's developing theory of mind in which mind was present in both states and was described as both manifest and unmanifest. Hu Hung may have saved Chu Hsi from a potential overemphasis on quietude and the unmanifest mind, but Chu Hsi went on to criticize Hu Hung's limitation of mind to the manifest mind and limitation of learning to the acquisition of external knowledge. Chu Hsi sought instead a theory of mind that recognized both its manifest and unmanifest capacities and a process of learning that recognized nourishing and preserving as well as study. By retaining both the *wei-fa* and the *i-fa*, Chu Hsi was able to make a place for the practice of quiet-sitting as part of his way of learning and self-cultivation, a part sensitive to both nourishing and preserving as well as study.

Patriarchal Authority for Quiet-Sitting

Though the contact with Hu Hung's teachings seems to have played an important role in shifting Chu Hsi from the early influence of Li Yen-p'ing, the practice of quiet-sitting continued to be discussed and included in his general framework of learning and self-cultivation. At least part of the reason for his own continued discussion of the practice may also be seen in the authority attributed to the founders of the Sung learning. Chou Tun-i, Ch'eng I, and Ch'eng Hao were patriarchs of the tradition, and the fact that they discussed the practice and advocated its use was something not easily dismissed by Chu Hsi. Had Lo Ts'ung-yen or Li Yen-p'ing themselves created the practice, that is, had it not been possible to trace it back to figures such as Chou Tun-i, Ch'eng I, or Ch'eng Hao, then Chu Hsi might have been even more wary of the practice than he at times appeared. But Lo and Li had learned it from their own teachers, Ch'eng I and Ch'eng Hao, and while there might be debate on whether it was Ch'eng I or Ch'eng Hao who was the primary source,[21] there is no debate over the fact that quiet-sitting was something practiced and discussed by the Ch'eng brothers, and that both Lo Ts'ung-yen and Li Yen-p'ing relied on their authority. That gave the practice a stature not easily ignored and placed Chu Hsi in the position of recognizing that, regardless of the reservations he may have had concerning the practice, the figures he himself looked to as the founders of the Sung learning advocated the use of quiet-sitting. This may well have been part of the reason that the Ch'eng brothers figured prominently in some of Chu Hsi's comments about the practice.

> People today are not willing to understand things in terms of the fundamentals [*ken-pen*]. They take note of a word such as reverent seriousness [*ching*] as something merely for future concern and are concerned even less for things of the past. The fundamentals have not been established and therefore the rest is fragmented and the moral effort [*kung-fu*] neither unified nor steady. [Ch'eng] Ming-tao and [Li] Yen-p'ing taught people quiet-sitting; from their perspective it was quiet-sitting that was essential.[22]

The passage is straightforward enough. Fundamentals (*ken-pen*) are being ignored. The importance of the past as a guide to learning and self-cultivation as well as the critical importance of the teaching of reverent seriousness (*ching*) are both disregarded. The result is the failure to establish the proper foundation for learning and thus the inability to proceed with learning itself. Chu Hsi then says that Ch'eng Hao and Li Yen-p'ing recommended quiet-sitting, presumably for the restoration of fundamentals. Does Chu Hsi himself recommend quiet-sitting? Were Chu Hsi thoroughly disenchanted with the practice of quiet-sitting, one would imagine that it would scarcely be mentioned; thus, its mention is at least a measured acceptance, though with qualifications. The most important of these in this passage is the inclusion of the reference to reverent seriousness (*ching*), a doctrine central to Ch'eng Hao's brother Ch'eng I, but of less significance to Ch'eng Hao. By placing quiet-sitting with reverent seriousness, Chu Hsi moved his own advocacy of the practice closer to the position of Ch'eng I, a major source of many of Chu Hsi's own ideas. The authority that is most respected in this sense is that of Ch'eng I, and Ch'eng I's own preference for reverent seriousness over quietude may be very suggestive of Chu Hsi's own proclivities. To the question of whether reverent seriousness is not the same as quietude Ch'eng I responded, "Once one speaks of quietude, one has fallen into the ways of Buddhism. Only use the word reverent seriousness; do not use the word quietude."[23] *The Chin-ssu lu* (Reflections on Things at Hand) records a similar comment by Ch'eng I: "One who is reverently serious is naturally vacuous and tranquil. But vacuity and tranquility cannot be called reverent seriousness."[24] Chu Hsi's comment on this passage draws the distinction between Ch'eng I and Chou Tun-i in terms of the issue of quietude and clearly shows his own preference.

> Master Chou considers tranquility to be fundamental, primarily because he wants people's minds to be tranquil and calm and he wants people to be their own master. Master Ch'eng, on the other hand, is afraid that if people merely seek tranquility they will not have anything to do with things and affairs. He therefore talks about reverent seriousness. If one is reverently serious, one is naturally vacuous and tranquil.[25]

In another discussion of quiet-sitting we find Chu Hsi critical of Li Yen-p'ing and what Chu Hsi perceived to be too great an emphasis on the practice, not unlike his explanation of Ch'eng I's qualifications on the practice and concept of quietude.

> A disciple asked: "When I recently saw Liao Tzu-hui[26] he told me that he had seen you this year and had asked about [Li] Yen-p'ing's discussion of quiet-sitting. [He said] that you were inclined to pay it little heed. Why would this be the case?" [Chu Hsi] said: "This matter is difficult to discuss. If through quiet-sitting one comprehends the Principle of the Way, there is naturally no harm in it. But when one merely pursues quiet-sitting one cannot comprehend the Principle of the Way or understand that the natural is tranquil. People today devote themselves to quiet-sitting so as to reduce [their involvement in] affairs, so that they are unable [to comprehend the Principle of the Way]."[27]

This is Li Yen-p'ing without the authority of the Ch'eng brothers, particularly Ch'eng I. It presents a teaching that, from Chu Hsi's point of view, needs to be criticized and corrected for it has subverted the very goals of learning itself, the understanding of the Principle of the Way, through a biased emphasis on quietude alone. It demonstrates Chu Hsi's critique of a doctrine of quietude, an issue discussed further below, and his criticism of the practice of quiet-sitting when that practice has departed sufficiently from what he understood as the practice of the patriarchs of the Sung learning and the qualifications they placed on the practice. This is further addressed in a letter to Chang Yüan-te.[28]

> [Ch'eng] Ming-tao instructed people in the practice of quiet-sitting. He taught them this practice because at that time his followers were pursuing study alone to the exclusion of internal affairs. Now if one practices quiet-sitting to the exclusion of affairs, holding to quiet-sitting and creating a special kind of effort, this is no different from Ch'an meditation. It is only through setting forth reverent seriousness which penetrates both activity and quiescence that the two will be uninterrupted so that one need draw no distinction between them.[29]

Ch'eng Hao's instruction itself cannot be faulted because he has put quiet-sitting in a context with other activities, in this case, studying. There is again, however, a very strong emphasis on reverent seriousness. The problem is not Ch'eng Hao's instruction to practice quiet-sitting; the problem arises when that teaching is placed in a different context, one where the only object of focus is quietude and quiet-sitting. The fault does not rest with Ch'eng Hao himself even though Chu Hsi would change his emphasis. Authority thus can still lie with Ch'eng Hao.

What begins to emerge from Chu Hsi's discussion is a sense that he intends to sustain the teachings of the patriarchs of the Sung learning: regardless of the changes Chu Hsi made as he moved toward his own "completion" of Neo-Confucianism,[30] he accepted the authority of the Sung patriarchs. This acceptance included quiet-sitting when it was practiced with an understanding of the role it could play in the learning process, not as an end unto itself. For the Ch'eng brothers and Chu Hsi alike it seems clearly identified with study and learning. It is a form of quiet-sitting conjoined with study that Chu Hsi addressed most frequently in his discussions of the practice.

The Balance of Quiet-Sitting and Study

Though the phrase "a half-day of quiet-sitting and a half-day of reading" is used only once by Chu Hsi, it clearly speaks to the necessary balance between quiet-sitting and study. Both of these activities were in pursuit of the learning of the Way, one facilitating the other when pursued together. This balance between quiet-sitting and study is addressed in several passages.

> For many persons there is a time of quiet-sitting without thought or recall, and there is a time for thought and measure of the Principle of the Way. How is it possible, however, to define these as two separate paths? If one speaks of a time of quiet-sitting and a time of book-learning, the moral effort involved [in the two] is different. Thus when one nourishes [*han-yang*] [one's nature] through quiet-sitting there must be at that very time a thorough investigation and scrutinizing of the Principle of the Way. Only in this way will there be real nourishment. . . . The defect of people today is that the effort they exert in quiet-sitting and in book-learning is not the same, and therefore they err.[31]

Several important issues are raised in this passage. Chu Hsi is addressing a common misunderstanding of quiet-sitting that suggests that its object is the cultivation of a quiet state reflective of the unmanifest dimensions of the mind discussed by Li Yen-p'ing and Lo Ts'ung-yen. Such a state is seen as different from study, different in a profound sense of no-activity within the inner dimensions of the unmanifest mind. Though, as de Bary has suggested, Li Yen-p'ing's focus on the unmanifest state of the mind did not mean that his conception of quiet-sitting was opposed to rationality or even scholarly activity, Chu Hsi remains wary of placing a priority on the unmanifest.[32] Chu Hsi seems to be suggesting that this interpretation of quietude fails to see its capacity for activity and, as a result, fails to see the basis for the incorporation of the practice with study.

To Chu Hsi quietude is itself a time for activity. It is not a vacuous, blank expression of no-thought. Within quietude the processes of investigating and scrutinizing of the Principle of the Way move forward. Quietude is best understood as a period for focusing such attention, not eliminating it. The moral effort of quiet-sitting can be said to resemble that of study. Quietude of this nature was immune from criticism as a form of quietism associated with a Buddhistic focus on no-thought and emptiness. To cultivate a state of quietude of the unmanifest mind placed one precariously close to Buddhist thought and practice. Those who indulged in such a practice ran the risk of being unable to return to study and the real affairs of the world. This was the excess of quietude Chu Hsi found in Li Yen-p'ing. Quietude had its place, but that place was defined in terms of a reflective capacity for study itself.

There are other passages as well in which Chu Hsi discusses the active or thought-reflective capacity of quietude in its balance and integration with study:

> Someone asked: "How is it that at the beginning of learning the spirit [*ching-shen*] can be so easily lost? How would it be to practice quiet-sitting?" [Chu Hsi] said: "This is all right too, but it is not only in quietude that one makes an effort. One must also seek to realize it in moral action [*kung-fu*]. One ought also to examine and embody what the sages and worthies teach people. How can one only concentrate upon forced meditative sitting [*ta-tso*]? If one sets forth energy in all areas, that is, in studying, in attending others and handling affairs, then whether active or quiet, speaking or silent, such a spirit can be preserved. When one is without affairs one can unify the quiet mind with rested thought [*hsi-nien*] and there need be no concern for other activities. And what of one's mind? If there be unsettled desires as well as scattered, chaotic and rambling activity, this is not related to learning. Mencius said: "The way of learning is none other than seeking the mind that has strayed." If this is not the case and the spirit is not recollected [*shou-shih*], then study will lack flavor and the performance of duties will lack unanimity. How can this be beneficial?[33]

Chu Hsi's point is a very simple one. Learning can be lost in quiet-sitting if quiet-sitting becomes an end unto itself. Quiet-sitting must be carefully balanced with moral action (*kung-fu*), which is defined across a range of activities. In addition, quiet-sitting is not the cultivation of a blank and empty quietude or the opportunity to dwell in no-thought. Quiet-sitting is instead the occasion for quiet and attentive thought. Rather than tie such mind cultivation to the unmanifest state of the mind, there is an appreciation of the active capacity of quietude as the opportunity for attention and thought. In fact, the retention of thought and attention is one of the important features of the correct practice of quiet-sitting.

> Chu Hsi asked Po-yü:[34] "How do you employ effort [in self-cultivation]?" He said: "To undertake the study of quiet-sitting, one should severely limit thought and deliberation." Chu Hsi said: "Such severe limiting cannot

simply mean driving it out entirely. If one shuts one's eyes completely and just sits, there is still thought."[35]

The object is not to drive thought from the mind, to make it blank and empty, but to recognize that thought is a natural part of the mental process. There is a legitimate place for a practice that creates a setting for quiet and reflective thought and thus a context that facilitates the ongoing effort of study directed toward acquiring knowledge of the Way of Principle. The passage concludes by saying: "The idea is not to be without thought, but to be without depraved thought."[36] Clearly, the practice of quiet-sitting is not to cultivate a state without thought.

One of Chu Hsi's descriptions of quiet-sitting suggests that it is virtually a form of study itself. Suggesting that quiet-sitting prevents the loss of the mind's energy, Chu Hsi says: "The mind that restfully studies old books and washes away worldly habits and dust begins to realize that it has returned to its resting place."[37] Merely to practice quiet-sitting without studying furthers only the state of quietude, not the learning of the Principle of the Way.

This is the reason that Chu Hsi is critical of the division between quiet-sitting and study. To divide the two rather than trying to integrate them is to run the risk of creating a separate category of quietude that can then become an end in itself. This same issue of the division between quiet-sitting and study applies equally to the division between quiet-sitting and moral action.

> [Someone] asked: "Does the [principle of] 'regarding quietude as funda-mental' create a place for moral effort?" [Chu Hsi] said: "Although we speak of 'regarding quietude as fundamental,' this does not mean the rejection of activities or affairs. Since to be a human being means that one sets forth service for superior and parent, communication with friends, comfort for wife and children and regulation of servants, one cannot cut oneself off completely, shutting the door and practicing only quiet-sitting. When there are matters to attend to, one does not simply leave, saying: 'Just wait until I have finished my quiet-sitting!' Not to respond is simply unacceptable. This is nothing more than doing only what one wishes. Between these two ways one must make a clear decision. From the very beginning it is essential to put real energy into the performance of moral effort. This cannot just be passed over as so much talk."[38]

The practice of quiet-sitting must remain accessible enough to permit the individual to attend to the performance of duties and responsibilities. His capacity for moral action must not be limited. If it is limited, then, from Chu Hsi's point of view, it has compromised the larger goal of learning and may be little different from Buddhism. Thus we find Chu Hsi cautioning against meditation alone, what he calls concentration upon forced sitting (*ta-tso*),[39] suggesting that "quiet-sitting need not be like sitting meditation (*tso-ch'an*) in Ch'an Buddhism, entering concentration and cutting off thought and cognition."[40] Stressing the preference for reverent seriousness over quietude, Chu Hsi asserts the corrective to a biased focusing on quietude. The practice of quiet-sitting must fit into a balance and serve the larger goal of learning itself. A problem occurs when one dominates over the other, and the more common error is found in the dominance of quietude.

This, for Chu Hsi, is one of the chief potential problems with Chou Tun-i's phrase "regarding quietude as fundamental." Quietude is not related to activity, and quiet-sitting is seen only as furthering quietude. As a result, the state of quietude alone is sought, and the cultivation of reverent seriousness as well as other major elements of learning, the investigation of things, the extension of knowledge, the exhaustive investigation, become secondary to the pursuit of quietude.

Time and again Chu Hsi recommends that the practice of meditation be in balance with other activities. It is only in this dependent relation that the true character of quietude for Chu Hsi can emerge. Apart from particular and unusual circumstances, quiet-sitting is a part of a life of moral duties and responsibilities. The degree to which it becomes a special and sought after practice isolated from other activities is the degree to which it is no longer judged to be part of the learning of the sage, and as such, for Chu Hsi, it is a practice to be abandoned before it creates the same separation from the world and its concerns that Chu Hsi sees as typical of a tradition such as Buddhism.

The Priority of Quiet-Sitting

Thus far the emphasis has been on the balance of quiet-sitting and learning and the necessity of seeing these two activities as thoroughly integrated. Quiet-sitting provides a quiet reflection on one's study, but it is the study that is emphasized. But in several passages the priority is placed on the quiet-sitting; it is the groundwork for study and learning. This is also a cause for wariness. One who begins without the balance between quiet-sitting and study constantly in mind can easily slip into too great an attention to quietude itself.

Replying to Chou Shen-fu's letter [Chu Hsi] said: "In general people who want to study should first collect together [*shou-shih*] body and mind in order to become quiet. Only after this can they open a chapter and have any real benefits. If anxieties disappear rapidly in this fashion, then the mind will accord with the Principle of the Way. If, however, things are not in complete accord, then how can one possibly read books? Nothing else need be said! Simply shut your door and begin sitting for half a month. After ten days have passed pick up a book to study and you will see the truth of these words."[41]

Formerly the teacher Ch'en Lieh had suffered from a loss of memory. One day he read Mencius' phrase "The way of learning is nothing other than seeking the mind that has strayed."[42] Suddenly he realized this and said, "If my mind has never been collected together [*shou-te*] then how could I possibly remember all these books?" Subsequently he shut his door and practiced quiet-sitting without reading any books at all. After about a hundred days he recovered the mind that had strayed and, though he had abandoned the study of books, not a single passage had been lost.[43]

Replying to Ts'ai Chi-t'ung's[44] letter [Chu Hsi] said: "Recently I have seen that study and reading can injure mind and eyes. Quiet-sitting as a way of examining the self is not like this. Since it has beneficial results you should practice it and then you will see its efficacy."[45]

In the first passage the context is learning, not its abdication. Chu Hsi suggests that learning will be of little use when it is dominated by worries and anxieties. Such distress must be minimized if learning is to proceed. This is the role assigned to quiet-sitting. It has the capacity to quiet and focus the mind and thus prepare it properly for learning. The context defines the balance of quiet-sitting and study essential to learning, but it also isolates a role for quiet-sitting, making the practice a precondition to study and the successful pursuit of learning.

In the second passage quiet-sitting is also given an important priority in the pursuit of learning. Someone who approaches learning without a mind that is centered or clear, lacks a basis for memory because there is no integration of knowledge in the mind. Reflecting on Mencius' comment on the mind that has strayed, Chu Hsi advocates a method to find the mind that has strayed. He appears to allow an extensive period of quiet-sitting alone. Where in this case is the balance between quiet-sitting and study? The context remains the pursuit of learning, and even though an extensive practice of quiet-sitting is recommended, its purpose is to return to learning itself. Still, when required, quiet-sitting can be employed in a strict and demanding regimen as a prerequisite for successful study.

The third passage also suggests a priority assigned to quiet-sitting, but one must be careful not to overread it. The context again is critical: there is an admission that the process of learning and study can be fatiguing, even injurious to mind and body. Quiet-sitting can serve as a respite to such fatigue, a calming of overextended mental activity and thus a refocusing and new attentiveness to the issues at hand. Chu Hsi is not advising that one desist from study, but that study can fatigue body and mind and quiet-sitting can be of benefit. In fact, in a condition of fatigue or even injury, priority should be given to quiet-sitting.

All three of these passages suggest that priority be given to quiet-sitting in its relation to study. This is not inconsistent with the larger goal of integrating quiet-sitting with study, but simply an indication that under certain circumstances quiet-sitting has a specific role to play in the larger context of learning. Its role is to facilitate learning, and where in other passages we have seen Chu Hsi critical of solitary use of quiet-sitting for fear of its eclipsing the role of learning, here its advocacy can be understood as a method to restore the goal of learning itself. Its practice did not result in the cultivation of a blank or empty state with an increasing attachment to quiet-sitting itself. It was a carefully prescribed role for the practice within the framework of learning.

Health and Quiet-Sitting

The previous passage, in addition to demonstrating the concern for quiet-sitting to restore a balance to study, also suggested, at least indirectly, a link between quiet-sitting and health. Quiet-sitting can remedy fatigue and even injury of mind and body. We have also seen the capacity of quiet-sitting for restoring memory. While there is no technical discussion of the relation of the practice to matters of health or its relation to the traditional Chinese view of physiology, there are several additional passages in which Chu Hsi describes the mental and physical benefits of the practice of quiet-sitting.

Replying to Lin Ching-po's[46] letter [Chu Hsi] said: "During the year I suddenly became exhausted and just did not feel up to my normal self. A number of different illnesses all seemed to strike me at the same time and in addition I was not able to sleep properly. I was taking medicine but it was only when I could obtain a day or two of quiet-sitting without reading or study that I could see any relief at all."[47]

Cheng-shu[48] was suffering from diffuseness of spirit [*chih-man*].[49] Chu Hsi sought a relief to his illness and Cheng-shu as a result practiced quiet-sitting. After this he again began his study, but tired of reading. Chu Hsi said: "You don't want to concentrate [only on quiet-sitting]. It has given you a rest but now you need to return to study."[50]

Replying to P'an Shu-ch'ang's letter [Chu Hsi] said: "After middle age how much vital energy and spirit are left . . . ? As the eyes dim it is difficult to put forth the effort. For this reason I practice quiet-sitting in the midst of reading in order to collect together [*shou-lien*] body and mind. As I feel the energy I go back to reading. Once in a while I cover my eyes, expecting to encounter the dwelling place of the mind, and I sigh."[51]

Replying to Huang Tzu-keng's[52] letter [Chu Hsi] said: "When you are ill it is not good to think strenuously. Everything possible should be put aside. You should pay attention only to preserving the mind and nourishing the vital energy. Increase the practice of quiet-sitting with the eyes focused upon the tip of the nose and the mind focused upon the abdomen. After a time it [i.e., the abdomen] will become warm and you will see results."[53]

In each of these passages Chu Hsi suggests that quiet-sitting serves to restore health. He describes exhaustion and fatigue, weakness of spirit and intellect, as well as aging and waning vitality, and in each case he suggests the use of quiet-sitting as either a curative or at least therapy for the particular malady. What is the strength of quiet-sitting in these areas? It would appear to be its capacity for providing complete rest and relaxation as well as its ability to reinvigorate a mental focus and attentiveness. Not unlike the rigors of study, weakness drains the vitality. Quiet-sitting is seen by Chu Hsi as a means for restorating such vitality. We have already seen this capacity in the context of study. Here Chu Hsi extends the same principle to the encounter with a weakness of spirit and vitality.

Such descriptions of quiet-sitting reinforce an emerging picture of Chu Hsi's view of the practice. It is not designed to be a strenuous practice demanding the rigors of mental and physical discipline. Had this been the case, such practices would in all likelihood have to have been suspended during illness because of their strain upon body and mind. In his discussion of Zen illness in the *Orategama*,[54] Hakuin (1686–1769) makes clear that during such illnesses the practice of *zazen* is virtually eliminated while other forms of practice are initiated. By contrast, for Chu Hsi quiet-sitting is a practice maintained, if not focused on, during periods of weakness because of its capacity for rest and reinvigoration. Not unlike Hakuin's description of curing his illness, however, Chu Hsi also suggests a certain technical form to meditative practice, particularly as it relates to the restoration of health.

Health, Breath Control, and Meditative Procedure

Little is usually said about the actual practice of quiet-sitting by Chu Hsi or for that matter most other Confucians who engaged in the practice.[55] The specific reasons for this are addressed below. The last passage, however, is an exception. I know of no other discussion of quiet-sitting by Chu Hsi that specifies the technical details of meditation. There is no evidence to indicate that this kind of procedure was routine for quiet-sitting; in fact, quite the contrary. With so much of the discussion focusing on the attempt to accommodate quiet-sitting to study as well as the constant fear that too much attention to quiet-sitting would result in little differentiation from Ch'an Buddhist practices, this passage seems very much at odds with the tradition of practice inherited and taught by Chu Hsi.

The explanation may very well lie in the larger context of the passage dealing with an attempt to heal an illness. One cannot help but wonder whether there was a common tradition of meditative procedure dealing with issues of illness and health, so that Chu Hsi might simply have been drawing on that tradition.[56] In such a capacity the tradition would carry little stigma of association with the Buddhist meditative tradition, though the case for Taoist techniques may be less easy to eliminate. For reasons I have discussed elsewhere, a solution in terms of syncretism seems less than satisfactory,[57] though interaction with Taoist techniques is conceivable.[58]

Relevant to the passage at hand is a poem by Chu Hsi found in the *Chu-tzu wen-chi* (Collection of Literary Works by Master Chu Hsi) that celebrates breath control procedures in meditation. A tentative translation of "T'iao-hsi chen" (Poem in Praise of Regulated Breathing) follows:

> There is white at the tip of the nose. When I observe it, no matter where or when, I become free and easy. Expelling the breath at the height of quietude is like fish in a spring pond. Drawing it in at the height of activity is

like the swarming of a hundred insects. The inhaling and exhaling, their mystery is limitless. Who can control it? It is an achievement without a ruler. Cloud resting and Heaven walking are not things I dare speak of. By maintaining singleness of mind and dwelling in peace I shall live to a thousand and two hundred years.[59]

In Chu Hsi's poem, as in his letter to Huang Tzu-keng, there is the same reference to the focusing of the eyes on the tip of the nose and apparently similar concentration on the abdomen. In the "T'iao-hsi chen" the reference to breath (*hsü*) is interpreted as breathing from the abdomen rather than normal breath from the lungs.[60] Such focusing on the abdomen may then be interpreted as a concentration on breathing from the abdomen. Obviously, however, much more is said in the "T'iao-hsi chen," and one can only speculate as to the degree to which further instruction in breath control was then implied or applied in the situation involving quiet-sitting. In this sense it is important to note that the poem does not refer to quiet-sitting. Its context of meditation remains unstated and possibly unclear, though the use of what may be Taoist terminology raises some interesting questions.

In general, Chu Hsi does not discuss meditative techniques. The only references seems to be limited to discussions of curing illness.[61] Not only is there an absence of attention to technical meditative procedures in Chu Hsi's frequent discussions of the practice, but the same is true for the later Neo-Confucian tradition, even in those periods where much emphasis was placed on the practice of quiet-sitting, for example, in the Tung-lin school at the end of the Ming dynasty (1368–1644),[62] with certain figures of the Ch'eng-Chu tradition during the Ch'ing dynasty (1644–1912),[63] and in the Yamazaki Ansai school in the Tokugawa period (1600–1867).[64]

It may be suggested that this was not merely a failure to talk about the techniques, but a disinclination to employ such techniques in practice. Were it the case that such techniques were viewed as a viable part of the practice, and particularly that Chu Hsi had upheld such an interpretation of quiet-sitting, then one might anticipate substantial discussion of such techniques in the later tradition. Short of occasional references to such techniques for the curing of illness and restoration of health, I find no association of these techniques with quiet-sitting as it is usually discussed. What one finds repeatedly in the later discussions of quiet-sitting are the very issues that dominate Chu Hsi's discussion of the practice, the balance of quiet-sitting with other activities.

Method and Practice in Quiet-Sitting

Chu Hsi's discussions of quiet-sitting contain very little, if any, description of the practice itself. They include no description of the physical position or posture for the practice. Later figures occasionally give some detail on this, but Chu Hsi does not discuss it. In addition, very little is said of the time duration for the practice apart from the phrase "a half-day of quiet-sitting and a half-day of reading." Even if this phrase were an indication of regular practice, it still tells us little in terms of the actual division of time, since the number of ways two half-days can be divided up is virtually unlimited. Other references are made to extended time periods, for example, "a day or two of quiet-sitting,"[65] "begin sitting for half a month,"[66] and "after about one hundred days he found the mind that had strayed."[67] These are, however, of little assistance even in the recommendations for an extended period of quiet-sitting,[68] because they do not indicate how the practice is incorporated into a given day. We are not told, for example, whether quiet-sitting is to be practiced exclusively or whether activity and quiet-sitting are always evenly divided.

Perhaps such lack of specificity should come as no surprise, for the practice of quiet-sitting is continually presented as a model of meditation without regimented practice. In this sense the very generality of the practice is a part of its inner content. One is not to set up rules and regulations regarding physical position and the time period for practice because this may regiment the practice too much. Such regimentation could separate its practitioner from the responsibilities of everyday affairs, and it could come to resemble the systems of meditation that the teachers of quiet-sitting criticize. Since its primary function is a support and complement to learning and moral action, one might suggest that the actual style and duration of practice are left largely to the practitioner himself to allow a flexibility of practice to suit the particular needs of the situation. In this way practice does not become an end in itself, and moral responsibilities can always be answered immediately.

The lack of specificity involved in the practice of quiet-sitting, however, has another, more subtle dimension. This involves a recognition of problems inherent in the formulation of specific "methods" of practice, problems that go beyond the attempt simply to integrate quiet-sitting and study or to avoid practices that appear to approach techniques used by Buddhists and others. This is suggested by the following example.

> Hu asked about the method [*fa*] for the practice of quiet-sitting. [Chu Hsi] said: "Quiet-sitting is just to sit quietly in this way. One does not need to

shut out affairs; one does not need to shut out thought and deliberation. It is without method."[69]

The point, of course, is to emphasize that quiet-sitting is not to be made a special object. Not being anything special, it therefore is not sought after. It is, after all, just quiet-sitting. The problem is that anything specifically designated becomes an object focused on in practice. However designated, it will remain an object, and this is where the problem lies. It is better not to focus on this practice called quiet-sitting, but simply to sit quietly. Such quiet-sitting is not attentive to quiet-sitting as a practice, it is just quiet, or more accurately, it is just attentive.

Someone asked: "Each day in my leisure time I do a little quiet-sitting in order to nourish my mind, but all I see are ideas spontaneously and confusedly arising. The more I desire to become quiet, the less quiet I become. [What can I do?]" [Chu Hsi] said: ". . . Adamantly to teach others not to think is unacceptable. However, if one thinks about quietude with already confused thought, how much more thought is added? One doesn't want to adhere to something or bind or oppress oneself. There needs to be time for rest."[70]

Chu Hsi's response to the question emphasizes again the difficulty created by seeking a specific goal. In this case the questioner is seeking a quiet mind. The only result, however, is the creation of ideas and the failure to produce quietude. Chu Hsi cautions that one can neither force the cessation of thought nor expect to quiet the mind by *thinking about* quietude. If the mind is already full of thought, then how will it help to add the additional thought of quietude? The only way to seek quietude is by not seeking it. That is, one does not adhere to quietude as an object and therefore is not bound or oppressed by it. Thus, as the earlier discussion suggested, all one can do is simply to sit quietly with no particular method or plan for the acquisition of quietude. Do not think about it; simply practice it. One should just sit, neither forcing the cessation of thought nor attempting the addition of more thought, and thought itself will be calmed. Of course, to think that thought is calmed only stirs more thought. And to think that one should not think about thought being calmed exacerbates the problem further.[71] Just sitting and not thinking about it are virtually all that Chu Hsi can recommend.

"Collecting Together" Body and Mind

While Chu Hsi recommends that one neither think about quietude and its cultivation nor make an object of the practice itself, he does describe part of what takes place within the practice. These descriptions are found primarily focused on two terms that appear to be used interchangeably and occur quite frequently in Chu Hsi's discussions of quiet-sitting. The terms *shou-shih* and *shou-lien* mean to collect together or to gather, and by extension to unify, to focus, and to make attentive. We have already seen the terms used. They are also prominent in the following passages.

> [Someone] asked how [Ch'eng] I-ch'uan taught people quiet-sitting. [Chu Hsi] replied: "When he saw people filled with anxiety and desire, he instructed them to collect together [*shou-shih*] the mind by means of this [i.e., quiet-sitting], just this and nothing else. If it is a matter of one just beginning learning, it should be like this as well."[72]

> Replying to Chou Shen-fu's letter [Chu Hsi] said: "In general people who want to study should first collect together [*shou-shih*] body and mind in order to become quiet. Only after this can they open a chapter and have any real benefits."[73]

> For this reason I practice quiet-sitting in the midst of reading, in order to collect together [*shou-lien*] body and mind.[74]

In these passages the uses of *shou-shih* and *shou-lien* seem obvious enough. They suggest a mind scattered and without focus, dealing with the array of affairs and events or simply the fatigue of study. In such a setting the purpose of quiet-sitting is to give the individual the opportunity of calming the mind or, as we might say, collecting oneself together. Chu Hsi expands upon the meaning of collecting together in the following passage.

> [Someone] asked: "Irrespective of the relation of quiet-sitting and the performance of duties, isn't it most important to focus upon oneness? [Chu Hsi] said: "On the contrary, quiet-sitting need not be like the sitting meditation [*tso-ch'an*] of Ch'an Buddhism, entering concentration and cutting off thought and cognition. It is just the gathering together [*shou-lien*] of this mind. Without diverse activities and idle thought the mind is naturally of its own clearly focused upon oneness. And if matters should arise, then it follows them, fulfills its duty, and returns to clarity. It is not necessary

because of one event to provoke two or three others. How will one be able to focus on oneness?"[75]

Chu Hsi's response again focuses upon "collecting together" (*shou-lien*). It is distinguished from any process of conscious concentration. Rather than a state of concentration, which, from Chu Hsi's point of view, would come to resemble Buddhist practice, one attends to nothing more than the gradual cessation of "diverse activities and idle thoughts." If this can be accomplished, then the mind is naturally calm and collected. Chu Hsi is also suggesting that a calm and collected mind is one that is naturally attentive and focused. This stands in sharp contrast to the cultivation of a kind of blank state. Here the direction is toward an increased attention and focus. In this context the term oneness is appropriate, not to describe an ultimate metaphysical union but, rather, a level of attentiveness. To focus upon oneness means to be single-minded and attentive.

In quietude, the mind is focused and attentive; it is single-minded and attentive. This is a form of quietude, not seeking after quietude but drawing one's attention to a single focus. This process of becoming attentive to a single focus is described in a quotation from Ch'eng I in the *Chin-ssu lu*.

People often cannot be tranquil in their thought because they have not calmly mastered their minds. The only way to master one's mind is to let it rest in the thing one is doing, as, when one is a ruler, one abides [rests] in humanity. . . . People cannot rest in the things they are doing because they grab many other things and cannot leave things as they are . . . "As there are things, there are their specific principles." One must rest in the thing one is doing.[76]

To focus on a single thing—to rest in the thing one is doing—is an attentiveness that Chu Hsi also sees as the result of quiet-sitting. It is also the way in which he frequently describes reverent seriousness (*ching*). Ch'en Ch'un (1159–1223), one of the most faithful interpreters of Chu Hsi, characterized *ching*, reverent seriousness, in the following terms in his *Pei-hsi tzu-i* (Neo-Confucian Terms Explained):

Master Ch'eng [Ch'eng I] said, "Reverent seriousness is concentrating on one thing, and oneness means not getting away from it." Wen Kung [Chu Hsi] combined the two and said, "Reverent seriousness is concentrating on one thing without departing from it," making the meaning especially clear.[77]

Or further:

When one is doing nothing and his mind is always present without going in an opposite direction, that is of course concentrating on one thing. When one is doing something and his mind responds to that thing without allowing a second or third thing to interfere, that is also concentrating on one thing.[78]

Reverent seriousness is an attentiveness both in quietude and in activity. As we have seen, the attentiveness of reverent seriousness is preferred to that of quietude. By focusing only on quietude there is much greater difficulty in seeing its application to both quietude and activity. Not unlike Ch'eng I's statement, reverent seriousness produces natural quietude, but quietude does not necessarily produce a state of reverent seriousness.[79] Such attentiveness can then serve the process of learning and study and provide the groundwork for the investigation of things and the exhaustion of principle, hallmarks of the specific learning methods associated with Chu Hsi.

For Chu Hsi quiet-sitting produces an attentiveness that is to be applied to quietude and activity alike. He sees quiet-sitting as that which produces this attentiveness or singleness of thought and prefers to describe this state in terms of reverent seriousness rather than quietude. Whether called single-mindedness, attentiveness, or reverent seriousness, each of these terms emphasizes the capacity of the mind to act in a state of quietude. This remains a dominant theme for Chu Hsi in his discussions of quiet-sitting, and it is consistent with the influence of Hu Hung on Chu Hsi, developing a model of learning far more concerned with the learning and cultivation of the manifest, *i-fa*, capacity of the mind.

Still, there are times in the writings of Chu Hsi on quiet-sitting when there are hints of the unmanifest and the suggestion that the practice of quiet-sitting leads not just to a singleness of thought or attentiveness but to a deep and profound foundation and resting place within the individual. The vocabulary of the manifest and unmanifest is not employed, but the depth hinted at might well suggest the deepest layers of the mind, the state before the arising of the feelings.

When one practices quiet-sitting, one nourishes the gradual calming of the original foundation [*pen-yüan*]. Even though one does not avoid worldly affairs or self-knowledge, there is still a collecting together [*shou-lien*] and a return to a point of rest. It is similar to a person going on a journey. He goes and he returns home and he still has a dwelling for himself to rest in. If there is not the preservation and nourishment of the original foundation [*pen-yüan*] and one just freely follows things in the world, then when one wants to collect together [*shou-lien*] and return, one will lack the dwelling place to rest in.[80]

According to Chu Hsi, this foundation will be established through the practice of quiet-sitting. This will provide what he describes as a resting place. How might we understand this resting place: is it a final state of quietude? Or, is one who attains it still attentive to the needs of action in the world? Obviously for Chu Hsi one may never withdraw from attending to the needs of the world. Thus it cannot be a state of ultimate quietude, for this would differ little in Chu Hsi's eyes from the Buddhist practices he so strongly rejects. Perhaps the metaphor he himself uses is the best clue. A person goes on a journey, and he has a home to which he can return. The journey is an extending of self, and it is accompanied by insecurity and uncertainty. Yet there is a home to return to, where one can find solace. Chu Hsi seems to be suggesting that quiet-sitting can create this foundation of solace. If it is truly realized, then the journey within and the journey without are little different from each other and there is a foundation from which to respond to the world, a solace found within.

Conclusion

This chapter examines several dominant issues for Chu Hsi in the practice and teaching of quiet-sitting. First is his continuing emphasis on the relation between quiet-sitting and study. Almost without exception Chu Hsi's discussion of quiet-sitting has placed the practice in the context of study and learning. In this context there is a reciprocal relation between quiet-sitting and study, with each benefiting the other.

Second, in this concern for the balance between quiet-sitting and study, there is a constant concern that the balance may falter and that too much attention may come to be placed on the practice of quiet-sitting. This is seen as becoming a quest for quietude itself and regarded as leading the individual away from learning and moral action. For this reason, much attention is placed on seeing quiet-sitting as including both quietude and activity.

Third, for Chu Hsi, as for Ch'eng I before him, reverent seriousness is given priority over quietude and quiet-sitting is related to the cultivation of reverent seriousness. If quiet-sitting can be related to reverent seriousness, then its practice can avoid slipping into a kind of quietism. Such reverent seriousness links quiet-sitting to both learning and moral action.

Fourth, quiet-sitting in its connection to reverent seriousness suggests the production of an active mind, not a blank and empty mind. This is expressed by Chu Hsi in terms of the mind's attentiveness and its focus, a single-mindedness. These images suggest an active response of the mind to learning and to moral action. The mind remains active though it is quiescent, and Chu Hsi's position reflects Ch'eng I's statement that reverent seriousness contains quietude, but quietude does not necessarily contain reverent seriousness. For Chu Hsi this set the limits of the practice of quiet-sitting and defined the errors of the way of the Buddhists who only sought the way of quietude.

Fifth, even with the focus on the active capacity of the mind in quiet-sitting, the cultivation of a state of constant attentiveness, there is also a sense expressed by Chu Hsi that quiet-sitting can permit the mind to find and express its deepest layers, its own original foundation, and its resting place. This, in turn, is presented by Chu Hsi as a source of strength and a profound depth of solace.

We have seen that Chu Hsi discussed quiet-sitting at some length, and it seems fair to say that quiet-sitting was not an inconsequential part of Chu Hsi's learning. He continued to advocate the use of quiet-sitting, and at times it played a very important role in the learning process. He did not discourage those who asked him about the practice, and he advocated and encouraged its use in a number of settings.

However, Chu Hsi also cautioned about the potential hazards in the misuse or misinterpretation of the practice of quiet-sitting. Much of his own attitude seems to have derived from the authority of his teachers, and thus the authority of the practice established by the lineage of patriarchs of the Sung learning. Chou Tun-i, Ch'eng I, Ch'eng Hao, and his own teacher Li Yen-p'ing considered quiet-sitting an important form of self-cultivation. Chu Hsi expressed his cautions about its misuse, clarified its limitations, and related it to his own central concerns in learning, but he also continued to advocate its use in a balanced setting with other activities. Quiet-sitting thus remained a part of the Transmission of the Way, and it was a practice that Chu Hsi in turn transmitted to those who came after him.

NOTES

1. This paper was first delivered at the Regional Seminar in Neo-Confucian Studies, Columbia University, March 1988. I am grateful to Professor Wing-tsit Chan for his extensive discussion of my paper in the seminar. I discovered at that point that he had been working on his own study of Chu Hsi and quiet-sitting, and I was able to benefit from our mutual interest in the topic. His work was first presented under the title "The New Fortune of Master Chu," at the Regional Seminar in Neo-Confucian Studies, Columbia University, April 1986, and later published under the title "Chu Hsi and Quiet-Sitting." See Wing-tsit Chan, *Chu Hsi: New Studies* (Honolulu: University of Hawaii Press, 1989), 255–70.

2. See Wm. Theodore de Bary, "Neo-Confucian Cultivation and the Seventeenth-Century 'Enlightenment,'" in Wm. Theodore de Bary, ed., *The Unfolding of Neo-Confucianism*, 141–216 (New York: Columbia University Press, 1975). On the emergence of Neo-Confucian orthodoxy, see Wm. Theodore de Bary, *Neo-Confucian Orthodoxy and the Learning of the Mind-and-Heart* (New York: Columbia University Press, 1981), pp. 1–66.

3. Chan, *Chu Hsi*, 255–70.

4. Ibid., 256–57.

5. Kuo Te-yüan is Kuo Yu-jen. For an account of Kuo, see Wing-tsit Chan, *Chu-tzu men-jen* (Master Chu's Disciples) (Taipei: Hsüeh-sheng shu-chü, 1982), 203–4.

6. *Chu-tzu yü-lei* (Classified Conversations of Master Chu Hsi), 1880 edition, 116:20 a–b (1473 ed., 116:17b[4474]) (hereafter referred to as *Yü-lei*). See Chan, *Chu Hsi*, 257.

7. See Chan, *Chu Hsi*, 257–60, for an excellent summary of the use and misuse of this phrase.

8. We are fortunate in having a rare work compiled by Yamazaki Ansai's disciple Yanagawa Gogi, *Shushi seiza shūsetsu* (Collection of the Sayings of Chu Hsi on Quiet-Sitting), 1717 edition, a comprehensive collection of passages by Chu Hsi primarily drawn from the *Chu-tzu yü-lei* and the *Chu-tzu wen-chi* (Collection of Literary Works by Master Chu Hsi). I have found no errors and little additional discussion of quiet-sitting not included in Yanagawa's work. This work has been the basis for the present study, and I would like to express my thanks to Okada Takehiko and Fukuda Shigeru for making it available to me.

9. For a review of these materials, see R. L. Taylor, *The Confucian Way of Contemplation: Okada Takehiko and the Tradition of Quiet-Sitting* (Columbia: University of South Carolina Press, 1988), 98.

10. *Chung-yung*, 1:4; Wing-tsit Chan, *A Source Book in Chinese Philosophy* (Princeton: Princeton University Press, 1963), 98.

11. Huang Tsung-hsi, *Sung Yüan hsüeh-an* (Philosophical Records of Sung and Yüan Scholars) (Taipei: Shih-chieh shu-chü, 1974), 10:63.

12. Ibid., 10:72.

13. Okada Takehiko, *Zazen to seiza* (Tokyo: Ofusha, 1972), 118–19, translated in R. L. Taylor, *The Confucian Way of Contemplation*, 140–41; Conrad Schirokauer, "Chu Hsi and Hu Hung," in W. T. Chan, ed., *Chu Hsi and Neo-Confucianism*, 480–502 (Honolulu: University of Hawaii Press, 1986).

14. See Taylor, *The Confucian Way of Contemplation*, 140, and Schirokauer, "Chu Hsi and Hu Hung," 483.

15. Ibid.

16. See Taylor, *The Confucian Way of Contemplation*, 141.

17. Quoted in Schirokauer, "Chu Hsi and Hu Hung," 484.

18. Ibid., 480.

19. A brief but excellent overview of Chu Hsi's theory of mind is provided in T'ang Chün-i, "The Development of the Concept of Moral Mind from Wang Yang-ming to Wang Chi," in Wm. Theodore de Bary, ed., *Self and Society in Ming Thought*, 93–97 (New York: Columbia University Press, 1970).

20. Schirokauer, "Chu Hsi and Hu Hung," 491–97.

21. See Taylor, *The Confucian Way of Contemplation*, 34.

22. *Yü-lei*, 12:11a–b (1473 ed., 12:9b–10a [334–35]).

23. *Erh-Ch'eng i-shu* (Written Legacy of the Two Ch'engs) (Ssu-pu pei-yao ed.), 8:6b.

24. Wing-tsit Chan, trans., *Reflections on Things at Hand: The Neo-Confucian Anthology Compiled by Chu Hsi and Lü Tsu-ch'ien* (New York: Columbia University Press, 1967), 143. Note that the translation of *ching* as "seriousness" has been changed to read "reverent seriousness."

25. Ibid.

26. Liao Tzu-hui is Liao Te-ming (*chin-shih* 1169). An account is found in Chan, *Chu-tzu men-jen*, 287.

27. *Yü-lei*, 103:2b–3a (1473 ed., 103:2a–b [4135]); Yanagawa, *Shushi seiza shūsetsu*, 7b–8a.

28. Chang Yüan-te is Chang Hsia (1161–1237). An account of him is found in Chan, *Chu-tzu men-jen*, 192.

29. *Chu-tzu wen-chi* in *Chu-tzu ta-ch'üan* (Great Collection of Literary Works by Master Chu Hsi) (Ssu-pu pei-yao ed.), 62:6a (hereafter referred to as *Wen-chi*); Yanagawa, *Shushi seiza shūsetsu*, 9b–10a.

30. See Wing-tsit Chan, "Chu Hsi's Completion of Neo-Confucianism," in Françoise Aubin, ed., *Etudes Song-Sung Studies: In Memoriam Etienne Balazs*, 59–90 (Paris: Mouton, 1973).

31. *Yü-lei*, 12:18b (1473 ed., 12:16a [347]); Yanagawa, *Shushi seiza shūsetsu*, 2a–b.

32. See Wm. Theodore de Bary, "Neo-Confucian Individualism and Holism," in Donald J. Munro, ed., *Individualism and Holism: Studies in Confucian and Taoist Values*, 343 (Ann Arbor: University of Michigan Press, 1985).

33. *Yü-lei*, 115:10b (1473 ed., 115:9a–b [4427–28]); Yanagawa, *Shushi seiza shūsetsu*, 1b–2a; quoting *Mencius*, 6A:11.

34. Po-yü is T'ung Po-yü (1144–1190 or after). See Wing-tsit Chan, *Chu-tzu men-jen*, 247–48.

35. *Yü-lei*, 118:1b (1473 ed., 118:1a [4525]); Yanagawa, *Shushi seiza shūsetsu*, 7a–b.

36. Ibid.

37. *Wen-chi*, 63:9b; Yanagawa, *Shushi seiza shūsetsu*, 6b.

38. *Yü-lei*, 45:13a–b (1473 ed., 45:11b [1844]); Yanagawa, *Shushi seiza shūsetsu*, 2b–3a.

39. *Yü-lei*, 115:10b (1473 ed., 115:9a–b [4427–28]); Yanagawa, *Shushi seiza shūsetsu*, 1b–2a.

40. *Yü-lei*, 12:17b (1473 ed., 12:15a–b [345–46]); Yanagawa, *Shushi seiza shūsetsu*, 3a–b.

41. *Wen-chi*, 63:37b–38a; Yanagawa, *Shushi seiza shūsetsu*, 4a.

42. *Mencius*, 6A:11.

43. *Yü-lei*, 11:2a (1473 ed., 11:1b [280]); Yanagawa, *Shushi seiza shūsetsu*, 4b.

44. Ts'ai Chi-t'ung is Ts'ai Yüan-ting (1135–1198). See Chan, *Chu-tzu men-jen*, 331–32.
45. *Chu-tzu hsü-chi* (Supplementary Collection of Writings by Master Chu), in *Chu-tzu ta-ch'üan*, 2:13a; Yanagawa, *Shushi seiza shūsetsu*, 5a–b.
46. Lin Ching-po is Lin Ch'eng-chi. See Chan, *Chu-tzu men-jen*, 148.
47. *Chu-tzu pieh-chi* (Additional Collection of Writings by Master Chu) in *Chu Tzu ta-ch'üan*, 4:14b; Yanagawa, *Shushi seiza shūsetsu*, 5a.
48. Cheng-shu is Yü Ta-ya. See Chan, *Chu-tzu men-jen*, 85.
49. The condition described is one of diffuseness or randomness of spirit or intellect.
50. *Yü-lei*, 113:16a (1473 ed., 113:13b [4384]); Yanagawa, *Shushi seiza shūsetsu*, 5b.
51. *Wen-chi*, 46:21b–22a; Yanagawa, *Shushi seiza shūsetsu*, 6a–b.
52. Huang Tzu-keng is Huang Hsün (1147–1212). See Chan, *Chu-tzu men-jen*, 262–63.
53. *Wen-chi*, 51:27a; Yanagawa, *Shushi seiza shūsetsu*, 6b–7a.
54. See Philip Yampolsky, trans., *The Zen Master Hakuin: Selected Writings* (New York: Columbia University Press, 1971), 84–86.
55. See Taylor, *The Confucian Way of Contemplation*, 31–55.
56. The only discussion I know of the relation of quiet-sitting to matters of health and well-being is that by Okada Takehiko, *Zazen to seiza*, 47–58.
57. See R. L. Taylor, "Proposition and Praxis: The Dilemma of Neo-Confucian Syncretism," *Philosophy East and West* (April 1982), 32(2):187–99.
58. See Julia Ching's chapter in this volume.
59. *Wen-chi*, 85:6a. An alternative translation may be found in Julia Ching's chapter in this volume.
60. Okada Takehiko, *Zazen to seiza*, 50.
61. Ibid., 52–55.
62. R. L. Taylor, "Meditation in Ming Neo-Orthodoxy," *Journal of Chinese Philosophy* (June 1979) 6(2):149–82.
63. I am referring particularly to Wm. Theodore de Bary's study of Ch'en Chien, Li Yung, Li Kuang-ti, and Chang Po-hsing. Wm. Theodore de Bary, *The Message of the Mind in Neo-Confucian Thought* (New York: Columbia University Press, 1989), 98–99, 155–61, 184, 189–91.
64. See Okada's study of the practice of quiet-sitting during this period, translated in Taylor, *The Confucian Way of Contemplation*, 123–61.
65. *Chu-tzu pieh-chi*, 4:15b; Yanagawa, *Shushi seiza shūsetsu*, 5a.
66. *Wen-chi*, 63:37b–38a; Yanagawa, *Shushi seiza shūsetsu*, 4a.
67. *Yü-lei*, 11:2a (1473 ed., 11:1b [280]); Yanagawa, *Shushi seiza shūsetsu*, 4b.
68. One of the few extended discussions is that by Atobe Ryōken, and even in it detail is at a minimum. See Okada Takehiko's treatment of this translated in Taylor, *The Confucian Way of Contemplation*, 154–55, 158–59.
69. *Yü-lei*, 120:4a (1473 ed., 120:3b [4608]); Yanagawa, *Shushi seiza shūsetsu*, 7a.
70. *Yü-lei*, 118:23a (1473 ed., 118:19b–20a [4562–63]); Yanagawa, *Shushi seiza shūsetsu*, 9a–b.
71. See my discussion of Kao P'an-lung and his comments on the practice of quiet-sitting; Taylor, "Meditation in Ming Neo-Orthodoxy," 155–62.
72. *Yü-lei*, 119:7a–b (1473 ed., 119:6b [4588]); Yanagawa, *Shushi seiza shūsetsu*, 1a–b.
73. *Wen-chi*, 63:37b–38a; Yanagawa, *Shushi seiza shūsetsu*, 4a.
74. *Wen-chi*, 46:21b–22a; Yanagawa, *Shushi seiza shūsetsu*, 6a–b.

75. *Yü-lei*, 12:17b (1473 ed., 12:15a–b [345–46]); Yanagawa, *Shushi seiza shūsetsu*, 3a–b.

76. Chan, *Reflections on Things at Hand*, 134–35.

77. Wing-tsit Chan, trans., *Neo-Confucian Terms Explained (The Pei-hsi tzu-i) by Ch'en Ch'un* (1159–1223) (New York: Columbia University Press, 1986), 100.

78. Chan, *Neo-Confucian Terms Explained*, 101.

79. Chan, *Reflections on Things at Hand*, 143.

80. *Yü-lei*, 96:12a–b (1473 ed., 96:10b [3926]); Yanagawa, *Shushi seiza shūsetsu*, 5b–6a.

GLOSSARY

Atobe Ryōken　跡部良賢

Ch'an　禪

Chang Po-hsing　張伯行

Chang Shih　張栻

Chang Hsia (Yüan-te)　張洽，元德

Ch'en Chien　陳建

Ch'en Ch'un　陳淳

Ch'en Lieh　陳烈

Ch'eng-Chu　程朱

Ch'eng Hao (Ming-tao)　程顥，明道

Ch'eng I (I-ch'uan)　程頤，伊川

Cheng Shu　正叔

Ch'ien Mu　錢穆

chih-man　支蔓

Chin-ssu lu　近思錄

ching　敬

Ch'ing　清

ching-shen　精神

ching-tso　靜坐

Chou Shen-fu　周深父

Chou Tun-i　周敦頤

Chu Hsi　朱熹

Chu Tzu hsü-chi　朱子續集

Chu Tzu men-jen　朱子門人

Chu Tzu pieh-chi　朱子別集

Chu Tzu ta-ch'üan　朱子大全
Chu Tzu wen-chi　朱子文集
Chu Tzu yü-lei　朱子語類
chu-ching　主靜
Chuang Tzu　莊子
Chung-yung　中庸
Dōgen　道原
Erh-Ch'eng i-shu　二程遺書
fa　法
Fukuda Shigeru　福田殖
Hakuin　白隱
han-yang　涵養
hsi-nien　息念
hsü　噓
Hu An-kuo　胡安國
Hu Hsien　胡憲
Hu Hung　胡宏
Huang Hsün (Tzu-keng)　黃營・子耕
Huang Tsung-hsi　黃宗羲
i-fa　巳發
Kao P'an-lung　高攀龍
ken-pen　根本
kung-fu　工夫
Kuo Yu-jen (Te-yüan)　享友仁・德元
Lao Tzu　老子
Li Kuang-ti　李光地
Li Yen-p'ing (T'ung)　李延平・侗
Li Yung　李容
Liao Te-ming (Tzu-hui)　廖德明・子晦
Lin Ch'eng-chi (Ching-po)　林成季・井伯
Lo Ts'ung-yen　羅從彥
Okada Takehiko　岡田武彥
Orategama　遠羅天釜
pan jih ching tso; pan jih tu shu　半日靜坐　半日讀書

P'an Shu-ch'ang　潘叔昌

Pei-hsi tzu-i　北溪字義

pen-yüan　本原

seiza　靜坐

Shih ching　詩經

shou-lien　收斂

shou-shih　收拾

shou-te　收得

Shushi seiza shūsetsu　朱子靜坐集說

Ssu-pu pei-yao　四部備要

Sung Yüan hsüeh-an　宋元學案

"*T'iao-hsi chen*"　調息箴

ta-tso　打坐

Ts'ai Yüan-ting (Chi-t'ung)　蔡元定，季通

tso-ch'an　坐禪

Tung-lin　東林

T'ung Po-yü　童伯羽

wei-fa　未發

Wen Kung　文公

Yamazaki Ansai　山崎闇齋

Yanagawa Gōgi　柳川剛義

Yü Ta-ya (Cheng-shu)　佘大雅，正叔

zazen　坐禪

Zazen to seiza　坐禪と靜坐

Chapter Three

SUNG NEO-CONFUCIAN VIEWS ON GEOMANCY

PATRICIA EBREY

> *Divination of the future, astrology, geomancy, physiog-*
> *nomy, the choice of lucky and unlucky days, and the lore of*
> *spirits and demons, were part of the common background of*
> *all Chinese thinkers, both ancient and medieval.*
>
> —JOSEPH NEEDHAM,
> *Science and Civilisation in China, vol. 2, p. 346*

Geomancy of graves is generally recognized to have had a profound influence on Chinese at all levels of education.[1] Both poor and rich consulted experts who could guide them to the best spots to bury their parents, believing the choice would affect their own lives and the lives of their children. Writing in the late nineteenth century, de Groot noted that "every right principled man is pretty familiar with Fung-shui matters," as they concerned filial duty. Even poor people "seldom neglect consulting a Fung-shui expert when they have to bury their father or mother."[2] Maurice Freedman, describing Hong Kong only a few years ago, noted the connection between geomancy and belief in social mobility:

> It is when a man begins to think of the possibility of increased success for himself and his issue, a measure of prosperity already having been achieved, that he takes to a concern with geomancy. On their side, those who are already successful cannot ignore the need to ensure their continuing prosperity by taking geomantic precautions.[3]

Belief in and practice of geomancy, in other words, was not confined to the more ignorant in Chinese society, tending if anything to be more prevalent among the prosperous.

Several scholars have recently attempted to disentangle and explain the ideas that constituted geomancy in late imperial times, most notably Feuchtwang, Marsh, and Bennett.[4] It is now widely recognized that geomantic ideas had close connections with other Chinese cosmological ideas and habits of correlative thinking.[5] Little attempt, however, has been made to look at geomantic ideas in historical context, probably because the sources have not lent themselves to this sort of treatment.[6] The classical texts of geomancy used in Ch'ing times, especially the *Chai-ching* (Classic of Sites), *Tsang-shu* (Book of Burials), and *Ch'ing-nang ao-yü* (Inner Sayings of the Green Sack), are all problematic, with attributions that are widely doubted, and they often exist in several versions.[7]

This essay examines some of the encounters between Neo-Confucianism and geomancy during the Sung dynasty. As a source for the study of geomancy, the writings of Neo-Confucians have the advantage that their dating is well established and the social and intellectual background of the authors well known. Neo-Confucian scholars' and philosophers' reactions to geomancy also illuminate their own thinking, for they show them responding to the culture around them. The diversity of scholars' responses can also highlight some fundamental differences in their philosophies.

The bibliographical chapters in the *Sung History* list dozens of books on geomancy with titles like *Yin-yang tsang-ching* (The Yin-Yang Burial Classic, three *chüan*), *K'an-yü ching* (The Classic of Geomancy, one *chüan*), *Ti-li hsin-shu* (The New Book of Earth Patterns, thirty *chüan*), and *Wu-yin ti-li chüeh* (Secrets of Five Sounds Geomancy, one *chüan*).[8] Texts surviving from this era are highly varied. In Tun-huang a few fragments of geomancy books have survived that give checkerboard-like diagrams listing the terms for each grave site, and the preferred sites for people according to the "note" of their surname. The *Book of Burials* contains aphorisms such as "Burial takes advantage of the production of *ch'i* [vital energy]" and "People receive their bodies from their parents. When the original bones obtain *ch'i* the transmitted body receives protection," explained in commentaries. The profusely illustrated, *New Book of Earth Patterns* covers the siting of both houses and graves and quotes many earlier authors. It is especially detailed on the theory of the five notes (discussed below) and regularly specifies the negative consequences of choosing a wrong site. For instance, one site might lead to the chief mourner's drowning, another to his being killed in a fight, another to the loss of the family property in a lawsuit.

The audience for these books and the knowledge they contained can be inferred from the many anecdotes recorded about graves and their influence on human destinies. Wang Ming-ch'ing (1127–1214+), an official from a prominent family, recorded the following anecdote about a court official of his father's generation, Fan T'ung (1097–1148):

> Fan Tse-shan (T'ung) passed the examinations in the Hsüan-ho period (1119–1125) and was made an educational officer in Chiang-hsi. On the journey to bring his two parents to his post, his father died in Shang-jao. Fan stopped at a Buddhist temple en route, unsure how to proceed. The head monk took pity on him and said, "It happens that there is a grave site in the mountain behind this temple. It would be best to bury your father there. Not only would you avoid the trouble of transportation, but in the past I have given some attention to geomancy [*feng-shui*] and know that this place is extraordinary. It really is an auspicious site." Tse-shan accepted his advice and buried [his father] there. Later Tse-shan became very eminent in the government, so he planned to move the coffin back to his ancestral grave yard. He requested a leave of absence to manage the move. At the time, the old monk was still [at the temple], and tried without success to dissuade him. Later Tse-shan got into trouble with Ch'in Kuei because of anonymous slander.[9]

In this anecdote we see several common themes: the connection between the geomancy of parents' tombs and success in office; the possibility of moving coffins to change geomancy; and geomantic knowledge as something possessed by experts who might also be religious specialists.

Hung Mai (1123–1202), an official and prolific author, also often mentioned geomancers.[10] One story concerned Yao Yu, a poor scholar who with his brother lived in the mansion of a rich family. The rich man was selecting a grave site and so invited a renowned geomancer to his house, and Yao Yu became friends with this man. The geomancer, deciding that one of the sites on his host's property was particularly auspicious, secretly advised Yao to ask for it. Yao did and was given it as a site to bury his father. The geomancer then even suggested that Yao get a written deed for the plot to prevent later disputes. When that was accomplished, the geomancer advised him:

> "In this place there are two sites [*hsüeh*]. If you take the upper one, you and your brother will pass the examinations as soon as you are out of mourning and will swiftly reach strategic posts, but I fear that your life spans will not

be long. If you take the lower site, then your progress will be slower, achieving eminence only after thirty years, but you will take charge of the government. Which of these two do you choose?"

Yao said, "Right now I am in dire straits with no way to feed myself morning or night. I will be satisfied with getting a salary soon. How do I have the leisure to plan for thirty years away? I wish to take the top site."

The visitor said, "Then let's do that for the time being. If things later turn out as I have predicted, you could still move the coffin to the lower site, but by then you would not be able to take charge of the government."

Later both brothers became officials, but when his elder brother died relatively young, Yao Yu remembered the geomancer's words. His father then came to him in a dream, his clothes soaking wet, asking to be reburied elsewhere. Yao opened the grave and found it full of water, as hot as soup. Needless to say, even though he moved the coffin, Yao never became a chief minister.[11]

These two stories may be apocryphal, but the fact that they circulated is evidence that they conformed to the knowledge people had of their social world: some people claimed expertise in the siting of graves, and the sorts of people who sought official careers paid attention to what such experts said. In their own accounts of how they buried their parents, men did not say they selected spots because they hoped for blessings for themselves, but they did sometimes describe the siting and location of the graves in geomantic terms.[12] They might also tell of moving coffins because the dead had returned in dreams to complain of water or other discomforts, or report declining the advice of geomancers because they preferred to be buried near loved ones rather than to pursue future blessings.[13] Some also discussed earlier generations' use of geomancers for selection of the family graveyard.[14]

Further evidence of the place of geomancy in Sung society is the support it received from the government. The Sung government used geomantic books and theories in selecting imperial graves and issued geomantic manuals. In 1004, for instance, an official assigned to the burial of Empress Dowager Ming-te used I-hsing's *Ti-li ching* (Classic of Earth Patterns) to explain how her tomb should be located with respect to a prior empress's tomb; in 1022 the officials in charge of Chen-tsung's tomb memorialized concerning the appropriate depth of burial, citing the conflicting figures given in Yu-wu's and I-hsing's respective *Burial Classics*.[15] The first Sung emperor commissioned the *Ch'ien-k'un pao-tien* (Treasury of Heaven and Earth), of which thirty parts were devoted to geomancy. Because many scholars perceived errors in this book, in 1034 a new book was commissioned. In 1051 this one was criticized as shallow, and Wang Shu (997–1057) was given the task of compiling another, the *New Book of Earth Patterns.*[16]

Neo-Confucian Critics

How did Neo-Confucian scholars, after they had devoted themselves to study of the classics and to the task of reforming their own society, interpret the practice of geomancy? One scholar who found virtually no merit in it was Ssu-ma Kuang (1019–1086). In 1063 after Emperor Jen-tsung died, Ssu-ma Kuang wrote a memorial protesting the plan to start a new imperial tomb area and use geomancers to choose the site. He began by arguing that geomantic books were pernicious superstition and geomancers ignorant folk:

> Books on yin-yang cause people to be constrained and fearful, and of these the most harmful concern burial. The families of literati and commoners may delay a burial for generations as they seek a site or a time for burial. Your subject has long been deeply troubled by this custom, but has not had the time to request that the state ban these books. Now the major task of the imperial tomb should be done according to the codified rituals of the former kings. The *Book of Burials* derives from vulgar, convoluted talk. The yin-yang officers of the directorate of astronomy are all ignorant folk of the market place. How are these [books and people] worth consulting?[17]

Ssu-ma Kuang next argued that the classics already prescribed when and where to bury:

> In ancient times, the Son of Heaven was buried after seven months, feudal lords after five months, great officers after three months, and gentlemen after a month. They were buried on the north side with their heads to the north. No one asked about the year or month or evaluated [*hsiang*] the hill or mound. Yet if one examines the luck or ill-fortune of their descendants, was it any different from today? . . .
>
>   In the *Chou li* (Rites of Chou) the tomb master took charge of the public graveyard. The first king was buried in the middle, and others were on the left and right in *chao-mu* order.[18] It is evident that the tomb master did not select according to topography [*ti-hsing*]. And yet Chou possessed the realm through the reigns of thirty-six kings, for 867 years. For kings receive their mandate from Heaven and their fate is based on constant principles. The

rise and fall of states resides in the quality of their virtues. It is definitely not tied to the auspiciousness of the place or time of burial.[19]

Ssu-ma Kuang knew that the classics called for divining to check the suitability of a grave site, and that these divinations were concerned with securing the peace or comfort (*an*) of the dead. But he saw no classical precedent for going further:

> Now, burial is hiding [two homonyms]. Basically it is to make the forebear's body comfortable. Any land will do so long as the soil is thick, the water low, and the land is high, level, and solid. How can descendants seek blessings through [burial]?[20]

Some twenty years later Ssu-ma Kuang compiled a guide to family rituals (*Ssu-ma shih shu-i*). He returned to the subject of geomancy, elaborating his earlier arguments:

> The *Hsiao ching* [Classic of Filial Piety] says: "Divine for the grave site to make them comfortable."[21] This means that one divined to decide if a spot was auspicious or ill-omened. It was not like today's yin-yang experts who inspect the geomancy [*feng-shui*] of hills and ridges. Kuo Tzu-kao said, "Burial is hiding." He also said, "When I die, select a place where no food grows to bury me."[22] It is evident that burials can be in any place.[23]

In this piece, Ssu-ma Kuang especially ridiculed the contradictions in the theories espoused by geomancers:

> The current custom is to place credence in the theories of burial specialists (*tsang-shih*) who select a year, month, day, and hour, and select a site by the configuration (*hsing-shih*) of mountains and waters. People believe that the wealth, rank, wisdom, and longevity of the descendants entirely depends on these choices. Moreover, the books used by burial specialists differ from one to the other. What one considers auspicious, the other will call ill-omened. With their confusing arguments they can never settle on an answer. . . . Those yin-yang masters say that the year, month, day, and hour of a person's birth is enough to set his life span and status. If this is to be believed, then a person's fate is already set at birth. How can it be changed by burial? These two theories are contradictory, and yet the custom is to believe them both. How ignorant![24]

In addition, Ssu-ma Kuang argued that geomancy was unfilial.

> [Because of geomancy] the coffin may be left in a temple, or in a distant place. Sometimes it reaches the point where a lifetime or even several generations pass without the burial taking place. Or perhaps when the descendants get old and decline they may forget the location of the coffin and abandon it without burying it. People want descendants in large part so that someone will take care of their physical remains. When descendants act like this, wouldn't [the dead] be better off if they had had no descendants and died by the road? Then some man of virtue might bury [their bodies].
> . . . If one really supposed that burial was able to affect human fortunes, how could sons and grandsons bear to cause their parents to rot and suffer exposure in order to seek profit for themselves? There are no perverse rituals that hurt moral principles more than these.[25]

Since the classics enjoined divination for tomb sites, Ssu-ma Kuang proposed selecting a few suitable sites and divining for the choice among them.

> The heart of a filial son is filled with deep and long-ranging worries. He fears that if the burial is shallow people will break in, and that if it is deep, moisture will speed decay. Therefore he must search for places where the dirt is rich and the water low to bury the body. He should select several spots, then divine to see if any are ill-omened.[26]

Ssu-ma Kuang returned to the subject of geomancy in 1084 when he wrote an essay criticizing contemporary burial practices. He repeated many of the arguments already given in the two pieces above, then added a personal example:

> When we were about to bury [my father] T'ai-wei Kung, my agnatic relatives all said, "Burials are major family events. Why are you not taking yin-yang into account? This is not proper." My elder brother Po-k'ang [Tan] had no alternative, so said, "It will be all right to consider yin-yang. How can we find a good burial specialist to consult?" A relative said, "In a nearby village there is a Master Chang who is a good specialist. The people of several counties all use him." My brother then summoned Master Chang and offered him 20,000 cash. Master Chang was a country fellow whose forebears had been burial specialists. When local people had burials, he never received more than 1,000 cash. Hearing this offer pleased him greatly.

My brother said, "If you do as I say, I will assign you the burial. If you do not, I will choose another specialist," to which Master Chang replied, "I will do whatever you say." Thereupon my brother told him his own ideas for the place, the time, the depth and width of the pit, and the route of the road. He had Master Chang dress it up according to the *Book of Burials* and pronounce it very auspicious. He then showed it to the relatives, who were all pleased, none voicing any objections.

Today my brother is seventy-nine, having retired as a minister. I am sixty-six and still hold a post in attendance on the emperor. Twenty-three of our agnatic relatives are serving in office. Others who have diligently used the *Book of Burials* are not invariably more successful than we are. Last year my wife died. Once the coffin was ready, we laid her out in it. Once the procession was arranged and the pit dug, her coffin was buried. Not one word was asked of a yin-yang expert. Yet nothing unexpected has happened so far. . . . Look at my family for evidence that the *Book of Burials* is not worth believing.[27]

Ssu-ma Kuang seems to have had no reservations about geomancy. At the level of theory, he saw it as convoluted nonsense. Moreover, it was not innocuous nonsense, for belief in it undermined virtue, leading to selfish and unfilial acts. The "experts" were vulgar men, easily bought off with money. The fact that his peers, even his relatives and court officials, were misled by these ideas only increased the danger they posed.

Books on geomancy often used the terms *ch'i* and *li*, terms whose philosophical meanings were most fully developed by Chang Tsai (1020–1077) and Ch'eng I (1033–1107) respectively.[28] Yet neither of these men had anything good to say about geomancers. Chang Tsai wrote:

One burial method is called "wind and water and hills and ridges." It is completely without any rational basis and should not be used. In the south they use *The Green Sack*, which can still be obtained. Westerners use I-hsing's manual, which is especially preposterous. Southerners test a burial spot by taking a multicolored piece of silk and burying it in the ground. After a year they take it out to look at it. If the soil is good the colors will not have changed, whereas if the *ch'i* of the soil is bad it will have changed. They will also put a small fish in a container of water and bury it for a year, divining for the quality of the land according to whether it lives or dies or whether plants flourish or wither.[29]

Ch'eng I wrote at greater length on geomancy and was almost as virulent in his condemnation as Ssu-ma Kuang. He wrote that the ancients divined for grave sites mostly because they did not know the location of underground water. "In later ages yin-yang masters have competed in producing wild theories, so that now there are 120 schools professing the techniques of the *Book of Burials*."[30] The most preposterous geomantic theory, in Ch'eng I's view, was the Five Notes or Surname [classes] (Kung, Shang, Chüeh, Chih, and Yü). For instance, the surnames Chang and Wang belonged to Shang, Liu to Kung, and Chao to Chüeh. As Ch'eng I noted, this classification matched neither rhymes nor tones.[31] Ch'eng I argued that this theory was without canonical basis, did not make sense in terms of the known history of surnames and, moreover, could be disproved by history. He noted that people seemed to have lived longer in ancient times before there were any geomancers, so their claim to increase life spans did not hold up to scrutiny.

Ch'eng I objected to moving bodies, noting, as Ssu-ma Kuang had, that "burial is hiding. Once the body is hidden, it cannot be moved. One must seek permanent rest."[32] He also criticized the theories that posited that the hours *ch'ien* and *ken* were most auspicious for burial, even though they were in the middle of the night, and that *ssu* and *hai* days were inauspicious, even though the *Ch'un-ch'iu* (Spring and Autumn Annals) records many cases of burial on those days without any sign of detrimental consequences. What those choosing grave sites should pay attention to was geneaological order (*chao-mu*): "If they are not divided into *chao* and *mu* ranks, it is easy to confuse seniority. If the dead have consciousness, how could they be comfortable with this?"[33]

Like Ssu-ma Kuang, Ch'eng I also used the example of his own family to prove geomancy's fallacies:

In the world today there are a lot of works on divination and numerology, and of them, the books on geomancy [*ti-li*] are the most preposterous. When my grandfather was buried, we used a geomancer [*ti-li jen*]. My elders all had faith in him; only my late elder brother and I did not. Later we simply used the *chao-mu* method [of burying in genealogical order]. . . . After I used the *chao-mu* method for one site, one of my elders summoned a geomancer to the burial place. This man said, "This place will cut off those in the Shang class [which apparently applied to the Ch'eng surname]. Why did you make the grave here?" I answered, "It was exactly because I knew it was a place that cuts it off [in your theory]. I want to test what will happen." Note that the members of my family have increased severalfold since then.[34]

Unlike Ssu-ma Kuang, Ch'eng I does not seem to have discounted all of the cosmological premises underlying geomancy. He allowed for a sort of amateur geomancy based on the idea that the comfort of the ancestors was linked to the comfort of the living descendants.

> Divining for a tomb site should be aimed at discovering the excellence of the land, not what the yin-yang specialists call fortune or misfortune. When the land is excellent, the spirits will be comfortable and the descendants will flourish; the principle is the same as the branches and leaves of a plant flourishing when dirt is banked around the roots. When the land is bad, the contrary occurs. But what is meant by the excellence of land? It is land that is bright and moist; a flourishing growth of plants and trees is the evidence.
>
> Father and grandfather, son and grandson, all share the same *ch'i*. According to this principle, when the one is at peace the other will be at peace; when the one is endangered the other will be endangered. Adherents of superstitions [*chü-chi*] are deluded into selecting the direction of the land and choosing days for their auspiciousness. Isn't this ignorant! The worst do not think in terms of serving the deceased but worry solely about their own future benefits. This is not at all what a filial son should be concentrating on in arranging a burial place.
>
> Nevertheless, there are five problems to which one must give attention when picking a burial site. One must see that the spot will never be made into a road, a city wall, or a ditch; that it will not be seized by the high-ranking or powerful; and that it will never be cultivated. Another text says that the five problems to be avoided are ditches, roads, villages, wells, and pits.[35]

Noticing whether trees and plants grew at a spot and its distance from settled areas did not require the services of experts or even any special theories. Anyone could select grave sites according to these criteria.

Chang Chiu-ch'eng (1092–1159), who had studied with Yang Shih (1053–1135), a leading disciple of the Ch'eng brothers, directed much of his criticism of geomancy to the theory of the green dragon and white tiger.[36] He explained that in this theory the left "shoulder" of either a building or grave was the "green dragon" and its right shoulder the "white tiger," and that whatever occupied the place of the dragon was auspiciously located while anything in the tiger's territory was inauspiciously located. He refuted this theory on the basis of the classics (*chao-mu* order would be nonsensical in this scheme), on the basis of logic (everything is to the left and right of innumerable other things), and morality (siting should not have more effect on future fortunes than good or bad deeds).[37]

When he was about to bury his father, Chang Chiu-ch'eng wrote a text for the sacrifice to the spirits of the soil and trees of that spot. In the text he explained why he had divined for the spot himself: "I am a Confucian scholar [*ju-che*] and so ought to believe the words of the former kings, not the theories of 'shamans and blind men.'"[38] He then offered classical citations to refute a whole series of geomantic theories, including the theory of the green dragon and white tiger, the theory of the five surnames, the theory that certain hours, days, and years should be avoided, and the theory that black and yellow clash.[39]

Let me end this section with a thirteenth-century critic of geomancy, Lo Ta-ching (*chin-shih*, 1226).[40] In an essay entitled "Geomancy" (*feng-shui*) Lo reiterated many of the arguments given by earlier writers but then went on to discuss the errors in the ideas of Kuo P'u (276–324, reputed author of the *Book of Burials*). According to Kuo P'u, descendants receive benefits depending on the way the ancestors' bones interact with *ch'i*. But, Lo argued, "Dried bones and rotting flesh can feel no pain. As the days and months add up, they are transformed through decomposition, becoming soil. How can they resonate [*hsiang-kan*] with the living to bring about disasters or blessings?"[41] In other words, Lo questioned the canonical notion that the dead can be comfortable or uncomfortable and also the belief in "interaction at a distance," a basic component of correlative thinking. If one accepts Lo's argument, geomancy cannot be reformed; it must be totally discarded. Like Ch'eng I, Lo brought in ancient history to prove his case. He also credited Yang Wan-li (1127–1206) with asking why Kuo P'u had been executed and his descendants so obscure if he had been such a good geomancer.[42]

Lo Ta-ching strengthened his argument by pointing to the social consequences of belief in geomancy: Not only would people leave their parents unburied for years, but they would dig them up and rebury them, sometimes three or four times. Moreover, when there were several brothers, they might be deluded by the theory of "separate geomancy for each collateral line," and become enemies because of fights over selection of the site.[43]

These critiques of geomancy brought in logical, canonical, historical, and ethical arguments. The logical arguments were often directed at specific elements in geomantic theory: How could the sounds of surnames matter when so many surnames had been changed over the centuries? How could placement to the right or left matter when everything was right or left of so many other things? But sometimes logic was also directed at the most fundamental premises of geomancy: Ssu-ma Kuang questioned the simultaneous belief that parents' burial location and moment of birth could both determine destinies, and Lo Ta-ching questioned the whole idea that the dead could be comfortable or uncomfortable and the state of their bodies have any influence on the living. The canonical objections to geomancy were that the classics gave contrary rules for siting graves. The historical argument against geomancy was that the descendants of those who had been buried in places considered bad by geomancers fared no worse than others. The ethical argument was that geomancy was motivated by selfish desires. In addition to these explicit arguments, there often seems to be an implied argument based on social origins: geomancy cannot be very good given the types of people who profess it.

Where these critics differed the most was in their understanding of the classical instruction to divine for a grave site to make the ancestors comfortable. Lo Ta-ching questioned the very notion of the ancestors' feeling anything. Ssu-ma Kuang accepted the idea that descendants should attempt to make their parents comfortable, but insisted that this was the common sense idea that they would want to be dry and undisturbed.[44] He moreover saw this effort as disinterested: sons did it for their fathers out of concern for them, not any belief that their own happiness was at stake. Ch'eng I acknowledged that there was a cosmological basis for believing the ancestors' comfort was linked to descendants' comfort; like Ssu-ma Kuang, however, he thought comfort could be determined in common sense ways and the search for it should not be selfishly motivated.

Supporters of Geomancy

Now I turn to the more difficult part of this essay: Sung Neo-Confucians who found value in geomancy. The important person here is none other than Chu Hsi (1130–1200).

Chu Hsi touched on geomancy in a variety of contexts. His *Chia-li* (Family Rituals) is closely based on Ssu-ma Kuang's *Ssu-ma shih shu-i* (Mr. Ssu-ma's Letters and Etiquette).[45] In it he quoted part of Ssu-ma Kuang's condemnation of geomancy, in particular, his objections to allowing burials to be postponed because of geomancy. From Ch'eng I he quoted the passage above that can be interpreted to provide a rationale for geomancy on the grounds that fathers and sons share the same *ch'i*, and therefore that when one is at peace the other will also be. Chu Hsi also quoted Ch'eng I's passage on avoiding places likely later to be made into roads, fields, ditches, and so on. After quoting from these two critics of geomancy, however, Chu Hsi added that since people no longer knew how to divine with stalks, it was all right to use customary methods for choosing grave sites and burial dates.[46] This can certainly be taken as acceptance of geomancy if it is not selfishly motivated and does not lead to postponing burials, as it was indeed interpreted in later times.[47]

Chu Hsi reported taking geomancy into account when burying several of his relatives. In 1170 he had his father's body moved from one site to another because when the first burial had been arranged he had been young and ignorant, "unfamiliar with divination of places."[48] In 1176, when his wife died, his friend Chang Shih (1133–1180) chided him for his concern with locating the grave according to geomancy.[49] When his eldest son died in 1191, Chu Hsi wrote to Ch'en Liang (1143–1194) that he was delaying burial on the advice of a geomancer.[50]

In discussions with his students, Chu Hsi defended geomancy on several occasions. The *Chu Tzu yü-lei* (Classified Conversations of Master Chu Hsi) quotes him as downplaying Ch'eng I's objections to geomancy.

> In a discussion of geomancy [*ti-li*], [Chu Hsi] said, "Master Ch'eng also selected a place where the grass and trees were flourishing, so it is not the case that he did not select spots. Po-kung [Lü Tsu-ch'ien] by contrast merely picked a flat place at random, then performed the burial. If he did not know the principle [of selecting sites], his action was wrong, but if he knew and purposely did not use it, his action was especially wrong.[51]

Apparently Lü Tsu-ch'ien (1137–1181), a friend and collaborator of Chu Hsi's, had concurred with Ssu-ma Kuang that one could bury virtually anywhere. Here Chu Hsi was defending a basic principle of geomancy by insisting that graves had to be selected, pointing out that even the critic of geomancy, Ch'eng I, had admitted this.

More of the cosmology of geomancy was accepted in the following conversation.

> "When wind acts on things, it enters into all of them. Today coffins are buried in the ground. To a small extent they get blown, some even blown over." Someone asked, "If one places an object on the ground, even a fierce wind will not necessarily be able to move it. Since the ground is so strong and solid, how could [wind] blow through it to move things?" [Chu Hsi] answered, "I think that in the ground when [wind] collects together and wants to come out, its power intensifies, but when it is out on the flat land,

its *ch'i* disperses." [The interlocutor] said, "Perhaps there is no such principle [i.e., perhaps you are wrong]." [Chu Hsi] said, "In Cheng-ho county, a man buried his parent at a certain place. After the burial he heard sounds from the grave from time to time. His family thought that these sounds occurred because the place was good. After a long time the family property slowly declined and the descendants became poor. They thought that the place was unfortunate [*pu-li*], so took [the coffin] out to look at it. They found that one side had been smashed and was ruined. The place it had been was exactly in the front part of the pit, the part formed by curved bricks, where the coffin enters." [The interlocutor] said, "Perhaps water caused this." [Chu Hsi] answered, "No. If water had entered, how could there have been the sound of hitting? I do not know what the explanation is."[52]

Here Chu Hsi not only showed interest in the lore of graves but entertained the possibility that underground wind would harm a coffin and that this could, in turn, lead the descendants of the one buried to suffer financial losses.

Where Chu Hsi laid out his views on geomancy most fully was in a memorial to the throne written in 1194. The issue was whether or not to bury the former Emperor Hsiao-tsung (r. 1163–1189, d. 1194) at the site of the earlier Southern Sung imperial tombs in Shao-hsing. An official inspecting the imperial tombs had reported that the earth was shallow and water and rocks had appeared. Emperor Ning-tsung (r. 1195–1224) asked for debate on the issue, and Chu Hsi, then briefly holding a court post, sent in a memorial proposing that a new site be selected.[53]

Your subject has heard that burial means hiding; it is the means by which to hide the physical remains of ancestors. . . . If the body is whole, the spirit [*shen-ling*] will attain peace, then the descendants will flourish and the sacrifices will not be cut off. This is a principle of how things happen of themselves. It was for this reason that the ancients always selected a site for burials, divining with stalks to make their decisions. If the site was not auspicious they would choose another and divine again. In recent times the method of divining with stalks has been lost but theories of how to select sites still exist. All literati and commoners with even modest resources when burying their forebears consult widely among experts [*shu-shih*] and visit famous mountains, comparing one site to the next to select the very best.

Only afterward do they use a spot for burial. Should the selection be defective, making the spot inauspicious, then there will surely be water, ants, and ground wind that will damage the contents and cause the body and spirit to be uncomfortable. And descendants also have worries about death and extinction [of the descent line], which are very frightening. Sometimes, although they obtain auspicious land, the burial is not solid enough or the coffin placed deep enough, with the result that during wars or disturbances the body cannot escape being exposed. This is another major cause for concern.

As to places that have been dug into many times, the *ch'i* of the earth will already be thin. Even if it is an auspicious spot, it will not have full power. Moreover, if one frequently carries out earth-work projects near the ancestral tombs, this will result in [the ancestors] being startled and shaken, which also leads to disasters. Although this is the theory of the experts [*shu-chia*], it is not without a rational basis.[54]

Chu Hsi then cited the *Li chi's* (Record of Rites) rule that the dead be buried with their heads to the north, explaining that this meant they would face south, thereby benefiting from the yang forces of sunshine. On this point he criticized geomancers who picked directions on other grounds. Chu Hsi also dismissed the theory of the five notes, remarking that former Confucians had already refuted it (undoubtedly referring to Ch'eng I) and that it was no longer so popular anyway. It had been used for the burial of previous emperors, but the repeated misfortunes of the imperial family — including the failure of two emperors to have direct descendants and the interruption of the imperial succession with the loss of the north — was evidence enough that it was not efficacious. Thus Chu Hsi substantiated the validity of geomancy through negative evidence: faulty geomantic theories had been followed, and undesirable things had happened.

Chu Hsi then argued that rather than improve the existing site in Shao-hsing, it would be better to bury the coffin in a new place altogether. Since several emperors and empresses had already been buried at Shao-hsing, the *ch'i* of the earth there was already thin, making selection of an entirely new spot preferable. He also argued for use of skilled experts for locating the new tomb.

The methods of geomancy [*ti-li*] are like those of acupuncture and moxibustion. There is a fixed site that cannot be off by a hair. If a doctor did his cauterizing the way the censors are presently choosing the grave site, then to "attack" one site the whole side of the body would be injured. How is this the correct way to get a site?[55]

Chu Hsi noted that there had to be some suitable places in the circuits of Che-tung and Che-hsi. He mentioned attractive places he had seen in his travels, including Fu-yang county, which had been the home of the Sun family (of the state of Wu in the Three Kingdoms period), implying that it must therefore have something auspicious about it. He also suggested that Hangchow itself would have similar qualities since the Ch'ien family (rulers of the state of Wu-Yüeh during the Five Dynasties) came from there. Chu Hsi again recommended calling in experts:

> If you wish to search [for a spot], then I venture to note that the most prominent scholars of geomancy in recent years have come from Kiangsi and Fukien. Even if they are not all fully proficient, surely there is one with a rough knowledge of the main points, who can make the tomb more or less flat and stable, who would be better than a couple of censors.[56]

Chu Hsi advised that an immediate search be made for five or six possible sites and an official sent out to inspect them. The official should be chosen not by official rank but according to his comprehension of geomancy. After doing a comparison he should select the most auspicious site.

Chu Hsi ended his memorial with some humble disclaimers:

> Your subject is basically a Confucian scholar who does not understand divination and numerology. I do not dare wildly confuse your sagely ears with the words of "shamans and blind masters." Although I am bringing ridicule on myself, I really cannot bear to think of the sage body of Shou-huang [i.e., Hsiao-tsung] put among water and pebbles, in a broken-down, shallow place. Therefore I have passionately expressed this all to your majesty. The situation is comparable to when my neighbors, relatives, or friends have something important to discuss. If I clearly recognize the advantages and disadvantages but do not express myself completely, they would have to consider me disloyal and untrustworthy. How much more so is this true in the case of a subject to his ruler or a son to his father! How could I bear to have advice that I silently keep to myself![57]

In this memorial Chu Hsi accepted both the philosophical premises of geomancy and the expertise of geomancers. He quite explicitly stated that faulty placement of a grave site can have dreadful consequences for descendants, including their early deaths and the consequent break in the descent line. He even went so far as to suggest that faulty geomantic theories had something to do with the succession problems of the imperial line. Chu Hsi did not elaborate on the connections between the discomfort of the ancestors and the problems their descendants will incur: he did not say the ancestors were angry or analyze the agency through which they punished their descendants. As observers of geomancy in modern times have noted, the role of ancestors as spirits can be downplayed, with geomancy treated as natural science, as the systematic analysis of the consequences that occur spontaneously when certain physical conditions prevail.[58]

Chu Hsi was taking an even bolder stance in arguing that those called experts (*shu-chia, shu-shih*) had some real expertise. Even though some theories expounded by some of them were false, that did not invalidate all their theories. Moreover, allowing others — such as censors — to decide on the siting of graves was reckless. Water and ants were widely acknowledged problems of burials, and geomancers had experience in finding places safe from these dangers. Ground wind and weakening of the earth's *ch'i* caused by too much cutting are probably best thought of as cosmological problems, and, as such, only those knowledgeable about geomancy could avoid them.

There is no reason to think Chu Hsi was less than sincere in his defense of geomancy. If he had been arguing for using the existing tomb site, one might have supposed he was promoting frugality in burials, a long tradition among Confucian scholars, and only cloaking his argument in a geomantic vocabulary in order to sway his audience. But his proposal for starting a new imperial tomb area could only add expense (and certainly violated Ch'eng I's emphasis on burying in *chao-mu* order).

Chu Hsi's failure to follow his many predecessors in condemning geomancy can be explained in both philosophical and social terms. The philosophical explanation is that, however much Chu Hsi revered Ch'eng I, his cosmological beliefs were quite different. As Professor Wing-tsit Chan has shown, Chu Hsi was much more concerned with the metaphysical issues of the relationship of *li* and *ch'i* and the Great Ultimate than the Ch'eng brothers had been.[59] Hsü Fu-kuan, in his analysis of the differences between Ch'eng I and Chu Hsi, stressed the contrast in their approach to the *I-ching* (Classic of Changes), a contrast applicable here as well. Ch'eng I was interested only in the philosophical principles implied in the ancient commentaries to this classic and did not believe in divination. Chu Hsi, on the contrary, saw divination as the way to reach beyond the current world.[60] In his studies of the *I-ching* Chu Hsi freely drew on Shao Yung (1011–1077), even though he had excluded him from his *Chin-ssu lu* (Reflections on Things at Hand). Chang Li-wen has shown how Chu Hsi in his studies of the *I-ching* combined Ch'eng I's moral views with Shao Yung's emblemology and numerology.[61] Stripped to its core, geomancy fits within the cosmology of the *I-ching*, which includes the geomancers' favorite classical allusion: "Look up to observe the patterns of heaven; look down to examine the principles of earth [*ti-li*]."[62] As Freedman put it, geomancy is "a complex of beliefs concerned with a central theme in Chinese metaphysics: man's place in nature and the universe."[63] Chu Hsi, as someone deeply concerned with metaphysics, who took the *I-ching* seriously, and who believed that all phenomena and their changes could be explained in terms of an organismic model of *li* and *ch'i*, could well have accepted the metaphysical assumptions of geomancy: that forces of the earth act on the remains of ancestors and these remains act at a distance on their descendants.

Chu Hsi's interest in cosmology may explain why he was willing to disagree with Ch'eng I, but does not account for the differences between him and Chang Tsai or Ssu-ma Kuang, each of whom had well-developed interests in cosmological issues. Ssu-ma Kuang even wrote a numerological treatise (*Ch'ien-hsü*) modeled on Yang Hsiung's *T'ai-hsüan ching* (Canon of Supreme Mystery). Here a social explanation is more compelling, Chu Hsi's friendship with Ts'ai Yüan-ting (1135–1198).[64] My hypothesis is that Chu Hsi's confidence in professional geomancers and their theories derived from his respect for Ts'ai Yüan-ting, well known in his own time and in later ages for his geomantic knowledge.

Chu Hsi wrote that Ts'ai Yüan-ting's father, Ts'ai Fa, had traveled widely in his youth, becoming fully proficient in divination according to the *I-ching*, in astrology/astronomy (*t'ien-wen*), and in geomancy (*ti-li*). After he settled down he taught his son the books of the Ch'eng brothers, Chang Tsai, and Shao Yung.[65] Later Ts'ai Yüan-ting went to study with Chu Hsi, but Chu Hsi, on meeting him, decided that he should be classed as a friend and not a disciple. Chen Te-hsiu (1178–1235) reported that whenever Chu Hsi ran into subtle points concerning "human nature or the Way of Heaven" he would discuss them with Ts'ai Yüan-ting, and that he only made up his mind on abstruse points after these conversations.[66] According to the *Sung History*, when Chu Hsi and Ts'ai Yüan-ting were together, "they would sit on opposite benches discussing the inner meaning of the classics into the middle of the night."[67] Ts'ai Yüan-ting acted as Chu Hsi's assistant, helping new students, assisting with Chu Hsi's scholarly books, and even drafting his *I-hsüeh ch'i-meng* (Introduction to the Classic of Changes).[68] Chu Hsi's maternal grandson, Li Yu-wu, recorded that Chu Hsi's analyses of the *I-ching*, the River Diagram and Lo Text, Shao Yung's *Huang-chi ching-shih shu* (Supreme Principles Governing the Ages) and *Hsien-t'ien t'u* (Prior Heaven Diagram) all drew from his discussions with Ts'ai Yüan-ting.[69] Yeh Shao-weng (ca. 1175–1230) reported that Chu Hsi had come "clearly to understand the numbers of Heaven and Earth, master musical theory, and incorporate knowledge from books on yin-yang and geomancy [*feng-shui*]" from his friend Ts'ai Yüan-ting.[70]

The *Sung-Yüan hsüeh-an* (Philosophical Records of Sung and Yüan Scholars) listed Ts'ai Yüan-ting first among Chu Hsi's followers.[71] When Chu Hsi was accused of "false learning" and heterodoxy in 1196, Ts'ai Yüan-ting was explicitly mentioned as "helping him in his diabolical activities."[72] At any rate, although a private scholar who had never held office, Ts'ai Yüan-ting was banished and forced to walk all the way to Hunan, where he died.

Intellectually, Ts'ai Yüan-ting was associated with Shao Yung because of his studies of numerology.[73] Ts'ai wrote a guide to three numerological/cosmological books: Shao Yung's *Huang-chi ching-shih shu*, Yang Hsiung's *T'ai-hsüan ching*, and Ssu-ma Kuang's *Ch'ien-hsü*.[74] John Henderson identifies Ts'ai as Shao Yung's major follower during the Southern Sung.[75]

From all accounts Chu Hsi was impressed by Ts'ai Yüan-ting's mastery of abstruse subjects, and this seems to have included his knowledge of geomancy. Yü Ch'eng reports that he was present at a conversation between Chu Hsi and several guests about geomancy. Chu Hsi praised Ts'ai Yüan-ting's knowledge, leading one of the guests to counter, "Ts'ai does not understand the attacks that have been made on yin-yang over the ages." Chu Hsi defended Ts'ai's knowledge of "dragon veins," noting that he got it from his father and grandfather. The guest rejoined by claiming that a family tradition of geomancy was hardly evidence of its efficacy. Chu Hsi laughed with the other guests at this argument and asked them not to repeat it to Ts'ai.[76] Another source reported that Chu Hsi had Ts'ai Yüan-ting help him look for a grave site and that they spent six days in the search.[77]

Ts'ai Yüan-ting's major contribution to Chinese geomancy is probably his editing of the standard edition of the *Book of Burials*, which may have led to the increased use of this book. Of the twenty sections in the edition then current, he removed twelve as inexact.[78] Ts'ai himself followed the geomantic teachings of his father and honored his text, *Fa-wei lun* (A Treatise on the Production of Subtleties).[79] As the editors of the *Ssu-k'u ch'üan-shu* (Complete Collection of the Four Libraries) noted, this treatise analyzed geomancy in terms of Neo-Confucian principles. It is divided into fourteen sections, each dealing with a set of complementary bipolarities: Hard and Soft, Movement and Rest, Concentration and Dispersal, Facing and Backing, Male and Female, Strong and Weak, Compliance and Defiance, Life and Death, Subtle and Obvious, Divided and Joined, Floating and Sinking, Shallow and Deep, Enhancement and Curtailment, Advancing and Withdrawing, Cutting Off and Completing, and Resonances. The language used draws from the *I-ching*, especially its "Commentary of Attached Verbalizations." Below are some representative passages.

The *Changes* says: "The way of establishing Heaven is called yin and yang."[80] Mr. Shao said, "The way of establishing earth is complete in hard and soft."[81] Therefore in geomancy nothing is more essential than hard and soft.[82]

With regard to the four phenomena of earth, water is the blood of the human body: it thus is "very soft." Fire is the breath of the human body; it thus is "very hard." Soil is the flesh of the human body; it thus is "slightly soft." Stone is the bone of the human body; it thus is "slightly hard." Joining water, fire, soil, and stone to make earth is like joining blood, breath, bone, and flesh to make human beings. The one near at hand draws from the body; the far one draws from things, but they have the same principle [*li*].[83]

An isolated yin does not give birth; solitary yang is not complete. Everything in the world wants its mate. When geomancers speak of male and female, they are generally referring to nothing more than the principle of pairing. . . . The yang dragon takes the yin grave site; the yin dragon takes the yang grave site. This is the pairing of dragon and grave site.[84]

The principle [*li*] of all under Heaven is fully expressed in centrality [*chung*]. . . . Geomancers must examine the *ch'i* of the endowment. If it leans toward softness, its nature is slow. If it leans toward hardness, its nature is quick. When the nature is quick the grave site should be in a slow place. If the grave site is located in a strong, fast place, there would surely be the calamity of the descent line dying out.[85]

Ch'i is what has no form; it belongs to yang. Veins [of the earth] are what have form; they belong to yin. Yang is clear and yin is muddy. Therefore *ch'i* is subtle and veins are obvious. But *ch'i* cannot complete itself; it must rely on veins; veins do not make themselves, but use *ch'i.* . . . Those good at inspecting *ch'i* and veins use what has form to examine what has no form. Those poor at inspecting use what has no form to obscure what has form.[86]

A geomancer examining veins is no different than a doctor examining veins [pulse]. A good doctor examines veins' yin and yang to prescribe medicine; a good geomancer examines how veins float or sink to set the grave site.[87]

One who divines for land must use shallowness and depth as the standard. If it ought to be shallow but is deep, the *ch'i* will pass from the top. When it ought to be deep but is shallow, the *ch'i* will pass from the bottom. This is the explanation of cases where the results are not appropriate even though one obtained an auspicious spot.[88]

This treatise does not talk of the five notes, the green dragon and white tiger, or any prohibited days or hours. It was written in the type of language that Chu Hsi used in discussing the *I-ching* or spirits and ghosts.[89] Considering Chu Hsi's other writings, it is not implausible that he found these geomantic theories compelling and played with the ideas himself.

I suspect that there were both direct and indirect connections between Ts'ai Yüan-ting and Chu Hsi's views on geomancy. The direct connection would be at the level of ideas. Sung observers already suggested that Chu Hsi's theories about the "principles of the earth" expressed in his memorial owe much to Ts'ai Yüan-ting.[90] The indirect connection concerns the practice of geomancy. The critics of geomancy quoted earlier all held its practitioners in contempt. Chu Hsi did not, insisting that some at least were proficient, probably because his brilliant friend was something of a geomancer and came from a family of geomancers.

Finally, let me bring in a highly speculative geographical explanation of Chu Hsi's receptiveness to geomancy. Chu Hsi grew up in Fukien and lived nearly all his life in the southeast. Geomancy goes back at least to the Han period and was certainly widely practiced in the north, but, in recent times at least, its appeal has been the strongest in the south. It has been plausibly argued that the hillier terrain of the south gave a greater abundance of sites to choose among for burials and that the greater diversity in topography fostered interest in the exact configuration of land forms. Could it be that a rational or moral rejection of geomancy was easier for northerners like Ssu-ma Kuang and Ch'eng I? Could the aesthetic appeal of geomancy have contributed to Chu Hsi's attachment to it?

Conclusions

What does this minor episode in the history of geomancy and the history of Neo-Confucianism tell us about either of them? Since so little has been written on the history of geomancy, the contribution there may be the larger. Critics and supporters document a wide variety of beliefs current in their age and place them in their social setting: the rustic geomancer, the family elders who hire him, the visits to numerous sites for inspections, the payments, the fights between brothers, the delays in burial, the exhumations and reburials. They mention the books most commonly in use and some regional variations.

Both critics and supporters of geomancy provide some insight into the long-term hold of geomantic practices. What Ssu-ma Kuang could condemn as irrational superstition, Chu Hsi could see as making sense in a cosmology of yin-yang, *li*, and *ch'i*. Thus the educated class itself was divided, a situation that continued through the rest of Chinese history. In later periods skeptics elaborated on the points made by Ssu-ma Kuang, Chang Tsai, and Ch'eng I.[91] Later scholars would sometimes explicitly condemn Chu Hsi for being misled by geomancy, especially for burying his mother far from his father, and reburying his father twice away from her.[92] At the same time, advocates could point to Chu Hsi as an authority. Professional geomancers also cited Chu Hsi.[93]

Philosophers' analyses of geomancy help illuminate Neo-Confucianism by pointing to the tensions in its rationalism. As Wm. Theodore de Bary wrote many years ago, one of the major themes in Neo-Confucianism is rationalism, a belief in a universe "characterized by order, regularity, and a harmonious integration of its parts," and a commitment to the effort to discern this order through study of things and events.[94] Geomancy was certainly rational in that it sought systematic explanations of recurrent phenomena. Its appeal to Chu Hsi, Ts'ai Yüan-ting, and others was in no small part on this ground.

Of course, the Neo-Confucians' commitment to rationalism did not lead them to accept any systematic explanation of the universe: Buddhism and even popular beliefs in a wide pantheon of deities provide systematic explanations of observed phenomena and yet were virtually unanimously rejected. Neo-Confucians sought a rationalism both grounded in the classics and directed against "superstition." These goals could come into conflict. Did a rational model of the universe have to explain the divinations, prophetic dreams, ghosts, spirits, and sacrifices in the classics? Must it also explain "uncanny" phenomena in their own day? The classics gave them no clear guidance on modern means of divination. Was a divinatory practice superstitious when its procedures were uncanonical? When people used it out of fear of unknown forces? When it was done for selfish purposes? When its efficacy could not be adequately demonstrated? When its primary practictioners were ill-educated? In the case of geomancy, at least, scholars could not agree.

NOTES

1. Geomancy is referred to in Chinese as *k'an-yü* (chariot and canopy, or Heaven and earth), *ti-li* (principles or science of earth), or *feng-shui* (wind and water). Geomancy may not be the best English rendering of these terms, but its use is by now conventional. Geomancers are referred to in Sung texts as "burial masters" (*tsang-shih*), "yin-yang masters" (*yin-yang chia*), "experts" (*shu-chia*), "land evaluators" (*hsiang-ti che*), and related terms.

2. J. J. M. de Groot, *The Religious System of China* (Leyden: Brill, 1892–1910), vol. 3, pp. 1017, 1034.

3. *The Study of Chinese Society*, ed. G. William Skinner (Stanford: Stanford University Press, 1979), 195.

4. Stephan D. R. Feuchtwang, *An Anthropological Analysis of Chinese Geomancy* (Vientiane: Vithagna, 1974); Andrew L. Marsh, "An Appreciation of Chinese Geomancy," *Journal of Asian Studies* (1968), 27(2):253–67; Steven J. Bennett, "Patterns of the Sky and Earth: A Chinese Science of Applied Cosmology," *Chinese Science* (1978), 3:1–26. See also de Groot, vol. 3, pp. 936–75; and Robert P. Weller, *Unities and Diversities in Chinese Religion* (Seattle: University of Washington Press, 1987), 173–84.

5. On this type of thinking, see Joseph Needham, *Science and Civilisation in China* (Cambridge: Cambridge University Press), vol. 2, pp. 216–345; John B. Henderson, *The Development and Decline of Chinese Cosmology* (New York: Columbia University Press, 1984).

6. Partial exceptions are Makio Ryōkai, "Fūsui shisō shōkō" (A Small Study of Geomantic Thought), in *Fukui hakushi shōju kinen Tōyō bunka ronshū* (Essays on East Asian Culture in Honor of Professor Fukui) (Tokyo: Waseda University Press, 1969); and "Dōkyō to fūsui shisō" (Daoism and Geomantic Thought), in *Yoshioka hakushi kanreki kinen Dōkyō ronshū: Dōkyō no shisō to bunka* (Essays on Taoism in Honor of the Sixtieth Birthday of Professor Yoshioka: Taoist Thought and Culture) (Tokyo: Kokusho Kankōkai, 1977); and Carol Morgan, "T'ang Geomancy: The Wu-hsing ('Five Names') Theory and Its Legacy," *T'ang Studies* (1990–91), 8–9:45–76.

7. Versions of these three texts are found in volume 808 of the *Ssu-k'u ch'üan-shu*, prefaced by comments on their history and authenticity.

8. *Sung shih* (Sung History), ed. T'o T'o et al. (Peking: Chung-hua shu-chü, 1977), 206. 5244, 5252, 5259, 5261. See also the list of titles in *T'ung-chih* (Comprehensive Record) (Kyoto: Chūbun, 1978 reprint of Shih-t'ung ed.), 68:807, which gives 149 titles all specifically on grave geomancy.

9. *Hui-chu lu* (Historical Notes) (Ts'ung-shu chi-ch'eng ed.), *hou-lu* 11, pp. 667–68. On Fan T'ung's official career, see *Sung shih*, 380:11712–13.

10. On Hung Mai's interest in popular religious practices and beliefs, see Valcrie

Hansen, *Changing Gods in Medieval China, 1127–1276* (Princeton: Princeton University Press, 1990).

11. *I-chien chih* (Records of the Listener) (Peking: Chung-hua shu-chü, 1981) *chih-ching* 10, p. 957. On Yao Yu's political career, see *Sung shih*, 354:11162–63. Hung Mai miswrites the "Yu" in Yao Yu's name, but the *tzu* (style) is the same.

12. See, for instance, Lou Yüeh, *Kung-k'uei chi* (Collected Works of Lou Yüeh) (Ts'ung-shu chi-ch'eng ed.), 60:810–11.

13. See Fan Tsu-yü, *Fan T'ai-shih chi* (Collected Works of Fan Tsu-yü) (Ssu-k'u ch'üan-shu ed.), 39:1b–2a; Ch'ao Pu-chih, *Chi-le chi* (Collected Works of Ch'ao Pu-chih) (Ssu-pu ts'ung-k'an ed.), 67:12a.

14. For example, Wen T'ien-hsiang, *Wen Wen-shan ch'üan-chi* (Collected Works of Wen T'ien-hsiang) (Taipei: Shih-chieh shu-chü ed.), 11:273; Hung Kua, *P'an-chou wen-chi* (Collected Works of Hung Kua) (Ssu-pu ts'ung-k'an ed.), 33:6b.

15. Hsü Sung, *Sung hui-yao chi-pen* (Sung Classified Documents) (Taipei: Shih-chieh shu-chü ed.), *li* 37:50a–54a (I-hsing is mentioned on 54a); 29:24a–b. I-hsing (683–727) was an eminent monk of the T'ang, known especially for his studies of the calendar. See *Chiu T'ang shu* (Old T'ang History) (Peking: Chung-hua shu-chü, 1995), 191:5111-13.

16. *Ti-li hsin-shu*, preface.

17. *Ssu-ma wen-cheng kung ch'uan-chia chi* (Collected Works of Ssu-ma Kuang Transmitted in his Family) (Kuo-hsüeh chi-pen ts'ung-shu ed.), 27:381.

18. *Chao-mu* order was the order used for the arrangement of ancestral tablets on an ancestral altar, with odd-numbered generations on one side and even-numbered generations on the other.

19. *Ssu-ma Wen-cheng kung ch'uan-chia chi*, 27:381.

20. Ibid.

21. *Hsiao ching* (Shih-san ching chu-shu ed.), 9:2b.

22. Allusions to *Li chi*, "T'an Kung" (Shih-san ching chu-shu ed.), 8:15b–16a.

23. *Ssu-ma shih shu-i* (Mr. Ssu-ma's Letters and Etiquette) (Ts'ung-shu chi-ch'eng ed.), 7:75.

24. Ibid.

25. Ibid.

26. Ibid., 7:75–76.

27. *Ssu-ma Wen-cheng kung ch'uan-chia chi*, 65:810–11.

28. See Ira E. Kasoff, *The Thought of Chang Tsai (1020–1077)* (Cambridge: Cambridge University Press, 1984), 36–43; and A. C. Graham, *Two Chinese Philosophers: Ch'eng Ming-tao and Ch'eng Yi-ch'uan* (London: Lund Humphries, 1958), 8–21.

29. *Chang Tsai chi* (Collected Works of Chang Tsai) (Peking: Chung-hua shu-chü, 1978), 299. De Groot, vol. 3, pp. 1018–19, reported that in his day people tested the soil by burying such things as pig bones or duck eggs.

30. *Erh-Ch'eng chi* (Collected Works of the Two Ch'engs) (Peking: Chung-hua shu-chü, 1981), *wen-chi* 10:624. Here Ch'eng I is borrowing from Lü Ts'ai of the early T'ang, who wrote a long critique of geomancy. See *Chiu T'ang shu*, 79:2723.

31. One geomantic manual of Sung or Yüan date explained that the classification was based on the position of the tongue when pronouncing the word. If the tongue was extended, it was *shang*, if against the teeth, *ch'eng*, etc. *Ta-Han yüan-ling mi-tsang ching* (Yung-le ta-tien, ch. 8199), 3b–4a.

32. *Erh-Ch'eng chi, wen-chi* 10:625.

33. Ibid., 625.

34. Ibid., *I-shu*, 22A:290.

35. Ibid., *wen-chi*, 10:623.

36. The green dragon, white tiger, red bird, and black turtle were used in geomancy to represent the four directions, and by Sung times had strong associations with burials. Tombs were often decorated with pictures of them or furnished with models of them and the "mock deeds" regularly placed in tombs generally said the site extended on the east to the green dragon, and so on.

37. *Heng-p'u chi* (Collected Works of Chang Chiu-ch'eng) (Ssu-k'u ch'üan-shu ed.), 19:6b–7b. It should perhaps be noted that even critics of geomancy like Chang Chiu-ch'eng did not claim that people believed this literally, that they thought mountains were dragons or were protected by dragon spirits, and so on. Chang seems to have accepted that people spoke of dragons to represent certain types of forces, much as the *I-ching* did.

38. This last phrase is an allusion to Liu Tsung-yüan's criticism of the belief in portents. See *Liu-Tsung-yüan chi* (Collected Works of Liu Tsung-yuan) (Peking: Chung-hua shu-chü, 1978), 1:30.

39. *Heng-p'u chi*, 20:5b–6b. Ch'en Fu-liang (1137–1203), a contemporary of Chang Chiu-ch'eng, also brought criticism of geomancy into a mortuary text, this time into a funerary inscription; *Chih-chai hsien-sheng wen-chi* (Collected Works of Ch'en Fu-liang) (Ssu-pu ts'ung-k'an ed.), 48:4a–5a.

40. Not much is known of Lo Ta-ching's biography, so his exact connections with Neo-Confucianism are unclear. However, as the editor of the recent edition notes in his preface, the internal content of Lo's *Ho-lin yü-lu* (Conversations of Lo Ta-ching) shows that he belonged to what was called in his time *tao-hsüeh*.

41. *Ho-lin yü-lu* (Peking: Chung-hua shu-chü, 1983), 6:344.

42. *Ho-lin yü-lu*, 344–45.

43. This seems often to have occurred in modern times. See Maurice Freedman, *Chinese Lineage and Society: Fukien and Kwangtung* (London: Athlone, 1966), 130–33.

44. In his critique of the idea of hell, however, Ssu-ma Kuang used language similar to Lo Ta-ching's in arguing that the dead could feel nothing. See *Ssu-ma shih shu-i*, 5:54.

45. See Patricia Buckley Ebrey, *Confucianism and Family Rituals in Imperial China: A Social History of Writing About Rites* (Princeton: Princeton University Press, 1991), esp. pp. 102–44.

46. *Chu Tzu chia-li* (Master Chu's Family Rituals) (Ssu-k'u ch'üan-shu ed.), 4:19b–20b. Cf. Patricia Buckley Ebrey, trans., *Chu Hsi's "Family Rituals": A Twelfth-Century Chinese Manual for the Performance of Cappings, Weddings, Funerals, and Ancestral Rites* (Princeton: Princeton University Press, 1991), 103–5.

47. See Li Wen-chao, *Chia-li sang-chi shih-i* (Collected Fragments on the Family Rituals of Funerals and Sacrifice), in *Tu-li t'ung-k'ao* (Taipei: Kuo-hsüeh chi-yao 1967 reprint of 1891 ed.), 18b.

48. Chu Hsi, *Chu Wen-kung wen-chi* (Collected Works of Chu Hsi) (Ssu-pu ts'ung-k'an ed.), 94:25a.

49. *Nan-hsüan chi* (Collected Works of Chang Shih) (Ssu-k'u ch'üan-shu ed.) 23:14a.

50. *Chu Wen-kung wen-chi, hsü* 7:8b.

51. *Chu Tzu yü-lei* (Chung-hua shu chü ed.), 90:2286. Cf. *Chu Wen-kung wen-chi* 63:1a–2a.

52. *Chu Tzu yü-lei*, 89:2287. For other minor references to geomancy in the *Yü-lei*, see ibid., 2:24; 4:75–76.

53. On this incident, see Ma Tuan-lin, *Wen-hsien t'ung-k'ao* (Comprehensive Study of Documents) (Taipei: Hsin-hsing shu-chü reprint of Shih-t'ung ed.), 126:1133b–1134a; *Sung hui-yao chi-pen*, *li* 37:24b–26a; Huang Kan, *Huang Mien-chai hsien-sheng wen-chi* (Collected Works of Huang Kan) (Ts'ung-shu chi-ch'eng ed.), 8:177–78; Makio Ryōkai, "Shushi to fūsui shisō" (Chu Hsi and Geomantic Thought), *Chizan gakuhō* (1974), 23–24:361–77.

54. *Chu Wen-kung wen-chi*, 15:34a–b.

55. Ibid., 15:36a–b.

56. Ibid., 15:37a. The tradition that Kiangsi and Fukien represent the two main schools of geomancy has continued into the present. See de Groot, vol. 3, pp. 1007–8.

57. *Chu Wen-kung wen-chi*, 15:37a–b.

58. Freedman, for instance, wrote that the dead were passive agents who "could choose neither to confer nor to withhold the blessings that flowed through their bones" (*Chinese Lineage and Society*, 126). Emily M. Ahern, by contrast, reported that ordinary peasants saw their ancestors as actively engaged in distributing geomantic benefits. (*The Cult of the Dead in a Chinese Village* [Stanford: Stanford University Press, 1973], 178–90).

59. "Chu Hsi's Completion of Neo-Confucianism," *Etudes Song, In Memoriam Etienne Balazs* (1973), 2(1):59–70.

60. "A Comparative Study of Chu Hsi and the Ch'eng Brothers," in Wing-tsit Chan, ed., *Chu Hsi and Neo-Confucianism* (Honolulu: University of Hawaii Press, 1986), 43–57. Many other articles in this volume deal with Chu Hsi's metaphysics, especially those by Stanislaus Lokuang, Yamanoi Yū, and Teng Ai-min.

61. "Chu Hsi's System of Thought of *I*," in *Chu Hsi and Neo-Confucianism*, 307.

62. *I-ching*, "Hsi-tz'u chuan" (Shih-san ching chu-shu ed.), 7:9a.

63. *The Study of Chinese Society*, 191.

64. On Ts'ai, see R. C. Pian's biography in Herbert Franke, ed., *Sung Biographies*, vol. 3, pp. 1037–39 (Wiesbaden: Franz Steiner Verlag, 1976); and Ch'en Jung-chieh [Wing-tsit Chan], *Chu-tzu men-jen* (Master Chu's Disciples) (Taipei: Hsüeh-sheng shu-chü, 1982), 331–32.

65. *Chu Wen-kung wen-chi*, 83:6b.

66. *Hsi-shan wen-chi* (Collected Works of Chen Te-hsiu) (Ssu-k'u ch'üan-shu ed.), 42:7b.

67. *Sung shih*, 434:12875.

68. Ibid., 434:12875–76. On Ts'ai's drafting the *I-hsüeh ch'i-meng*, see also Li Ch'ing-fu, *Min-chung li-hsüeh yüan-yüan k'ao* (Study of the Evolution of Neo-Confucianiom in Fukien) (Ssu-k'u ch'üan-shu ed.), 25:24a.

69. *Sung ming-ch'en yen-hsing lu* (Records of the Works and Deeds of Famous Officials of the Sung Dynasty), *Wai chi* (1638 ed.), 17:3a.

70. *Ssu-ch'ao wen-chien lu* (Literary Records of Four Reigns) (Ts'ung-shu chi-ch'eng ed.), 38.

71. *Sung-Yüan hsüeh-an*, 48:1.

72. *Ch'ing-yüan tang-chin* (Proscription of the Ch'ing-yüan Era) (anon.) (Ts'ung-shu chi-ch'eng ed.), 16. How much Ts'ai Yüan-ting was to blame for Chu Hsi's troubles was still

debated in the Ch'ing period. See Wang Fu-chih, *Sung lun* (Essay on the Sung Dynasty) (Ts'ung-shu chi-ch'eng ed.), 204–6.

73. Lo Ta-ching defended such studies: "In Heaven and Earth, where there are patterns [*li*], there must be numbers: they cannot be separated." He regretted that so few people paid attention to Shao Yung's and Ts'ai Yüan-ting's works. *Ho-lin yü-lu*, 271–72.

74. Parts of this book are preserved in the commentary to the current edition of the *Huang-chi ching-shih shu*. See Chung-kuo tzu-hsüeh ming-chu chi-ch'eng ed.

75. *The Development and Decline of Chinese Cosmology*, 120.

76. *Ying-hsüeh ts'ung-shuo* (Collected Conversations of Yü Ch'eng) (Ts'ung-shu chi-ch'eng ed.), 1:10.

77. See Ch'iu Chün, *Chia-li i-chieh* (Family Rituals with Specification of the Procedures) (1618 ed.), 5:46b. Cf. *Ts'ai-shih chiu-ju shu* (Works of the Nine Confucian Scholars of the Ts'ai Family) (San-yü shu-hang 1868 ed.), 2:157a–158a.

78. See *Ssu-k'u ch'üan-shu tsung-mu t'i-yao* (Taipei: Commercial Press 1971 reprint), vol. 21, p. 2245; *Liu Chiang-tung chia-ts'ang shan-pen Tsang-shu* (Rare Edition of the Book of Burials Preseved by the Family of Liu Chiang-tung) (Pai-pu ts'ung-shu chi-ch'eng ed.), prefaces.

79. This treatise is also sometimes attributed to Ts'ai Yüan-ting, an attribution the editors of the *Ssu-k'u ch'üan-shu* accepted. However, the prefaces included in *Ts'ai-shih chiu-ju shu* show that Ts'ai Fa wrote it. In 1166 Ts'ai Yüan-ting brought a copy of it to Chang Hsien, asking him to write a preface for it (*Ts'ai-shih chiu-ju shu*, 1:45b–46a). The name *Fa-wei lun* was also used by Ssu-ma Kuang for the appendix to his *Ch'ien-hsü*.

80. *I-ching* (Shih-san ching chu-shu ed.), 9:3b.

81. Cf. *Huang-chi ching-shih shu*, 3:1a, which is worded slightly differently.

82. *Fa-wei lun* (Ssu-k'u ch'üan-shu ed.), 1a.

83. Ibid., 1b. This is based on *Huang-chi ching-shih chi*, 3:3a–6b.

84. *Fa-wei lun*, 3a–b.

85. Ibid., 4b.

86. Ibid., 6b–7a.

87. Ibid., 8a–b.

88. Ibid., 9a.

89. See Ch'ien Mu, *Chu Tzu hsin hsüeh-an* (New Studies of Master Chu) (Taipei: San-min shu-tien, 1971), vol. 1, pp. 283–344. A eighteenth-century Korean book on geomancy, *T'agokpu*, attributes to Ts'ai Yüan-ting a list of auspicious and inauspicious directions for tomb sites, using the *pa-kua* and the stems and branches. See *P'ungsu chiri ch'ongsŏ* (Seoul, 1969).

90. *Ssu-ch'ao wen-chien lu*, i, 38; Ma Tuan-lin, in *Wen-hsien t'ung-k'ao*, 126:1133c, also noted that Chu Hsi's ideas in this memorial resembled Ts'ai Yüan-ting's.

91. See Paul S. Ropp, *Dissent in Early Modern China* (Ann Arbor: University of Michigan Press, 1981), 164–85; Hsü Ch'ien-hsüeh, *Tu-li t'ung-k'ao* (Comprehensive Inquiry into Readings on Ritual) (Ssu-k'u ch'üan-shu ed.), 83:22b–41a; Ho Ch'ang-ling, *Huang-ch'ao ching-shih wen-pien* (Documents on Government Management of the Ch'ing Dynasty) 63:1a–12b; Wu Jung-kuang, *Wu-hsüeh lu*, 19:5a–15b.

92. See Hu Han, *Hu Chung-tzu chi* (Collected Works of Hu Han) (Ts'ung-shu chi-ch'eng ed.), vol. 4, pp. 52–53, in which he laments that a certain book refuting geomancy had not been available to Chu Hsi two hundreds years earlier. See also Wang Fu-li, *Chia-*

li pien-ting (Family Rituals Discriminated) (1707 ed.), 7:44b–50a, which quotes four Ch'ing scholars who criticized Chu Hsi.

93. During the eighteenth century, Li Wen-chao reported that a chart used by geomancers in his day derived from the ideas of Chu Hsi and Ts'ai Yüan-ting (*Chia-li sang-chi shih-i*, 19a). See also de Groot vol. 3, p. 1011.

94. "Some Common Tendencies in Neo-Confucianism," in David S. Nivison and Arthur F. Wright, eds., *Confucianism in Action*, 39 (Stanford: Stanford University Press, 1959).

GLOSSARY

an　安

Chai-ching　宅經

Chang　張

Chang Chiu-ch'eng　張九成

Chang Shih　張栻

Chang Tsai　張載

Chang Tsai chi　張載集

Chao　趙

chao-mu　昭穆

Ch'ao Pu-chih　晁補之

Che-hsi　浙西

Che-tung　浙東

Chen Te-hsiu　真德秀

Ch'en Fu-liang　陳傅良

Ch'en Liang　陳亮

Ch'eng I　程頤

Chi-le chi　雞肋集

ch'i　氣

Chia-li　家禮

Chia-li i-chieh　家禮儀節

Chia-li pien-ting　家禮辨定

Chia-li sang-chi shih-i　家禮喪祭拾遺

Chiang-hsi　江西

ch'ien　乾

Ch'ien   錢

Ch'ien-hsü   潛虛

Ch'ien-k'un pao-tien   乾坤寶典

Ch'ien Mu   錢穆

Chih-chai hsien-sheng wen-chi   止齋先生文集

Chin-ssu lu   近思錄

Ch'in Kuei   秦檜

Ch'ing-nang ao-yü   青囊奧語

Ch'ing-yüan tang-chin   慶元黨禁

Ch'iu Chün   丘濬

Chiu T'ang shu   舊唐書

Chou li   周禮

chü-chi   拘忌

Chu Hsi   朱熹

Chu Tzu chia-li   朱子家禮

Chu Tzu hsin hsüeh-an   朱子新學案

Chu Tzu men-jen   朱子門人

Chu Tzu yü-lei   朱子語類

Chu Wen-kung wen-chi   朱文公文集

Ch'un-ch'iu   春秋

chung   中

Dōkyō to fūsui shisō   道教と風水思想

Erh-Ch'eng chi   二程集

Fa-wei lun   發微論

Fan T'ai-shih chi   范太史集

Fan Tse-shan   范擇善

Fan Tsu-yü   范祖禹

Fan T'ung   范同

feng-shui   風水

Fukien   福建

Fukui hakushi shōju kinen Tōyō bunka ronshū   福井博士頌壽記念東洋文化
論集

Fūsui shisō shōkō   風水思想小考

Fu-yang   富陽

hai 亥

Heng-p'u chi 橫浦集

Ho Ch'ang-ling 賀長齡

Ho-lin yü-lu 鶴林玉露

Hsi-shan wen-chi 西山文集

hsiang 相

hsiang-kan 相感

hsiang-ti che 相地者

Hsiao-ching 孝經

Hsiao-tsung 孝宗

hsing-shih 形勢

Hsü Ch'ien-hsüeh 徐乾學

Hsü Sung 徐松

hsüeh 穴

Hu Chung-tzu chi 胡仲子集

Hu Han 胡翰

Huang-ch'ao ching-shih wen-pien 皇朝經世文編

Huang-chi ching-shih shu 皇極經世書

Huang Kan 黃榦

Huang Mien-chai hsien-sheng wen-chi 黃勉齋先生文集

Hui-chu lu 揮麈錄

Hung Kua 洪适

Hung Mai 洪邁

I-chien chih 夷堅志

I-ching 易經

I-hsüeh ch'i-meng 易學啟蒙

I-hsing 一行

Jen-tsung 仁宗

ju-che 儒者

k'an-yü 堪輿

K'an-yü ching 堪輿經

ken 艮

Kung-k'uei chi 攻媿集

Kung, Shang, Chüeh, Chih, and Yü 宮商角徵羽

Kuo P'u　郭璞

Kuo Tzu-kao　國子高

li　理

Li chi　禮記

Li Ch'ing-fu　李清馥

Li Wen-chao　李文炤

Li Yu-wu　李幼武

Liu Chiang-tung chia-tsang shan-pen Tsang-shu　劉江東家藏善本葬書

Liu　柳

Liu Tsung-yüan　柳宗元

Liu Tsung-yüan chi　柳宗元集

Lo Ta-ching　羅大經

Lou Yüeh　樓鑰

Lü Ts'ai　呂才

Lü Tsu-ch'ien　呂祖謙

Ma Tuan-lin　馬端臨

Makio Ryōkai　牧尾良海

Min-chung li-hsüeh yüan-yüan k'ao　閩中理學淵源考

Nan-hsüan chi　南軒集

Ning-tsung　寧宗

pa-kua　八卦

P'an-chou wen-chi　盤洲文集

Po-kung　伯恭

pu-li　不利

P'ungsu chiri ch'ongsŏ　風水地理叢書

shang　商

Shao-hsing　紹興

Shao Yung　邵雍

shen-ling　神靈

Shou-huang　壽皇

shu-chia　術家

Shushi to fūsui shisō　朱子と風水思想

shu-shih　術士

ssu　巳

Ssu-ch'ao wen-chien lu　四朝聞見錄

Ssu-k'u ch'üan-shu　四庫全書

Ssu-k'u ch'üan-shu tsung-mu t'i-yao　四庫全書總目提要

Ssu-ma Kuang　司馬光

Ssu-ma shih shu-i　司馬氏書儀

Ssu-ma Tan (Po-k'ang)　司馬旦（伯康）

Ssu-ma Wen-cheng kung ch'uan-chia chi　司馬文正公傳家集

Sung hui-yao chi-pen　宋會要輯本

Sung lun　宋論

Sung ming-ch'en yen-hsing lu　宋名臣言行錄

Sung shih　宋史

Sung-Yüan hsüeh-an　宋元學案

T'agokpu　琢玉斧

Ta-Han yüan-ling mi-tsang ching　大漢原陵祕葬經

T'ai-hsüan ching　太玄經

T'ai-wei Kung　太尉公

T'an Kung　檀弓

tao-hsüeh　道學

ti-feng　地風

ti-hsing　地形

ti-li　地理

Ti-li ching　地理經

Ti-li hsin-shu　地理新書

ti-li jen　地理人

t'ien-wen　天文

Ts'ai Fa　蔡發

Ts'ai-shih chiu-ju shu　蔡氏九儒書

Ts'ai Yüan-ting　蔡元定

tsang-shih　葬師

Tsang-shu　葬書

Tu-li ts'ung-ch'ao　讀禮叢鈔

Tu-li t'ung-k'ao　讀禮通考

tzu-jan chih li　自然之理

Wang　王

Wang Fu-chih　王夫之

Wang Fu-li　王復禮

Wang Ming-ch'ing　王明清

Wang Shu　王洙

Wen-hsien t'ung-k'ao　文獻通考

Wen T'ien-hsiang　文天祥

Wen Wen-shan ch'üan-chi　文文山全集

Wu-hsüeh lu　吾學錄

Wu Jung-kuang　吳榮光

Wu-yin ti-li chüeh　五音地理訣

Yang Hsiung　楊雄

Yang Shih　楊時

Yang Wan-li　楊萬里

Yao Yu　姚祐

Yeh Shao-weng　葉紹翁

yin-yang　陰陽

yin-yang chia　陰陽家

Yin-yang tsang-ching　陰陽葬經

Ying-hsüeh ts'ung-shuo　螢雪叢説

Yoshioka hakushi kanreki kinen Dōkyō kenkyū ronshū: Dōkyō no shisō to bunka
　吉岡博士還曆記念道教研究論集——道教の思想と文化

Yü Ch'eng　俞成

Yu-wu　由五

Chapter Four

CHU HSI AND TAOISM

JULIA CHING

In the philosophical writings of Neo-Confucian thinkers, Buddhism and Taoism tend to be spoken of together. This is also true of Chu Hsi's writings. Like many of the others, he had in his youth been interested in both Buddhism and Taoism before he turned seriously to the philosophy of principle (*li*) and nature (*hsing*). What, then, about Chu Hsi and Taoism?

The topic is a vast one, in part because of the nebulous significance of the word *Taoism*. Its meaning is ambiguous, both in English and in Chinese, whether as *Tao-chia* (Taoist philosophy) or *Tao-chiao* (Taoist religion). This is especially the case when we speak of the Taoist religion, often an umbrella term for everything from the practice of *ch'i-kung* (breathing exercises) to religious beliefs in gods and spirits as well as religious rituals, sometimes including shamanic practices. And yet for many people the term refers particularly to the quest for immortality or at least for physical longevity, with its side interests in scientific and medicinal inquiry.

It is not possible here to cover everything about Chu Hsi and the whole range of beliefs and activities customarily associated with the term *Taoism*. This chapter focuses instead on a few concepts and writings considered central to its philosophy and religion: Chu Hsi's reactions to those philosophical texts as important to Taoist philosophy and religion as the *Lao-tzu*, the *Chuang-tzu*, and the *I ching* (Classic of Changes), as well as the *Ts'an-t'ung-ch'i*, which is associated with that last-mentioned classic. The chapter also discusses Chu's personal feelings about the quest for longevity and immortality, sometimes identified with Taoist religion.[1]

Chu Hsi had acknowledged a youthful interest in Taoism — among other things. He said that he was engrossed with "Buddhism and Taoism" for "over ten years." This lasted until he met Li T'ung (1093–1163) and decided to concentrate on "the learning of the sages."[2] He also held sinecures involving the supervision of Taoist temples for several decades.[3] What then was his understanding and evaluation of Taoism, and to what extent did Taoism influence his thinking?

In seeking to answer this question, I explain below how, on the one hand, Chu tried to transform religious beliefs into philosophical concepts without always succeeding in doing so completely, thereby showing certain apparent contradictions in his own thinking. On the other hand, I show how this criticism of Taoism was a selective and nuanced one. My concern remains the history of ideas rather than persons or institutions.

Chu Hsi associated with many Taoist priests as well as with Buddhist monks. He made occasional sojourns in Taoist temples, exchanged words and poetry with individual priests, and sought their care when he was ill.[4] Among Chu's more than four hundred disciples, one, who came to him through Ts'ai Yüan-ting (1135–1198), has been identified as a Taoist priest versed in astrology, fortune-telling, and the art of war.[5]

But Chu's association with Taoist priests was different from his relations with Buddhist monks. For example, we have no reason to suppose, for example, that Chu ever took lessons from any Taoist priest, as we know he did from Buddhist monks. This study briefly compares his interest in Taoism with his interest in Buddhism. Indeed, it is my opinion that Chu was much more influenced by Ch'an Buddhism in his youth than he was by Taoism and that as he matured he moved away from Buddhism, eventually gravitating toward Taoism through an increasing interest in practices of longevity, which he developed because of practical health needs. If we compare Chu Hsi with Wang Yang-ming (1472–1529), we shall find that in his youth Wang had much stronger interests in Taoism — indeed, he was engrossed in Taoist longevity practices — but with age moved closer to Ch'an Buddhist ideas.

Chu Hsi and Taoist Philosophy

Chu Hsi is known for his breadth of knowledge. He was obviously conversant with Taoist philosophical works, including *Lao-tzu*, *Chuang-tzu*, and others, and commented on selected chapters from each. He also appears to have a better than usual knowledge of religious Taoism, being the alleged author of two influential treatises, each a study of a Taoist religious text: the *Ts'an-t'ung-ch'i k'ao-i* (A Study of the *Ts'an-t'ung-ch'i*) and the *Yin-fu ching k'ao-i* (A Study of the *Yin-fu ching*).[6]

Like his philosophical predecessors Chang Tsai (1020–1077) and Ch'eng I (1033–1107), Chu's general attitude toward Taoism is a critical one. He refers to it by the terms *Lao-Chuang* (Lao-tzu and Chuang-tzu), regards it as a kind of "heresy," and attacks it as Mencius had also criticized Yang Chu (for disregard of the ruler/subject relationship) and Mo Ti (for disregard of the father/son relationship). Indeed, Chu explains that if Mencius had not explic- itly criticized Lao-tzu, it was because Mencius had already shown his opposi- tion to what Lao-tzu represents in his critique of Yang Chu.[7] Thus it may be said that Chu's own general disapproval of Taoism, like that of Buddhism, is rooted in his conviction of the primary importance of social and political responsibility. In addition, we also find a critique of religious Taoism grounded in Chu's basically rationalist outlook.

Without using such words as *philosophy* and *religion*, Chu makes a careful distinction between the Taoism of Lao-tzu and Chuang-tzu and the cult of immortality that developed later on. He asserts that the quest for immortality replaced the earlier interest in a philosophy of nonaction until "shamans [*wu-chu*] took over and only paid attention to the use of charms and talismans, praying for blessings, and averting or ameliorating disasters."[8] In this way, he voices greater disapproval of the latter practices with their magico-religious associations.

CHU HSI ON LAO-TZU

Chu Hsi's criticisms of Taoist philosophy are generally restrained and discern- ing. In responding to disciples' questions, he even defends Yang Chu from the charge of being superficial and considers his teaching similar to that of Lao- tzu. He says, "Lao-tzu has said many things. How can we say there is nothing worthwhile in his book? Even in the case of Buddhism, there is much that is worthwhile. But they err regarding human destiny."[9]

Chu regards Lao-tzu's condemnation of rituals and music as mistaken. While less severe than Ch'eng I, he echoes Ch'eng's criticism of the amoral and Legalist implications of Lao-tzu's thought,[10] singling out Lao-tzu's facile preference for survival. He also distinguishes carefully between Lao-tzu and Chuang-tzu, finding more depth in the former. Acknowledging that both teach a philosophy of withdrawal and retirement, he points out that, unlike Chuang-tzu, Lao-tzu is still concerned with social and political realities. He regards Chuang-tzu as the less rational and less responsible of the two:

> Lao-tzu's learning is generally focused on emptiness, tranquility, and nonaction. . . . What is said about straddling the sun and the moon and holding up the universe . . . comes from Chuang-tzu's nonsense,[11] while what is said about that which is full of light, reflecting all and penetrating all . . . comes from Buddhist empty talk. Where could you find such in the original Lao-tzu? In our own times, those who discuss Lao-tzu always mix up what is common between [Buddhism and Taoism] as though they were one school.[12]

In discussing the *Lao-tzu* text, Chu points out that he likes the sixth chapter best. He pays special attention to the two sentences:

> The spirit of the valley never dies.
> This is called the mysterious female.[13]

Chu offers a metaphysical interpretation of that passage. According to him, the empty valley's ability to echo represents a divinely or mysteriously transformed nature (*shen-hua chih tzu-jan*), whereas the so-called mysterious female refers to what is receptive and life-giving. He even adds: "This most marvelous meaning contains the idea of *sheng-sheng* (literally: life-giving life, generation and regeneration). It is what Ch'eng [I] learned from Lao-tzu."[14]

Surprisingly, Chu attributes Ch'eng I's doctrine of a dynamic universe of spontaneous generation to Lao-tzu. Ch'eng I had asserted that "the Way (*Tao*) spontaneously generates and regenerates [*sheng-sheng*] without end." Ch'eng himself had not referred to Lao-tzu and his philosophy has usually been said to show more Buddhist than Taoist influence.[15]

But Chu can appreciate the *Lao-tzu* for its positive teachings. In these cases, he tends to offer a Confucian interpretation of Lao-tzu, as Wing-tsit Chan has especially pointed out.[16] For example, Chu quotes from chapter 28 of *Lao-tzu*:

Know the male,
but keep to the female
And be a ravine to the empire. . . .
Know the white
but keep to the black
And be a model to the empire.[17]

According to him, "the ravine and the valley both refer to a lowly place." The *Lao-tzu* speaks of being content in a lowly place, without seeking to move higher, which is a very rare and difficult task. And yet, "with such effort, one could govern the country, or apply strategy in warfare, or take over the world without [appearing] to do anything." Here, Chu appears to shift to a practical teaching in the *Lao-tzu*, that of keeping modest and humble.[18]

Chu Hsi echoes Chang Tsai's criticism of Lao-tzu for saying "being comes from nothingness." They both point out that such thinking was not found in the *Classic of Changes*. And Chu Hsi adds: "In saying being comes from nothingness, Lao-tzu errs."[19]

He does admit, however, that Lao-tzu is not a nihilist since the text also says:

Have nothing [*wu*], to observe its secrets;
Have something [*yu*, i.e., being], to observe its manifestations.[20]

Comparing Lao-tzu to the Buddhists, he claims that the latter regard Heaven and Earth as illusions and the Four Phases as fantasy.[21]

Chu Hsi opposes the division of the text into two parts, *Tao ching* and *Te ching*, and for saying:

When the Way was lost there was virtue;
When virtue was lost there was benevolence;
When benevolence was lost there was righteousness.[22]

His comment is: "Lao-tzu says *te* comes after the loss of *tao*. These are not understood but divided into two things. . . . [Besides,] without benevolence and righteousness, there is no *tao-li* (meaning). How can one yet speak of the Tao?"[23]

He criticizes Lao-tzu as a person who refuses to take responsibility, who wishes to protect his own life selfishly, not caring about the world around him. He also criticizes Lao-tzu's proclivity to Legalism. He points out that Lao-tzu's teachings have led to the emergence of such Legalists as Shen Pu-hai and Han Fei-tzu, as well as to the military strategists connected with the *Yin-fu ching*.[24]

When asked whether one should be permitted to read *Lao-tzu* and *Chuang-tzu* at all, Chu answers that there is no harm in reading them, provided that one knows one's own mind. "What is important is to understand where their meaning differs from that of the sages."[25] Here, Ch'ien Mu points out that Chu's readiness to learn from both Lao-tzu and Chuang-tzu marks a departure from Ch'eng I, who refused to read these texts, showing him to be rather closer to Ch'eng Hao (1032–1085).[26]

CHU HSI ON CHUANG-TZU

Chu Hsi appears to have a special regard for Chuang-tzu. Chu says that while one does not know where Chuang-tzu learned what he knew, he had greater knowledge than many scholars coming after Mencius, including Hsün-tzu. Indeed, he adds that whatever is positive in Buddhism comes from Chuang-tzu.[27] Chu praises both the *Chuang-tzu* and the *Mencius* for being good literature. He finds much that is positive or appealing in Chuang-tzu, including the cosmological explanations of yin and yang, which he considers a key to understanding the *Classic of Changes*. In particular he cites the chapter on "The Turning of Heaven." The cosmological questions posed there seem to have fascinated him:

> Who masterminds all this? Who pulls the strings? Who, resting inactive himself, gives the push that makes it go this way? I wonder, is there some mechanism that works it and won't let it stop? I wonder if it just rolls and turns and can't bring itself to a halt? Do the clouds make the rain, or does the rain make the clouds? Who puffs them up, who showers them down like this? Who, resting inactive himself, stirs up all this lascivious joy?[28]

Chu several times also appreciatively cites a long passage from "The Secret of Caring for Life." Following is a quotation from this famous story:

> Cook Ting was cutting up an ox for Lord Wen-hui. At every touch of his hand, every heave of his shoulder, every move of his feet, every thrust of his knee — zip! zoop! He slithered the knife along with a zing, and all was in perfect rhythm, as though he were performing the dance of the Mulberry Grove or keeping time to the Ching-shou music.[29]

When the lord expressed admiration at the cook's skill, he received the following response, which also impressed Chu:

> What I care about is the Way, which goes beyond skill. When I first began cutting up oxen, all I could see was the ox itself. After three years I no longer saw the whole ox. And now . . . I've had this knife . . . for nineteen years and I've cut up thousands of oxen with it, and yet the blade is as good as though it had just come from the grindstone.[30]

Chu sees here a hidden lesson about the gradual acquisition of *li*:

> When a student first reads the text, he only sees the whole thing. After a long while he sees several pieces in it, even more than ten pieces. Only then is he making progress. This is like the cook cutting up the ox, who no longer sees the whole ox.[31]

Significantly, this corroborates Chu Hsi's preference for gradual cultivation over sudden enlightenment.

But he criticizes *Chuang-tzu*'s saying "If you do good, stay away from fame. If you do evil, stay away from punishments."[32] He points out that fear of the disadvantages fame and punishment might bring causes Chuang-tzu to advocate "not doing too much good, and not doing too much evil," since philosophical Taoism is less interested in moral norms and more concerned with assuring personal security.[33]

According to Chu, the teaching of the sages is that one should do as much real good as possible, neither seeking fame nor running away from it. Indeed, a scholar seeking fame is not pursuing study for its own sake, what has been called *wei-chi chih hsüeh*.[34]

> For to study for the sake of acquiring a reputation is not to study for oneself [*wei-chi*]. . . . To fear that fame might injure oneself and for that reason not to do one's best in studying is [to show] that one's mind is already not right and has even turned slightly to evil.[35]

Although there are only a few sentences of criticism of Chuang-tzu in Chu Hsi's recorded conversations, more appears in Chu's letters to friends and disciples.[36] Chuang-tzu is often mentioned together with Lao-tzu as "crazy," "partial," and "without truth."[37] Chu Hsi says, however, that Chuang-tzu was a well-educated man who understood many things, but did not wish to do anything. In fact, Chuang-tzu liked to use Confucius as a mouthpiece but did not wish to imitate Confucius. Chu compares Lao-tzu and Chuang-tzu, saying that while Lao-tzu was willing to do a few things, Chuang-tzu was unwilling to do anything—it was not a case of his not being able to do anything; rather, "he was unwilling to do anything."[38]

Lieh-tzu is another Taoist text that Chu explicitly discussed, but in only a few words. He considered Lieh-tzu to have lived before Chuang-tzu and the latter to have modeled his writings on the former.[39] He also expressed the opinion that the hedonist teaching of Yang Chu issued from Lao-tzu and is reflected in Chuang-tzu.[40]

A text that Chu does not appear to have discussed formally is the *Huai-nan-tzu*, with its discourse on the old Chinese concept of *ch'i*, which we find in Chu's philosophy. But whereas *ch'i* figured in ancient philosophy independently as "ether" (matter/energy), the "stuff" of the universe, it re-emerged in both Ch'eng I and Chu Hsi in association with *li*, "principle" (essence or "form"), a term with Hua-yen Buddhist overtones.

CHU HSI AND THE CLASSIC OF CHANGES

A philosopher driven by great intellectual curiosity, Chu formulated the doctrine of investigating things and examining principles. His appreciation of things Taoist shows his desire to understand the origin and structure of the universe. His inclination was to use the theory of yin and yang and the Five Phases[41] as well as explanations deriving from the theory of numbers to present his own philosophy of nature. This is especially seen in his treatment of the *Classic of Changes*, a text considered a classic by both Confucians and Taoists. Chu regarded it as both a book of divination and a cosmological treatise.

Chu wrote two books on the *Classic of Changes*: the *Chou I pen-i* (The Original Meaning of the *Classic of Changes*, 1177) and the *I-hsüeh ch'i-meng* (Introduction to the *Classic of Changes*), in four *chüan* (1186). Chu said that the *Classic of Changes* was originally a divination manual, using notions of fortune and misfortune for its own didactic purposes.[42] In the *Chou I pen-i*, he included a section giving instruction on how the text may be used for divination with the help of milfoil stalks.[43] In both works he combined the mathematical and numerological interpretations of Shao Yung (1011–1077) and the metaphysical interpretations of Ch'eng I. His own interpretation was thus a kind of synthesis that has since been regarded as orthodox.[44]

To the head of *Chou I pen-i*, Chu Hsi appended nine diagrams, including the legendary *River Chart* (*Ho-t'u*) and *Book of Lo* (*Lo-shu*).[45] The *locus classicus* for the *River Chart* is the *Classic of History*, "Ku-ming," that for the *Book of Lo* is allegedly "Hung-fan," at least according to an explanation predating Chu. The "Appended Remarks" to the *Classic of Changes* makes reference to both these diagrams as corroborating the teaching of the *Classic of Changes* itself.[46]

In this light we can understand his acceptance of such legendary materials as the *River Chart* (allegedly carried out of water by dragon horses at the time of the mythical Fu-hsi) and the *Book of Lo* (allegedly borne up by sacred turtles in the River Lo and offered to the legendary Yü, the Flood-controller).[47] As Chu himself put it:

> Heaven and Earth cannot speak and rely on the sage to write books for them. Should Heaven and Earth possess the gift of speech, they would then express themselves better. The *River Chart* and the *Book of Lo* are [examples of] what Heaven and Earth have themselves designed.[48]

The *River Chart* and the *Book of Lo* have been represented as diagrams. When both are compared with the numbers and emblems of the *Classic of Changes*, it is found that the emblems in the former are round, while those in the latter are square. According to the *River Chart*, "The heavenly numbers are the odd ones of yang, the earthly numbers are the even ones of yin."[49] Chu Hsi discussed them in mathematical terms also in his letters and in his essay on these diagrams.[50]

CHU HSI AND THE *TS'AN-T'UNG-CH'I*

The *Chou I Ts'an-t'ung-ch'i* (or *Ts'an-t'ung-ch'i*), like the *Yin-fu ching* (Harmony of the Seen and the Unseen) is a short text (one *chüan*) ascribed to the Yellow Emperor and included in the Taoist Canon.[51] It purportedly shows how the *Classic of Changes* tallies with the alleged teachings of the Yellow Emperor and of Lao-tzu, that is, with the cult of immortality. As such, it was highly regarded by Confucian scholars of the Sung dynasty together with the *Lao-tzu* and the *Chuang-tzu*. Apparently having read many Buddhist and Taoist texts, Chu wrote a textual commentary on the *Ts'an-t'ung-ch'i*. He did this work while he was old and sick, and officially under a cloud. It was one of his final works, together with the *Ch'u-tz'u chi-chu*, a comentary on the "Songs of Ch'u," and the *I-li ching-chuan t'ung-chieh*, his work on the ritual text called the Ceremonials. Both the *Ts'an-t'ung-ch'i* and the *Ch'u-tz'u chi-chu* have Taoist concerns, the latter because of the shamanic character of some of its contents as well as its references to longevity and immortality.

Though old and sick, Chu chose to labor over these texts. The work with the ritual text represents his continual commitment to Confucian social values. The immersion in the *Ch'u-tz'u chi-chu* reminds us of his sympathies for Ch'ü Yüan, who had also experienced public disgrace in old age and allegedly searched for longevity techniques. The interest in the *Ts'an-t'ung-ch'i* expresses the same quest in Chu's own case, even if he would find in it more in terms of cosmological understanding than anything pertaining to health and longevity.[52]

Like the *Yin-fu ching k'ao-i* (A Study of the *Yin-fu ching*), the *Chou-I Ts'an-t'ung-ch'i k'ao-i* (1197) bears the pen-name of K'ung-t'ung tao-shih, literally, the "empty-same Taoist priest," as well as the assumed name Tsou Hsi. Tsou refers to a small state of the Warring States period, which could have been Chu's ancestral home, whereas Hsi is a homophone of his actual name. The title, however, merits some analysis. To be sure, Taoist writers usually give their titles as well as their real or assumed names. In the case of Chu, while "emptiness" signifies possible Taoist belief, the "empty-same" title may also suggest that he was *not* a real Taoist priest. Nevertheless, his use of an assumed name could also be due to his preference for not openly favoring Taoism.[53]

The problem with any discussion of this work is its triple implication: it is a text about another text, which in turn discusses an earlier text, that is, the *Classic of Changes*. The whole task is complicated by the coded character of the language of both the *Classic of Changes* and the *Chou I Ts'an-t'ung-ch'i*. In itself, Chu's text is not easy either, not only because it discusses the other two but also because of the mathematical or, rather, numerological implications of his interpretation.

Reputed to be the first alchemical text, the *Ts'an-t'ung-ch'i* borrows the highly symbolic language of the *Classic of Changes* to explain what appear to be alchemical processes. *Ch'ien* and *k'un* (the first and second hexagrams, respectively) represent the tripods, *k'an* and *li* (the fifty-sixth and eighteenth hexagrams) the elixir, and the other sixty hexagrams the fire. It also offers a system called *na-chia*. Basically this is an elaborate correlation between the eight trigrams (*kua*), which constitute the foundation of the *Classic of Changes* and from which the sixty-four hexagrams are derived, and the cyclical calendrical signs called ten "heavenly stems" (*kan*).[54] These represent the various stages of the movements of the sun and moon and the supposed fluctuations of yin and yang. Since the ambiguity of the language opens the text to all kinds of interpretations, it has been variously understood as teaching spiritual cultivation, sexual hygiene, or alchemy. Thus it has been regarded by some scholars as dealing mainly with outer alchemy, that is, the quest for immortality through the making of an elixir in the furnace. Other scholars closer to Chu's time regard it as dealing mainly with inner alchemy, that is, the same quest, but one experienced through the discovery of inner enlightenment, euphemistically called the "inner elixir." Among other things, the problem is that the language of inner alchemy is basically the same as that of outer alchemy, which it is suppose to reflect.[55]

The *Ts'an-t'ung-ch'i* has played an important role in the development of Sung Neo-Confucianism. It also influenced Chou Tun-i's (1017–1073) *T'ai-chi-t'u shuo* (Explanation of the Diagram of the Great Ultimate), which refers to the four above-mentioned hexagrams as well as Shao Yung's theory of numbers.[56] Chu's treatise on the *Ts'an-t'ung-ch'i* came twelve years after his work on the *Yin-fu ching*.

Today it is widely accepted that the *Classic of Changes* is a divination text that owes its original inspiration to early mathematical speculation wherein the divided and undivided lines of the hexagrams embody the principles of binary arithmetic.[57] This is reflected in Shao Yung's reordering of the sequences of the hexagrams, starting from the primordial divided and undivided lines and moving to complexes of two, three, four, five, and, finally, of six lines making up the hexagrams. Shao arranged the sixty-four hexagrams one after the other in a square of eight by eight or in a circle, half of which was separated and inverted to harmonize with an alleged earlier arrangement known as the *Hsien-t'ien t'u* (Diagram of What Antedates Heaven). In either case, his sequence makes manifest the mathematical foundations of the *Classic of Changes*, which had been forgotten for centuries.[58]

For Shao Yung, however, the diagram manifests more than just a mathematical sequence. It also represents the forces of yin and yang and the alternating processes of growth and decay that govern their movement. Indeed, Shao elaborated a complex and mind-boggling cosmological chronology illustrating the cycle of growth and decay to which the universe itself is subject.[59]

Chu called his work *Chou I ts'an-t'ung-ch'i k'ao-i*. The title *k'ao-i* makes it sound like a work of textual criticism, but it is really more of a textual commentary. Chu probably completed it in 1197, having worked on it while he was under severe pressure because of the official condemnation of his teaching. Moreover, he was experiencing health problems in his old age and sought help for the cultivation of life. In this context, he also wrote a short piece on breath circulation, although he had disdained such practices earlier.[60]

Chu worked on the text with the help of Ts'ai Yüan-ting. Chu described how he and Ts'ai discussed the treatise together, often working late at night and neglecting sleep.[61] Chu used the text that was accompanied by P'eng Hsiao's commentary (974 A.D.). He admired the prose but acknowledged that the text was extremely difficult to understand because of its coded language. He admitted that it was an esoteric work: "It was probably thought that a clear exposition would entail a disclosure of heavenly secrets [*t'ien-chi*]; on the other hand, refraining completely from speaking of it would have been a pity."[62]

He indicated that "I had many times wanted to study it, but, not having received any [special] transmission, I did not know [for a long time] where to begin."[63]

Here, too, Chu dismisses the alleged authorship of the Yellow Emperor and decides, on the basis of style, that it was probably the work of a late Han author, pointing thereby to Wei Po-yang (second century C.E.).[64] He does not believe that the *Ts'an-t'ung-ch'i* was originally related to the so-called *Lung-hu shang-ching* (Classic of the Dragon and Tiger), which he thinks was a later forgery, very much dependent on the *Ts'an-t'ung-ch'i*, and attributed to Wei Po-yang.[65]

As mentioned above, Chu was suffering from ill health and old age as well as from the effects of political persecution at the time he was working on the *Chou I Ts'an-t'ung-ch'i k'ao-i*. Presumably, such work was done in the hope of finding a cure for his health problems and to calm his mind in a time of great stress. This is also reflected in Chu's commentary on the *Ch'u-tz'u* ("Songs of Ch'u," also known as "Songs of the South"), which he completed in 1198–99. The text, ascribed to the third-century B.C. poet Ch'ü Yüan, expressed a yearning for immortality. This is especially visible in the chapter entitled "Yüan-yu" (Far-Off Journey), a kind of response to the famous "Li-sao" ("Encountering Sorrow"), another chapter in the collection. This describes a celestial journey, and often refers to immortals and yogalike techniques. In the commentary, Chu says:

> Ch'ü Yüan . . . contemplates the universe, despises the abjectness and narrowness of worldly customs, laments the shortness of [human] lifespan and so composes this section. He was hoping to control and cultivate his body and soul, sway the *k'ung* [emptiness] and ride the *ch'i* [air]. . . . Although this is an allegory . . . it is actually an essential teaching of longevity.[66]

And then, he comments on the quest for immortality and longevity techniques:

Where theories about immortals are concerned, it is clear that they are unreasonable and [immortality is] not to be expected. But why, then, did Ch'ü Yüan still show such attachment to these ideas? Because the past is no longer within reach and the future is yet unknown; he wants to live longer while awaiting [what is yet to come].[67]

Later, commenting on another section, "Summoning the Soul," traditionally regarded as a ritual performed after death, Chu Hsi says of the alleged author, Sung Yü, Ch'ü's disciple:

Sung Yü laments Ch'ü Yüan's undeserved exile and fears that his upper and lower souls may depart and not return. So, following the customs of the country, he relies on the command of the Lord-[on-high] and uses a shaman's words to summon it. From the point of view of ritual, it is rather vulgar. But it is a prayerful expression of great love, recording the surviving intentions of the ancients.[68]

Let us, however, return to the *Chou I Ts'an-t'ung-ch'i*. The term *k'ao-i* means a work that "examines differences." Chu explains in an essay that many persons had made arbitrary changes in Wei Po-yang's original text. Hence he himself read and compared many editions and commentaries to seek to establish a correct version.[69] However, from beginning to end, Chu felt that he was not sure he understood the text. Indeed, only twelve days before his death, he wrote to a disciple about his new work, adding:

I could not find a key to understanding this book. But I love its ancient and elegant style, and for that reason I did the study of it.[70]

As it happened, Chu found the text's instructions about cultivation of life, including breath circulation and inner alchemy, especially ambiguous. He therefore increasingly turned to interpreting it in mathematical terms in connection with the *Classic of Changes*. In doing so, Chu tends to follow Shao Yung's judgments, understanding the language of cyclical signs to refer to seasonal and calendrical changes with which a Taoist adept must remain in harmony. This is especially important in the careful choice of precise times at which to conduct experiments. He even theorizes that Shao had learned much of what he knew from the Taoist Ch'en T'uan (d. 898), who in turn had learned from the *Ts'an-t'ung-ch'i* itself.[71]

For example, Wei Po-yang had utilized *na-chia* to explain the making of elixirs. He considered the hexagrams of Heaven (*ch'ien*) and Earth (*k'un*) as representing the furnace in which experiments were made and those of *k'an* and *li* as representing the elixir itself. All the other hexagrams represented the fire that activated the experiment and were themselves in turn coordinated with the ten heavenly stems, allegedly with a view to finding the propitious time for the experiments.

> Within the universe, *ch'ien* . . . stands for Heaven above, *k'un* for Earth below, while the transformations of yin and yang and the beginning and end of the ten thousand things all occur in between them. Within the human body, *ch'ien* as yang remains above, *k'un* as yin remains below, while the transformations of yin and yang and the beginning and end of the ten thousand things within the body all occur between them. . . . In using the word *change* [*i*], we are always pointing to the transformations of yin and yang; in speaking of human beings, [we are referring] to what is called the golden elixir and the great medicine. Are not therefore *ch'ien* and *k'un* the furnace and the tripod?[72]

Chu Hsi understood well this primary meaning of the text, which interprets the *Classic of Changes* as offering the coordination of the forces of yin and yang in the universe as the explanation for cosmic change. He criticizes the then popular assumption that the text dwells mainly on outer alchemy, especially the manner of finding the right time for experiments in the furnace. He considers this unnatural and irrational, a later interpretation not in conformity with Wei Po-yang's original intention.

> My feeling is that the essential meaning of this book dwells in the two words *k'an* and *li*. Should we obtain the crucial idea there, then we could also acquire the meaning of Wei's words about the effort [*kung-fu*].[73]

Presumably, what the text says about the cyclical movements of yin and yang in the universe is also mirrored in the human organism. Thus the correct method of breath circulation is implicit as well. For the order of the universe is also to be reflected in the proper functioning of the human body. However, Chu was unable to follow through on this supposition. In the end, he would move in the opposite direction from many of his contemporaries, who were interpreting the text in much more alchemical terms.[74]

Chu Hsi, to a greater extent than Shao Yung, maintained a strictly mathematical-astronomical interpretation for such a coordination and used it to interpret the basic meaning of the *Classic of Changes*. He probably did this in part better to understand the mathematical context of the *Ts'an-t'ung-ch'i*. Chu worked on the "theory of numbers" (a combination of mathematics and astronomy) even after the completion of the *Ts'an-t'ung-ch'i k'ao-i*. His further insights were incorporated in an essay on the *Ts'an-t'ung-ch'i*. Here too, while Chu acknowledged that Taoists had used the text for alchemical purposes, he asserted his preference for interpreting it scientifically and cosmologically.[75]

CHU HSI AND TAOIST RELIGION

In Chu's own days, Taoist philosophy was no longer dominant, having been largely absorbed into Ch'an Buddhist philosophy. But Taoist religion, focusing mainly on the cult of immortality, had many adherents. Several Sung emperors were patrons of Taoism, the best known being Hui-tsung (r. 1101–1125), who favored the priest Lin Ling-su and promoted Lin's Shen-hsiao sect.[76] He also ordered the assembly and editing of Taoist texts, which led to the first printing (in Fukien) of the Taoist canon in 5,481 *chüan*, a collection that survived intact through the Southern Sung and into Yüan times.[77] This was a real landmark in the history of the Taoist religion. Also, during Chu Hsi's lifetime, two important Taoist "morality books" were published and began to gain wide acceptance, the *T'ai-shang kan-ying p'ien* (Treatise of the Most Exalted One on Moral Retribution) (1164) and the *T'ai-wei hsien-chün kung-kuo ko* (Ledgers of Merit and Demerit of the Immortal Lord of T'ai-wei) (preface dated 1171). The former deals with the retributions one will suffer in the hereafter for deeds committed in this life; the latter tells how to keep an account of one's good and bad deeds.[78]

Chu Hsi describes the Taoist religion of his day as having evolved from a philosophy of nonaction to an immortality cult. This in turn gave way to the practices of shamans and "prayermen" (*wu-chu*) who made incarnations and prognostications.[79] He describes the evolution from philosophy to religion in negative terms, as something moving from what is more credible to what is much less so.[80] He also laments the Taoist custom of indiscriminate borrowing from Buddhism by setting up scriptural and doctrinal structures that parallel those of the Buddhists.

> The Taoists have *Lao-tzu* and *Chuang-tzu*, but do not know how to study them. Instead, they allow them to be stolen and used by Buddhists, while they themselves compile scriptures and doctrines in imitation of Buddhism. They act like children of a wealthy house who allow their own treasures to be stolen but go to others' properties to pick up potsherds.[81]

Chu criticizes Taoist deities, not only as evidence for confused borrowing from Buddhism but also for a manifest lack of logical consistency: "What the Taoists call the Three Pure Ones is an imitation of the Three Bodies of the Buddha." Chu claims that Lao-tzu was being honored in the Three Pure Ones, without clarifying whether the first of these Pure Ones represents the *dharmakāya*, the second the *samboghakāya*, and the third the *nirmanakāya*. Besides,

> In honoring . . . the Primal Celestial (Yüan-shih T'ien-tsun), the Supreme Lord Tao (T'ai-shang Tao-chün), and the Supreme Lord Lao (T'ai-shang Lao-chün) . . . they place below these the supreme Lord-on-high. Can one find a greater act of usurpation and treason?[82]

His reasoning was that Lao-tzu, as a former human being, should not, even when deified, rank higher than the Lord-on-high of antiquity. And he concluded that both Buddhism and Taoism should, if possible, be abrogated. In case this was not possible, the Taoists could continue to pay reverence to Lao-tzu, Chuang-tzu, and other Taoist figures. But the cult honoring heavenly and earthly deities should revert to the sacrificial agencies of the government since they did not legitimately belong to religious Taoism.[83]

CHU HSI AND THE QUEST FOR IMMORTALITY

Living as they did during the Southern Sung period, Chu Hsi and his disciples could hardly ignore the beliefs and practices of religious Taoism. The *Classified Conversations* offer questions and answers between Chu and his disciples on many subjects pertaining to the Taoist religion. Generally speaking, Chu shows himself not totally opposed to the quest for longevity, even if he had reservations about physical immortality as such.

On the question of whether there are real Immortals, Chu is rational and cautious:

> People say that immortals don't die. [But I think that] it is not that they don't die, but that they pass away very gradually. . . . Since they know how to cultivate their forms and their *ch'i* and dissolve the sediments in this *ch'i*, only what is pure *ch'i* is left so that they are able to levitate and change. . . . After a long time, [however,] dissipation [and death] still take place.[84]

Chu describes as strange and "uncanny" the Taoist explanation of the "apparent death" of the immortal. This refers to various explanations of what happens to the immortal at the hour of apparent death, called "liberation from the corpse." It is sometimes said that the immortal leaves his corpse behind, other times that he leaves behind only a sword to represent his former body so that such apparent death is called *chien-chieh* or "liberation by sword," leaving people to guess how he died and what became of him. Chu poses a somewhat trivial question, which is nevertheless indicative of his rationalist outlook.

At the moment of death, a sword and a medicinal elixir are placed at the bedside. Should it be asked, if the sword is what has become of oneself, what has the medicine become when one's self has gone somewhere else?[85]

Chu explained Taoist practices — presumably relating to inner or outer alchemy — as playing games with the "psyche" (*ching-shen*) and "fooling the people" to attract their faith.[86] He explains the practice of divination in similar terms: the mind reaching out to be the "contracting and expanding" *ch'i*.[87] When told that in Taoist quiet-sitting, the effort of "making the mind force the *ch'i* to rise up" had resulted in death by asphyxiation, Chu replied that he did not believe this was what was taught and offered another explanation according to his own investigation. He described Taoist circulation of breath (*tao-yin*) as an "inferior effort,"[88] yet he appeared reasonably familiar with Taoist meditation. He even wrote a short piece on "watching the white on the nose," a Taoist technique with Buddhist antecedents, explored further below.[89]

CHU HSI AND BREATH REGULATION

Before proceeding further, we should pause to discuss breath circulation in general. Basically, there are two ways of breathing: through the lungs and through the diaphragm. While breathing through the lungs is faster paced, breathing through the diaphragm is alleged to be more natural and relaxing. It is, indeed, what many physicians in the West also counsel their patients to do. If, today, many people are too rushed to attend to diaphragmatic breathing, in Chu Hsi's time, this appeared to be the known practice.[90]

The practice of "watching the tip of the nose" is mentioned in a forged Buddhist classic, the *Śūraṅgama Sutra*. It reflects Taoist influence, recalling the "fasting of the mind" in *Chuang-tzu* and the development of the teaching of inner alchemy in the Sung dynasty.[91]

In his exchanges with disciples, Chu Hsi criticized the Taoist practice of counting the breath together with Buddhist meditation practices. His objection had to do with the tendency to seek only peace and tranquility, while ignoring active involvement in things and affairs. In other words, he believed that there was a time for meditation and a time for action. And he preferred the kind of meditation that is morally motivated.[92] Still, this did not stop him from seeking to learn from both Buddhist and Taoist instructions and experience. His interest in "yoga" or breath regulation is a good example.

In his conversations with disciples, Chu mentioned the practice of "watching the tip of the nose." Once, when asked what to use as a focus in quiet-sitting, he recommended the Taoist method of "counting the inhaling and exhaling of breath while watching the white tip of the nose."[93]

His brief piece on breath circulation contains only sixty-four words, with four words in each of sixteen sentences. Entitled *T'iao-hsi chen*, it represents a kind of "motto" or "watchword" (*chen*), and is written in rhyme for easy remembrance. It may be translated as follows:

The nose has a white tip:
I can see it.
At all times and places,
It moves with the face.
In utmost quiet, breathe out,
Like a fish in a spring pond.
In utmost action, breathe in,
As insects between summer and fall.

We find here an echo of Chou Tun-i's *T'ai-chi-t'u shuo*, where he mentions utmost stillness followed by utmost activity. The fish is happy to swim in a pond free of ice while the insects prepare for hibernation between summer and autumn.[94]

Opening and closing—
Who is there to move such?
That's the work of no master.
Its marvels are without limit.

The first image is about the opening and closing of the gates of Heaven (*ch'ien*) and Earth (*k'un*) of the *Classic of Changes*. It also echoes what Ch'eng I has to say about breathing.[95] We then find a reference to *Chuang-tzu* about "who is there to move such?" Earlier some lines are quoted from the chapter "The Turning of Heaven," which begins:

Does Heaven turn? Does the earth sit still? Do sun and moon compete for a place to shine? Who masterminds all this?[96]

The response to the question is that no one is in charge of the natural process of breathing. It refers to Ch'eng Hao's words.[97] The piece goes on:

They sleep on clouds and fly in heaven —
That's not my problem.
Holding on to the One is harmony:
And a thousand and two hundred years' [life]!

So Chu asserts that he does not expect to become immortal. But he speaks of the practice of "holding on to the One," and expresses his desire to live a very long life.[98]

Where Taoists are preoccupied with the cultivation of life, Neo-Confucian philosophers have concentrated on the cultivation of the mind. Nevertheless, as human beings, they also have afflictions of the body. Should they resist Taoist methods as "heretical," or try to learn from them? Could not the cultivation of life help the cultivation of mind and vice versa?

In a letter, Chu Hsi speaks about what to do in times of sickness: that one should forget all worry and anxiety and pay attention to the cultivation of breath. This could be done during quiet-sitting with legs crossed, fixing one's gaze on the tip of the nose and focusing the mind on the abdominal area. After a while, one would feel warmer and gradually experience positive effects.[99]

CHU HSI AND THE YIN-FU CHING

Chu Hsi is the alleged author of two influential treatises, each a study of a religious Taoist text: the *Yin-fu ching k'ao-i* (1175) as well as the *Ts'an-t'ung-ch'i k'ao-i*. We have discussed the second of these texts. What about the first?

The authorship of the *Yin-fu ching* was attributed to the legendary Yellow Emperor and is said to have commentaries by celebrated ancient figures, the last of whom was the late T'ang military strategist Li Ch'üan (eighth century) It is a brief text of one *chüan* consisting of 384 characters. Li says of the book, that it "first gives the Way of the Immortals embracing the One, then gives the meaning of enriching the country and giving peace to the people, and finally gives the art of maintaining a strong army and gaining military victories." In this sense it is alleged to comprehend the teachings of Taoism and Legalism as well as the art of war. For this reason he divided the text into three parts, a topical division customarily followed by later commentators.

Shao Yung regarded this text as coming down from the Warring States period and Ch'eng I dated it even earlier, in the late Shang or early Chou.

The author of the *Yin-fu ching k'ao-i* believes that the *Yin-fu ching* was written by the man who allegedly "discovered" it, Li Ch'üan himself.[100] If today we cannot agree with his opinion, we should remember that in Chu's day it represented a step forward. Chu also makes an attempt to separate the text from its various alleged commentaries.

Before proceeding further, however, I would like to point out a problem with the authorship of *both* the *Yin-fu ching* itself and the commentary allegedly written by Chu Hsi. As already mentioned, this question has particularly been raised by the Japanese scholar Sueki Yasuhiko, who believes the commentary to be the work of Chu's collaborator, Ts'ai Yüan-ting.

The problem with attributing the *Yin-fu ching k'ao-i* to Chu is that in his other writings there is no mention of such authorship. This is in contrast to the good evidence available concerning his writing of the *Chou I Ts'an-t'ung-ch'i k'ao-i*, which he also completed with the collaboration of Ts'ai. Moreover, the *Yin-fu ching k'ao-i* is not usually listed among Ts'ai's own works.

Sueki also has something to say about the assignment of authorship of the *Yin-fu ching* itself. While Li's name is associated with two extant versions of this work, a short one (one *chüan*) and a somewhat longer one (three *chüan*), the two texts are completely different. Sueki claims that Li's commentary is exactly the same as that of one Yüan Shu-chen (in three *chüan*), whom he regards as the actual author of the work. Yüan probably lived in the tenth century and ascribed his own work to Li, presumably because Li was better known than he was.[101]

Other scholars had previously questioned Li's authorship of the *Yin-fu ching*, especially the Chinese scholar Liu Shih-p'ei (1884–1919).[102] Contemporary Chinese scholars have echoed and partly endorsed this opinion.[103] We cannot settle the question of authorship here, but to the extent that Chu and Ts'ai were probably in agreement about what the *Yin-fu ching* represented, we can still analyze the text as representative of opinions that Chu would support.

The preface to the *Yin-fu ching k'ao-i* (1175) says:

> The three hundred words of the *Yin-fu ching* which Li Ch'üan was alleged to have received in a cave are supposed to be [the words of] the Yellow Emperor which had been preserved by K'ou Ch'ien-chih. Shao [Yung] . . . thought it a work of the Warring States period; Ch'eng [I] . . . regarded it as coming from either the later part of Shang dynasty or the early part of the Chou dynasty. On account of the long lapse of time, we know little for sure. Judging from its language and style, this could not be a very ancient text.

But it must have been written by someone who had a profound knowledge of the Tao.[104]

The Preface goes on to assert that, of the three hundred words making up the *Yin-fu ching*, a hundred explain the Tao, another hundred explain the *fa* (law), and a third hundred words explain *shu* (method, i.e., political craftsmanship). Should we combine these three senses, we would have a teaching that appeals to all:

Above there is the *Tao* of the immortals embracing the One; in the middle there is the *fa* for enriching the country and giving peace to men; below there is the *shu* for having a strong army and military victory.[105]

The author of the *Yin-fu ching k'ao-i* emphasizes that the "three senses" are all invisibly present in the same words, yet the text should be read as a whole, rather than divided into three parts.[106] He also acknowledges the text as alchemical, even if he also offers a philosophical interpretation for its content:

Essentially it takes supreme nonbeing as the principal doctrine and the culture and principles of Heaven and earth as *shu* [numbers], saying that in all under Heaven being [*yu*] comes from nonbeing [*wu*]. Should someone be able to return being to nonbeing, the universe would be in his hands.[107]

A difficult word in the text is that of "thief" (*tao*). Where the *Yin-fu ching* speaks first of the Way (*Tao*) of Heaven and then of the "Five Thieves" of Heaven, the *k'ao-i* understands these to refer to the Five Agents, which produce and overcome one another.[108] A similar explanation is given for a later part of the text, which says:

Heaven and Earth are the robbers of the myriad things; the myriad things are the robbers of man; man is the robber of the myriad things.[109]

The comment is:

Heaven and Earth engender the myriad things and also kill the myriad things. The myriad things engender human beings and also kill human beings. Human beings engender the myriad things and also kill the myriad things. What engenders is also what kills. That is why we can reverse it and call it "thief." It is like the talk of the "five thieves." But if the engendering and the killing are each proper, then the three robbers are in harmony. And when the three robbers are in harmony, Heaven and Earth are in their proper places and the myriad things are nurtured.[110]

The text also later speaks of "stealing the secret" (*tao-chi*). Taoists derive the slogan "stealing the secret of Heaven and Earth" from this expression. It refers to their efforts to find the secret of immortality.

The term *chi* also deserves some elaboration. The text cites the *Classic of Changes* as saying that the gentleman acts according to the *chi* that he sees, but that such *chi* are easy to see and yet difficult to know.[111] Azuma refers to it as a sign that foretells great events. It can be perceived, but needs reflection to be properly understood.[112]

The comment here is:

The reason the Yellow Emperor, Yao, and Shun gained their reputations and longevity, and . . . Shen Pu-hai and Han Fei-tzu lost their lives and their clans was all the Tao.[113]

However, Sueki maintains that the *k'ao-i* does not support the importance of the concept of *chi*, preferring to understand the text more as a way of understanding a world that follows a pattern of regularity. He quotes from the *k'ao-i* itself:

Heaven, Earth, and the myriad things are controlled by human beings. . . . If [human beings] can move according to the secret [*chi*] of Heaven and Earth, the myriad transformations will be in peace. Such is the Tao of thieves. The times refer to spring and autumn, early and late. The secret refers to birth, killing, growth, and nurture.[114]

In this light, we may better appreciate why the author expresses a particular liking for the sentences near the end of the *Yin-fu ching*:

The way of nature is quiet, producing heaven and earth and the myriad things; the way of heaven and earth is gradual, allowing yin and yang to overcome each other; the reciprocity between yin and yang permits harmonious transformation.[115]

Before Chu Hsi, these words influenced both Shao Yung and Chou Tun-i. Chou's *T'ai-chi-t'u shuo* offers a mixture of ideas coming from the

Classic of Changes and the *Ts'an-t'ung-ch'i*. Obviously Chu would recognize this. The author of the *Yin-fu ching k'ao-i*, whether it was Chu himself or Ts'ai, was a philosopher who attempted to interpret the original text cosmologically.

Chu Hsi's Contributions to Taoism

Chu Hsi's studies have helped to make the *Classic of Changes* as well as the *Ts'an-t'ung ch'i* — which is certainly a *Taoist* text — better known to Confucian scholars. They have also become important in Taoist circles as well. In the case of the *Ts'an-t'ung-ch'i*, his having written the study under a pen-name did not prevent others from recognizing him as the author, especially since evidence in his other writings points to this. The same is not true of the study on the *Yin-fu ching*, although the extant version bears the same pen-name.[116]

Here, if we pause to ponder Chu's reasons for commenting on these Taoist texts, especially the *Ts'an-t'ung-ch'i*, the obvious and undeniable reason would be his intellectual curiosity, which was unbounded by orthodoxy. But was it also an indication of his belief in Taoist assertions? Certainly, his statements in the *Classified Conversations* and elsewhere lead us to believe that he himself did not totally discount the efficacy of Taoist practices with respect to peace of mind, health, and longevity. His use of a pen-name shows his sensitivity to public expectations, which would also explain, if only in part, his general consistency in criticizing Taoism.

And we should not forget that Chu was struggling under persecution, being regarded officially as a "heretic," as someone not quite within the pale of Confucian orthodoxy. That was an important reason for using a pen-name for his Taoist writings. Basically, we have to wait for the emergence of Wang Yang-ming (1472–1529) to find a Confucian thinker who would offer philosophical reasons for going beyond traditional limits.[117]

Basically, Chu Hsi is an original interpreter, learning from yet transforming and making his own the ideas of others who preceded him. He did this with Chou Tun-i's idea of *t'ai-chi*, rendering it not only transcendent and full of *li*, but also immanent in each particular person and thing as well as in the universe as a whole. He also did this with Chang Tsai's philosophy of *ch'i* and Ch'eng I's philosophy of *li*, rendering them consistent and giving them a central place in his own synthesis. With respect to the text of the *Ts'an-t'ung-ch'i*, he transposed its meaning to a higher level of understanding without entirely violating the literal sense of its highly ambiguous wording.

Taoist Influence on Chu Hsi: Extent and Limitations

In discussing Chu's criticism of both philosophical and religious Taoism, we can see at work the mind of a man with a commitment to Confucian social values and a scholar with sound historical judgment as well as logical and rationalist propensities. Chinese ethnocentrism played a part in Chu's displeasure with Taoist borrowings from Buddhism. But we can also discern his scholarly disappointment with the lack of philosophical consistency in the Taoist concept of the Three Pure Ones compared to that of the Buddha's Three Bodies as well as his distaste for the lack of religious sensitivity and the ahistorical nature of the subordination of the Lord-on-high to a divinized Lao-tzu.

> The . . . Primal Heavenly Celestial is not Lao-tzu's *dharmakāya* . . . ; the Supreme Ruler of Tao is not Lao-tzu's *samboghakāya*. To erect two images . . . and to have Lao-tzu himself as the . . . Supreme Ruler Lao, is to imitate a Buddhist mistake and make of it another mistake.[118]

Chu claims correctly that Taoists "stole" from Buddhists such doctrines as hell and reincarnation. He also asserts that the early sixth-century Taoist sacred text *Chen-kao*, allegedly recording fourth-century revelations, contains a chapter that borrows heavily from the *Sutra of Forty-two Sections*.

> I once told the [Taoist] followers: You have your own precious pearl, which they (the Buddhists) have stolen. Yet you pay no attention to that. . . . Instead, you steal from their corners and crevices broken cans and bottles. This is quite amusing.[119]

Even where he acknowledges the possibility of other modes of understanding, Chu prefers, whenever possible, to interpret things in metaphysical terms. We have seen this preference in his rendering of the meaning of *kuei-shen*. He admits the presence of "ghosts and spirits" while seeking to understand them in terms of a philosophy of *li* and *ch'i*, even reinterpreting the terms themselves to allow for a scientific understanding of natural phenomena. We also discern this in the analyses of the Taoist texts such as the *Ts'an-t'ung-ch'i* and possibly the *Yin-fu ching*. He detects in each a false attribution of authorship and acknowledges alchemical content. Yet he also seeks—and finds—a metaphysical interpretation of the universe. This in turn he integrates into the cosmology of *li* and *ch'i* and of the Non-Ultimate (*wu-chi*), which is also the Great Ultimate (*t'ai-chi*).

Chu Hsi was open to learning from both Taoist philosophical and religious texts; at the same time he was critical of the practical thrust of Taoist teachings. He felt that they caused people to withdraw from the world and society, or engulfed them in the nonrational pursuit of immortality for its own sake. Generally speaking, Chu's criticism of Buddhism is much stronger than that of Taoism since he recognizes that the former had a deeper and wider influence among the populace, especially the intellectuals. However, his philosophy was much more influenced by Buddhist ideas than by Taoist ones — to the extent that we can distinguish one from the other.

Moreover, to the extent that Chu read Taoist texts and tested certain methods of cultivation, we may say that he was influenced by Taoism. But to the extent that he also transformed what he found in Taoism and incorporated it into his own thinking — which we know as the Neo-Confucian synthesis of thought and philosophy — we must say that Taoist influence on Chu was limited. He used the data and material he found to create something new — his own philosophical system, in which metaphysical ideas are dominant. Within this system a place could be found for cosmology and metaphysics as well as for the philosophy of human nature and the practical doctrine of cultivation. Chu had turned primarily to Taoist philosophy and religion for expanding his understanding of the universe as well as to find ways to improve his health. He integrated what he learned from them into something different: a new Confucian *Weltanschauung* with its rational-intuitive perspective on the cosmic and the human and an unchanging commitment to social responsibility.

Chu criticized Taoism, both the philosophical and the religious varieties. But his criticism was limited and nuanced and less severe than his criticism of Buddhism. He was essentially a moralist. He worked with conventional distinctions of orthodoxy and heterodoxy and was not afraid to change and evolve. We might safely conclude that while a younger Chu Hsi had been immersed for some years in Ch'an Buddhist practices, a mature Chu Hsi became a Neo-Confucian scholar and synthesizer. Furthermore, an older Chu Hsi turned more and more to Taoist practices for the cultivation of life without giving up his basically Confucian convictions and commitments.

NOTES

1. For secondary sources, consult Wing-tsit Chan, *Chu Hsi and Neo-Confucianism* (Honolulu: University of Hawaii Press, 1986). Professor Chan has concentrated on Chu and

Taoist philosophy in "Chu Hsi's Appraisal of Lao-tzu," *Philosophy East and West* (1975), 25: 131–44; *Chu-tzu hsin t'an-so* (New Essays on Master Chu Hsi) (Taipei: Student Book Company, 1981); as well as *Chu Hsi: New Studies* (Honolulu: University of Hawaii Press, 1989), 486–503. The Japanese scholar Sakai Tadao concentrated on Chu Hsi and Taoist religion, in "Shushi to Dōkyō" (Chu Hsi and Religious Taoism), in Morohashi Tetsuji et al., comp., *Shushigaku nyūmon* (Introduction to the School of Chu Hsi), *Shushigaku taikei* series, 1:411–27 (Tokyo: Meitoku, 1974). An older Japanese work deals with both in a wider context: Tokiwa Daijō, *Shina ni okeru Bukkyō to Jukyō Dōkyō* (Buddhism, Confucianism, and Taoism in China) (Tokyo: Tōyō Bunko, 1966). Consult also Yoshikawa Kōjirō and Miura Kunio, *Shushi shū* (Chu Hsi's Works) (Tokyo: Asahi shinbunsha, 1976), ch. 6. The author wishes also to acknowledge Professor Kristofer Schipper and Professor Liu Ts'un-yan for their help.

2. *Chu-tzu yū-lei* (Classified Conversations of Master Chu Hsi), 1270 edition (Taipei: Cheng-chung reprint, 1973), abbrevation as CTYL, 104:8b.

3. Chu was overseer of at least six different Taoist temples during his life. See his chronological biography, ch. 2–3, in Wang Mao-hung, *Chu-tzu nien-p'u*, abbreviated as CTNP, *Ts'ung-shu chi-ch'eng* (TSCC) edition.

4. *Chu Wen-kung wen-chi* (Collected Writings of Chu Hsi), abbrevation as CWWC, Ssu-pu pei-yao (SPPY) ed. 6:22b, 76:27a–b, 9:10b.

5. Wang Tzu-ts'ai et al., *Sung-Yüan hsüeh-an pu-i* (Supplement to the Records of Sung and Yüan Scholars), Ssu-ming ts'ung-shu edition, 69:176a–b; see Wing-tsit Chan, *Chu-tzu men-jen* (Chu Hsi's Disciples) (Taipei: Student Book Company, 1982), 99. The priest's name was Wu Hsiung.

6. For a rather recent study of these texts, see Azuma Jūji, "Shu Ki 'Shūeki sandōkei kōi' ni tsuite" (A Study of the *Chou I Ts'an-t'ung-ch'i k'ao-i* by Chu Hsi), *Nippon Chūgoku gakkaihō* (1984), 36:175–90; and Sueki Yasuhiko, "Inbukei kōi no shisō" (The Thought of *Yin-fu-ching k'ao-i*), *Nippon Chūgoku gakkaihō* (1984), 36:175–90. Sueki expresses the opinion that the *Yin-fu-ching k'ao-i* is not from Chu's pen but is the work of his friend and contemporary, Ts'ai Yüan-ting.

7. CTYL, 126:1a–b.

8. CTYL, 12:14b.

9. CTYL, 125:7b.

10. See CTYL, 125:3b; *Erh-Ch'eng ch'üan-shu* (The Complete Works of the Two Ch'engs), abbreviated as ECCS, SPPY ed., *Ts'ui-yen* (Selected Words), 1:8a–b, 9a; *I-shu* (Surviving Works), 18:39b.

11. Allusion to the description of the Perfect Man in *Chuang-tzu*, ch. 2, "On Making All Things Equal"; see Burton Watson's translation, *The Complete Works of Chuang Tzu* (New York: Columbia University Press, 1968), 46.

12. CTYL, 125:1b.

13. English translation from D. C. Lau, *Lao tzu: Tao Te Ching* (Harmondsworth: Penguin, 1963), 62.

14. CTYL, 125:9a. Chu's interpretation is actually close to Wang Pi's; see Wang's commentary on *Lao-tzu*, SPPY ed., part 1, 4a.

15. ECCS, *I-shu*, SPPY ed., 12:5b.

16. Chan, *Chu-tzu hsin t'an-so*, 615–16; idem, *Chu Hsi*, 494–97.

17. English translation adapted from Lau, *Lao tzu*, 85.

18. *CTYL*, 125:9a.

19. *CTYL*, 125:10a; *Chang-tzu ch'üan-shu* (Complete Works of Chang Tsai), SPPY ed., *Cheng-meng* (On Correcting Youthful Ignorance), "Ta-I p'ien" (On the Classic of Changes), 3:11a. The reference is to *Lao-tzu*, ch. 40.

20. *Lao-tzu*, ch. 1.

21. *CTYL*, 126:5b. The Four Phases are earth, water, fire, and wind.

22. *Lao-tzu*, ch. 38; English trans. adapted from Lau, *Lao-tzu*, 99.

23. *CTYL*, 13:8b.

24. *CTYL*, 126:9b.

25. *CTYL*, 97:16b.

26. Ch'ien Mu, *Chu-tzu hsin hsüeh-an* (A New Record of Chu Hsi's Philosophy) (Taipei: San-min, 1971), 612.

27. *CTYL*, 16:44b–45a; Chan, *Chu Hsi*, 498–502.

28. Translated by Burton Watson, *The Complete Works of Chuang Tzu*, 154.

29. Ibid., 50.

30. Ibid., 50–51; for Chu, see *CTYL*, 20:9a–b; 125:11a–b.

31. *CTYL*, 10:2a; see also 57:6a.

32. *Chuang-tzu*, ch. 2; see Watson, *Complete Works of Chuang Tzu*, 50.

33. "Yang-sheng chu shuo" (On Cultivating Life), in *CWWC*, 67:23b–24b.

34. Ibid.

35. *CWWC*, 67:24a. To study for one's own sake is very close to discovering truth for oneself (*tzu-te*) which Professor Wm. T. de Bary highlights in several thinkers (including Chu Hsi) in *Neo-Confucian Orthodoxy and the Learning of the Mind-and-Heart* (New York: Columbia University Press, 1981).

36. Chan, *Chu-tzu hsin t'an-so*, 627.

37. *CWWC*, 46:16b, 67:23b, 38:35a.

38. *CTYL*, 125:3b.

39. *CTYL*, 126:2a.

40. *CTYL*, 125:2a. There is a chapter on Yang Chu's hedonism in the *Lieh-tzu*.

41. The Five Phases refer to fire, water, wood, metal, and earth.

42. See an anonymous treatise, *Chou I pen-i k'ao yü ch'i-ta* (An Examination of the Original Meaning of the Classic of Changes and Other Works) (Changsha: Commercial Press, 1937), 3–4.

43. "Shih-i" (Divination Ritual), in *Chou I pen-i*, Four Libraries (Ssu-k'u ch'üan-shu) ed., 6th Collection, No. 001. For the *I-hsüeh ch'i-meng*, I have consulted the edition in the *Chu-tzu i-shu* (Surviving Works of Chu Hsi) (Pao-kao-t'ang ed., Taipei reprint, I-wen, 1969), vol. 12.

44. Chu Hsi's friend and disciple, Ts'ai Yüan-ting (1135–1198), was very influential in the making of the *I-hsüeh ch'i-meng*, possibly writing portions of it. See Chang Liwen, "An Analysis of Chu Hsi's System of the Thought of *I*," in Chan, ed., *Chu Hsi and Neo-Confucianism*, 308, note 2. Chu discussed with Ts'ai many of his own works in preparation, including those on the Four Books, the *Classic of Poetry*, and the *Classic of Changes*. We have about fifty extant letters from Chu to Ts'ai, who also suffered for his association with Chu during the persecution that was waged against Chu's school and died in exile soon after. Ts'ai published some works of his own, including the *Lü-lü hsin-shu* (A New Study of Musical Notations), for which Chu wrote a preface. A scholar's scholar, Ts'ai was well

versed in a whole range of subjects, including music, astronomy, mathematics, and geography as well as rituals and the art of war. Chu allegedly made the remark, "People find it hard to read easy books; Ts'ai Yüan-ting finds it easy to read hard books." For more on Ts'ai, see *Sung shih* (Sung History), *Erh-shih-wu shih* (Twenty-five Dynastic History Series), K'ai-ming ed., 434:5595–96; *SYHA, SPPY* ed., ch. 56.

45. Chu's biographer, Wang Mao-hung, has given the opinion that Chu did not himself append the diagrams to his book. But many disagree with Wang. See Chang Li-wen's article, "An Analysis of Chu Hsi's System of the Thought of *I*," in Chan, ed., *Chu Hsi and Neo-Confucianism*, 293. The other seven diagrams are various versions of the Eight Trigrams and the Sixty-four Hexagrams.

46. *Shang-shu cheng-i* (Correct Meaning of the *Classic of History*), SPPY ed., 12:2a, 18:11b; *Chou-I pen-i*, Appended Remarks, pt. 1, 7:12b.

47. Ibid. The explanatory note concerning the *Book of Lo* came from K'ung Ying-ta, the exegete for the *Classic of History*. See also Chang Liwen, in Chan, ed., *Chu Hsi and Neo-Confucianism*, 294.

48. *CTYL*, 65:9a; consult *CWWC*, 38:1a–2b.

49. *Chou-I pen-i*, ch. 3, commentary on "Appended Remarks," pt. 1, ch. 9.

50. See *CWWC*, 38:1a–5a; 84:3b–4a; consult Hu Wei, *I-t'u ming-pien* (An Explanation of the Diagrams of the *Book of Changes*), Ts'ung-shu chi-ch'eng, 1st series, ch. 1; Chang Liwen, in Chan, ed., *Chu Hsi and Neo-Confucianism*, 301–6.

51. For the Yellow Emperor, consult Yün-hua Jan, "The Change of Images: Yellow Emperor in Ancient Chinese Literature," *Journal of Oriental Studies* (1981), 19:117–37.

52. Miura mentions this fact and asserts that to the end of his life Chu was balancing concern for the physical self with his effort to transcend the self. See *Shushi shū*, 517–18.

53. For the *Ts'an-t'ung-ch'i k'ao-i*, I have consulted the edition in the *Chu-tzu i-shu* (Surviving Works of Chu Hsi), Pao-kao-t'ang ed. (Taipei reprint, I-wen, 1969), vol. 12.

54. See Joseph Needham, *Science and Civilisation in China* (Cambridge: Cambridge University Press, 1956), vol. 2, p. 441.

55. The scholarly divergence continues today. Azuma supports Ch'en Kuo-fu who prefers to understand the text more in terms of inner alchemy; see Azuma, "Shu Ki 'Shūeki sandōkei kōi,'" 188–89, note 2. Ch'en Kuo-fu, *Tao-tsang yüan-liu k'ao* (An Examination of the Sources and Transmission of the Taoist Canon) (Beijing: Zhonghua, 1963), Appendix 6, 438–53.

56. Sakai Tadao, "Shushi to Dōkyō." 417.

57. On this subject, I remember a paper presented by the archaeologist Li Xueqin at a conference on Chinese culture organized by Fudan University, Shanghai, in January 1986.

58. It was in Shao's circular sequence that the German philosopher Leibniz discovered his own dyadic or binary numeral system. I have done a recent study of this, included in Julia Ching and Willard G. Oxtoby, *Moral Enlightenment: Leibniz and Wolff on China*, Monumenta Serica Monograph Series, no. 26 (Nettetal: Steyler Verlag, 1992). See also Helmut Wilhelm, *Eight Lectures on the I-ching* (Princeton: Princeton University Press, 1960), 90–91.

59. See Fung Yu-lan, *A History of Chinese Philosophy*, trans. Derk Bodde (Princeton: Princeton University Press, 1953), vol. 2, pp. 459–70.

60. Azuma, "Shu Ki 'Shūeki sandōkei kōi,'" 179–80.

61. *Ts'an-t'ung-ch'i k'ao-i*, Preface, 3a. For Ts'ai, see Chan, *Chu-tzu men-jen*, 331–32.

62. *Ts'an-t'ung-ch'i k'ao-i*, 1b–2a. The reference to transmission alludes to Chu's not belonging to any esoteric circle in which such texts were orally transmitted.

63. Ibid.

64. *CTYL*, 125:13a.

65. Ibid., 5a–b. Chu's judgment is based on mistakes he found in the "Classic of the Dragon and Tiger." As far as the authorship of the *Ts'an-t'ung-ch'i* is concerned, Kristofer Schipper thinks it could be an apocryphal text of the Han dynasty appended to the *Classic of Changes*. For this and other opinions, see Fukui Kojun, "A Study of *Chou-i Ts'an t'ung-ch'i*," *Acta Asiatica* (1974), 27:19–32.

66. *Ch'u-tz'u chi-chu* (Collected Commentaries on the Songs of Ch'u), T'ing-yü-chai edition (1900), 5:2a. For an English translation of the *Ch'u-tz'u*, see David Hawkes, *The Songs of the South: An Ancient Chinese Anthology* (London: Oxford University Press, 1959).

67. Chu Hsi, *Ch'u-tz'u chi-chu*, 5:1a.

68. *Ch'u-tz'u chi-chu*, 7:1b.

69. *CWWC*, 84:26b.

70. *CWWC*, 45:15a.

71. Actually, Shao had studied with Li Chih-ts'ai, a Taoist from Ch'en's circle. See *Sung shih*, 427:5580–81. For Ch'en T'uan, see also Livia Knaul, *Leben und Legende des Ch'en T'uan* (Frankfurt: Peter Lang, 1981), Würzburger Sino-Japonica, 9.

72. *Ts'an-t'ung-ch'i k'ao-i*, 2b.

73. *Ts'an-t'ung-ch'i k'ao-i*, 2a.

74. Azuma, "Shu Ki 'Shūeki sandōkei kōi,'" 187–88.

75. See *CWWC*, 67:25a–26b.

76. See Chin Chung-shu, "Lun Pei-Sung mo-nien chih ch'ung-shang Tao-chiao" (On the Favoring of Religious Taoism During the Last Years of the Northern Sung), an article in two parts, *Sung shih yen-chiu chi* (Collected Essays on Sung History), edited by the Symposium on Sung History (Taipei: Chung-hua ts'ung-shu pien-sheng wei-yüan-hui, 1974/76), 7:291–392, and 8:207–78.

77. Ch'en Kuo-fu, *Tao-tsang yüan-liu k'ao*, 1:135–36, 147–49.

78. Sakai Tadao, "Shushi to Dōkyō," 426–27. Chu Hsi said nothing about these two texts, although a later scholar of his school, Chen Te-hsiu (1178–1235), would write a preface for the *T'ai-shang kan-ying p'ien*.

79. *CTYL*, 125:14b.

80. *CTYL*, 125:14a.

81. *CTYL*, 125:15a.

82. *CTYL*, 128:15a.

83. *CTYL*, 128:15b.

84. *CTYL*, 125:13a–b.

85. *CTYL*, 125:16a. For the problems of "liberation from the corpse" or "liberation by sword," see Michel Strickmann, "On the Alchemy of T'ao Hung-ching," in *Facets of Taoism* (New Haven: Yale University Press, 1979), 130–31.

86. *CTYL*, 128:15b.

87. Chu wrote on the practice of divination according to the *Book of Changes*. See *CWWC*, 66:11b–27b.

88. *CTYL*, 125:13b.

89. See *T'iao-hsi chen* (On Regulating Breath) in *CWWC*, 85:6a. For more information on this subject, consult Miura Kunio, "Shushi to kokyū" (Chu Hsi and Breath Control), in

Kanaya Osumu, ed., *Chūgoku ni okeru ningensei no kenkyū* (Studies of Human Nature in China), 499–521 (Tokyo: Sōbunsha, 1983).

90. *CTYL*, 1:6b. For more information about Taoist cultivation of health through breath circulation, consult Chiang Wei-ch'iao's autobiographical treatise, *Ying-shih-tzu ching-tso fa* (Master Ying-shih's Method of Meditation), in Hsiao T'ien-shih, comp., *Tao-tsang ching-hua* (Taipei: Tzu-yu ch'u-pan she, 1984), 2nd Collection, No. 9.

91. For the Buddhist source, consult *Taishō* 19, No. 945, p. 126c. For the fasting of the mind. see *Chuang-tzu*, "In the World of Men," trans. in Watson, *The Complete Works of Chuang Tzu*, 57–58.

92. *CTYL*, 126:10b.

93. *CTYL*, 120:3b.

94. For Chou-Tun-i, see *SYHA*, SPPY ed., ch. 9. The last two sentences hide a reference to a Taoist work on inner alchemy, the *Hsing-ming kuei-chih* (The Essential Meaning of Nature and Destiny), ascribed to the school of the Taoist Yin, in Hsiao T'ien-shih, comp., *Tao-tsang ching-hua* (1981), Collection 1, No. 5, part *"heng,"* p. 175. The last sentence refers also to dragons and serpents hibernating. See the *Classic of Changes*, "Appended Remarks," part 2. See *Chou I pen-i*, 8:4a.

95. See *Chou I pen-i*, "Appended Remarks," part 1, 7:12a. Consult *Erh-Ch'eng ch'üan-shu*, *I-shu*, SPPY ed., ch. 15.

96. Consult Watson, *Complete Works* of Chuang Tzu, 154. Reference to Lau, *Lao-tzu*, ch. 51, p. 112, and to *Ch'u-tzu*, "T'ien-wen" (The Heavenly Questions). Consult Chu's *Ch'u-tz'u chi-chu*, ch. 3.

97. *ECCS*, *I-shu*, ch. 11.

98. For "holding on to the one," which became a method of meditation, see *Lao-tzu*, ch. 10, in Lau, *Lao-tzu*, 66. Also see *Pao-p'u-tzu*, ch. 18; English translation by James Ware, *Alchemy, Medicine, Religion in the China of* A.D. *320: The Nei-P'ien of Ko Hung* (Cambridge: M. I. T. Press, 1966), pp. 303–4. Among the famed immortals, Kuang-ch'eng tzu was a legendary ancient described in *Chuang-tzu*. See Watson, *The Complete Works of Chuang Tzu*, 118–20.

99. *CWWC*, 51:27a.

100. Ibid.

101. Sueki, "Inbukei kōi no shisō," 163–64.

102. Liu Shih-p'ei, *Tu Tao-tsang chi* (Reading Notes on the Taoist Canon), in *Liu Shen-shu hsien-sheng i-shu* (Surviving Works of Liu Shih-p'ei) (Ning-wu: Nan-shih, 1934–36).

103. Sueki refers to Wang Ming and Chang Tai-nien, who doubt Li's authorship at least for part of that work. See "Inbukei kōi no shisō," 173, notes 4 and 6.

104. *Yin-fu-ching k'ao-i*, 1b, in *Chu-tzu i-shu*, vol. 12. For more information on that text, see Needham, *Science and Civilisation in China*, vol. 2, pp. 447–48.

105. Preface to *Yin-fu ching k'ao-i*, 1a.

106. Ibid.

107. *Yin-fu ching k'ao-i*, 6a.

108. Ibid., 4a.

109. Ibid., 6a.

110. *Yin-fu ching k'ao-i*, 6a. See also *CTYL*, 125:14a–b.

111. *Yin-fu ching k'ao-i*, 6b. Reference is to the "Appended Remarks" (Pt. 2) to the *Classic of Changes*. See *Chou I pen-i*, 8:5b.

112. Azuma, "Shu Ki 'Shūeki sandōkei kōi," 166–67.

113. *Yin-fu ching k'ao-i*, 7a.

114. *Yin-fu ching k'ao-i*, 6a.

115. For an English translation, consult Wm. T. de Bary, ed., *Sources of Chinese Tradition* (New York: Columbia University Press, 1960), vol. 1, pp. 221–22.

116. Chu was criticized by others, includng the Ming scholar Hu Chü-jen (1434–84) for advocating "watching the tip of the nose" and writing these treatises on Taoist texts, that is, for leading others "into heresy." See Hu Chü-jen, *Chü-yeh lu* (1633 ed.), 3:10a–11b, 7:11b–12a.

117. Julia Ching, *To Acquire Wisdom: The Way of Wang Yang-ming* (New York: Columbia University Press, 1976).

118. *CTYL*, 125:15a–b.

119. *CTYL*, 126:4a–b.

GLOSSARY

Azuma Jūji　吾妻重二

Chan, Wing-tsit　陳榮捷

Chang Liwen　張立文

Chang Tai-nien　張岱年

Chang Tsai　張載

Chang-tzu ch'üan-shu　張子全書

Chen-kao　真誥

Ch'en Kuo-fu　陳國符

Ch'en T'uan　陳搏

Cheng-meng　正蒙

Ch'eng Hao　程顥

Ch'eng I　程頤

chi　機

ch'i　氣

ch'i-kung　氣功

chien-chieh　劍解

ch'ien/k'un　乾坤

Ch'ien Mu　錢穆

Chin Chung-shu　金重書

ching　精

ching-shen 精神

Ch'ien Mu 錢穆

Ch'in Chia-i 秦家懿

Chou I 周易

Chou I pen-i 周易本義

Chou I pen-i k'ao yü ch'i-ta 周易本義考與其他

Chou Tun-i 周敦頤

Chu Hsi 朱熹

Chu-hsüeh lun-chi 朱學論集

chu-tsai 主宰

"Chu-tzu chih tsung-chiao shih-chien" 朱子之宗教實踐

Chu-tzu hsin hsüeh-an 朱子新學案

Ch'u-tz'u chi-chu 楚辭集註

Chu-tzu hsin t'an-so 朱子新探索

Chu-tzu i-shu 朱子遺書

Chu-tzu men-jen 朱子門人

Chu-tzu nien-p'u 朱子年譜

Chu-tzu ta-ch'üan 朱子大全

Chu-tzu wen-chi 朱子文集

Chu-tzu yü-lei 朱子語類

Chuang Tzu 莊子

Chūgoku ni okeru ningensei no kenkyū 中國における人間性の研究

Chü yeh lu 居業錄

Ch'ü Yüan 屈原

Erh-Ch'eng ch'üan-shu 工程全書

Erh-shih-wu-shih 二十五史

fa 法

Fung Yu-lan 馮友蘭

Fu-hsi 伏羲

Han Fei-tzu 韓非子

Ho-t'u 河圖

Hsiao T'ien-shih 蕭天石

Hsien-t'ien t'u 先天圖

Hsin-ya hsüeh-shu chi-k'an 新亞學術集刊

hsing　性

hsing-erh-hsia　形而下

hsing-erh-shang　形而上

Hsing-ming kuei-chih　性命圭旨

Hsün-tzu　荀子

Hu Chü-jen　胡居仁

Hu Wei　胡渭

Hua-yen　華嚴

Huai-nan-tzu　淮南子

Hui-tsung　徽宗

hun/p'o　魂魄

"Hung-fan"　洪範

I-hsüeh t'ao-lun chi　易學討論集

I-li ching-chuan t'ung-chieh　儀禮經傳通解

I-shu　遺書

I-t'u ming-pien　易圖明辨

"Inbukei kōi no shisō"　陰符經考義の思想

Jan Yün-hua　冉雲華

kan　干

Kanaya Osamu　金谷治

k'an/li　坎離

Kinsei kanseki sōkan　近世漢籍叢刊

Ko Hung　葛洪

K'ou Ch'ien-chih　寇謙之

"Ku-ming"　顧命

kua　卦

kuei-shen　鬼神

K'ung-t'ung tao-shih　空同道士

"Lai-pu-ni-tz'u ti *Chou-I* hsüeh"　萊甫尼茲的周易學

Lao-tzu　老子

li　理

Li Cheng-kang　李證剛

Li-chi cheng-i　禮記正義

Li Chih-ts'ai　李之材

Li Ch'üan　李銓

"Li-sao"　離騷

Li T'ung　李侗

Li Xueqin　李學勤

Lieh-tzu　列子

Lin Ling-su　林靈素

Liu Pai-min　劉百閔

Liu Shih-p'ei　劉師培

Lo　洛

Lo-shu　洛書

"Lun Pei-Sung mo-nien chih ch'ung-shang Tao-chiao"　論北宗末年之崇尚
　道教

Lung-hu shang-ching　龍虎上經

Lü-lü hsin-shu　律呂新書

Miura Kunio　三浦國雄

Mo Ti　墨翟

Morohashi Tetsuji　諸橋轍次

na-chia　納甲

Nihon Chūgoku gakkaihō　日本中國學會報

nü-tao　女道

Okada Takehiko　岡田武彦

Ou-yang Hsi-hsün　歐陽希遜

Pao-p'u-tzu　抱朴子

P'eng Hsiao　彭曉

Sakai Tadao　酒井忠夫

Shang-shu cheng-i　尚書正義

Shang Ti　上帝

Shao Yung　邵雍

Shen Pu-hai　申不害

shen　伸

Shen-hsiao　神霄

shen-hua chih tzu-jan　神化之自然

sheng-sheng　生生

Shina ni okeru Bukkyō to Jukkyō Dōkyō　支那にオ‍ける佛教と儒教道教

shu　術

"Shu Ki 'Shūeki Sandōkei kōi' ni tsuite"　朱熹『周易參同契考異』に就いて

Shushi shū　朱子集

Shushi to Dōkyō　朱子と道教

Shushi to kokyū　朱子と呼吸

Shushigaku nyūmon　朱子學入門

Shushigaku taikei　朱子學大系

Sueki Yasuhiko　末木恭彦

Sung Yü　宋玉

Sung shih　宋史

Sung shih yen-chui chi　宋史研究集

t'ai-chi　太極

T'ai-chi-t'u shuo　太極圖説

T'ai-shang kan-ying p'ien　太上感應篇

T'ai-shang Lao-chün　太上老君

T'ai-shang Tao-chün　太上道君

T'ai-wei hsien-chün kung-kuo ko　太微仙君功過格

Tao　道

tao-chi　盜機

Tao-chia　道家

Tao-chiao　道教

Tao-te ching　道德經

Tao-tsang yüan-liu k'ao　道藏源流考

tao-yin　導引

T'ao Hung-ching　陶弘景

te　德

T'ien　天

t'ien-chi　天機

T'iao-hsi chen　調息箴

Tokiwa Daijö　常盤大定

Ts'ai Yüan-ting　蔡元定

Ts'an-t'ung-ch'i k'ao-i　參同契考異

Tsou Hsi　鄒訢

Ts'ui-yen　粹言

Tu-jen Chung　杜仁仲

Tung Shu-chung　董叔重

tzu-te　自得

Wang Mao-hung　王懋竑

Wang Ming　王明

Wang Pi　王弼

Wang Tzu-ts'ai　王梓材

Wang Yang-ming　王陽明

wei-chi chih hsüeh　為己之學

Wei Po-yang　魏伯陽

wu　無

wu-chi　無極

wu-chu　巫祝

Yang Chu　陽朱

"*Yang-sheng chu shuo*"　養生主説

Yin-fu ching k'ao-i　陰符經考異

yin-ssu　淫祠

yu　有

Yü　禹

Yüan Chi-chung　袁機仲

Yüan-shih T'ien-tsun　元始天尊

Yüan Shu-chen　袁淑真

"Yüan-yu"　遠遊

Chapter Five

THE CULT OF KUAN-YIN IN MING-CH'ING CHINA: A CASE OF CONFUCIANIZATION OF BUDDHISM?

CHÜN-FANG YÜ

Like all celestial bodhisattvas in Mahayana Buddhism, Kuan-yin cannot be said to possess any gender characteristics, although in India, Southeast Asia, Tibet, and China up until the T'ang the deity is usually depicted as a handsome and princely young man. From the time of the Five Dynasties, however, Kuan-yin began to undergo a process of feminization. By the Ming this process reached completion, and Kuan-yin became a completely sinicized goddess.

The feminine transformation of Kuan-yin is, of course, not entirely a Chinese innovation, but has a firm scriptural basis. According to chapter 25 of the *Lotus Sutra*, "The Gateway of the Bodhisattva Sound-Observer" (known in Chinese as "P'u-men p'in" and circulated separately since the fourth century as the "Kuan-yin Sutra") Kuan-yin can appear in as many as thirty-three different forms in order to save different types of people. Among these forms, seven are feminine: nun, lay woman, wife of an elder, householder, official, Brahman, and girl (*Scripture of the Lotus Blossom of the Fine Dharma*, 314–15). But in China Kuan-yin did not simply appear as such an undefined woman. In fact, a key factor in the successful indigenization and feminization of this Buddhist deity in China is that through various myths and legends the Chinese managed to transform Avalokiteśvara, the ahistorical bodhisattva who transcended temporal and spatial limitations as depicted in the Mahayana scriptures, into Kuan-yin, who, known by different Chinese names, led lives in clearly definable times and locations on the soil of China. Only in this way could Kuan-yin conform to the model of Chinese deities. For in China, not only were popular gods such as Kuan-ti and Chi-kung or the goddess Ma-tsu real people who once lived in specific times and places, but, as Derk Bodde suggested many years ago, through the process of "euphemerization," even mythical figures were turned into historical cultural heroes who were venerated as the founding fathers of Chinese civilization (1961:367–408). Unlike ancient Greece, where human heroes were turned into Olympian gods, in China, gods were depicted as real human beings. As recent studies by Valerie Hansen and Kenneth Dean have demonstrated, many new deities whose cults began during the Sung were once ordinary men and women who became deified after death (Hansen 1990; Dean 1993). On the other hand, if the god was not originally a human being, as, for instance, in the case of Wen-ch'ang, there were, starting in the Sung, concerted efforts of personification designed to turn him into a human being (Kleeman 1993). In the case of Kuan-yin, the same process occurred in reverse. Kuan-yin had to become Miao-shan, a living woman, so that she could be worshiped as a Chinese goddess.

Although bodhisattvas, including Kuan-yin, were not given birthdays in the Buddhist sutras (for, unlike Śākyamuni, they were not historical personages), in China, the nineteenth day of the second month became known as Kuan-yin's birthday. Like the birthdays of all Chinese deities, this day has been the most important festival for her devotees. This serves as a powerful example of the Chinese transformation of Kuan-yin. A similar example may be found in the identification, over time, of the island P'u-t'o, located off the shore of Chekiang Province, with the mythical Potalaka, the transtemporal and trans-spatial realm mentioned in the *Hua-yen Sutra*. Following the development of the cult of Nan-hai Kuan-yin (Kuan-yin of the South Sea), this originally desolate and obscure island came to be celebrated as the native home of Kuan-yin and was established as a national and international pilgrimage center (Yü 1992).

Of the various feminine manifestations Kuan-yin assumed in China, by far the most familiar one, especially for people in the Ming-Ch'ing period, was the chaste and filial daughter represented by Princess Miao-shan. As Glen Dudbridge has demonstrated, the core of the legend can be traced to the stele inscription entitled *Ta-pei P'u-sa chuan* (Biography of the Bodhisattva of

Great Compassion), composed by Chiang Chih-ch'i (1031–1104), who came to Ju-chou, Honan, as its new prefect in 1099. He became friends with the abbot of Hsiang-shan Temple in Pao-feng County, which housed a Ta-pei (Thousand-eyed and Thousand-armed Kuan-yin) Pagoda and was the pilgrimage center for the Kuan-yin cult. The fame of the temple and the pagoda rested on the legend that Princess Miao-shan, who was an incarnation of Kuan-yin, underwent an apotheosis at this very site. Based on what the abbot told him, Chiang wrote the account, which was penned by the famous calligrapher Ts'ai Ching (1046–1126) and inscribed on a stele in 1104. When Chiang served as the prefect of Hangchow during 1102–3, he brought the story with him, and the monk of Upper T'ien-chu Monastery, another pilgrimage center for Kuan-yin worship, had the same story carved on a stele in 1104 (Dudbridge 1978:10–15; 1982:589–94).[1]

Although the legend of Miao-shan was already known in the Sung, the fully developed story was set forth in the Ming novel *Nan-hai Kuan-yin ch'üan-chuan* (The Complete Story of Kuan-yin of the South Sea), the Ming *ch'uan-ch'i* drama *Hsiang-shan chi* (Story of Hsiang-shan), and the early Ch'ing sectarian text *Kuan-yin chi-tu pen-yüan chen-ching* (True Scripture of Kuan-yin's Original Vow of Universal Salvation, preface dated 1667). All the works cited above, moreover, were in turn based on the *Hsiang-shan pao-chüan* (Precious Volume of Hsiang-shan). The earliest surviving edition was from the Ch'ien-lung era, although it bore a preface dated 1103 written by a monk named P'u-ming of Upper T'ien-chu Monastery, who cannot be otherwise identified. Even if the preface was spurious, the *pao-chüan* was clearly written by the Ming, for it was already referred to this title in the 1550s. The story, in short, is the following.[2]

Miao-shan was the third daughter of King Miao-chuang. She was by nature drawn to Buddhism, keeping a vegetarian diet, reading scriptures by day, and practicing Ch'an meditation at night from an early age. The king had no sons and hoped to choose an heir from his sons-in-law. When Miao-shan reached the marriageable age of nineteen, she refused to get married, unlike her two elder sisters, who had both obediently married the men chosen by their father. The king was greatly angered by her refusal and punished her with various ordeals. She was first confined to the back garden and subjected to hard labor. When, with the aid of gods, she completed the tasks, she was allowed to join a nunnery to undergo further trials in the hope of discouraging her from pursuing the religious path. She persevered, and the king burned down the nunnery, killed the five hundred nuns, and had Miao-shan executed for her unfilial behavior. While her body was safeguarded by a mountain spirit, Miao-shan's soul toured hell and saved beings there by preaching to them. She returned to the world, went to Hsiang-shan, meditated for nine years, and achieved enlightenment. By this time, the king had become seriously ill with a mysterious disease that resisted all medical treatment. Miao-shan, disguised as a medicant monk, came to the palace and revealed the only remedy that could save the dying father: a medicine concocted with the eyes and hands of someone who had never felt anger. She further told the astonished king where to find such a person. When the king's messengers arrived, Miao-shan willingly offered her eyes and hands. The father recovered after taking the medicine and came to Hsiang-shan with the royal party on a pilgrimage to offer thanks to his savior. He recognized the eyeless and handless ascetic as none other than his own daughter. Overwhelmed with remorse, he and the rest of the royal family all converted to Buddhism. Miao-shan was transformed into her true form, that of the thousand-eyed and thousand-armed Kuan-yin. After the apotheosis, Miao-shan passed away and a pagoda was erected to house her relics.

Earlier in the story, Miao-shan's refusal to get married was the major crime for which she had to suffer many hardships and even death. Later in the story, the selfless sacrifice of her hands and eyes to save her father made possible the reconciliation and her eventual transfiguration. Why was marriage refused and virginity glorified? Why was the supreme act of filial piety conceived as the offering of parts of one's own body to be consumed and incorporated by one's parent? These were bold and provocative messages that challenged the Confucian value system. The Confucian ideal of filial piety was grounded firmly on the continuance of the family and ideologically opposed to extreme acts of self-mutilation as exemplified by the behavior of Miao-shan. In the myth of Miao-shan, the central themes are clearly Buddhist: the heroine opted for a life of austerity and renunciation instead of carrying out her familial obligations as a wife and mother. Even though she did not remain a member of a monastery but carried out her religious cultivation by herself, she followed the Buddhist ascetic ideal.

The rejection of marriage was based on two powerful arguments. The first one had to do with a negative attitude toward sexuality and physical desire, and the second was a negative evaluation of the married condition itself. Both reflected the values of Buddhism, which always regarded the monastic and ascetic life as preferable to that of a householder. When Miao-shan was challenged by her father to explain her disobedience, she reminded him of the brevity of human life and the pains of transmigration. She dwelled particularly on the horrors of hell. Even if loyal subjects and filial sons should be willing to suffer on behalf of the king, such torments could not be endured by anyone else. "Love of life is the cause, and sexual desire is the consequence. When cause and consequence are intertwined, one undergoes ten thousand births and ten thousand deaths. Changing one's heads and faces, one wanders in the six realms of rebirth and sees no beginning for deliverance" (*Hsiang-shan pao-chüan*, 16a). Marriage was explicitly linked to hell, for "when man and woman get married, they plant a tree of bitterness and broadly cast seeds that take root only in hell" (18a). The *True Scripture of Kuan-yin's Original Vow of Universal Salvation* expanded on the same theme but went into greater detail. Miao-shan set forth the bitterness of a woman's fate in a memorial that she presented to her father.

> Due to the sins I committed in my previous lives, I am now born with a woman's body. How sad!
>
> I have to listen to my father before I get married. If I get married, I must obey my husband and can have no opinion of my own.
>
> Should the husband die an early death from illness, I must then guard my chastity and listen to my son. . . .
>
> The "three obediences" and "four virtues" are serious matters, for hell awaits the woman who dares to ignore them. In this world, only women have to suffer so much for their sins: Killing animals after giving birth is very sinful. Coming to the kitchen before a full month's confinement is over pollutes the stove. Going to the front hall with an impure body offends the family altar.
>
> Washing and pounding blood-stained clothing in the river is a great sin against gods in the watery region.
>
> Exposing dirty garments under the sun angers deities who pass by. Pouring bloody water into open space pollutes heaven, earth, and the three bodies of light [sun, moon, and stars]. Who keeps track of all these offences? Lord Yama examines me most carefully after my death. (27a–b)

Such a lament over the subservient position of women was not new—it was, in fact, a leitmotif found in the literature of the time. More interesting are the specific taboos affecting women after childbirth, as emphasized by popular religion. Although sexual desire is declared to be the driving force behind rebirth, and therefore to be avoided (a teaching much stressed in Buddhism), the revulsion against marriage expressed in such popular religious literature is not only an indictment of sexuality per se but is also linked with the fear of loss of autonomy and the unavoidable eventuality of childbirth.[3]

Was Miao-shan's example followed by women in Ming-Ch'ing China? When we examine the cult of Kuan-yin in late imperial times as represented by the lives of religious women and men, there is clear evidence that Miao-shan's messages received mixed responses. Although a woman could become a nun and, with the increasing influence of the cult of chaste widowhood, she could remain single with great social prestige, there was no large-scale movement of resistance to marriage. On the contrary, we can speak of the rise of a kind of "domesticated religiosity" in late imperial times. In a recent study of seventeenth-century gentry women in the Kiangnan area, Dorothy Ko uses the term "domestic religion" to describe the "religious rituals and sentiments which were embedded in everyday life in the inner chambers and were integral to the women's worldviews and self-identities" (Ko 1994:198). While devotion to Kuan-yin was very common among the gentry women Ko studied, they were not exclusively Buddhists but, rather, were syncretic in their religious practices. Furthermore, these sentiments and rituals, expressed through poetry writing, painting, and appreciation of drama, were often secular in nature. Prayers to Taoist deities, participation in seances, immersion in dream interpretations, and even intense emotional attachments to Tu Li-niang, the heroine of *Mu-tan t'ing* (The Peony Pavilion), all constituted elements of the domestic religion and the cult of *ch'ing* (feelings).

I use the term *domesticated religiosity*, however, in a somewhat different, yet more definable sense. What I mean by this term can be illustrated by two distinct though related phenomena. In the first instance, the home was literally the physical arena where one performed one's religious activities. One did not have to leave home and join a monastery. This could be seen as a natural extension of the lay Buddhist ideal. But unlike the literati Buddhist laymen who followed the leading Buddhist masters such as Chu-hung and Te-ch'ing in the late Ming, many women did not become affiliated with a particular monk or monastery.

A case in point is provided by the short biographies of some 140 women practitioners of Buddhism found in the *Shan nü-jen chuan* (Biographies of Good Women) compiled by P'eng Shao-sheng (1740–1796) in the eighteenth century.[4] Sixty-six, or about half, of the women lived in the Ming and Ch'ing, the last of the biographies being that of T'ao Shan, the daughter-in-law of the author's own brother. These women were wives and mothers who recited the Buddha's name, worshiped Kuan-yin, kept to a vegetarian diet, chanted sutras, or practiced meditation. All of them carried out their primarily Pure Land practices at home. They were not disciples of monks. On the other hand, some of them could be said to have led lives similar to those of nuns, as when they did not have sex with their husbands. Even though they were laywomen, they often exhibited the spiritual authority of a Buddhist master. For instance, they could predict the times of their deaths, and they often passed away in full control of their faculties without any sign of pain or distress. In a way, Miao-shan herself can be seen more as a lay Buddhist woman than a nun. Except for a short time when she worked as a menial laborer at the White Sparrow Nunnery, she practiced meditation by herself. She did not seek instruction from any monk, nor did she join any religious establishment. In a recent study of religious lives of members of lay Buddhist groups of the Sung and Yüan, ter Haar notes some characteristics that could be applied to the life-style of Miao-shan. Those whom he called the "activist lay Buddhists," for example, carried out their Buddhist activities parallel to, but not subordinated under, the organized *sangha*. They performed good deeds for society as well as ritual activities such as chanting sutras for the benefit of people in need, a specialty normally reserved for monks. They identified themselves as a distinct group by adopting affiliation names that included, among others, the character *miao* (ter Haar 1992:16–43).[5]

Another example of what I call "domesticated religiosity" is the case of the woman visionary T'an-yang-tzu (b. 1558), whom Ann Waltner has been study-ing. We know her primarily through the biography written by Wang Shih-chen (1526–1590), who regarded her as his master. Aside from Wang and his brother, who knew her family well, her own father Wang Hsi-chüeh (who became a grand secretary after her death) and her brother were also fervent followers. She claimed four other literati who obtained their *chin-shih* degrees in 1577 as her disciples as well. She had visions of Kuan-yin and the Queen Mother of the West, who taught her meditational techniques to attain immor-tality. Although she did not want to get married, she did not refuse the marriage arranged by her father with the son of a fellow townsman who had received the *chin-shih* degree the same year as her father, 1558, the year she was born. But the man died before the wedding could take place. She mourned him grievously as a wife and served him as his widow. After she finished her meditational regimen, she retired to the grave of her dead hus-band where she lived and then died (or "cast off the corpse") in a neighboring shrine. Her religious pursuit was carried out completely in a domestic setting. She was said to do embroidery and care for her parents (including the cure of her father by giving him pure water, over which she cast spells), living the life of a dutiful daughter before her betrothal and that of a chaste widow after her fiancé's untimely death. When she went spirit-wandering, she asked her father to guard her inert body. Before she left the world as an immortal, there was a farewell scene, full of pathos, between parents and daughter (Waltner 1987:105–27). Her religious calling was fulfilled through familial obligations. The home, not a Taoist convent, provided the setting for her religious career. There were other examples of "domestic goddesses," talented women who died tragically young and who, as a result of being promoted by their male kinsmen, as in the case of T'an-yang-tzu, also became immortalized. The gifted seventeenth-century poet Yeh Hsiao-luan (1616–1632) was such an example (Ko 1994:200–202).

The second meaning of "domesticated religiosity" is illustrated in the phenomenon whereby in Ming-Ch'ing times one could achieve religious sanctification by performing one's domestic obligations to the fullest degree. The cult of chaste widowhood is an obvious example. But *ko-ku* (slicing off a piece of flesh from one's thigh) should be viewed in the same light. Through rendering extreme acts of fidelity and filial piety to one's husband and parents, who were in this process transformed into religious absolutes, a woman attained a kind of sainthood.[6] Miao-shan's offering of her eyes and hands found resounding resonances in the practice of *ko-ku*. To what extent can one speak of this aspect of "domesticated religiosity" as an example of the "Confucianization" of Buddhism?

A final example of this "domesticated religiosity" was the widespread worship of Kuan-yin as a fertility goddess by Ming-Ch'ing men and women. Despite the general fear and loathing connected with childbirth, found in precious scrolls and popular religious tracts, the cult of Kuan-yin as "Giver of Sons" (Sung-tzu) was vigorously promoted by literati in the late Ming. Instead of posing as a potential threat to the Confucian family as the story of Miao-shan implied, Kuan-yin was transformed into a patron saint of the domestic hearth and a savior of infertile Confucian literati who hoped, through their worship of her, to escape the worst sin of unfiliality. The unambiguous Buddhist messages in the legend of Miao-shan became Confucianized by these two examples, which may be regarded as key components of a new type of family-centered religion. On the other hand, one may ask to what extent the Confucian ethical system was also simultaneously Buddhicized by taking these new directions. It is for this reason that the title of this essay takes the form of a question.

Ko-ku and Kuan-yin

The highlight of the Miao-shan legend is assuredly the offering of her eyes and hands to save her dying father. This extraordinary act of self-sacrifice not only cancels out her crime of unfiliality but triggers her miraculous metamorphosis into a goddess. Let us look at this image of Miao-shan and the cult of filial piety exemplified by *ko-ku* in Ming-Ch'ing times. In an earlier article I discussed the Buddhist antecedents for Miao-shan's sacrifice (1993:3–5). There are many stories about the self-sacrifice of bodhisattvas and, especially, of the Buddha in his previous lives recorded in Buddhist scriptures. They offered parts of their bodies either as food or medicine to save sentient beings in dire straits. But in most cases, the recipients were not their parents. Among the cases that I discovered, the one most closely resembling that of Miao-shan is the story of Prince Patience, one of the previous incarnations of the Buddha, who offered his eyes and bone marrow to cure his dying father. This story was undoubtedly familiar to the Chinese of the Sung period, for it is not only recorded in a popular Buddhist scripture, the *Ta-fang-pien Fo pao-en ching* (The Sutra of Buddha's Repaying Parental Kindness with Great Skillful Means); the scene was also carved on the cliff of Pao-ting Shan in Ta-tsu, Szechuan by Chao Chih-feng (1159–122?), the founder and architect of this flourishing pilgrimage center (*Ta-tsu shih-ke yen-chiu* 272:257–64). It may not be coincidental that Chao chose to carve this particular scene to illustrate the highest deed of filial piety, for by the Sung the ideal of *ko-ku* probably had already become well known to Chao, the unknown author of *Hsiang-shan pao-chüan*, as well as ordinary men and women.

The origin of *ko-ku* lies with Chinese medical lore. Chinese historical sources generally identified Ch'en Tsang-ch'i as the legitimator of this belief, for he claimed in his medical text, *Ts'ao-mu shih-i* (Corrected Pharmocopeia), written in 739 that human flesh could cure diseases. Among the dynastic histories, the *Hsin T'ang shu* (New History of the T'ang) is the first to contain three accounts, and subsequently, more cases are recorded in the *Sung shih* (Sung History) and *Yüan shih* (Yüan History). By the Ming, such acts were reported not only in historical sources but in literature. Both men and women chose to show their utmost filial piety toward their parents by resorting to this drastic action. Typically, the filial child was usually a commoner from an obscure background. The actions of such persons attracted the attention of local officials and literati who wrote commemorative essays and poems to glorify their deeds and requested commendation from the government. The literati themselves, however, were ideologically opposed to such behavior, for, according to the dictum of the Confucian *Hsiao ching* (Classic of Filial Piety), the body was a gift from one's parents and one must never do any damage to it. An early condemnation came from Han Yü (768–824) in the T'ang. He strongly argued that filial action consisted of securing medicine for the sick parents but should not involve any harm to one's body. If self-mutilation were really permissible, he ironically asked, why was it not done by former sages and worthies? Moreover, if such acts resulted in death, it could lead to the extinction of the family line — a most unforgivable sin (*Hsin T'ang shu* 195:2a–b). With rare exceptions, notably Chen Te-hsiu (1178–1235)[7], most Neo-Confucian thinkers echoed this sentiment. For instance, Wang Ken (1483–1540), in his essay "Clear Wisdom and Self-Preservation," argued:

> If I only know how to love others and do not know how to love my self, then it will come to my body being cooked alive or the flesh being sliced off my own thighs, or to throwing away my life and killing my self, and then my self cannot be preserved. And if my self cannot be preserved, with what shall I preserve my prince and father? (*I-chi* 1:12b–13a, quoted in de Bary 1970:165)

Li Shih-chen, the Ming medical specialist, was another typical literatus. In the *Pen-ts'ao kang-mu* (Classified Materia Medica), he at first mentioned that *ko-ku* and the related practice of *ko-kan* (slicing off a piece of liver) already existed before the T'ang, so they did not really originate with Ch'en Tsang-ch'i. But he still blamed Ch'en, for the latter gave it credence by writing it down in his book instead of exposing it as a fallacy. Li then took it upon himself to educate his readers, "Alas, we receive our hair, skin, and body from our parents and do not dare to harm or damage them. Even when the parent is seriously ill, how can one allow the children to injure their bodies, not to mention eating the flesh of one's own flesh and blood? This is truly the opinion of foolish people" (Li Shih-chen 52:110).

Partly because of literati ambivalence, this practice, though widely known in China, has so far received little scholarly attention.[8] The only recent substantive article treating this topic is that by Jonathan Chaves, who translated poems written by Wu Chia-chi (1618–1684) glorifying his contemporaries, including his own niece, who practiced *ko-ku*.[9] Literati ambivalence was also responsible for the government's sporadic attempts to discourage such practices among the common people by legislation. Both the Yüan and the Ming issued prohibitions to this effect.[10] But judging from the increasing number of cases mentioned in local gazetteers, popular literature, and collections of miracle tales compiled in the Ming and Ch'ing, such governmental attempts were apparently not effective.

The theory of *ko-ku* is a peculiar one. It was believed that, when a parent (or parent-in-law) was critically ill and all known medical recourse had failed to yield any cure, the flesh (from the thigh or the arm) or a piece of the liver cut from the body of a filial son, daughter, or daughter-in-law could unfailingly gain the patient's miraculous recovery. I had at first thought of calling this "filial cannibalism" (or "cannibalistic filiality"), for the cure is effected specifically by the consumption of the flesh of the child. But upon further consideration, the use of the term "cannibalism" would not be appropriate here. In societies where cannibalism is practiced, the central focus is on the "consumer" who sets about consciously and deliberately to capture, prepare, and eat the flesh of his or her victim, acts usually carried out in a ritual setting. The reason for eating the flesh is to incorporate the life force or spiritual power of the victim. Except in cases of famine, the act does not serve a utilitarian purpose (Sunday 1986; Brown and Tuzin 1983). In the Chinese case, although the beneficiary was the receiving parent, the central focus is always the "victim," the filial child. The parent invariably did not know that he or she was eating human flesh, for it was always prepared with other ingredients and disguised as a soup or broth. It was the child who received the exclusive attention from the chronicler and eulogy writer. Detailed description was sometimes lavished on the painful and elaborate ritual of cutting off the flesh, the hasty preparation of the life-saving broth, and the return from near death caused by the mortal wound effected with divine help. Finally, it was the child who became sanctified by having part of him or herself reincorporated by the parent. One became spiritually strong by feeding the other and not, as in cannibalism, by consuming the same.

The relationship between Miao-shan's offering her eyes and hands and the Chinese cult of ko-ku is obviously a very close one. But it is difficult to establish either causality or priority. The rationale for Miao-shan's action has a logic that is less discernible in the many cases of ko-ku found in dynastic histories and local gazetteers. By refusing to get married and produce an heir, Miao-shan committed the most unfilial action imaginable in Confucian society. The breach in familial and cosmic harmony could be mended only by having herself reincorporated by her father through the latter's eating of her flesh. This is an act of redemption. Her rebellion did not lead to a real separation, but ended with her reincorporation into the family. The legend of Miao-shan, in the final analysis, did not challenge the hegemony of Confucian ethical discourse. Moreover, although in most cases it was Heaven or the kitchen god who was moved by this act of utmost sincerity and came to the filial child's rescue, in some stories of ko-ku of the Ming and Ch'ing, it was Kuan-yin who acted as the inspiration and guide for filial children who had difficulty in carrying out or completing this act. At other times she was the savior who protected them from sure death.

Let us look at a few of such cases. The first two are from the Ming.

Weng Ch'iang-chiang was the niece of a military commander, rank 3b, and, unlike most protagonists of this type of story, she was not a lowly commoner. When she was nine, her father was mortally ill. She prayed to Kuan-yin behind closed doors and sliced her left thigh to get a piece of flesh which she immediately gave to her mother, née Huang, to make into a soup for her father. He soon recovered. The local people wanted to report this event but she refused to allow them to do so. After her father died, she married a man named Hsi Chia-jui. Her mother became ill within six months of her wedding and she again sliced her thigh as before to save her (*Ku-chin t'u-shu chi-ch'eng* 397:42a).

The next story was about a man, and it was described in gruesome detail:

Filial son P'eng Yü-yüan of the Ming was a native of Yi-yang, Hu-kuang. He had the habit of chanting scriptures of Kuan-yin, the Three Officials, and other deities in the hope of prolonging his parents' life. Once his father was very ill and he cut off a piece of flesh from his arm to cure him. The father recovered and lived for more than ten years after that. In the autumn of 1636 his mother became too ill to get up from her bed. Yüan was worried day and night. One night he dreamt of Kuan-yin telling him that the mother's lifespan had come to an end, but if she ate human liver she could survive. When he woke up the next morning, the mother told him that she would like to have some sheep liver. Realizing the significance of his dream, he knelt down and thanked Kuan-yin tearfully. During the night he saw Kuan-yin come to him surrounded by many saints carrying banners. He woke up with a start and was drenched all over with perspiration. After bathing and worshiping, he took up the knife and aimed at the place where his liver and lung were located. Blood gushed out after one cut. The rib cage was exposed after the second cut. After the third and fourth cuts, there was a resounding sound, and after the sixth cut, the heart leaped out. Following the heart he groped for the lung, and after the lung he found the liver. By then he nearly fainted because of the extreme pain. After a moment's rest, he called his wife and told her quickly to cook the liver [the text is not clear whether it was the whole liver or a piece of it] to serve his mother. Not knowing what it really was, the mother ate it happily and soon became well. People from near and far came to know the story and were all greatly moved. Because his wounds did not heal and his lung could still be seen, some people prayed to gods for help. They dreamt of Kuan-yin, who told them, "It is not difficult to heal the wound, but because few people are filial in this degenerate age, I let the lung hang out for a hundred days so that everyone can view it." The above was recorded by Wang Wen-nan, a second-degree holder (Chou K'e-fu 1980:425a–b).

This story conforms to a general pattern: the filial son was a poor commoner, and the one who recorded and broadcast the story was a local gentryman. Kuan-yin played an active role from beginning to end. It was she who gave him the idea in the first place. It was she who guided him in the "operation." And it was she who allowed the wound to remain unhealed for a hundred days as an object lesson for the masses.

Three stories about filial daughters and daughters-in-law in which Kuan-yin appeared took place in the Ch'ing.

The filial daughter-in-law Liu was a native of Hsün County, Hupeh. Her husband was not at home. When her mother-in-law was ill and no medicine could cure her, she cut flesh from her thigh and made a congee with it to feed her. The mother-in-law recovered after eating it, but became ill again ten days later. Liu cut more flesh from her thigh and prepared meat balls to feed her. The mother-in-law became well, but then had a relapse several weeks later. Liu prayed to Kuan-yin and wished to offer herself in place of her mother-in-law. The doctor, moved by her sincerity, took pity on her and told her that ordinary pills could not help the patient, whose illness could be cured only by eating a piece of human liver. Liu believed him deeply and, secretly cutting open her underarm with a sharp knife, she got hold of the liver that had become exposed and cut off a few inches. She then fainted. In semiconsciousness, she seemed to see Kuan-yin come to her. Caressing her body, Kuan-yin said, "My child, you have suffered much!" and put medicine on her wound. Liu woke up and immediately cooked the liver. After eating it, the mother-in-law recovered and the illness never returned. This happened in the sixth month of the *yi-hai* year of Ch'ien-lung (1779). (*Kuan-shih-yin P'u-sa ling-kan lu*, 3a–b)

This woman was a believer in Kuan-yin. Therefore, when she saw that her mother-in-law was still sick, even after she had tried to cure her by performing *ko-ku* twice, she prayed to Kuan-yin and offered herself as a substitute. For her, Kuan-yin was the supreme authority who had control over life and death. It is also interesting that in this story, it was the doctor who told her that human liver was the miracle drug. Apparently, despite Li Shih-chen's condemnation, some doctors in the Ch'ing shared the same belief as their less-educated countrymen. In this miracle tale, Kuan-yin was not merely an inspiration and guide but a savior, for she applied medicine to the wound and saved the filial woman's life.

Another Ch'ing case also presents Kuan-yin as a controller of the human lifespan.

> Sun Fu-ju's wife had the surname of Chin. She was a native of Wu-chin, Kiangsu, and filial by nature. . . . Her husband died when she was twenty-four, and she kept her integrity. When her father-in-law became ill, she served him day and night for sixty days without sleeping. She prayed to Kuan-yin and cut off flesh from her thighs in the hope of curing him. It just so happened that the patient wanted to eat rice dumplings, so she mixed the flesh with rice flour and served him with broth. After he ate five dumplings, he went to sleep. The next morning, after waking up, he said to her, "I am not going to die. Just now I saw the White-Robed Kuan-yin who told me that your sincerity had moved Heaven, and I was given another *chi* [300 days] to live." He soon recovered and lived to be seventy-seven, exactly three hundred days after this happened. (*Kuan-shih-yin P'u-sa ling-kan lu*, 3b)

The last one was a little girl of ten years old who received inspiration and courage from Kuan-yin.

> Fang Fu-chu was the daughter of Fang Yü-ch'ing by his concubine. In K'ang-hsi 33 [1694] when she was only ten, her mother, née Feng, became ill and did not respond to medical treatment. She cried day and night and tried to think of all ways to save her mother. At night she dreamed of a woman in white carrying a barber's knife. She woke up with a start. The next morning, when she saw the mother had become worse, she went upstairs, lighted incense and lamp, prayed and sliced her left arm. She cooked a soup with the flesh and served the mother, who, upon eating, immediately improved. Officials bestowed on her silver and cloth as a reward. (*Ku-chin t'u-shu chi-ch'eng*, 398:5a–b)

The practice of *ko-ku* had apparently become so widespread that contemporary popular literature often contains it as part of the plot. One *pao-chüan* written probably in the Ch'ing, the *Kuan-yin shih-erh yüan-chüeh ch'üan-chuan* (Complete Biographies of Kuan-yin's Twelve Completely Enlightened Ones) is about how Kuan-yin took different disguises and helped twelve people become enlightened. One of them, a filial daughter-in-law named Chou, was about to perform *ko-ku* in order to save her ailing mother-in-law. Her sincerity moved Kuan-yin, who decided to protect her:

> Kuan-yin sighed saying, "Wonderful, wonderful! Such a daughter-in-law is very rare in the world. I fear though that she will die if she opens her stomach and cuts her liver." She ordered Wei-t'o to cover her with a copy of the *Scripture of Saving One from Suffering* [*Chiu-k'u ching*] so that her life might be protected. (*Kuan-yin shih-erh yüan-chüeh ch'üan-chuan*, 43a–b)

Contemporary records, on the other hand, include anecdotes about Kuan-yin, who appeared as a real person to filial children and gave them a certain miraculous pill that could save them from death should they one day slice their thighs. We read, for instance, in the *Ch'ien-chü lu* (Record of Living as a Hermit), the following:

> Hsieh Fen-lan was extremely filial by nature and she had worshiped Kuan-yin all her life. One day an old nun took out some pills from her sleeve and gave them to her, saying, "These pills can cure injuries resulting from the knife." Fen-lan took them and forgot about it. The following year her mother-in-law became seriously ill and no doctor could help her. She prayed to heaven and asked for help. She then secretly stole into her room and cut flesh from the thigh in order to cook a soup for the mother-in-law. The wound became unbearably painful, and she suddenly remembered the pills from before. So she asked her maid to get them and apply them to her wound. As soon as they were applied, new flesh began to grow, and it looked as if the thigh had never been cut. The old nun must be the "Great Being" and filial piety can indeed move the divinity (*Ku-chin t'u-shu chi-ch'eng*, 398:10b).

Although in these stories Miao-shan's name does not appear, and Kuan-yin is always referred to as *ta-shih* (Great Being), in view of the fact that the legend of Miao-shan had become widely disseminated throughout society by way of plays and popular texts in the Ming, it is safe to assume that the practitioners of *ko-ku* were aware of the model set by her. The image of Miao-shan as the chaste and filial daughter might not give rise directly to the cult of filial piety as exemplified by *ko-ku*, but it most likely helped to sustain its attraction. If Kuan-yin herself not only practiced it but showed her approval by protecting the filial sons and daughters in their ordeal, surely *ko-ku* was a religious act that would please Kuan-yin and Heaven as well as save one's parent. By lending legitimacy to this practice, Kuan-yin was made to uphold the central value system of Confucianism instead of challenging it by offering an alternative. The religiosity of *ko-ku* in late imperial China turned the parent into the highest object of devotion. The child achieved religious sanctification by worshiping the parent to the point of sacrificing his or her flesh. The parent, symbolically representing the entire Confucian family system, became the unquestioned moral absolute. Although men also participated in this, women seemed to favor this mode of filial behavior even more (T'ien 1988:159–61). Seen together with the parallel cult of female chastity, which turned widowhood into a religious calling, *ko-ku* possessed an inner logic despite what at first sight appears to be fanatical and bizarre behavior. Female religiosity became domesticated.

Kuan-yin as a Fertility Goddess

In the development of the cult of Kuan-yin in China, the bodhisattva appeared in several forms. Among them, the White-Robed (*Pai-yi*) Kuan-yin is one of the most familiar to her devotees. The White-Robed Kuan-yin began to appear in sculpture, paintings, poetry, founding myths of monasteries, miraculous tales, and pilgrims' visions from the tenth century on (Yü 1990). The deity is clearly feminine. She wears a long, flowing white cape, the hood of which sometimes covers her head and even arms and hands. The conventional view in Buddhist scholarship traces her to Tantric female deities such as White Tara or Pāṇḍaravāsinī, the consort of Avalokiteśvara and one of the chief deities of the World of Womb Treasury Mandala (Garbhakośadhātu, *t'ai-tsang chieh*) (Ch'en 1964:342; Stein 1986:27–37). The received wisdom in art historical circles has, on the other hand, identified this figure as a typical subject of the so-called Zen paintings, symbolizing the serenity and wisdom of Ch'an meditative states (Matsumoto 1937:350–51).

The time has come to reconsider the above interpretations. The popularity of the White-Robed Kuan-yin was not simply due to promotion by Ch'an monks and literati painters. Moreover, instead of tracing her to Tantric Buddhism, the origin of this deity may lie in a group of indigenous scriptures that portray her primarily as a fertility goddess. Although Kuan-yin's power of granting children is already mentioned in the *Lotus Sutra*, these indigenous scriptures are noteworthy on two accounts: they emphasize Kuan-yin's power to grant sons, and they call attention to Kuan-yin's protection of pregnant women and assurance of safe childbirth. These texts also provide the basis for the iconography of Child-Giving (Sung-tzu) Kuan-yin, which is indeed a variant of the White-Robed Kuan-yin.

Indigenous scriptures celebrating Kuan-yin have had, of course, a long history in China. Since 1970, chiefly through the work of Makita Tairyō, we have known that many such scriptures were composed during the Six Dynasties (420–581) and later. Although their titles remain in various catalogues, many did not survive. Of those that did, Makita studied extensively two: the *Fo-shuo Kuan-shih-yin san-mei ching* (Kuan-shih-yin Samadhi Sutra as Spoken by the Buddha) and the *Kao Wang Kuan-shih-yin ching* (Kuan-shih-yin Sutra [Promoted by] King Kao) (Makita 1970 and 1976). Instead of dismissing these scriptures as "forged," Makita regarded them as valuable documents revealing contemporary understandings of Buddhism. His sympathetic attitude has elicited similar responses among scholars in recent years (Buswell 1989, 1990; Kapstein 1989; Strickmann 1990). Studying similar apocryphal scriptures in other Buddhist traditions, they also see these scriptures as creative attempts to synthesize Buddhist teachings and adapt them to the native cultural milieu.

One indigenous scripture bearing the title *Pai-yi Ta-pei wu-yin-hsin t'o-lo-ni ching* (The Dharani Sutra of the Five Mudras of the Great Compassionate White-Robed One) enjoyed particular popularity among the Chinese people who hoped to have sons in late imperial China. Although the exact date of its composition cannot be established, there is a clear indication that it was already being circulated by the eleventh century at the latest. A stele dated 1082 with the White-Robed Kuan-yin holding a baby and the text of this sutra penned by Ch'in Kuan (1049–1100) has survived (Toshio Ebine 1986: plate 13). Since this scripture is not included in any existing edition of the Buddhist canon, its existence came to light as a result of happy coincidences. I first came across a handwritten copy of this text in the Rare Book Collection of the Palace Museum in Taipei, Taiwan, in the summer of 1986. It was written by the famous Ming dynasty calligrapher Tung Ch'i-ch'ang in 1558 and bore seals of both Emperors Ch'ien-lung and Chia-ch'ing. A few months later, while I was doing research in the rare book section of the Library of Chinese Buddhist Cultural Artifacts located at the Fa-yüan Monastery in Beijing, I found thirty-five copies of this scripture. They were all printed during the Ming, the earliest one in 1428 and the majority during the Wan-li period, around 1600–1610.

Literati living in the late Ming, during the sixteenth century, appeared to have given the cult of the White-Robed Kuan-yin new life. The following evidence shows that men, especially literati, were also devotees of Kuan-yin, the Giver of Sons, and promoted the popularity of this *dharani* sutra. Although Kuan-yin has been widely worshiped by Chinese women, her cult was never limited to women. In fact, it is difficult to think of any deity who is gender specific in relation to the worshipers in China. The common assumption that because Kuan-yin was a fertility goddess only women would appeal to her was not correct.

Yüan Huang (1533–1606), the literatus who promoted morality books, did not have a son until he was forty. He started to chant this scripture and had a son in 1580. When he compiled a collection of texts to help people in obtaining heirs, entitled *Chi-ssu chen-ch'üan* (True Instructions for Praying for an Heir), he put this text at the very beginning. He also identified the *dharani* contained in the scripture as the *Sui-hsin t'o-lo-ni* (Dharani Conforming to the Heart's Desire), the same *dharani* the great pilgrim Tripiṭaka relied on in crossing the perilous desert on his way to India. The *dharani*, according to Yüan, was therefore a translation from Sanskrit and was contained in the Buddhist canon, even though the scripture as it now stood could not be found there. Ch'ü Ju-chi (1548–1610) and his friend Yen Tao-che, two scholars responsible for the compilation of an important Ch'an chronicle, the *Chih-yüeh lu* (Record of Pointing to the Moon), were also faithful chanters of this *dharani*.

The copies of this scripture were printed in Beijing and distributed free of charge by donors who wanted to bear witness to White-Robed Kuan-yin's efficacy and promote her cult. Depending on the economic ability of the donors, who ranged from members of the royal family, literati-officials, and merchants, all the way down to obscure men and women, the quality and quantity of the printing varied greatly. But in all cases the donors provided accounts of miracles that happened either to others or to themselves. The former, which sometimes run to several pages, are appended immediately after the scripture, while the latter, which are usually no more than a few lines, are enclosed within a dedicatory plaque. One such plaque dated 1599, for instance, recorded the following:

> Mrs. Chao, née Shen, prayed for a male heir a few years ago and made a vow promising the printing of the "White-Robed Kuan-yin Sutra." Thanks to divine protection, twin boys Feng-kuo and Feng-chüeh were born to me on the twelfth day of the ninth month, 1597. Now I have finished printing one canon [*i-tsang*, i.e., 5,048 copies] of this scripture and donate them to fulfill my earlier vow. I pray that the two boys will continue to receive blessings without end. Donated on New Year's Day, 1599.

A great number of miracles accumulated around this text. The chanting of the *dharani* of the White-Robed Kuan-yin was believed to lead to the miraculous arrival of a long-awaited baby boy who would be born doubly wrapped in white placenta (*pai-yi ch'ung-pao*),[11] which indicated that he was a gift from the White-Robed Kuan-yin. The earliest testimony of this was traced to the T'ang, and miracles attributed to this scripture were reported during the six hundred years from the twelfth through the seventeenth centuries.

We conclude with a few selected testimonials appended to a copy of the sutra printed in 1609, all of literati background.

Wang Meng-pai, a metropolitan graduate from Ch'ing-chiang [in present-day Kiangsi province] was born because his parents faithfully chanted this sutra. When he was born, he had the manifestation of the "white robe." He himself also chanted the sutra and in 1214 had a "white-robed son" [*pai-yi-tzu*] whom he named "Further Manifestation" [*keng-hsien*].

Hsieh Tsung-ning, a native of Kuang-yang [Ta-hsing, present-day Beijing], who worked in the Central Drafting Office, came from a family that had only one son for the past five generations. In 1579 he and his wife, née Kao, started to chant the sutra, which they had also printed and distributed for free. In 1582 they had a son whom they named Ku, in 1585 another son whom they named Lu, and in 1586 twin boys Ch'u and Ying. All were born with double white placenta.

Ting Hsien of Yi-pin, Nan-yang [in present-day Honan Province] was fifty years old and had no son. So he decided to print this sutra and distribute it for free. He also had a thousand catties of iron melted down in the South Garden of the city to make an image of Kuan-yin, which was then gilded. It stood over six feet. At the same time, in order to acquire a son, Hsing Chien, the Grand Commandant, had a shrine dedicated to the White-Robed Kuan-yin erected in the northern part of the city. So the image was moved there to be worshiped. The local official set aside several thousand acres of good farmland to provide for the shrine's upkeep so that people could continue to offer incense in future generations. Not long after this, Ting dreamed one night of a woman who presented him with a white carp. The next morning, a son was born wrapped in a white placenta. That was the fourth day of the twelfth month, 1583. Earlier, when the image was moved to the White-Robed Kuan-yin Shrine, the gardener had a dream in which the bodhisattva appeared to him looking rather unhappy. When he told Ting about his dream, Ting had another image cast looking exactly like the first one in the South Garden. He invited a monk of repute to stay in the temple to take care of it. He subsequently dreamed of an old man wearing a white gown who came to visit him. The day after he had this dream, while he was relating it to his friend, a man suddenly came to the house seeking to sell the woodblocks of this sutra. Ting bought them and printed a thousand copies for distribution. He also hired a skilled painter to paint several hundred paintings of the White-Robed Kuan-yin to give to the faithful as gifts. In the fourth month of 1586, he had another son. By then, Hsing Chien, the Grand Commandant, had also a son and a daughter born to him and his wife.

Chao Yung-hsien, the son of a Grandee of the Tenth Order [the eleventh highest of twenty titles of honorary nobility conferred on meritorious subjects] was a native of Ch'ang-shu [in Kiangsu Province]. His wife, née Ch'en, chanted this sutra with great sincerity. On the sixteenth day of the seventh month in 1586, a daughter was born. She was covered with a piece of cloth as white as snow on her face, head, chest, and back. When the midwife peeled it away, the baby's eyes and eyebrows could then be seen. The parents already had sons, but only this daughter had the miraculous evidence of the "white cloth." It was for this reason that it was written down.

Yüan Huang, the metropolitan graduate who served in the Ministry of Rites, was a native of Chia-shan [in Chekiang Province]. He was forty but had no son. After chanting this sutra, in 1580, a son was born. He named the son Yüan-sheng ("Born from Universal Penetration") because he believed that the boy was a gift from Kuan-yin, the Universally Penetrating One (Yüan-t'ung). The boy had a very distinguished appearance and was unusually intelligent.

Ch'ü Ju-chi wrote a postscript to the sutra that appeared at the end of the 1609 text. He described how he and a group of friends chanted it for the sake of securing sons, what religious experiences he had, and why he wanted to promote this sutra. Although the text is rather long, it is translated here in its entirety, for it provides a rare glimpse of the private religious life of a highly educated literatus. It also offers important information about the networks of literati worshipers of Kuan-yin.

I began to chant this *dharani* in the second month of 1580 together with my friends Li P'o-shu and Yen Tao-che. Soon afterward Li had a son, and three years later Yen also had a son. I alone failed to experience a divine response.

I often blamed myself for my deep karmic obstructions, for I could not match the two gentlemen in their piety. Then one evening in the third month of 1583 I dreamed that I entered a shrine and a monk said to me, "In chanting the *dharani*, there is one Buddha's name you have not chanted. If you chant it, you shall have a son." Upon waking up, I could not understand what he meant by the missing Buddha's name, for I had always chanted the various names of Kuan-yin on the different festival days of her manifestation. In the winter of 1585 I traveled north and was stuck at a government post-house because the river was frozen. On the twelfth day of the twelfth month I entered a small temple and saw this sutra by the side of the *hou* animal mount on which Kuan-yin sat. It was donated by Wang Chi-shan, a judicial clerk. When I opened and read it, I saw the name of Lord Iśvara Buddha of Precious-Moon Wisdom-Splendor-Light-Sound, a name I had never heard of until that time. I had a sudden realization. I knelt down and kowtowed to the seat. I started to chant the name of the Buddha upon returning, and after only three days a son was born. It accorded perfectly with my dream.

In 1586 I went to the capital. Hsü Wen-ch'ing, Yü Tsung-pu, and other friends were all chanting the *dharani* in order to obtain sons. Yü's wife, furthermore, became pregnant after she had a strange dream. So we discussed plans to print this sutra to promote its circulation. I had earlier consulted the catalogues of the Northern and Southern Tripiṭakas [two collections of Buddhist scriptures compiled in the Ming] but did not find it listed in either one. I thought this must be a true elixir of life, secretly transmitted by foreign monks. Later Yüan Huang told me that this was actually the same *dharani* as the "*Dharani* Conforming to the Heart's Desire," two versions of which were included in the Tripiṭaka. When I learned about this, I rushed to Lung-hua Monastery to check the Tripiṭaka kept in the library. Although there were some variations in the sequence of sentences and the exact wordings of the mantra between the text found in the Tripiṭaka and that of the popular printed version, the efficacy of chanting the *dharani* was universally warranted. I could not help but feel deeply moved by the wonder of Kuan-yin's universal responsiveness and the divinity of the faithful chanters' sincere minds. The text in the Tripiṭaka promised not only sons but the fulfillment of many other desires in accordance with the wishes of sentient beings. According to the instruction given in the sutra contained in the Tripiṭaka, this *dharani* should be revealed only to those who are in possession of great compassion. If given to the wrong person, there might be disastrous results, for bad karma caused by hatred might be created if the person used the *dharani* to subdue enemies or avenge past wrongs. Taking this warning to heart, my friend Hsü and I decided that instead of reprinting the version found in the Tripiṭaka, we would print the *dharani* alone together with the stories about obtaining sons included in the popular versions of this text that were in circulation. After fasting and bathing, Hsü wrote out the sutra and gave it to an engraver to make the woodblocks for printing.

The term *dharani* means to keep all virtues completely. The extended meaning of the term, then, is the keeping of all virtues. For this reason, the merit of keeping the *dharani* is indeed limitless. With this Kuan-yin teaches people to do good. Therefore, if the practitioner does good, when he chants the words of the *dharani*, blessings as numerous as the sands of the Ganges will instantly come to him. But if he does not dedicate himself to goodness, he will lose the basis of the *dharani*. Even if he chants it, the benefit will be slight. I cannot claim to have realized this ideal, but I am willing to work hard toward it together with fellow practitioners. The conventional view of the world says that the ordinary people are totally different from sages and a person cannot be transformed into a holy person. Because he narrows his potentiality this way, he cannot keep the *dharani*. On the other hand, if a person falls into the other extreme of nihilism and thinks that in emptiness there is no law of causality, he also cannot keep the *dharani* because of his recklessness. When one realizes that the common man and the sage possess the same mind and there is not the slightest difference at all, one has left the conventional view. When one realizes that this one mind can be manifest as either ordinary or saintly, and that this is due to the clear working of the law of causality, one has then abandoned the nihilistic view. Leaving behind these two erroneous views and following the one mind in teaching the world, one can then chant the *dharani*. Like blowing on the bellows for wind or striking the flint for fire, the effect will be unfailingly efficacious.

Concluding Thoughts

In the above pages, two feminine forms of Kuan-yin have been discussed: the chaste and filial Miao-shan and the White-Robed Kuan-yin, giver of sons. The worshipers of Kuan-yin clearly cut across both gender and class lines in late imperial China. This is another example of the fact that conventional terms, such as *elite* and *popular* culture, are no longer very useful heuristic devices in analyzing the religious situation of that time.

Did the female Kuan-yin offer more options to Chinese women? It is often assumed that when a religion provides goddesses to worship, it can empower women. When Avalokiteśvara was transformed into Kuan-yin, the "Goddess of Mercy," new forms and expressions of religiosity became available to women and men in China. But as long as the traditional stereotypical views about women's pollution or inferiority remained unchallenged, the feminine images of Kuan-yin had to be either more or less than real women. They were not and could not be endowed with a real woman's characteristics. It is for this reason that the White-Robed Kuan-yin, though a fertility goddess, is devoid of sexuality. Like the Great Goddess in the Hindu tradition, she is "both a virgin and a mother" (Erndl 1993:144), a condition that no real woman can attain. Real women, in the meantime, together with their male countrymen, worshiped Kuan-yin as the "child-giving" Kuan-yin who saw to it that the family religion would never be disrupted by the lack of a male heir. Or, they would call upon her for help when they performed *ko-ku* and carried out this most fanatical ritual in the religion of filial piety. Chinese women, like Miao-shan, never really left the patriarchal home.

But, on further reflection, one may ask, what kind of home was it? Clearly, something close to a sea change occurred after the Sung in both Chinese religion and the Chinese family system. Patricia Ebrey has pointed out the increasing emphasis from the Southern Sung period and after on the lineage ideal, particularly on genealogies and generation markers (1986:32–39, 44–50). By the mid-Ming, around the fifteenth century, with fierce competitiveness in the examinations increasing, lineages became even more important, for they supported individuals to survive as successful degree candidates (ter Haar 1992:113). The desperate need to secure a male heir, the frantic effort to keep the head of the household alive, and the fanatical adherence to the ideal of chaste widowhood — all the disparate elements of a "domesticated religiosity" mentioned above — began to take on a new significance. The cult of Kuan-yin indeed served Confucian family values, and in this sense we can speak of a Confucianization of Buddhism. While it is true that because of the "diffused" character of Chinese religion, the family was never a completely secular institution, separated from the transcendent and devoid of religious status, it was still primarily Confucian in its orientations (Yang 1961:28–57, 294–340). In the end, the influence went both ways. As a common saying familiar to many Chinese goes, "Kuan-yin is enshrined in every household" (*chia-chia feng Kuan-yin*); it was ultimately a home where Kuan-yin was very much present. Kuan-yin had indeed found a home in China.

NOTES

1. The stele still stands in Hsiang-shan Monastery. The inscription was recarved in 1308 because the original one was damaged by erosion. The discovery of the stele, which had until 1991 been assumed by scholars to be lost, was described by Lai Swee-fo (Lai Jui-ho) in his article, "Wan-li hsün-pei chi" (Searching for a Stele in Ten Thousand Miles), published in *Chung-kuo shih-pao* (April 6, 7, 8, 1993). I owe this information to Professor Glen Dudbridge. I would also like to thank Dr. Lai for sharing his handwritten copy of the stele inscription with me.

2. This could be said to be the *ur*-myth of the Chinese Kuan-yin. All other legends of feminine incarnations of Kuan-yin involve elements of this myth. The general outline I summarize here is familiar to many women in China today. I interviewed women pilgrims in Hangchow, P'u-t'o, Yünnan, and Taiwan in 1987. When I asked them about Miao-shan, they told me stories about her that contained most, if not all, of the key elements from this outline. The story of Miao-shan that I learned at the age of five from my maternal grandmother corresponded faithfully to this summary.

3. I have not been able to find explicit statements to this effect in writings by women in the Ming-Ch'ing period. However, I often encountered similar sentiments expressed by women pilgrims I met in Chekiang. These village women sing songs glorifying Kuan-yin, which are called "Kuan-yin Sutra." They express their admiration for Kuan-yin/Miao-shan's independence and courage in refusing marriage. They envy her independence and freedom. One goes like this:

There is a truly chaste woman in the household of King Miao-chuang.
First, she does not have to bear the ill humor of her parents-in-law.
Second, she does not have to eat the rice of her husband.
Third, she does not have to carry a child in her womb or in her arms.

4. Yuet Keung Lo of the University of Minnesota is finishing an annotated translation and study of this work. I am grateful to him for showing me his draft manuscript.

5. Ter Haar notes the prevalence of affiliation names of women with the character *miao*: "The obvious precedent was of course the name of Guanyin (Miaoshan), in the legend of the female Guanyin with the thousand arms and eyes, where *miao* seems to function in the same way in her name and in the names of her two sisters (Miaoyan and Miaoyin). The popularity of Guanyin, as she appears in the Miaoshan legend, among women in general, and female members of religious groups in particular, has been noted before. One suspects some kind of connection between the change from the original male into a female Guanyin, the spread of the use of *miao* as an affiliation character and the popularity of lay Buddhism among women" (1992:40–41). It is indeed intriguing that the female lay Buddhists shared the same character in their religious names as the heroine of the Miao-shan legend. The monk who inspired the lay Buddhist movement and instituted the use of affiliation characters was Mao Tzu-yüan (circa 1086/8–1166). He was thus active during the first decades of the Southern Sung, the same time period when the written form of the Miao-shan legend started to spread from Honan to Hangchow. The choice of Miao-shan as the heroine's name might not be accidental, but reflected a current practice among

pious lay women of the time. On the other hand, as the legend became increasingly popular, more women might want to use not only the character *miao* but also the name *Miao-shan* (as indeed was the case, as evidenced by contemporary epigraphical records), just as many girls in Catholic countries would be named Mary or Maria.

6. One index of the enthusiasm surrounding female chastity is the overwhelming proportion of the section devoted to "female chastity" (*kuei-chieh*) in the *Ku-chin t'u-shu chi-ch'eng* (Synthesis of Books and Illustrations of Ancient and Modern Times), which covers 206 *chüan*. There are 8 *chüan* devoted to "female filiality" (*kuei-hsiao*). They contain short biographical accounts of women in pre–Sung time who did this; 14 out of 51 (about one-quarter of) women in the Sung, 306 out of 632 Ming women (about half) and 226 out of 340 Ch'ing women (two-thirds) did it.

7. Chen Te-hsiu promoted filial piety among the people of Chuang-chou when he became the prefect there in 1217 and asked for names of filial children. Among those reported to him, Huang Chang, a commoner, saved his mother by offering his liver; another commoner, Liu Hsiang, saved his father by doing the same, and Liu Tsung-ch'iang, a low-level government official, cured his mother by offering flesh sliced from his thigh. Chen Te-hsiu commented that, although such acts were not recommended by holy scriptures, they nevertheless deserved commendation because they issued from real sincerity of filial hearts (*Hsi-shan hsien-sheng Chen Wen-chung kung wen-chi*:40). In 1219 he wrote an inscription for an arch memorializing the filial behavior of an eighteen-year-old girl named Lü Liang-tzu. When her father became hopelessly ill, she prayed to her ancestors and asked them to take her instead because her father, being addicted to books, would be of little use to them in the other world. She then sliced flesh from her thigh and cooked a gruel with it. The father, after imbibing it, soon recovered (*Wen-chi*:24). Chu Ron-Guey, who wrote a dissertation on Chen Te-hsiu, told me that he had come across similar cases of Chen's great admiration of *ko-ku*.

8. *Ko-ku* and medical use of human flesh are treated in J. J. M. de Groot, *The Religious System of China*; the focus of Robert Des Rotours' two articles (1963, 1968) is cannibalism; T'ien Ju-k'ang discusses this in an appendix to his book, *Male Anxiety and Female Chastity* (1988:149–61); and finally, Kuwabara Jitsuzō wrote an article on this subject (1919) and another extended version of the same title later (1924; the section on the medical use of human flesh appears on pp. 51–59).

9. I am grateful to Professor Pei-yi Wu, who alerted me to a presentation of this article at the Columbia University Seminar on Traditional China.

10. For instance, in Chih-yüan third year (1266) and seventh year (1270), people were told not to cut pieces of liver or flesh from their thighs or gouge out their eyes (*Yüan-tien chang*, *chüan* 33). In Hung-wu twenty-seventh year (1394), not only were such actions discouraged, but those who engaged in them were not to receive any government commendation (*Li-pu chih-kao*, *chüan* 24).

11. This phrase is very ambiguous and difficult to understand. *Pai-yi* usually refers to the White-Robed Kuan-yin, but it may also refer to the color of the placenta (*t'ai-yi*). From the context, this phrase definitely describes the appearance of the baby. The baby should somehow emerge from the mother covered with something white, and this peculiarity would make him in the eyes of the faithful a gift from the White-Robed Kuan-yin. Medical literature has reported that in rare cases "the membranes remain intact until the time of delivery of the infant. If by chance the membranes remain intact until completion of

delivery, the fetus is born surrounded by them, and the portion covering his head is sometimes referred to as the caul." Jack A. Pritchard and Paul C. Macdonald, *Williams Obstetrics*, 16th ed. (New York: Appleton-Century-Crofts, 1986), p. 386. The caul appears whitish in color. I owe this information to Dr. Mary B. Jones of the University of Texas Health Sciences Center.

WORKS CITED

Bodde, Derk. 1961. "Myths of Ancient China." In Samuel N. Kramer, ed., *Mythologies of the Ancient World*, 367–508. Garden City: Doubleday.

Brown, Paula, and Donald Tuzin, eds. 1983. *The Ethnography of Cannibalism*. Washington, D.C.: Society for Psychological Anthropology.

Buswell, Robert E. 1989. *The Formation of Ch'an Ideology in China and Korea*. Princeton: Princeton University Press.

Buswell, Robert E., ed. 1990. *Chinese Buddhist Apocrypha*. Honolulu: University of Hawaii Press.

Chaves, Jonathan. 1986. "Moral Action in the Poetry of Wu Chia-chi (1618–84)." *Harvard Journal of Asiatic Studies* (December), 46(2):387–469.

Ch'en, Kenneth. 1964. *Buddhism in China, A Historical Survey*. Princeton: Princeton University Press.

Chou K'e-fu. 1980. *Kuan-shih-yin ching-chou ch'ih-yen chi* (Records of Miraculous Responses through Chanting Sutras and *Dharanis* of Kuan-yin), vol. 2. In Hui-men, ed., *Ssu-ta P'u-sa sheng-te ts'ung-shu* (Collections of the Saintly Virtues of the Four Great Bodhisattvas), vol. 1. Taiwan: Mi-le Ch'u-pan-she.

Dean, Kenneth. 1993. *Taoist Ritual and Popular Cults of Southeast China*. Princeton: Princeton University Press.

de Bary, Wm. Theodore. 1970. "Individualism and Humanitarianism in Late Ming Thought." In Wm. Theodore de Bary, ed., *Self and Society in Ming Thought*. New York: Columbia University Press.

De Groot, J. J. M. 1969. *The Religious System of China*, vol. 4, 357–406. Taipei: Ch'eng-wen, reprint.

Des Rotours, Robert. 1963. "Quelques notes sur l'anthropophagie en Chine." *T'oung Pao* 50(4–5):486–527.

———. 1968. "Encore quelques notes sur l'anthropophagie en Chine." *T'oung Pao* 54(1–3):1–49.

Dudbridge, Glen. 1978. *The Legend of Miao-shan*. Oxford Oriental Monographs, no. 1. London: Ithaca Press.

———. 1982. "Miao-shan on Stone." *Harvard Journal of Asiatic Studies* 42(2):589–614.

Ebine Toshio. 1986. "Chinese Avalokiteśvara Paintings of the Sung and Yüan Periods." In *The Art of Bodhisattva Avalokiteśvara — Its Cult-images and Narrative Portrayals — International Symposium on Art Historical Studies* 5:94–100. Department of the Science of Arts, Faculty of Letters, Osaka University.

Ebrey, Patricia. 1986. "The Early Stages in the Development of Descent Group Organization." In Patricia Buckley Ebrey and James Watson, eds., *Kinship Organization in Late Imperial China*, 16–61. Berkeley and Los Angeles: University of California Press.

Erndl, Kathleen M. 1993. *Victory to the Mother: The Hindu Goddess of Northwest India in Myth, Ritual, and Symbol.* New York and Oxford: Oxford University Press.

Hansen, Valerie. 1990. *Changing Gods in Medieval China, 1127–1276.* Princeton: Princeton University Press.

Hsiang-shan pao-chüan (Precious Volume of Hsiang-shan). 1866. Hsi-shan ta-wen-t'ang.

Hsi-shan hsien-sheng Chen Wen-chung kung wen-chi in *Chen Wen-chung kung ch'üan-chi* (Taipei: Wen-yu Bookstore, 1967 reprint), vol. 7, 3989–3995.

Hsin T'ang shu. Beijing: Chung-hua shu-chü, 1975.

Kapstein, Mathew. 1989. "The Purificatory Gem and Its Cleansing: A Late Tibetan Polemical Discussion of Apocryphal Texts." *History of Religions* (February), 28(3):217–44.

Kleeman, Terry. 1993. "Expansion of the Wenchang Cult." In Patricia Buckley Ebrey and Peter N. Gregory, eds., *Religion and Society in T'ang and Sung China.* Honolulu: University of Hawaii Press.

———. 1994. *A God's Own Tale: The Book of Transformations of the Divine Lord of Zitong.* Albany: State University of New York Press.

Ko, Dorothy. 1994. *Teachers of the Inner Chambers: Women and Culture in Seventeenth-Century China.* Stanford: Stanford University Press.

Kuan-shih-yin P'u-sa ling-kan lu (A Record of the Efficacious Responses from Kuan-yin Bodhisattva). Shanghai, 1923.

Kuan-yin chi-tu pen-yüan chen-ching (True Scripture of Kuan-yin's Original Vow). 1925 printed edition.

Kuan-yin shih-erh yüan-chüeh ch'üan-chuan (Complete Biographies of the Twelve Perfectly Enlightened Ones of Kuan-yin). 1938 edition.

Ku-chin t'u-shu chi-ch'eng (Synthesis of Books and Illustrations of Ancient and Modern Times). First published 1728; Shanghai, 1934 reprint.

Kuwabara Jitsuzō 1919. "Shina no shokujinniku fūshū' (The Custom of Eating Human Flesh in China). *Taiyō* (June), 25(7):121–24.

———. 1924. *Tōyō gakuhō* 14(1):1–61.

Li Shih-chen. *Pen-ts'ao kang-mu* (Classified Materia Medica). In *Kuo-hsüeh chi-pen ts'ung-shu ssu-pai chung* (Four Hundred Selections of Basic Books in Sinology). Taipei: Commercial Press, 1968, vol. 146.

Makita Tairyō, ed. 1970. *Rikuchō koitsu Kanzeon ōkenki no kenkyū* (Studies on the Ancient and Lost Records from the Six Dynasties of Kuan-shin-yin's Miraculous Responses). Kyoto: Hyōrakuji shoten.

———. 1976. *Gikyō kenkyū* (Studies on Apocryphal Sutras). Kyoto: Kyōto daigaku Jinbun kagaku kenkyūjo.

Matsumoto Eiichi 1937. *Tonkōga no kenkyū* (Studies on Paintings of Tun-huang Caves). 2 vols. Tokyo. Tōhō bunka gakuin Tōkyō kenkyūjo.

Scripture of the Lotus Blossom of the Fine Dharma. 1976. Trans. from the Chinese of Kumārajīva by Leon Hurvitz. New York: Columbia University Press.

Stein, Rolf A. 1986. "Avalokiteśvara/Kouan-yin, un exemple de transformation d'un dieu en déesse." *Cahiers d'Extreme-Asie* 2:17–77.

Strickmann, Michel. 1990. "The Consecration Sutra: A Buddhist Book of Spells." In Robert E. Buswell, Jr., ed., *Chinese Buddhist Apocrypha*, 75–118. Honolulu: University of Hawaii Press.

Sunday, Peggy Reeves. 1986. *Divine Hunger: Cannibalism as a Cultural System*. Cambridge: Cambridge University Press.

Ta-tsu shih-ke yen-chiu (Studies on Cliff Sculptures of Ta-tsu). 1985. Edited by Liu Chang-chiu, Hu Wen-ho and Li Yung-ch'iao. Chengdu: Sichuan Academy of Social Sciences Press.

ter Haar, Barend J. 1992. *The White Lotus Teachings in Chinese Religious History*. Leiden: E. J. Brill.

T'ien Ju-k'ang. 1988. *Male Anxiety and Female Chastity*. Leiden: E. J. Brill.

Waltner, Ann. 1987. "T'an-yang-tzu and Wang Shih-chen: Visionary and Bureaucrat in the Late Ming." *Late Imperial China* (June), 8(1):105–27.

Yang, C. K. 1961. *Religion in Chinese Society*. Berkeley and Los Angeles: University of California Press.

Yü, Chün-fang. 1990. "Feminine Images of Kuan-yin in Post-T'ang China." *Journal of Chinese Religions* (fall), 18:61–89.

———. 1992. "P'u-t'o Shan: Pilgrimage and the Creation of the Chinese Potalaka." In Susan Naquin and Chün-fang Yü, ed., *Pilgrims and Sacred Sites in China*, 190–245. Berkeley and Los Angeles: University of California Press.

———. 1993. "Pao-chüan wen-hsüeh chung ti Kuan-yin yü min-chien hsin-yang" (Kuan-yin and Popular Beliefs as Reflected in *Pao-chüan* Literature). In *Min-chien hsin-yang yü Chung-kuo wen-hua kuo-chi yen-t'ao-hui lun-wen chi* (Collected Papers of the International Symposium on Popular Beliefs and Chinese Culture), vol. 1, 336–40. Taipei: Center for Chinese Studies.

GLOSSARY

Chao Chih-feng   趙智風

Chen Te-hsiu   真德秀

Chen Wen-chung kung ch'üan-chi   真文忠公金集

Ch'en Tsang-ch'i   陳藏器

chi   紀

Chi-kung   濟公

Chi-ssu chen-ch'üan   祈嗣真詮

chia-chia feng Kuan-yin   家家奉觀音

Chiang Chih-ch'i   蔣之奇

Ch'ien-chü lu   潛居錄

Chih-yüan   至元

Chih-yüeh lu   指月錄

Ch'in Kuan　秦觀

chin-shih　進士

ch'ing　情

Chiu-k'u ching　救苦經

Chou K'e-fu　周克復

Chu-hung　袾宏

ch'uan-ch'i　傳奇

Chung-kuo shih-pao　中國時報

Ch'ü Ju-chi　瞿汝稷

Ebine Toshio　海老根敏郎

Fo-shuo Kuan-shih-yin san-mei ching　佛說觀世音三昧經

Gikyō kenkyū　疑經研究

Han Yü　韓愈

hou　吼

Hsiang-shan chi　香山記

Hsiang-shan pao-chüan　香山寶卷

Hsiao ching　孝經

Hsi-shan hsien-sheng Chen Wen-chung kung wen-chi　西山先生真文忠公文集

Hsin T'ang-shu　新唐書

Hu Wen-ho　胡文和

Hung-wu　洪武

i-tsang　一藏

Kao Wang Kuan-shih-yin ching　高王觀世音經

keng-hsien　更顯

ko-kan　割肝

ko-ku　割股

Ku-chin t'u-shu chi-ch'eng　古今圖書集成

Kuan-shih-yin ching-chou ch'ih-yen chi　觀世音經咒持驗記

Kuan-shih-yin P'u-sa ling-kan lu　觀世音菩薩靈感錄

Kuan-ti　關帝

Kuan-yin　觀音

Kuan-yin chi-tu pen-yüan chen-ching　觀音濟度本願真經

Kuan-yin shih-erh yüan-chüeh ch'üan-chuan　觀音十二圓覺全傳

kuei-chieh　閨節

kuei-hsiao 閨孝

Kuo-hsüeh chi-pen ts'ung-shu ssu-pai chung 國學基本叢書四百種

Kuwabara Jitsuzō 桑原隲藏

Lai Swee-fo (Lai Jui-ho) 賴瑞和

Li-pu chih kao 禮部志稿

Li Shih-chen 李時珍

Li Yung-ch'iao 李永翹

Liu Chang-chiu 劉長久

Makita Tairyō 牧田諦亮

Ma-tsu 媽祖

Mao Tzu-yüan 茅子元

Matsumoto Eiichi 松本榮一

Miao-chuang 妙莊

Miao-shan 妙善

Min-chien hsin-yang yü Chung-kuo wen-hua kuo-chi yen-t'ao-hui lun-wen chi
民間信仰與中國文化國際研討會論文集

Mu-tan t'ing 牡丹亭

Nan-hai Kuan-yin ch'üan-chuan 南海觀音全傳

Pai-yi 白衣

pai-yi ch'ung-pao 白衣重胞

Pai-yi Ta-pei wu-yin-hsin t'o-lo-ni ching 白衣大悲五印心陀羅尼經

pai-yi-tzu 白衣子

"*Pao-chüan wen-hsüeh chung ti Kuan-yin yü min-chien hsin-yang*" 寶卷文
學中的觀音與民間信仰

Pao-ting Shan 寶頂山

Pen-ts'ao kang-mu 本草岡目

P'eng Shao-sheng 彭紹升

"*P'u-men p'in*" 普門品

P'u-ming 普明

P'u-t'o 普陀

Rikuchō koitsu Kanzeon ōkenki no kenkyū 六朝古逸觀世音應驗記の研究

Shan nü-jen chuan 善女人傳

"*Shina no shokujinniku fūshū*" 支の食人肉風習

Ssu-ta P'u-sa sheng-te ts'ung-shu 四大菩薩聖德業書

Sui-hsin t'o-lo-ni 隨心陀羅尼

Sung shih　宋史

Sung-tzu　送子

Ta-fang-p'ien Fo pao-en ching　大方便佛報恩經

Ta-pei　大悲

Ta-pei P'u-sa chuan　大悲菩薩傳

ta-shih　大士

Ta-tsu shih-ke yen-chiu　大足石割研究

t'ai-tsang chieh　胎藏界

t'ai-yi　胎衣

Taiyō　太陽

T'an-yang-tzu　雲陽子

Te-ch'ing　德清

T'ien Ju-k'ang　田汝康

Tonkōga no kenkyū　敦煌畫の研究

Ts'ai Ching　蔡京

Ts'ao-mu shih-i　草木拾遺

Tu Li-niang　杜麗娘

Tung Ch'i-ch'ang　董其昌

"Wan-li hsün-pei chi"　萬里尋碑記

Wang Hsi-chüeh　王錫爵

Wang Ken　王艮

Wang Shih-chen　王世貞

Wen-ch'ang　文昌

Wen-chi　文集

Wu Chia-chi　吳嘉紀

Yeh Hsiao-luan　葉小鸞

Yü Chün-fang　于君方

Yüan Huang　袁黃

Yüan shih　元史

Yüan-tien chang　元典章

Chapter Six

TA-HUI'S INSTRUCTIONS TO TSENG K'AI: BUDDHIST "FREEDOM" IN THE NEO-CONFUCIAN CONTEXT

KOICHI SHINOHARA

The collection of Ta-hui's letters, *Ta-hui shu*, begins with a section on the exchanges between Ta-hui and Tseng K'ai.[1] The section is designated in the subheading provided by an editor as "[Ta-hui's] Answers to Vice Minister Tseng."[2] Tseng K'ai served as vice minister of rites; his biography is found in the official dynastic history, *Sung shih* (Sung History), *chüan* 382.[3] A passage on Tseng K'ai is found in the *Sung Yüan hsüeh-an* (Philosophical Records of Sung and Yüan Scholars), *chüan* 26 ("Chih-shan hsüeh-an"),[4] indicating that Tseng K'ai was also considered a scholar who was inspired by the emergent Neo-Confucian movement. The section on the exchanges between Ta-hui and Tseng K'ai in the *Ta-hui shu* begins with a letter from Tseng K'ai to Ta-hui, which is followed by Ta-hui's letters. It is my opinion that the edited text that appears in the Taishō collection and elsewhere marked as Ta-hui's first three independent letters is, in fact, one long letter in which Ta-hui comments in detail on Tseng K'ai's initial letter.[5]

Neither Tseng K'ai's initial letter nor Ta-hui's long response bears explicit dates, but the content of Ta-hui's letter enables us to date it as a letter he wrote while he was staying at the Yün-men an temple in Hai-hun (in Kiangsi province) and after he had begun his attack on the "Silent-illumination

Ch'an" in the fourth year of Shao-hsing period (1134) at the age of forty-six.[6] According to Araki Kengo, the letter was written when Ta-hui was forty-six years old.[7] For reasons presented below, I date Tseng K'ai's letter slightly later, in the fifth year of the Shao-hsing period (1135).

I would like to examine in some detail this first exchange between Tseng K'ai and Ta-hui in order to investigate the nature of the religious instruction that a Buddhist monk offered to an educated and high-ranking civil servant in the Sung dynasty. Tseng K'ai's initial letter illustrates how a man who held high official appointments and lived in the midst of political turmoil approached a monk, requesting instruction. Ta-hui's extensive comments on that letter in his reply contain many of the central themes in this influential monk's teaching. A distinctly Buddhist idea of "freedom" appears in his teaching.

Tseng K'ai's Letter

Since Tseng K'ai's letter is relatively short, and Ta-hui's response takes the form of a discussion of several points made in passing in this letter, I will translate the entire letter here:

I, Tseng K'ai, received a letter from my teacher Yüan-wu when I was in Ch'ang-sha. In this letter he praised you by saying that although you had come to him relatively late in your life, your attainments were indeed extraordinary. I have recalled this comment many times [thinking that I should come to you to receive instruction?], yet eight years have passed since then. Constantly I deplore the fact that I have not been able to receive instruction directly from you. I singlemindedly yearn for you.

As a young boy I entertained the aspiration for the Way, and I have studied under teachers, seeking instruction on "this matter." After undergoing the capping ceremony at the age of twenty, I have been busy with my family and official services; I have neglected spiritual cultivation and lived my life like this until the present moment. I have gotten old, and yet I have not learned anything worthwhile. I am always ashamed about this. The aspiration and vow to seek salvation are not matters that can be dealt with in the realm of shallow knowledge and understanding. If I were to give up seeking enlightenment, then there would be nothing more to do. But if I am to seek enlightenment, then I must directly reach the state that ancient men realized themselves. Only after I reach this state will I be able to consider that as the ground on which to stop finally and rest [*ta hsiu-hsieh chih ti*]. Though in my mind I have never even for a moment taken a step backward, I am aware that my spiritual cultivation has not yet been pure and concentrated [*ch'un-i*] at all. My condition may be described as "What I aspire to is great, but my capacity is small."

Formerly I earnestly entreated my teacher Yüan-wu, and he gave me a statement in six sections. At the beginning of this statement he pointed directly to "the matter," and then he presented Yün-men's *kung-an* story about Mount Sumeru and Chao-chou's *kung-an* statement "Drop it" [*fang-hsia-che*].[8] He told me to work on them steadily and to hold on to them constantly. He said that if I were to work in this way, I would eventually get to the point of entering enlightenment. He was so kind and thoughtful in his instruction, but I am so excessively dull and slow, and I have not been able to do very much. Luckily, my private family affairs have all been taken care of now, and I live quietly, having no other distracting concerns. Now is the time to whip myself hard and return to my original aspiration. I only regret the fact that I cannot receive your instruction face to face. I have described in detail all the failures of my life. You will surely be able to penetrate into this mind of mine and illuminate it; would you please kindly provide me with detailed instruction? How should I conduct spiritual cultivation in the middle of everyday life? My wish is to avoid being misled into wrong pathways and directly to become one with the original "true state." What I mentioned above includes many instances of failure. But I am here to present my condition sincerely; I should not hide things from you. Please take pity on me. Sincerely.[9]

The text of the statement that Yüan-wu is said to have given to Tseng K'ai is preserved in fascicle 1B of a collection of Yüan-wu's similar statements, *Fo-kuo K'e-ch'in ch'an-shih hsin-yao* (The Essential Teachings of Meditation Master Fo-kuo K'e-ch'in).[10]

Ta-hui's Answer

In response to Tseng K'ai's initial letter Ta-hui appears to have written a long letter, in which he commented on a number of points in Tseng K'ai's letter. I will here briefly summarize Ta-hui's response by focusing on the specific points in Tseng K'ai's letter on which Ta-hui commented:

(i) The first point on which Ta-hui comments extensively is Tseng K'ai's concern that he had neglected his spiritual cultivation because of his responsibilities to the government and to his family. Ta-hui first notes that educated civil servants cannot avoid these responsibilities and that it was not Tseng K'ai's fault that he had let these prevent him from making progress in his spiritual cultivation. This is a fault that even sages and worthies (*sheng hsien*) could not avoid.

Ta-hui then shifts the ground of his discussion and comments as follows:

> You should only know that everything in this world is empty illusion and not the ultimate reality. Turn your mind to "this teaching," wash away with the water of *prajna* wisdom the defilements you are covered with, settle down in cleanliness, incisively cut down deluded thoughts from their very base, and do not let them continue on in succeeding thoughts — this is all that is necessary. There is no need to think about and be bothered by the past and the future.[11]

The succeeding paragraphs elaborate on the two basic themes introduced in this statement: (a) the world that exists in the continuum of past, present, and future, and that is constituted by such things as official appointments, wealth, and human affections, as well as Heaven, Hell, defiling passions, ignorance, and karmic retribution is illusory; (b) if one perseveres in his cultivation, hoping to encounter a good teacher and hoping that the teacher will give him a statement that will enable him to overcome life and death suddenly and realize the supreme wisdom, then eventually he will experience such an awakening. Ta-hui explains this by describing the example of the story, taken from the *Hua-yen ching* (Flower Garland Sutra), of the youth Shan-ts'ai (Sudhana) who traveled everywhere, from teacher to teacher, seeking salvation, and who achieved awakening under Maitreya and Manjusri. At one point Ta-hui elaborates further on the idea that the world is illusory by saying that the disease of illusion is cured by the medicine of illusion. Once the disease is cured, the medicine is also removed, and the person who is cured is no different from the one before the cure.[12] There is no visible difference between the deluded and the awakened in the final analysis.

In this discussion Ta-hui establishes the ground of engagement between a man of the world, who is eagerly seeking spiritual instruction, and himself. Ultimately the only thing that matters is spiritual cultivation; the world that distracts and draws one into its entanglements — that persists through past, present, and future — is not real. It is not the context that affects one's spiritual cultivation directly. Ta-hui uses this basic position positively by instructing

Tseng K'ai not to be excessively troubled by the fact that he had neglected spiritual cultivation because of worldly responsibilities.

Ta-hui's well-known willingness to instruct lay followers may be a consequence of this line of reasoning. If one's past involvement in worldly affairs does not constitute an obstacle to one's spiritual endeavor, and the world of such involvement is only illusory, then it might not matter whether the particular student happens to be a monk or a layman. All that matters is determined and persistent cultivation, which is here taken out of the context of history and worldly engagements onto an entirely different plane. It might be helpful in this context, however, to remember that Ta-hui elsewhere also says that once one has achieved awakening, "he gains power over the paths of life and death, and if he on another day is to be placed in charge of the government, he will turn the ruler into a ruler superior to Yao and Shun as easily as pointing at something that is in his own palm."[13]

Although spiritual cultivation takes place on a different plane from worldly activities, its attainments can be turned to effective use in performing worldly duties.

(ii) Ta-hui warns Tseng K'ai that those who are intelligent "throw down and place in front of themselves the mind that objectifies, and thus cannot get to the crucial point that the ancients reached directly, cut all defilements in half with one strike of a sword, and immediately rest securely [*hsiu-hsieh*]."[14] By the expression "intelligent" people, Ta-hui probably means the secular intellectuals who served as civil servants. In the context of this discussion, Ta-hui refers to the *kung-an* stories such as Chao-chou's "Put it down" or Yün-men's "Mount Sumeru," which had been mentioned in Tseng K'ai's letter as *kung-an* assignments given to him by the teacher Yüan-wu. Ta-hui says "intelligent" people treat these stories as reified teachings (*shih-fa*: "real teaching"). What is contrasted here with the objectifying and reifying understanding is the phrase "one sentence" (*chü*): "Yen-t'ou Ch'üan-huo (828–887) had said 'To reject things is superior; to chase after things is inferior.' Yen-t'ou also said 'To speak broadly about the fundamental, we must know the [ultimate] one sentence.'"[15] Paraphrasing Yen-t'ou's long explanation, Ta-hui then describes this expression "one sentence" in a variety of ways, as "the time when one does not think any thought," "residing at the peak" (*chü-ting*), "able to stay firm"(*te-chu*), "clearly," "lucidly," and "such a time." All affirmations and negations are broken up with this "such a time"; so, if it is "such," then it is immediately not "such"; it is like a "pile of fire, which will burn one's hand if he touches it; it is entirely unapproachable."[16] After a passage in which Ta-hui gives the example of Lü Pen-chung (Lü Chü-jen, 1084–1145) as someone who suffers from the disease of intellectualizing, he elaborates on his points by giving a variety of quotations and references. One quotation from an "ancient worthy" reads:

"You cannot seek this matter with the mind that objectifies [yu hsin], nor with a mind that annihilates [wu hsin]; one cannot reach it with words, nor can one penetrate into it wth silence." This is an extremely kind explanation, which the teacher offered, getting himself covered with mud and drenched. Frequently, those who study Ch'an memorize such statements but fail to look into the principle expressed in them. If a worthy person hears them in passing, he immediately takes the treasure sword decorated with the king of diamonds, and incisively cuts apart the tangled paths of conflicting words. Then the paths of life and death are cut down, the spiritual and worldly paths are cut down, discriminating and calculating thought is cut down, the thoughts of gains and losses or of affirmations and negations are cut down. Where that man stands on his feet, there is absolutely nothing, and there is nothing to grab onto. Isn't this marvellous? Isn't this wonderful?[17]

Ordinary beings are caught in the flow of "conscious thought" (shih-ch'ing), which goes through life and death, and they experience fear and agitation. Students are all submerged in it and therefore are ignorant of their original appearance and original face. If we "drop it," "lose footing," and "step on its nose," this "conscious thought" is itself "the marvellous truth of true emptiness" (chen-k'ung miao-chih), and there is no other truth to obtain, and nothing else to realize. This "marvellous truth of true emptiness" is like empty space. Nothing in empty space obstructs the space itself, preventing it from pervading everywhere; the space does not obstruct anything from moving about within itself. The "marvellous truth of true emptiness" is exactly like this. It is entirely free from defilements that result from attachment to such dichotomies as life and death and worldly and holy. Although it is not attached, it moves freely in the midst of life and death and the worldly and the holy. Only if a person has reached this advanced stage, has he realized something of the teaching in Chao-chou's "drop it," and Yün-men's "Mount Sumeru."[18]

This discussion, presented in the section designated as Ta-hui's second letter in Araki's translation, centers on the topic of the kung-an of Chao-chou and Yün-men. It may thus be read as Ta-hui's comment on Tseng K'ai's reference to these two kung-an mentioned in the instruction that he received personally from Yüan-wu. Ta-hui appears to be saying something like the following: 'I am glad that you received these *kung-an* from Yüan-wu. But make sure you do not misunderstand the nature of Yüan-wu's instruction and mishandle these *kung-an*. The point of the these *kung-an* is . . .'"

Ta-hui's description of the "marvellous truth of true emptiness" may be read as a picture of absolute and radical "freedom," where one is free from all obstructions and at the same time does not obstruct anything. We should note here that this state is envisioned as a state that is attained after all entanglements and attachments have been cut down. Ta-hui's letter is filled with prohibitions. He is constantly exhorting Tseng K'ai and others not to do wrong things. Ta-hui's instruction is paradoxical, or "irrational," in a way that is familiar in Ch'an teachings: the ideal of absolute and radical freedom is taught in a manner that takes away virtually all conceivable forms of freedom.

(iii) In the passage commenting on the failings of those who intellectualize issues, Ta-hui criticizes the mistake of "placing the mind that seeks enlightenment and realization in front of oneself, thus creating an obstacle for oneself."[19] "If you set your mind up and wait for enlightenment, and if you set your mind up and wait for resting in peace, then even if you study until Maitreya is born in this world, you will not be enlightened and you will not rest in peace."[20] The expression "resting in peace" (*hsiu-hsieh:* "stop finally and rest") appears in Tseng K'ai's letter, in which it is used in a positive sense,[21] and Ta-hui also uses it in one passage in a similar sense.[22] But in the passage quoted above criticizing intellectualizing students, the expression appears to be differently nuanced.

The idea of "resting in peace" is turned into a major theme in Ta-hui's critique of the "Silent-illumination Ch'an" (*mo-chao Ch'an*) that is presented in the last major section of this letter:

> A kind of heterodox Buddhist teaching is around today. Although their spiritual eyes have not been opened, yet they busy themselves with teaching others to quiet their minds and rest in peace. Even if one thousand Buddhas appeared in this world, with such "resting in peace" one can never really rest in peace. Rather, the mind is led further and further astray.[23]

Ta-hui appears here to have taken a formulation in Tseng K'ai's letter and subjected it to critical examination in the light of the attack he had recently launched against the "Silent-illumination Ch'an." In the letter the theoretical basis for this criticism appears to be the fault of intellectualizing and reifying the mind. This argument is presented in the form of a quotation from Huang-po.[24]

A similar twisting of Tseng K'ai's comment may be detected in Ta-hui's remarks on "setting your mind up and waiting for enlightenment." In his letter Tseng K'ai mentions his teacher Yüan-wu's comment to the effect that "if I work in this way, I will eventually get to the point of entering enlightenment. He was so kind and thoughtful in his instruction." He also describes his situation in a manner that might indicate that he was "waiting for enlightenment": "Though in my mind I have never even for a moment taken a step backward, my spiritual cultivation has in the end not been pure and concentrated." Ta-hui also sometimes spoke in a similar fashion. Noting that when he sent his first letter to Ta-hui, Tseng K'ai burned incense for Buddhas and patriarchs and bowed down in the direction of Ta-hui's residence, Ta-hui says this is an expression of supreme sincerity, and that if Tseng K'ai practices spiritual cultivation in this manner, "he will undoubtedly fully realize the supreme wisdom in the future."[25]

In the passage in his letter on intellectualizing understanding, Ta-hui is nevertheless very explicit in condemning the attitude of waiting for enlightenment. Here he might have been commenting on a potential danger that he had detected in Tseng K'ai's letter.

After referring to the goal of "resting in peace," Tseng K'ai reflects on himself and notes: "I am aware that my spiritual cultivation [*kung-fu*] has not yet been pure and concentrated [*ch'un-i*] at all."[26] In the last section of his letter which, according to Araki, forms a part of Ta-hui's third letter, he turns to the issue of "purity and concentration of practice" (*kung-fu ch'un-i, pu ch'un-i*): "You should not concern yourself about the purity or impurity of your practice."[27] The reason for this prohibition is not stated explicitly, but the context of this letter suggests that Ta-hui might again have been thinking about reifying "practice" (or "cultivation").

If we follow the reading proposed here, Ta-hui responded to Tseng K'ai's initial letter requesting instruction by (a) noting that Tseng K'ai should not be overly concerned about his past failures (and, at least by implication, about his status as a lay follower); by (b) giving detailed comments on the proper way of studying the *kung-an* that his own teacher Yüan-wu had given to Tseng K'ai, emphasizing the danger of intellectualizing (and repeating his criticism of the then popular "Silent-illumination Ch'an" in this context); and by (c) encouraging Tseng K'ai that if he continued in the right way he would attain the supreme wisdom, though of course he should not reify enlightenment nor wait for it to arrive.

The Biographical Context of Tseng K'ai's Letter

The *Sung shih* biography of Tseng K'ai (*chüan* 382: 11769–71) states that he died at the age of seventy-one, but does not mention the date of his death, nor does it mention specific dates for many of the incidents in his life that are mentioned in the biography. Yet the broad chronological framework of his life can be reconstructed indirectly from the political context of the important events described in the biography.

The biography states that at the beginning of the Chien-yen period (1127–1130) he held the position of the military commissioner of T'an-chou region (Ch'ang-sha) and Hu nan, and in the following year he requested reassignment and was granted this request. If the expression "the beginning of the Chien-yen period" (*Chien-yen ch'u*) refers to the first year of that period (1127), the above letter, which is said to have been written eight years after Tseng K'ai received a letter in Ch'ang-sha from his teacher Yüan-wu, would have been written in the fifth year of the Shao-hsing period (1135). This happens to be the year after Ta-hui began his attack on the "Silent-illumination Ch'an."[28]

It is not clear what concrete circumstances Tseng K'ai had in mind when he said in his letter that he was no longer troubled by family affairs.[29] According to his *Sung shih* biography, after his assignment in Ch'ang-sha, Tseng K'ai held a few other appointments, and after the two years he spent in Ch'ao-yang (Kwangtung province) pacifying the area, he was given an appointment as supervisor of the Taoist temple T'ai-p'ing kuan (*t'i-chü T'ai-p'ing kuan*). Later, he was again given an appointment in the central government as secretarial drafter and played an active role in policy debates. The appointment as supervisor of the T'ai-p'ing kuan was largely an honorary one, and Tseng K'ai may have felt that he was free to pursue his spiritual cultivation without the hindrances of worldly affairs at this time.[30]

The pivotal historical event in the life of this generation of Chinese leaders was the loss of North China to the Tungusic Jurchen power (Chin) in the first year of the Ching-k'ang period (1126). This humiliating incident was followed by turbulent debates and conflict in the court of the Southern Sung between those who favored the realistic policy of concluding a peace treaty with the Chin (which was accomplished finally in the eleventh year of the Shao-hsing period [1141]) and those who advocated a militant policy of attempting to recapture the North. The grand councilor Ch'in Kuei favored the pacifist policy. According to his biography, Tseng K'ai, like others who had been inspired by founding figures in the Neo-Confucian movement, was an advocate of a militant policy toward the Chin and opposed Ch'in Kuei openly.[31]

Later, Junior Secretary of the Palace Secretariat Hu Ch'üan is said to have presented a sealed memorial to the throne that criticized Ch'in Kuei and praised Tseng K'ai.[32] The text of Hu Ch'üan's memorial is quoted extensively in his biography that is found in *chüan* 374 of the *Sung shih*.[33] Here the date of this memorial is given explicitly as the eighth year of the Shao-hsing period (1138). Hu Ch'üan was stripped of his position and was about to be exiled to Shao-chou region (Kwangsi province) for this conduct. It is said that many officials came to Hu Ch'üan's assistance.[34]

As a consequence of Hu Ch'üan's memorial praising Tseng K'ai, Tseng K'ai was also reassigned to the position of edict attendant of the Pao-wen ke and governor of Wu-chou region (Chekiang province). He argued forcefully against this punishment, and he was again reassigned as supervisor of the T'ai-p'ing kuan and governor of the Hui-chou region (Anhui province). In the end Tseng K'ai was excused from this assignment because of illness and is said to have lived as a private citizen for over ten years after this incident.

In the biography of Fo-hai Hui-yüan (1103–1176) of the Ling-yin ssu (temple) in the Lin-an superior prefecture in the fifteenth fascicle of the *Chia-t'ai p'u-teng lu* (Universal Lamp Record Compiled During the Chia-t'ai Period),[35] it is said that Chao Ling-chin[36] and Tseng K'ai visited Hui-yüan. Hui-yüan was also an important disciple of Yüan-wu and had inherited the latter's teaching.[37] A later source, called *Fo-fa chin-t'ang pien* (Defenders of the Castle of the Buddhist Teaching),[38] contains a section on Tseng K'ai and dates Tseng K'ai's visit to Hui-yüan as the *hsin-wei* year during the Shao-hsing period, which corresponds to the twenty-first year of that period (1151).[39] In a yet later source, *Chü-shih fen-teng lu* (Record of the Lamp Transmitted Among Laymen),[40] the entry on Tseng K'ai contains a longer account of his exchange with Hui-yüan, and Tseng K'ai is said to have declared that by that time he had been studying Ch'an for thirty years. Tseng K'ai's *Sung shih* biography notes that before his death he requested to be returned to a government position on account of his advanced age and was appointed to the relatively humble position of senior compiler of the Imperial Archives. It was only after Ch'in Kuei's death in the twenty-fifth year of the Shao-hsing period (1155) that Tseng was restored posthumously to the position of edict attendant. It appears that Tseng K'ai's visit to Hui-yüan took place shortly before Tseng's death, after he had spent many years out of government and in official disgrace.

Thirty years back from the twenty-first year of the Shao-hsing period (1151) would take us to the year 1121 (the third year of the Hsüan-ho period). By then many years had passed since he had passed the presented scholar (*chin-shih*) examination (sometime during the period 1102–1107); he had probably started receiving instruction from Yüan-wu K'e-chin. This information about Tseng K'ai's visit to Hui-yüan indicates that Tseng K'ai remained interested in Ch'an cultivation until the end of his life.[41]

If we follow the dating suggested above, the incident in the eighth year of the Shao-hsing period that led to Tseng K'ai's downfall would have occurred about three years after he presented his initial letter to Ta-hui in the fifth year of the same period. It is tempting to speculate that Tseng K'ai's spiritual cultivation under Ch'an master Yüan-wu and Ta-hui's letters to him might have served as a helpful preparation for his difficult career as a Confucian statesman in the turbulent years that followed. The exercise of political "freedom" in the face of anticipated difficulties, a well-attested Confucian tradition, might in the case of Tseng K'ai also have been supported by the spiritual "freedom" that he cultivated under Ch'an masters Yüan-wu and Ta-hui. As noted above in quoting a passage from Ta-hui's letters to Fu Chih-jung, Ta-hui himself spoke in broad terms about such a connection between spiritual cultivation and the task of ruling.

The nature of the available evidence suggests a connection between Tseng K'ai's Ch'an cultivation and his political career only as a theoretical possibility that might help to explain why many leading statesmen were attracted to the kind of Ch'an teaching that Ta-hui offered. Ta-hui's instructions to Tseng K'ai interest us as an example of a clearly recognized type of interaction between Ch'an and Neo-Confucianism. Tseng K'ai stood close to Neo-Confucian thinkers who actively practiced Ch'an. This engagement in Ch'an was an important episode in the early history of the Neo-Confucian movement. It is a testimony to the importance of this position that Chu Hsi (1130–1200) found it necessary to refute it carefully in his restatement of the Neo-Confucian position and, further, that despite his efforts, the relationship of Neo-Confucianism to Buddhism, or Ch'an, resurfaced repeatedly as an important issue in the long history of the Neo-Confucian movement. The remainder of this chapter places Ta-hui's instructions to Tseng K'ai within this larger context, first by investigating briefly Tseng K'ai's Neo-Confucian learning, and then by consulting Yanagida Seizan's perceptive discussion of Chu Hsi's relationship to Ta-hui. Yanagida's discussion delineates the significance of Chu Hsi's position in the context of Ch'an Buddhist intellectual history.

Tseng K'ai's Neo-Confucian Learning and His Profile as a Statesman

The *Sung shih* biography of Tseng K'ai notes that while he held an appointment in Li-yang, he studied with Yu Tso (1053–1123) and read the *Analects* every day: "When he could not understand a point by referring to the text, he referred to his mind, which always yielded the meaning; he was then overjoyed and forgot his meals."[42] Early in his career Tseng K'ai served the administrator of Ho-chou region. The date of this appointment is not given, but it is listed among Tseng K'ai's early appointments: he held these appointments after he passed the *chin-shih* examination sometime during the Ch'ung-ning period (1102–1106) and before Ch'in-tsung rose to the throne in 1126. Mount Li-yang was located in the Ho-chou district in Anhui province. According to Yu Tso's tomb inscription composed by Yang Shih (1053–1135), a fellow student under the Ch'eng brothers, Yu Tso settled in Li-yang and died on the twenty-third day of the fifth month of the fifth year of the Hsüan-ho period (1123) at the age of seventy-one.[43]

As noted earlier, Tseng K'ai sent his letter to Ta-hui around the fifth year of the Shao-hsing period (1135), and he had been told about Ta-hui by his teacher eight years prior to that, around the year 1127. Even if we assume that Tseng K'ai had been studying under Yüan-wu for some time by the time Yüan-wu mentioned Ta-hui's name, as indicated by the fact that he mentions the written instruction given by this teacher to him in that letter, it is probably safe to assume that Tseng K'ai's study under Yu Tso might have either preceded or been roughly contemporaneous with his study of Ch'an. His Ch'an studies, furthermore, continued long after Yu Tso's death. A brief examination of the biography of Yu Tso indicates that, in fact, Tseng K'ai's study under Yu Tso may have had something to do with Tseng K'ai's later involvement in Ch'an studies.

Yu Tso, whose biography is found in the *Sung shih, chüan* 428, was an important student of the Ch'eng brothers. Chu Hsi's collection of historical documents concerning the Ch'eng brothers' school, entitled *I-Lo yüan-yüan lu* (Record of the Origins of the School of the Two Ch'engs), contains a section on Yu Tso, and preserves the text of Yang Shih's tomb inscription mentioned above.[44] The scholarly community around Yu Tso is described in the twenty-sixth fascicle of the *Sung-Yüan hsüeh-an* (Philosophical Records of Sung and Yüan Scholars), and this chapter contains a passage devoted to Tseng K'ai as a student of Yu Tso. Kusumoto Bun'yū, who has studied the Ch'an background of early Neo-Confucian thinkers, notes that toward the end of his life Yu Tso appears to have studied under the Ch'an teacher K'ai-fu Tao-ning who died in 1113 at the age of sixty-one, six years after Ch'eng I (Ch'eng I-ch'uan) died.[45] Tao-ning was a fellow student of Yüan-wu under Fa-yen of Mount Wu-tsu (?–1104).[46] Furthermore, the section on Yu Tso in the *I-Lo yüan-yüan lu, chüan* 9, contains an exchange between Lü Pen-chung that took place during the Ta-kuan period (1107–1110);[47] answering Lü Pen-chung, Yu Tso states that he first studied under the Ch'eng brothers and then under many Ch'an masters.[48] Kusumoto speculates that this probably meant that Yu Tso was in contact with many contemporary Ch'an masters, including eminent disciples of Fa-yen such as Yüan-wu, Ch'ing-yüan, Hui-ch'in, and Ta-hui himself, who was thirty-five years old at the time of Yu Tso's death.[49]

This brief review of the involvement of Tseng K'ai's teacher Yu Tso in Ch'an studies shows that Yu Tso's own interest appears to have shifted from the Neo-Confucianism of the Ch'eng brothers to Ch'an around the time Tseng K'ai studied the *Analects* under him, and that it may well have been under Yu Tso's influence that Tseng K'ai also began his study of Ch'an under Yüan-wu. It is important in this context to keep in mind that Yu Tso and his students probably did not conceive of their Ch'an studies as something that implied rejecting Confucianism. In the exchange during the Ta-kuan period mentioned above, Lü Pen-chung once posed a question in a letter to Yu Tso saying,

> According to the Confucian way, we attain sagehood within the framework of the five basic human relationships [father and son, ruler and subject, husband and wife, older and younger brothers, and friends]; according to the Buddhist way, we attain sagehood only after we have rejected these relationships. Yet you first studied under the two Ch'eng brothers and then followed elders of the Ch'an teaching. [In your opinion,] there must be nothing that prevents one from moving freely from one to the other. Please explain the basis on which the two teachings can be distinguished.

Yu Tso answered this question by saying that Confucian scholars are ignorant about Buddhism and that one can discuss the similarities and differences only after he has studied Buddhism intimately. The implication here appears to be that superficial differences between Confucianism and Buddhism are misleading, and that the two teachings are ultimately more harmonious with each other than they appear.

Yu Tso was not unique among early Neo-Confucians in leaning toward Ch'an cultivation after Ch'eng I's death. In a recent article on Chu Hsi's essay on "miscellaneous teachings" (*Tsa-hsüeh pien*) Ichiki Tsuyuhiko noted that representative disciples of the Ch'eng brothers, such as Hsieh Liang-tso (1050–c. 1120), Yu Tso, Yang Shih, and Yin Ch'un (1071–1142), all developed their masters teaching in the direction of the learning of mind: in their thought the "subject" that investigates rather than the "principle" that is investigated through the world of objects is emphasized; the focus is on the experience of "penetration" (*kuan-t'ung*) rather than on the cumulative culti-vation (*chi-hsi*).[50] As the first- and second-generation disciples of the Ch'eng brothers developed the teaching of their teachers in the direction of the learning of mind, they moved closer to Ch'an Buddhist teaching.

It is important to keep in mind that the teaching of Ch'eng brothers first underwent this interpretation before it was reconstituted later by Chu Hsi. Among the second generation disciples were Chang Chiu-ch'eng (1092–1159), who studied under Yang Shih, and Lü Pen-chung (Lü Chü-jen), who associ-ated with Yang Shih, Yu Tso, and Yin Ch'un.[51] Both Chang and Lü had been profoundly affected by the tendency to interpret the teaching of the Ch'eng brothers with an emphasis on the subject and the mind, and this is one important context in terms of which their close relationship to Ta-hui needs to be interpreted. According to Ichiki, it was because of this widespread tendency that Chu Hsi, a fourth-generation disciple of the Ch'eng brothers, had to conduct a detailed critique of the views of such influential thinkers as Chang Chiu-ch'eng and Lü Pen-chung a few years before he finally estab-lished his own position (*ting-lun*) at the age of forty.

Kusumoto summarizes Yu Tso's teaching by focusing on his statement "In their study they [i.e., Ch'eng Hao's students] all realized the meaning of what they studied in their mind [*hsin tao tzu-te*], and did not seek it outside the mind." This statement appears in the biographical essay on Ch'eng Hao (Ch'eng Ming-tao) that Yu Tso composed to supplement the biography Ch'eng I had composed for his elder brother.[52] This emphasis on mind may be derived from Ch'an, and in Yu Tso's biographical material it echoes the answer that his teacher Tao-ning gave to him when Yu Tso asked for a summary teaching (*hsin-yao*): "The Way is not to be shown in speech. What-ever is shown in words is only an indirect means of instruction [*fang-pien*, i.e., "expedient means"]. You must look for the goal in yourself. If you look for outward expressions, you will end up not having anything to do with the Buddha [*fo yü ju pu hsiang-ssu yeh*]."[53] It may have been this emphasis on the mind that is reflected in the comment quoted above that Tseng K'ai studied the *Analects* under Yu Tso and that he learned to seek the meaning of its teaching in his mind.

It is important in reflecting on Tseng K'ai's Confucian learning to note that in his *Sung shih* biography he appears as a learned Confucian. He held such appointments as edict attendant, vice director of the Ministry of Justice and of the Ministry of Rites, auxiliary Hanlin academician, and senior compiler of the Imperial Archives; in all these cases Confucian learning must have been an important requirement. Furthermore, the biography admiringly quotes some of Tseng K'ai's statements with obvious Confucian content: "What Confucians struggle to obtain is righteousness." "Establish the government on the basis of the cultivation of virtue, be rigorous in defense, confront the enemy's lack of humanity [*jen*] with our humanity, their lack of righteousness with our righteousness, their arrogance with our caution" (p. 11770). The profile of Tseng K'ai depicted in the *Sung shih* biography is clearly that of a Confucian: "When he served at the court and ran into calamities, he confronted them squarely and could not be compromised."[54] It is important in reading biographies in dynastic histories to keep their biases in mind, and in the present case Tseng K'ai's profile as a Confucian might have been colored by the basic orientation of its source. Nevertheless, it would be a mistake to attribute this side of Tseng K'ai entirely to these biases. It would be more appropriate to assume that the two aspects of Tseng K'ai's life reviewed here, that of a student of Ch'an masters and that of an orthodox Confucian active in government, were held together more or less harmoniously throughout his life.

Concluding Comments: Yanagida Seizan on Ta-hui's Ch'an and Chu Hsi

In his magisterial essay exploring the Buddhist contexts of Chu Hsi's thinking, Yanagida Seizan showed that Ta-hui was the real opponent that Chu Hsi wrestled with in his critique of Buddhism.[55] Chu Hsi had an ambivalent attitude toward Ta-hui: he was strongly attracted to Ta-hui's powerful teaching,[56] and yet he also firmly rejected Ch'an, noting that it destroyed moral principles (*i-li*). This criticism appears to have been, in fact, directed against Ta-hui himself.[57]

Ta-hui's critique of the "Silent-illumination Ch'an" thematized the polarities of contemporary Ch'an. On the one hand, there was the understanding of Ch'an as "a training to get back to the world of the original nature where mind does not arise,"[58] or as an effort to seek the self before the world came into existence. Tan-hsia Tzu-ch'un (1064–1117) asked his disciple Chen-hsieh Ch'ing-liao (1089–1151), who later became the target of Ta-hui's critique of the "Silent-illumination Ch'an": "What is the self prior to the World Age of Destruction?"[59] This world of the original nature does not simply mean silence, since the wisdom that illuminates silently is at work there.[60] Yanagida shows that this understanding, in fact, represented the main line tradition of Ch'an, illustrated, for example, in Shen-hui's *Tun-wu wu-sheng pan-jo sung* (Verses on the Supreme Wisdom of Sudden Enlightenment); this idea of the "nature" is even found in Lin-chi (d. 866).[61]

Yet the criticism against the quietist tendency in Ch'an, that accuses it of reifying the negative state described by such terms as "no thought" or "no action," is also a part of the Ch'an tradition: Shen-hui's critique of the Northern school is a classic example, and Lin-chi's critique of the practice of "seeing the mind" and "seeing purity" (*k'an hsin, k'an ching*) is another.[62] Ta-hui saw that in practice the quest by the "Silent-illumination Ch'an" for the original "nature" ended up as an impossibility and resulted in an inconsistent flight from reality.[63] The effort to get back behind the phenomenal world of everyday life ended up by being nothing but an artificial activity, which was itself a part of everyday life. In addition, withdrawal from everyday life entailed the consequence that efforts at spiritual cultivation could not offer any positive guidance for living in this everyday life.

In answer to this dilemma, the Ch'an based on "past cases" (*k'an-hua* Ch'an), as advocated by Ta-hui, was a deliberate attempt to reproduce past and actual experiences of enlightenment. The record of past enlightenment was rewritten in a way that precluded superficial abstract rational understanding and explanation. What had been natural and spontaneous in the Ch'an of the T'ang period was deliberately reproduced through manipulation of past records as the foundational human experience.[64] Since truth was now understood to be found only in actual historical instances and nowhere else, the emphasis shifted radically from transcendental *li* ("principle") to historical *shih* ("event") or the "case" of the *kung-an*. Yanagida describes the logic of the *k'an-hua* Ch'an as follows:

> The word "*kung-an*" [*kōan*] was not originally a Ch'an term. It was a colloquial expression that meant legal precedents. It is a thoroughly historical concept, in the sense that it refers to facts that happen only once. It represents a viewpoint that values the concrete facts of the human mind and of human words. History does not repeat itself. The living events in history only happen once. Therefore, in order fully to understand the historical meaning of a particular precedent, an operation was required that would trace the record back to the historical point at which that event occurred.

Through such operations, infinitely numerous precedents, while being horizontally infinite in number, at the same time become vertically identical with the working of the one and only truth. If we borrow the concepts of substance [*t'i*] and function [*yung*], the substance is embodied deeply in historical occurrences, and this substance never loses function. The *kung-an* grasps the principle [*li*], which is understood as this unity of substance and function, in the form of specific facts/events [*shih*]. Once examples are chosen arbitrarily from the precedents, which are infinitely numerous, they become the one and only fact of reality. Once this is done, the example is no longer merely a precedent from the past. It is at the same time the newest fact itself. The fact of the *kung-an* and the fact of the existing self become one. The experience called "the great awakening that opens up suddenly" [*huo-jan ta-wu*] is nothing but this confirmation of self-existence. There is a precedent that would work in this way for each and every person. The *k'an-hua* Ch'an movement that began with Ta-hui was an attempt to discover such a precedent.[65]

Yanagida explains in this theoretical way the historical development that led Ta-hui to formulate his critique of the "Silent-illumination Ch'an." Behind the two opposing views lies the fundamental dilemma of Ch'an: the ultimate goal of Ch'an, difficult to realize in practice, splits into the two strategies of "Silent-illumination Ch'an" and "*k'an-hua* Ch'an" (or the Ch'an that relies on *kung-an*), each of which is accompanied by serious dangers.

Chu Hsi understood contemporary Sung Ch'an thought deeply and formulated his critique of Buddhism as a critique of two interrelated theses. On the one hand Ch'an falls into "the dualism of *t'i* and *yung*." Ch'an Buddhists think that "when the function of the six sense organs [*yung*] ceases, the original nature [*t'i*] appears spontaneously."[66] This is Chu Hsi's critique of the "Silent-illumination Ch'an." On the other hand, they advocate "the identity of function [*yung*] and nature [*hsing*]," and thus fail to cultivate the moral principles that govern the relationships between father and the son, ruler and the subject, husband and wife, young and old. Yet it is these principles that make human relationships different from those of animals. For, on the level of "function," of nourishing, for example, human relationships are no different from those of animals. The Buddhist thesis of the identity of function and the nature is, in fact, no different from Kao-tzu's view on human nature.[67] This is Chu Hsi's most pointed criticism of Ch'an, and the opponent here is the *k'an-hua* Ch'an of Ta-hui.

Yanagida observes that Ta-hui's "identification of function and the nature" in his *k'an-hua* Ch'an made it necessary for Chu Hsi to formulate a new critique of Ch'an. In one passage Chu Hsi explicitly named Chang Tzu-shao (Chang Chiu-ch'eng), a disciple of Ta-hui mentioned earlier, and commented on his well-known statement: "In serving your parent, only if you realize [*t'i-jen-ch'ü*] what you yourself are who serves the parent, do you understand what humanity [*jen*] is; in serving your elder brother, only if you realize what you yourself are who serves the brother, do you understand what rightness [*i*] is." As Chu puts it:

> In my view this would mean that in front you posit this mind [of Ch'an cultivation] as you serve the parent, and in the back you grope for this humanity; that in front you posit this mind as you serve your brother, and in the back you desperately grope for this rightness. The mind is here divided into two [namely, the mind of Ch'an cultivation and the Confucian mind in which Confucian moral virtues inhere]. Ch'an people are like this. They say, "You should chase yourself into a corner quickly. You must corner yourself to that point." So they raise their eyebrows, express anger in their eyes, raise the stick, and yell; they make you right away accept everything and believe. They call that the technique of Ch'an teaching (*Ch'an chi*). . . . I once asked my teacher Li [Li T'ung, 1093–1163] about Tzu-shao's teaching. I said, "'In serving your parent, you must realize [*t'i-jen*] what humanity is in yourself; in serving your brother you must realize what rightness is in yourself'—this would mean that the service to your parent and brother is not the important thing, but rather that you are only using it as a means for realizing humanity and rightness." Teacher Li said, "This is not an easy point to understand. You see the matter very clearly."[68]

Yanagida notes that a new and more fundamental critique of Buddhism became necessary after Ta-hui, because his identification of function with nature reduced humanity and rightness to abstract entities.[69] If it is assumed that humanity and rightness can only be attained through Ch'an teaching, humanity and rightness become a secondary matter.[70]

Yanagida ends his discussion by suggesting that the common ground that connected Ch'an and Sung Neo-Confucianism might have been their shared character as reflections on the ordinary life (Jap. *heijō*; Ch. *p'ing-ch'ang*).[71] Chu Hsi's teaching on practice was based on a critique of Ch'an. He had penetrated deeply into its logic and learned from it critically. Yet Yanagida notes towards the end of this perceptive discussion that Ta-hui's *k'an-hua* teaching, or the "public case" of "nonbeing" (*wu*) "remained beyond Chu Hsi's control."[72] Chu Hsi taught the "principle" (*li*), but that "principle" was only posited in the *a priori* and metaphysical realm and was nothing more than an hypothesis in the real world of experience. The a priori entity cannot be grasped directly in experience. What Chu Hsi did was simply to posit an a priori realm of rationality (*li*) outside the realm of experience. The irrational reality of the life of experience was simply ignored by Chu Hsi. This irrational reality is what Ta-hui's Ch'an was all about. Chu Hsi conducted a systematic critique of Buddhism, and by putting his finger on its ultimate bases, he critically absorbed virtually all its thinking. Yet, in the end one thing remained as a "strange heterodox teaching" (*ikyō*) that Chu Hsi could not absorb into his philosophical universe, and that was Ta-hui's *k'an-hua* Ch'an. Thus, Yanagida suggests that Chu Hsi's critique of Ta-hui is closely related to the most fundamental and essential aspects of Chu Hsi's learning.

Yanagida's discussion of the complex relationship between Ta-hui and Chu Hsi throws considerable light on our study of Tseng K'ai. Tseng K'ai's situation might have been something very similar to that of Chang Chiu-ch'eng, who was criticized by Chu Hsi.[73] As noted above, Chang's thought represented a widely shared tendency among the first and second generations of the Ch'eng brothers' disciples. This chapter attempts to explore the possibility that Tseng K'ai's courageous political stand (his "free discussion"), for which he paid heavily in his worldly career, may have been supported by his Ch'an cultivation. Ta-hui's instruction mapped the path of this cultivation as a combination of "prohibitions" that cut off easy options and the radical "freedom" to which one awakens as a consequence. Tseng K'ai's free and courageous stand, if inspired by this Ch'an vision, was nevertheless at least publicly presented and understood as an admirable example of Confucian statesmanship. To use Chang Chiu-ch'eng's formulation criticized by Chu Hsi, here we may have an example of a man who "realized" (*t'i-jen*) through Ch'an cultivation what he himself was who served the ruler, and then acted in an admirably Confucian manner in public life. The model of Ch'an cultivation and Confucian practice as conceived by Chang Chiu-ch'eng, and also by Ta-hui, though only as a secondary concern in the case of the latter, may have borne positive fruits in the case of Tseng K'ai.

Chu Hsi, as analyzed by Yanagida, was not prepared to accept this as a viable model. He would limit the radical "freedom" implied by those who saw the identity of substance and function in the "*kung-an*" teaching, and he rejected its "irrationalism" in favor of the grounding of morality in a theory of "principle" (*li*). Yet Chu Hsi had also learned a great deal from the opponent he thus rejected.

Chu Hsi was a profound thinker, and his objection to Ch'an derived from a perceptive theoretical reflection. At the same time his objection also bore a more thoroughgoing ideological character: he would not allow the "free" and "open-minded" combination of Ch'an and Confucian practices envisioned by such figures as Chang Chiu-ch'eng and Tseng K'ai. This side of Chu Hsi's position may have left a problematic legacy that would later evolve into the complex historical configurations of Neo-Confuciansim. In the introduction to his annotated translation of Ta-hui's letters, Araki Kengo points out that the formation of Sung Neo-Confucianism through Chu Hsi and Lu Hsiang-shan was mediated by Ta-hui's Ch'an; Ta-hui's Ch'an served as a catalyst that triggered the creativity of these Neo-Confucian thinkers. Thus, when Ta-hui was forgotten, their Neo-Confucianism also lost vitality. Araki believes that this fundamental relationship lies behind the advocacy in the Ming period of the thesis that if you want to know Confucianism you must study Buddhism.[74]

NOTES

1. The *Ta-hui shu* (Letters of Ta-hui) is reproduced in *chüan* 25–30 of the *Ta-hui P'u-chüeh ch'an-shih yü-lu* (Record of the Sayings of Meditation Master Ta-hui P'u-chüeh), *Taishō shinshū daizōkyō*, vol. 47, pp. 916b–942b. Araki Kengo published a superior annotated translation of this work titled *Daiesho* as vol. 17, *Zen no goroku* series (Tokyo: Chikuma shobō, 1969).

2. According to Araki, early printed editions of the *Ta-hui shu* are accompanied by two phrases, "Recorded by disciple Hui-jan" and "Secondarily edited by layman Ching-chih, Huang Wen-ch'ang." In an old edition, which appears to be a Korean reprint edition reproducing a Sung edition, there is a colophon that mentions the date of the eighth month of the second year of the Ch'ien-tao period (1166), indicating that the original Sung edition had appeared four years after the death of Ta-hui. Huang Wen-ch'ang's postscript states that toward the end of his life Ta-hui gave in to the request of his congregation and permitted records of his teaching to circulate widely. This suggests that a collection of Ta-hui's letters might have been published while Ta-hui was still alive, and that the existing collection called *Ta-hui shu* was a second edition compiled by Huang Wen-ch'ang who added new materials and edited the earlier collection. Araki, however, also notes that the same postscript by Huang Wen-ch'ang is also found at the end of the *Ta-hui fa-yü* (Ta-hui's Instructions on the Dharma), and the content of the postscript fits that of this work better. Thus, Huang Wen-ch'ang's postscript might have originally been written for the *Ta-hui fa-yü* and not the *Ta-hui shu*. This would mean that the material that was published during Ta-hui's

lifetime was not the collection of his letters. On the basis of this discussion Araki cautiously concludes only that the *Ta-hui shu* must have appeared more or less in the form we know today shortly after Ta-hui's death. Araki, ibid., 252.

3. This biography is found in *Sung shih* (History of the Sung) (Beijing: Chung-hua shu-chü, 1977), vol. 34, pp. 11769–71. All references to the *Sung shih* below will be based on the Chung-hua shu-chü edition.

4. *Sung Yüan hsüeh-an* (Taipei: Shih-chieh shu-chü, 1973), vol. 1, pp. 575–76. References from the *Sung Yüan hsüeh-an* below will be based on the Shih-chieh shu-chü edition.

5. According to Araki Kengo's annotated translation of the *Ta-hui shu* in the *Zen no goroku* series, the section on Ta-hui's answer contains six letters. The *Taishō shinshū daizōkyō* edition of the *Ta-hui shu*, which is given as a part of the Recorded Sayings of Ta-hui (twenty-fifth to thirtieth fascicles), also contains the mark *yu*, breaking down Ta-hui's letters in this section into six items. These sections also appear to be treated as separate letters in Muchaku Dōchū's *Daiesho kōrōju* (15 fascicles), which Araki praises as a superior and scholarly traditional commentary on the *Ta-hui shu* (Araki, 3).

A careful examination of these letters, however, indicates that Ta-hui's reply in fact consisted of four letters: what Araki designates as the first, second, and third answers of Ta-hui to Tseng K'ai probably formed one long letter (or possibly large quotations from a very long letter). I show in some detail below that these three letters may be understood as commenting in detail on different parts of Tseng K'ai's initial letter. The following fact might also serve to corroborate my hypothesis. Four of Ta-hui's letters, designated by Araki as his first, fourth, fifth, and sixth letters, begin by indicating that Ta-hui had received a letter from Tseng K'ai; all these letters of Ta-hui are Ta-hui's "responses" (*ta*) to letters from Tseng K'ai. The two passages designated by Araki as the second and third letters, and marked in the same fashion in the *Taishō* edition ("*yu*" in 917b14 and 918a19) do not begin with a similar acknowledgment. Thus, there is no clear indication in the text itself that suggests indisputably that the so-called second and third letters were in fact independent documents.

6. In this letter Ta-hui refers to himself as "Yün-men" (Taishō, 917b11; 918b1, 4), indicating that he was staying at the Yün-men an at the time he composed this letter. The section of Ta-hui's letter designated as his third letter by Araki contains criticisms of the followers of the "silent illumination" (*wang-ch'ing mu-chao*, 918a24). According to Araki's summary of Ta-hui's life, Ta-hui, who had achieved the great awakening under Yüan-wu at the T'ien-ning temple in the northern capital, fled from the capital when it fell to Chin forces in the first year of Ching-k'ang (1126), and moved to the Yün-men an in the fourth year of the Chien-yen period (1130) when he was forty-two years old; in the fourth year of the Shao-hsing period (1134), he went to Yang-yü (Fukien province) and began his attack on the "Silent-illumination Ch'an"; he was staying at the Yün-men an when he received the news of the death of his teacher Yüan-wu on the sixteenth day of the fourth month in the sixth year of the Shao-hsing period (1136). In the seventh year of the Shao-hsing period (1137) he was placed in charge of the Neng-jen ch'an-yüan temple in Ching-shan at the Lin-an superior prefecture; he was forty-seven years old at that time (ibid., 248).

7. This is the date he gives for what he calls Ta-hui's first letter responding to Tseng K'ai (ibid., 12). Araki notes that in some cases the dates of the letters included in the *Ta-hui shu* can be determined precisely by consulting the *Ta-hui P'u-chüeh ch'an-shih nien-p'u*, com-

piled by Ta-hui's disciple Tsu-yung and first published in the tenth year of the Ch'un-hsi period (1183–84); in others, the rough date can be inferred from the content of the letter, but that in a few cases there is no clue for determining the date (p. 253). As noted above, the contents of the letter enable us to narrow the letter's date to the short period after the fourth year of the Shao-hsing period and the seventh year of the same period when he moved to Ching-shan.

8. The *kung-an* story about Yün-men Wen-yen's (864–949) answer "Mount Sumeru" is included as case 19 in the *Ts'ung-jung lu*, a collection of *kung-an* stories that Hung-chih Cheng-chüeh (1091–1157) compiled during the Shao-hsing period (1131–1162): "A monk asked Yün-men, 'When not even one thought arises, does fault still exist?' Yün-men answered, 'Mount Sumeru.' " (*Taishō shinshū daizōkyō*, 48: 239b4,5). By this answer Yün-men is said to have pointed to the state beyond the dualism of good and evil. The *kung-an* story about Chao-chou Ts'ung-shen's (778–897) answer "Drop it" is given as case 57 in the same collection: "Honorable Yen-yang [Yen-yang Shan-hsin, dates unknown, who inherited Ts'ung-shen's teaching] asked Chao-chou, 'What if I don't bring even one thing?' Chao-chou said, 'Drop it.' Yen-yang said, 'I am not bringing even one thing. What am I to drop?' Chao-chou said, 'Then carry it away.' " (*Taishō shinshū daizōkyō*, vol. 48, p. 263a24–27). The message here is said to be that Yen-yang needed to drop the very awareness that he was bringing not even one thing. These two *kung-an* are briefly explained in the *Zengaku daijiten* (Tokyo: Daishūkan shoten 1978), pp. 77cd and 555bc respectively.

9. *Taishō shinshū daizōkyō*, vol. 47, 916b12–c5. I relied heavily on Araki's annotated translation of the *Ta-hui P'u-chüeh ch'an-shih yü-lu*, vol. 17, Daiesho, in the *Zen no goroku* series. The translation of Tseng K'ai's letter is found on pp. 3–6.

10. *Hsü Tsang ching*, vol. 120, p. 372Aab. Though the content of the passage preserved here under the subheading "Given to the Edict Attendant Tseng" (*shih Tseng tai-chih*) corresponds largely to Tseng K'ai's description of Yüan-wu's statement, there are also some grounds to believe that what is preserved in the *Hsin-yao*, fascicle IB may not have been the entire statement. Araki Kengo mentions Muchaku Dōchū's commentary on this: Muchaku noted that the *Hsin-yao*, fascicle IB passage contained only four sections, while the letter describes the statement as consisting of six sections; Muchaku suspected that the two other sections had been lost (*Daie fukaku zenji sho, kan jō, kōrōju, kan* 1, no page number). There is another statement in fascicle IIB of the same work that bears the same heading as that in fascicle IB ("Given to the Edict Attendant Tseng"). The relationship between these statements remains obscure.

11. *Taishō*, vol. 47, 916c14–17; Araki, *Daiesho*, 6.

12. *Taishō*, 916c17–22; Araki, *Daiesho*, 7. I interpreted the expression "*ts'ung chiao-hsia ch'ü i-tao liang-tuan*" to mean "cut [deluded thought] down from the very base or root." Araki translates the phrase more literally as "cut [deluded thought] down incisively from the base of one's own feet." I found Araki's translation somewhat obscure and attempted to read the passage taking the word *foot* (*chiao*) to mean the root or base of deluded thoughts. To cut something down from its roots is an expression that is frequently used in Buddhist texts, particularly with reference to eradicating completely evil thoughts or passions.

13. This sentence is found in the section on Ta-hui's answers to Fu Chih-jung, Minister in charge of the Bureau of Military Affairs ("Fu Shu-mi"), *Taishō*, 922a11–13; Araki, *Daiesho*, 55. I followed Araki in translating "*chih chang*" as "pointing at something that is in his own palm." The expression comes from *Analects*, 3:11. Although there is little doubt that the

expression illustrates something that can be easily done, its exact meaning is somewhat unclear. In D. C. Lao's translation the original *Analects* passage reads "(The Master said, 'whoever understands it [i.e., the theory of the *ti* sacrifice] will be able to manage the Empire) as easily as if he had it here,' pointing to his palm."

14. *Taishō*, 917b17; Araki, *Daiesho*, 13.

15. *Taishō*, 917b24, 25; Araki, *Daiesho*, 13. The two sentences that are given here in quotation marks are found in Yen-t'ou's sermon that is placed at the beginning of the larger collection of earlier masters' sayings that Ta-hui compiled under the title *Cheng-fa yen-tsang* (*Hsü Tsang ching*, vol. 118, pp. 2Ba9, 17, 18). Yen-t'ou's sermon continues and explains the "one sentence" in a variety of ways.

16. *Taishō*, 917b29; Araki, *Daiesho*, 13, 14.

17. *Taishō*, 917c13–22; Araki, *Daiesho*, 15–16.

18. *Taishō*, 918a1–18; Araki, *Daiesho*, 17.

19. *Taishō*, 917c8; Araki, *Daiesho*, 15, 16.

20. *Taishō*, 917c10–12; Araki, *Daiesho*, 15.

21. *Taishō*, 916b19; Araki, *Daiesho*, 4.

22. *Taishō*, 917b17; Araki, *Daiesho*, 13. It is translated above as "rest securely."

23. *Taishō*, 918a21–24; Araki, *Daiesho*, 19.

24. The passage is quoted from Huang-po's *Ch'uan-hsin fa-yao*, *Taishō shinshū daizōkyō*, vol. 48, 382c4–12; Iriya Yoshitaka, *Denshin hōyō*, *Enryōroku* (Tokyo: Chikuma shobō, 1969), 61 (63). The passage reads as follows:

As it has been transmitted from generation to generation, our Ch'an teaching has always rejected intellectualized understanding ("seeking knowledge and seeking understanding"). We speak only of "studying the Way," but even this is a provisional means for guiding [beginning students]. The Way cannot be "studied," either. If you deliberately try to study and understand it, you end up being lost in it. The Way has no direction and location — this is [the truth that is] called the mind of the Great Vehicle. This mind does not exist "inside," or "outside," or "in the middle." Truly it has no location. Under no circumstances should you engage in intellectualized understanding and speak from the perspective of ordinary thinking. Only if such ordinary thinking has ceased, does the mind become freed of location. This Way is the Original Truth and is inherently nameless. Only because people in this world fail to recognize this and remain lost in the ordinary world, Buddhas appeared in the world and taught the truth of this matter. They feared that you might not understand their teaching thoroughly, and so they provisionally used the name, the "Way." You must not cling to this name and give rise to intellectualized understanding.

25. *Taishō*, 917b10–13; Araki, *Daiesho*, 11. Ta-hui twice, 917b1,2 and 10, 11 (Araki, *Daiesho*, 10 and 11), gives this description of how Tseng K'ai sent his letter to him. Both descriptions are found in the last section of what Araki calls Ta-hui's first letter. In the first instance, Ta-hui says explicitly that he has been informed ("*ch'eng*," 917b1; Araki, *Daiesho*, 10). I take this to mean that someone other than Tseng K'ai, possibly the person who brought the letter from Tseng K'ai to Ta-hui, described to Ta-hui what Tseng K'ai did before entrusting the letter to him. It seems unlikely that Tseng K'ai himself would have informed Ta-hui of the things he is said to have done in sending the letter, although he might have performed the elaborate gesture, at least half expecting that the messenger might describe them to Ta-hui as a way of communicating Tseng K'ai's sentiments toward

Ta-hui. Ta-hui also talks about enlightenment as something that will come soon if one practices in the proper way in 916c29; Araki, *Daiesho*, 7.

26. *Taishō*, 916b20; Araki, *Daiesho*, 4.

27. *Taishō*, 918b26; Araki, *Daiesho*, 22.

28. This dating differs slightly from that of Araki Kengo mentioned above: Araki indicates that Ta-hui's first letter to Tseng K'ai, which was sent as a reply to this first letter from Tseng K'ai, was composed when Ta-hui was forty-six years old (ibid., 12). Ta-hui would have been forty-six years old in the fourth year of Shao-hsing (1134). As I noted above, a criticism of the Silent-illumination Ch'an appears in the last section of what I consider Ta-hui's first letter; this section is designated as Ta-hui's third letter by Araki. The slightly later date proposed here for Ta-hui's first letter harmonizes better with my general hypothesis that the first three sections of the part in the *Ta-hui shu* containing Ta-hui's answer to Tseng K'ai form one long letter. If we follow Araki's reading, the first letter was written in the fourth year of the Shao-hsing period in the year when Ta-hui began his critique of the Silent-illumination Ch'an; the third letter including a passage criticizing the Silent-illumination Ch'an would have been written slightly later. I believe that the long letter which included the critique of the Silent-illumination Ch'an was written in fifth year of the Shao-hsing period, i.e., the year after Ta-hui began his open attack on the Silent-illumination Ch'an.

Araki discusses Ta-hui's critique of the Silent-illumination Ch'an in pp. 256–259; his dating is based on the section on the fourth year of the Shao-hsing period in the *Ta-hui P'u-chüeh ch'an-shih nien-p'u*, *Shukusatsu daizōkyō*, teng 8, pp. 8–9.

29. 916b28; Araki, *Daiesho*, 4.

30. The honorary appointment as supervisor of Taoist temples is discussed in the "Taoist temple" (*kung-kuan*) section of the *Sung shih*, chüan 170, pp. 4080–4084. The "T'ai-p'ing kuan in Chiang-chou" is mentioned in that context, ibid., 4081.

31. Miyazaki Ichisada mentions the example of Yang Shih's school, in which the *Spring and Autumn Annals* was studied, and Sinocentric and anti-barbarian sentiments prevailed. Yang Shih was an influential student of the Ch'eng brothers and was also known as someone who had Buddhistic tendencies. Miyazaki Ichisada, ed., *Sekai no rekishi 6* (Tokyo: Chuōkōron-sha, 1975), vol. 6, p. 269. For a recent study of Yang Shih, see Araki Kengo, "Yō Kizan shōron," *Tetsugaku nenpō* (1981), 40:1–21. This article is also found in Araki Kengo, *Chūgoku shisōshi no shosō* (Fukuoka: Chūgoku shoten, 1989), 1–25.

32. A passage on Hu Ch'üan appears in the thirty-fourth fascicle of the *Sung Yüan hsüeh-an* ("Wu-i hsüeh-an," which lists those who were influenced by Hu An-kuo; the Hu Ch'üan passage is found on p. 680). Tseng K'ai's name is also mentioned in this section, suggesting that Hu Ch'üan and Tseng K'ai were close to each other.

33. See *Sung shih*, pp. 11580–82. The reference to Tseng K'ai's opposition to Ch'in Kuei is mentioned explicitly in this memorial, p. 11582, line 2.

34. Tseng K'ai's conflict with Ch'in Kuei is also mentioned in the biography of Tseng's younger brother Chi in the *Sung shih*, which immediately precedes that of Tseng K'ai in fascicle 382. As a result of this conflict Tseng Chi also lost his appointment (p. 11767).

35. This work was compiled by Lei-an Cheng-shou (1146–1208); the work was begun in 1185 and ended in 1201.

36. His biography is found in the *Sung shih*, chüan 244, pp. 8683–85. Morohashi notes (*Dai Kan-Wa jiten*, vol. 10, p. 882b) that an entry on him is also found in the *Sung shih hsin-*

pien, chüan 63, and the *Nan-Sung shih, chüan* 18, but I have not been able to check this information. There is also an entry on him in the nineteenth fascicle of the *Wu-teng hui-yüan,* p. 385.

37. The *Zengaku daijiten* mentions Hui-yüan's recorded sayings, called *Fo-hai Hui-yüan ch'an-shih kuang-lu,* but I have not been able to locate this work; the text of the *stupa* inscription for Hui-yüan composed by Chou Pi-ta is found in the *Yün-lin ssu chih, ch.* 5. Chou Pi-ta's biography is found in the *Sung shih, chüan* 391, pp. 11965–72, and in this biography Chou Pi-ta is said to have died in the fourth year of the Ch'ing-yüan period (1198) at the age of seventy-nine. See also *Fo-tsu li-tai t'ung-tsai, chüan* 20 (692bc); *Shih-shih chi-ku lüeh, chüan* 4 (894abc).

38. This work was completed in the nineteenth year of the Hung-wu period (1386) according to Ch'ing-chün's preface, *Hsü Tsang ching,* vol. 148, p. 482Aa5.

39. This work is accompanied by a preface by the compiler Chu Shih-en dated the *hsin-wei* year of the Ch'ung-chen era i.e., the fourth year of that period (1631), *Hsü Tsang ching,* vol. 147, p. 428B.

40. Tseng K'ai's name is miswritten here as Hui K'ai.

41. Araki Kengo notes that he achieved the great awakening under Hui-yüan of the Ling-yin ssu temple (*Daiesho,* 5). This information may have been based on Muchaku Dōchū's comment on the 11th sheet of the *Kōrōju, kan* 1, section 1, where Tseng K'ai is said to have inherited the teaching (*ssu-fa;* Jap. *shihō*) from Ch'an Master Hui-yüan (J. Eon) of the Fo-hai hsia-t'ang (J. Bukkai katsudō) hall of the Ling-yin temple. Araki states elsewhere that he benefited greatly from Muchaku's commentary (ibid., 3). The source from which Muchaku obtained this information is not mentioned in his commentary.

42. This same passage is reproduced in the *Sung Yüan hsüeh-an* passage on Tseng K'ai, p. 575. Yu Tso wrote a commentary on the *Analects,* called *Lun-yü tsa-chieh,* in one fascicle, and this work has been preserved in his collected works (*Yu Ting-fu hsien-sheng chi*). Passages from Yu Tso's commentary are also included in the *Lun-yü ching-i,* Chu Hsi's compilation of early Neo-Confucian commentaries on the *Analects,* and Chu Hsi's critical comments on these passages are found in his *Lun-yü huo-wen.* An examination of Yu Tso's commentary should enable us to reconstruct how Tseng K'ai studied the *Analects* under Yu Tso: what was meant by the comment that Tseng K'ai looked for the understanding of the *Analects* in the mind? Yu Tso's commentary on the *Analects* is mentioned in Yang Shih's inscription, p. 379, and the *Sung Yüan hsüeh-yüan,* 574. I have not had the opportunity to examine this work at this time, and hope to return to this subject at some later date in connection with a group project on Chu Hsi's commentaries on the *Analects* that I have been organizing for some years within the framework of the Chinese Commentaries Workshop at the Canadian Society for the Study of Religion.

43. The text of the inscription composed by Yang Shih is preserved in Chu Hsi's *I-Lo yüan-yüan lu, chüan* 9 (*Chu-tzu i-shu,* p. 379). This information concerning Yu Tso's residence in Li-yang is also repeated in the *Sung Yüan hsüeh-an, chüan* 26, p. 574.

44. This work in fourteen fascicles is preserved in a collection of Chu Hsi's writings called *Chu Tzu i-shu.* In a recently reproduced photo-offset edition published by the Chūbun shuppansha (Kyoto, 1976), the work is found on pp. 333–405. The section on Yu Tso is found on pp. 379–80.

45. Kusumoto Bun'yū, *Sōdai Jugaku no Zen shisō kenkyū* (Studies on Ch'an/Zen Thought in Neo-Confucian Learning During the Sung) (Nagoya: Nisshindō, 1980), pp. 317–20.

46. The collected records of Tao-ning's sayings, entitled *K'ai-fu Ning ch'an-shih yü-lu* (Recorded Sayings of Ch'an Master Ning of the K'ai-fu Temple), in two fascicles, is found in the *Hsü Tsang ching*, vol. 120, pp. 225–41. Sections on him are found in the *Lien-teng hui-yao* (The Synthetic Summation of the Lamp Lineage), *chüan* 16 (vol. 136, pp. 347Bb13–348Aa18); *Wu-teng hui-yüan* (The Five Lamp Records Synthesized), *chüan* 19 (vol. 138, pp. 373Ab11–Bb6).

47. This date indicates that the exchange of letters between Yu Tso and Lü Pen-chung took place shortly after Ch'eng I's death.

48. *Chu Tzu i-shu*, 380. The source for this statement is given as the *Lü-shih tsa-lu* in the *I-Lo yüan-yüan lu*; the same passage is found in the *Ts'ung-shu chi-ch'eng* edition of the *Tung-lai Lü Tzu-wei shih-yu tsa-chih* compiled by Lü Pen-chung, p. 6. This edition in the *Ts'ung-shu chi-ch'eng* (Beijing: Shang-wu yin-shua-kuan, 1935–) is based on the *Shih-wan-chüan-lou ts'ung-shu* that was compiled by Lu Hsin-yüan during the Kuang-hsü period of the Ch'ing dynasty (1875–1908). Lü Pen-chung (Lü Chü-jen) appeared in Ta-hui's letter to Tseng K'ai, summarized above, as an example of an intellectualizing student of Ch'an. Ta-hui's letters to Lü Pen-chung and his younger brother Lung-li are preserved in the *Ta-hui shu*, *chüan* 2, pp. 930–933a (Araki, *Daiesho*, 127–44). Lü Pen-chung's name is given as that of Yu Tso's leading student in the twenty-sixth fascicle of the *Sung Yüan hsüeh-an*, devoted to Yu Tso's school, and the thirty-sixth fascicle of the *Sung Yüan hsüeh-an* is devoted to Lü Pen-chung and his disciples.

49. According to Araki, Ta-hui begun his study under Yüan-wu K'e-chin in the fourth month of the seventh year of the Hsüan-ho period (1125), and achieved the "great awakening" less than a year after this. Ta-hui would have been thirty-six or thirty-seven years old at that time. Yüan-wu valued him highly and appointed him as the monastic secretary (*chi-shih*). Ta-hui's reputation grew rapidly, and later he received the imperial title "Fo-jih ta-shih" ("The Great Master Buddha's Sunlight"). This might mean that in the fifth year of the Hsüan-ho period (1123) when Yu Tso died, Ta-hui was staying at P'u-jung Tao-p'ing's temple in the capital city Pien-ching, waiting for Yüan-wu K'e-chin to come back to the capital. Ta-hui may not have had the kind of reputation at this time that might have motivated Yu Tso to contact him, as Kusumoto speculates.

50. Ichiki Tsuyuhiko, "Shushi no 'Zatsugakuben' to sono shūhen," *Sōdai no shakai to shūkyō* (Tokyo: Kyūko shoin, 1985), 7–10. The focus of Ichiki's discussion in this article is Chu Hsi's essay called "Tsa-hsüeh pien," *Chu wen-kung wen-chi*, *chüan* 72, pp. 16–46, in *Chu Tzu ta-ch'üan*, vol. 9 (Taipei: Chung-hua shu-chü, 1970, Ssu-pu pei-yao ed.). I would like to thank Mr. Tao Gang for calling my attention to this important article.

51. For recent study of Chang Chiu-ch'eng, see Araki Kengo, "Chō Kusei ni tsuite," *Chūgoku shisōshi no shosō*, 44–59.

52. The work was entitled "Shu hsing-chuang hou," and is preserved in the third fascicle of the *I-Lo yüan-yüan lu*, *Chu-tzu i-shu*, 343–44. The line appears in 344A4. Kusumoto's reference to this passage is found in ibid., 321.

53. *Fo-fa chin-t'ang pien*, *Hsü Tsang ching*, vol. 148, p. 478Ab4–6.

54. *Sung shih*, 11771. This phrase used in a passage summarizing Tseng K'ai's life at the end of his biography is a quotation from the *Analects*, 8:6. The phrase is translated by D. C. Lau as "without his being deflected from his purpose even in moments of crisis" (Confucius, *The Analects* [Harmondsworth: Penguin Classics, 1979], 93).

55. Yanagida Seizan, "Bukkyō to Shushi no shūhen," *Zen bunka kenkyūjo kiyō* (1976), 8:1–30. The point is made, for example, on p. 18. Chu Hsi's relationship with Ta-hui is discussed from a different point of view in Wing-tsit Chan, *Chu Hsi: New Studies* (Honolulu: University of Hawaii Press, 1989), 509–15.

56. Yanagida, "Bukkyō to Shushi," 3–4, 7.

57. Ibid., 5, 6.

58. Ibid., 13.

59. Ibid., 11.

60. Ibid., 13. Ta-hui's critique of "silent illumination" is discussed in some detail in Carl Bielefeldt, *Dōgen's Manual of Zen Meditation* (Berkeley and Los Angeles: University of California Press, 1988), 99–104.

61. Yanagida, "Bukkyō to Shushi," 12–13.

62. Ibid., 15.

63. Ibid., 14.

64. Ibid., 18.

65. Ibid., 11.

66. Ibid., 20.

67. Ibid., 24, 25.

68. Ibid., 25–26. The original passage is found in the *Chu Tzu yü-lei* (Taipei: Cheng-chung shu-chü ed., 1962), 1498–99. I found parts of this important passage somewhat obscure, even in Yanagida's translation. The comments included in square brackets are mine.

69. Yanagida, "Bukkyō to Shushi," p. 26 top, line 14: *"jingi o chūshō suru."* I took this expression to mean that with the intrusion of Ch'an into Confucian cultivation, as in the case of Chang Tzu-shao, "humanity" and "rightness" become abstract entities, cut off from the real cultivation of the mind in everyday life; "humanity" and "rightness" are no longer directly and fully present in everyday life.

70. Ibid., 26.

71. Ibid., 26.

72. Ibid., 28–29.

73. I quoted above a short passage from the *Chu Tzu yü-lei*, where Chu Hsi refers to his exchange with his teacher Li T'ung concerning the fundamental flaw of Chang Chiu-ch'eng's teaching as they saw it. Recently Ichiki Tsuyuhiko discussed Chu Hsi's critique of Chang Chiu-ch'eng in considerable detail in the above mentioned article, entitled "Shushi no 'Zatsugakuben' to sono shūhen," 16–31.

74. Araki, *Daiesho*, 2.

GLOSSARY

Araki Kengo 荒木見悟

"Bukkyō to Shushi no shūhen" 仏教と朱子の周邊

Ch'an chi 禪機

Chang Chiu-ch'eng (Tzu-shao)　張九成(子韶)

Chang Tzu-shao, see Chang Chiu-ch'eng

Chao Ling-chin　趙令衿

Chao-chou　趙州

Chao-chou Ts'ung-shen　趙州從諗

Ch'ao-yang　潮陽

Chen-hsieh Ch'ing-liao　真歇清了

chen-k'ung miao-chih　真空妙智

Cheng-fa yen-tsang　正法眼藏

ch'eng　承

Ch'eng　程

Ch'eng Hao (Ming-tao)　程顥(明道)

Ch'eng I (I-ch'uan)　程頤(伊川)

Ch'eng I-ch'uan, see Ch'eng I

Ch'eng Ming-tao, see Ch'eng Hao

Chi, see Tseng Chi

chi-hsi　積習

chi-shih　記室

Chia-t'ai p'u-teng lu　嘉泰普燈錄

chiao　腳

Chien-yen　建炎

Chien-yen ch'u　建炎初

Ch'ien-tao　乾道

chih-chang　指掌

Chih-shan hsüeh-an　鷹山學案

Chin　金

chin-shih　進士

Ch'in Kuei　秦檜

Ch'in-tsung　欽宗

Ching-chih　淨智

Ching-k'ang　靖康

Ching-shan　徑山

Ch'ing　清

Ch'ing-yüan　清遠

Hai-hun　海昏

Ho-chou　和州

Hsieh Liang-tso　謝良佐

hsin tao tzu-te　心到自得

hsin-wei　辛未

hsin-yao　心要

hsing　性

hsiu-hsieh　休歇

Hsü Tsang ching　續藏經

Hsüan-ho　宣和

Hu An-kuo　胡安國

Hu Ch'üan　胡銓

Hua-yen ching　華嚴經

Huang-po　黃蘗

Huang Wen-ch'ang　黃文昌

Hui-ch'in Hui-chou　慧懃徽州

Hui-jan　慧然

Hui K'ai　會開

Hung-chih Cheng-chüeh　宏智正覺

huo-jan ta-wu　豁然大悟

ikyō　異教

i-li　義理

I-Lo yüan-yüan lu　伊洛淵源錄

Ichiki Tsuyuhiko　市來津由彥

Iriya Yoshitaka　入谷義高

jen　仁

jingi o chūshō suru　仁義を抽象する

K'ai-fu Ning ch'an-shih yü-lu　開福寧禪師語錄

K'ai-fu Tao-ning　開福道寧

kan　卷

k'an-hsin, k'an-ching　看心，看淨

k'an-hua　看話

Kao-tzu　告子

kuan-t'ung　貫通

Kuang-hsü　光緒

kung-an　公案

kung-fu　工夫

kung-fu ch'un-i, pu ch'un-i　工夫純一，不純一

kung-kuan　宮觀

Kusumoto Bun'yū　久須本文雄

Lei-an Cheng-shou　雷庵正受

li　理

Li　李

Li T'ung　李侗

Li-yang　歷陽

Lien-teng hui-yao　聯燈會要

Lin-an　臨安

Lin-chi　臨濟

Ling-yin ssu　靈隱寺

Lu Hsiang-shan　陸象山

Lu Hsin-yüan　陸心源

Lun-yü ching-i　論語精義

Lun-yü huo-wen　論語或問

Lun-yü tsa-chieh　論語雜解

Lung-li see Lü Lung-li

Lu Chü-jen, see Lü Pen-chung

Lü Lung-li　呂隆禮

Lü Pen-chung (Chü-jen)　呂本中（居仁）

Lü-shih tsa-lu　呂氏雜錄

Miyazaki Ichisada　宮崎市定

Morohashi Tetsuji　諸橋轍次

mo-chao Ch'an　默照禪

Muchaku Dōchū　無著道忠

Nan-Sung shih　南宋史

Neng-jen ch'an-yüan　能仁禪院

Pao-wen ke　寶文閣

Pen-chung, see Lü Pen-chung

Pien-ching　汴京

p'ing-ch'ang (heijō) 平常

P'u-jung Tao-p'ing 普融道平

Sekai no rekishi 世界の歴史

Shan-ts'ai 善財

Shang-wu yin-shua-kuan 商務印刷館

Shao-chou 昭州

Shao-hsing 紹興

Shen-hui 神會

sheng hsien 聖賢

shih 事

shih Tseng tai-chih 示曾待制

shih-ch'ing 識情

shih-fa 實法

Shih-shih chi-ku lüeh 釋氏稽古略

Shih-wan-chüan-lou ts'ung-shu 十萬卷樓叢書

Shu hsing-chuang hou 書行狀後

Shukusatsu daizōkyō 縮刷大藏經

Shun 舜

Sōdai Jugaku no Zen shisō kenkyū 宋代儒學の禪思想研究

Sōdai no shakai to shūkyō 宗代の社會と宗教

ssu-fa 嗣法

Sung shih 宋史

Sung shih hsin-pien 宋史新編

Sung Yuan hsüeh-an 宋元學案

ta 答

ta hsiu-hsieh chih ti 大休歇之地

Ta-hui fa-yü 大慧法語

Ta-hui P'u-chüeh ch'an-shih nien-p'u 大慧普覺禪師年譜

Ta-hui P'u-chüeh ch'an-shih yü-lu 大慧普覺禪師語錄

Ta-hui shu 大慧書

Ta-kuan 大觀

Taishō shinshū daizōkyō 大正新修大藏經

T'an-chou 潭州

Tan-hsia Tzu-ch'un 丹霞子淳

te-chu 得住

t'eng 滕

Tetsugaku nenpō 哲學年報

t'i 體

t'i-chü T'ai-p'ing kuan 提舉太平觀

t'i-jen 體認

t'i-jen-ch'ü 體認取

T'ien-ning ssu 天寧寺

ting-lun 定論

Tsa-hsüeh pien 雜學辨

Tseng Chi 曾幾

Tseng K'ai 曾開

ts'ung chiao-hsia ch'ü i-tao liang-tuan 從腳下去一刀兩段

Ts'ung-jung lu 從容錄

Ts'ung-shu chi-ch'eng 叢書集成

Tun-wu wu-sheng pan-jo sung 頓悟無生般若頌

Tung-lai Lü Tzu-wei shih-yu tsa-chih 東萊呂紫微師友雜誌

Tzu-shao, see Chang Chiu-ch'eng

wang-ch'ing mu-chao 忘情默照

wu 無

Wu-chou 婺州

wu-hsin 無心

Wu-i hsüeh-an 武夷學案

Wu-teng hui-yüan 五燈會元

Wu-tsu 五祖

Yanagida Seizan 柳田聖山

Yang Shih 楊時

Yang-yü 洋嶼

Yao 堯

Yen-t'ou Ch'üan-huo 嚴頭全豁

Yen-yang Shan-hsin 嚴陽善信

Yin Ch'un 尹焞

"Yō Kizan shōron" 楊龜山小論

yu 又

yu hsin 有心

Yu Ting-fu hsien-sheng chi 游定夫先生集

Yu Tso 游酢

yung 用

Yüan-wu 圜悟

Yüan-wu K'e-chin 圜悟克勤

Yün-lin ssu chih 雲林寺志

Yün-men 雲門

Yün-men an 雲門庵

Yün-men Wen-yen 雲門文偃

Zen no goroku 禪の語錄

Zen bunka kenkyūjo kiyō 禪文化研究所紀要

Zengaku daijiten 禪學大辭典

Chapter Seven

WHEN THEY GO THEIR SEPARATE WAYS: THE COLLAPSE OF THE UNITARY VISION OF CHINESE RELIGION IN THE EARLY CH'ING

JUDITH A. BERLING

In eighteenth-century China, the unity of the Three Teachings, like sex, was not mentioned in polite society. It was not a major religious trend; the general cultural milieu simply did not support positive religious interaction. Yet this period was preceded by centuries in which such unity and interaction were both presupposed and invoked as a cultural cliché.

From at least the time of the Han dynasty, the Chinese had held a deep sense of cultural unity, sufficiently broad to embrace the recognized regional and linguistic differences in the vast Middle Kingdom. The reconciliation of various ancient cosmological traditions into one cosmology served to undergird and facilitate this unity. Various Chinese "religions" (Confucian, "Taoist," and local) were formed out of this common core.

The introduction of Buddhism was the first major challenge to this unity, and for a time Buddhism was attacked as a foreign religion. It was only through accommodation — conveying teachings in Taoist terminology, absorbing local deities, acceding to deep-rooted Confucian/cultural values, and blending with Chinese patterns of practice — that Buddhism succeeded in rooting itself in Chinese soil and was eventually claimed by the Chinese as one of the Three Teachings. Buddhist cosmology was never perfectly reconciled with native categories, but the remaining differences were not belabored and the Buddhists succeeded in melding into Chinese patterns of religious practice and behavior.

Thus although there were Three Teachings (Confucianism, Buddhism, and Taoism) — each with distinctive bodies of literature and lineages of teachers as well as a host of local cults — these various strands of Chinese religion were in a very real sense a single "religious economy." They drew from a common pool of myths, symbols, ideas, deities, and practices, borrowing liberally from one another. Moreover, major festivals and religious celebrations involved an entire community, regardless of patterns of affiliation or patronage. There was, to be sure, competition between teachers for disciples and temples for patronage, but the competition was carried on within the parameters of a "Chinese religious economy," and it was not unheard of for teachers or temples to cross "denominational" boundaries.

From the Sung (960–1279) through the Ming (1368–1644), and again in the mid-nineteenth century, intentional movements to embrace a unitary vision of Chinese religion were at the very heart of religious attempts to cope with a changing society and culture. These attempts became more desperate in the mid-nineteenth century, when the increasing internal disintegration of society and the external threat of the West combined to challenge the very heart of traditional Chinese civilization. Nineteenth-century attempts to revitalize Chinese tradition from elite or popular perspectives did not create the base for the kind of reform necessary to cope with the problems of the day. It is an oversimplification to see the failure of China to modernize only as a religious or ideological failure. Nonetheless the breakdown of patterns of unitary religious discourse in the eighteenth century helped set the stage for the inability of late nineteenth-century thinkers to find a new vision that might have revitalized traditional culture.

The retreat in the eighteenth century from attempts to articulate and institutionalize the religious unity of China may have made it more difficult for those in the nineteenth century who were searching for some vision to unite China against its internal and external threats. Or, one might argue that the intentional attempts of Sung and Ming leaders to inspire and solidify the religio-cultural unity in the response to societal changes were checked in the nineteenth century when the deep actual divisions in society resurfaced.[1]

Peter Nosco's chapter in this volume traces the temporary breakdown of a single scholarly discourse in eighteenth-century Japan. I hope that future scholars will investigate whether the nativist and polarizing impulses in China and Japan during this same period are related more than superficially. They seem at first glance to follow a rather different course, but the issue merits further investigation.

The Changing Context for A Unified Religious Discourse

The history of Chinese religions involved not only Confucianism, Buddhism, and Taoism (known collectively as the Three Teachings) but also a variety of popular cults. None of these traditions developed in isolation; as they responded to the same historical and cultural circumstances they interacted in various ways. On the one hand, religious teachers competed for adherents and scored one another in doctrinaire polemics; on the other, they borrowed from and influenced one another. Some religious leaders even attempted a partial religious synthesis of several religions, reconciling them by means of symbols or patterns of practice. Study of these interactions can help us to define the changing boundaries and issues between religious communities and to understand the religious *problematik* of various periods and persons.

The Sung dynasty was a period of religious ferment that supported positive religious interaction. The new movements within the Three Teachings (particularly Neo-Confucianism and Inner Alchemy Taoism) were marked by an openness to a broader vision and a fundamental reformulation of "orthodoxy." These developments were paralleled by the appearance of openly syncretic and popular Three Teachings cults and Three Teachings halls.[2]

The height of mainstream intellectual religious unity movements came in the mid-Ming. In the fifteenth and sixteenth centuries, thinkers of every major religious tradition were proclaiming the unity of the Three Teachings. Yüan Huang (1533–1606) advocated use of the Taoistic ledgers of merit and demerit (*kung-kuo ko*) as part of Confucian ethical cultivation.[3] Buddhists like Te-ch'ing (1546–1623) and Ta-kuan (1544–1604) proclaimed the unity of the Three Teachings in Buddhism, and Chu-hung (1532–1612) sought to unite Confucian and Buddhist ethics, thought, and practice in his lay Buddhist organizations.[4] Wang Yang-ming (1472–1529), the great light of Ming Neo-Confucianism, did not entirely rule out the contributions of Buddhism and Taoism, saying, "If learned correctly, even a heretical teaching could be useful in the world, but if learned incorrectly, even Confucianism would be accompanied by evils."[5] His disciple Yüan Tsung-tao (1560–1600) went even further: "It is not irresponsible to assert that we can understand Confucianism for the first time only after we have studied Ch'an."[6] While not all Ming thinkers shared this unitary vision, there was in the Ming a sense of a shared spiritual goal, a search for the realization of sagely mind, which drew thinkers beyond the boundaries of schools and doctrines. They did not accept the beliefs of other schools wholesale, but their stress on the attainment of the spiritual goal rather than on the definition of orthodox means opened them to new ideas. As Araki Kengo has written, Wang Yang-ming believed that "as long as it pertains to the essence of human existence, it is not subject to judgment in terms of the distinction between orthodoxy and heterodoxy."[7]

The mid-Ming was also a period rich in religious experimentation. Ho Hsin-yin (1517–1579) tried to revitalize Neo-Confucianism through clan reform.[8] Members of the T'ai-chou school, such as Wang Ken (1483–1540), believed that the streets were full of sages; they sought to bring the truths of Neo-Confucianism to the streets through public lectures.[9] Buddhist lay associations and vegetarian halls sought with new vigor to provide a viable praxis for the lay believer. Lin Chao-en (1517–1598) established a unitary religion of the Three Teachings for students of all religions and social classes. Lin's teaching took a Taoist form of meditation and interpreted it in Neo-Confucian terms, infused with Ch'an imagery. By radically reinterpreting and "explaining" the true meaning of many popular beliefs, he brought them into line with what he considered orthodox Neo-Confucianism.[10] In all these cases, members of the elite sought to make the truth of the Way accessible to the persons of more modest education in their own clans or in society at large.

Experimentation with religious unity in the Ming was stimulated by two factors. First, a considerable number of scholars for one reason or another did not pursue official careers. Some could not pass the government examination. Others passed, but fell prey to the stormy political scene. Still others resigned or refused to serve for political, moral, or personal reasons. These scholars who were not officials[11] taught in private academies, among friends, or in the streets. They represented a strain of Confucian thought and spirituality independent of official "state" orthodoxy. Second, the spread of literacy to a broader base of the population created an audience for a simplified elite ideal; these new "folk intellectuals" were too literate to be at home in the oral religious traditions, but not sophisticated enough to wend their way through the subtleties of classical studies or philosophy.[12] Confucians who followed the Way outside official service and official orthodoxy found a potentially large audience among the nonelite literate population.

The situation among the educated elite in the Ch'ing (1644–1912), however, was not nearly so hospitable to attitudes and activities espousing religious unity. For one thing, several prominent early Ch'ing scholars held the "wild Ch'an" speculations and religious openness of the Ming thinkers partly responsible for the fall of China to the Manchus; many charged that while Ming thinkers were lost in Buddhistic speculation, the barbarians had been able to snatch away the Middle Kingdom. In response to the "wild" speculations and subjectivism of the Ming, Ch'ing Confucians attempted to find a solid and substantial basis for Confucianism in the classics, history, and philosophy.[13] This scholarly turn also tended to undermine the eclecticism of earlier periods, for in strict classical and philological studies it was hard to find any common ground between Confucianism and other traditions. Moreover, the Manchu governors of China propagated an official Neo-Confucian orthodoxy more rigid than that of their Ming predecessors. Since the Manchus needed to employ Confucian scholars as efficient and loyal bureaucrats, but wanted to avoid independent groups of intellectuals who might be a base of opposition to the regime, they defined behavioral codes and orthodox attitudes ever more strictly, climaxing in the Ch'ien-lung (1736–1796) censorship of heretical books. Unorthodox ideas and behaviors were suppressed as potential causes of social disruption.

The Ch'ien-lung campaign against heterodox doctrines also included a legal ban in 1774 on Three Teachings movements in South China, alleging that the Three Teachings taught heterodox doctrines, neglected the Three Bonds and Five Constant Virtues,[14] and incited the people to discontent.[15] Laws like these, which were part of the Ch'ing policy of keeping peace in the provinces, help to account for the lack of information about eclectic tendencies and movements in the Ch'ing. Such groups there were driven into hiding in order to save their scriptures from the eyes of ambitious local bureaucrats who could impress the central government by zealous persecution of heresy. The legal bans and stricter definitions of orthodoxy tended to isolate scholar-officials from those who still courted a vision of the unity of Chinese religions; it was not politically wise to dabble in heresy. Thus not only were the intellectual trends of Confucianism flowing in directions away from common ground with Buddhism and Taoism, but the legal and social pressures of official orthodoxy made going against the stream a risky proposition.

The constriction of Confucianism from within and its restriction from without placed severe limits on the possibilities for espousing religious unity. This chapter explores some of the scope and implications of those constraints. Beginning in the early nineteenth century, with an example of a critique by a Confucian scholar-official of Buddhist millenarian scriptures, I then move backward in time to the eighteenth century and examine the work of several more eclectic thinkers whose writings illustrate how a syncretic impulse, while still present, had begun to falter in the eighteenth century as a more expansive religious spirit was undermined by social and political realities.

First, in the absence of the elite espousal of religious unity, the more blatantly popular forms of eclecticism were pitted against the increasingly rigid Confucian orthodoxy. The result was a particularly virulent form of doctrinaire Confucian polemic that exhibited in a striking way the incompatibility between the values held by many Ch'ing Confucians and the Ming vision of a broad Way that would encompass all under Heaven. Second, while certain lay Buddhists tried to build a basis for compatibility with Confucianism on the foundation of moral retribution, their efforts really amounted to a critique of certain weaknesses in the Confucian moral system and constructed at best a fragile basis for a broader religious synthesis. Buddhist teaching on spiritual transformation through meditation and faith was no longer seen as compatible with Confucian orthodoxy. Third, within Confucianism the turn away from the particular kind of religious openness and expansiveness associated with the School of the Mind left a religious vacuum that some scholars with Confucian training filled by turning to lay Buddhism. Although these scholars were in many ways the most open of their age, the constraints of the intellectual milieu cast their shadow over the extent and the impact of their unitary vision. Although a careful reading of the full scope of their writings reveals the power of both Buddhism and Neo-Confucianism in shaping their lives and thought, they did not systematically attempt to reconcile and synthesize these two aspects of their spiritual life. Further, in their essays and commentaries, as opposed to letters to friends, there was no public defense or even discussion of a unity of Chinese religion. The reader senses throughout their public writings the negative effects of the cultural ethos; compared to the vision of scholars in the previous century, their unitary vision cannot help but seem a bit limp and pallid.

The Unitary Vision of Millenarian Buddhism

One source that richly documented Confucian constraints on unitary vision was Huang Yü-p'ien's criticisms of millenarian Buddhist scriptures. Huang Yü-p'ien (fl. 1830–1840) served as a local official in two areas that had produced Buddhist sectarian "bandits." Although he was not directly involved in the official suppression of major sectarian uprisings, he was very concerned about the danger to the social order he perceived in millenarian sects. He started an all-out campaign to extirpate the remnants of the sects, to uncover believers and temples, and to confiscate scriptures. The latter he published with refutations in the *P'o-hsieh hsiang-p'ien* (Detailed Refutation of Heresies) in 1834, with sequels in 1839 and 1841.[16] Although the collection was published in the early nineteenth century, the sects had been active throughout the eighteenth century. The White Lotus uprising of 1795–1804 was able to ride the crest of a strong wave of eschatological belief. Huang's refutations of millenarian views were in perfect accord with eighteenth-century Confucianism.

Recent scholarship on Buddhist millenarian movements, beginning with the work of Daniel Overmyer, has greatly enhanced our understanding of millenarian sects by insisting on their religious character. Earlier writers, following traditional Confucian historiography or the "revisions" of other modern doctrinaire theorists, assume that the sects could be analyzed most fruitfully in political terms. The sectarians have been portrayed either as deluded bumpkins led by rabble-rousing and ambitious outlaws into rebellions against the great Confucian social order, or (from another political point of view) as oppressed masses lashing out against the injustice of the system, albeit not in an ultimately effective way. Overmyer, however, insisted on the religious intention and significance of these organizations. The primacy of their religious nature, he argued, is supported by several facts: (1) the sects persisted over long periods in which there were no rebellions; (2) even during rebellions the religious character of the sects was never lost; and (3) only a small percentage of peasant rebellions were led by religious groups. These were religious organizations that could, in extreme circumstances, become channels for overt political or military rebellion, but they were primarily and fundamentally religious communities.[17]

The millenarian or eschatological Buddhist sects[18] assumed full form in the late Ming with a new vision of Buddhism. Buddhist millenarianism was a combination of Amidist piety and faith in the future Buddha Maitreya,[19] enriched with a new element of belief in the Venerable Mother (Wu-sheng lao-mu), the creator of the world and the mother of the human race.[20] According to this tradition, the Venerable Mother had watched her human children go astray and fall victim to their sins and desires. No longer remembering their home in Heaven, they did not know enough to long for salvation. As the Mother wept in heaven, the Jade Emperor, ruler of Heaven, became angry with humans for having hurt their Mother, and wished to punish them. The Buddha intervened and prayed for mercy; he begged to be allowed to go to the earth to reform those errant sons and daughters and call them home. Thus it was that three Buddhas (Lamplighter, Śakyamuni, and Maitreya) were sent into the world, each in charge of the salvation in a different era. In the first two eras some souls had found their way home, but a huge remnant remained to be saved by Maitreya, who would soon come with a new emperor to destroy the corrupt world and establish a new, perfect order.

As the *eschaton* approached, the Venerable Mother dispatched various divine beings to warn her children. The Ancestor of True Emptiness (Chenk'ung lao-tsu) was sent to reveal the scriptures of the Venerable Mother and spread her teachings; he was incarnated as the son of a man named Chang and was known to believers by the secret name Kung Ch'ang.[21] It was also said in the late Ming, that the Venerable Mother herself was incarnated in the body of a woman who spread the call to salvation.[22] These avatars of compassionate deities warned of moral retribution in heavens and hells designed to recompense justly and graphically the virtues and vices of all beings. Only those who declared their faith in the Venerable Mother and had their names inscribed on the registers of the faithful in Heaven would be saved from having to pay for the sins of many lives and could go straight home.

The teachings of these millenarian sects were influenced by the Chinese heritage of religious unity, although the dominant world view was Buddhist. Heaven was not seen as a Buddhist monopoly; it was open to all who saw the truth regardless of religious affiliation. The founders of all Three Teachings, five sects, nine limbs, and eighteen branches (i.e., all religious traditions) had received the teachings of the Venerable Mother at the Lung-hua Assembly in Heaven,[23] and sayings by them were included in the scriptures of the eschatological sects. The pantheon of the sect included a Bodhisattva of the Three Teachings, who would lead people of all faiths back to the true Way.[24]

Millenarian scriptures proclaimed the compatibility of their faith with the true teachings of Confucianism and Taoism. They argued in the manner of earlier Buddhists that by achieving enlightenment and realizing one's true nature, one could repay one's Confucian debt of filiality to one's parents, for not only the believer but his ancestors and descendants would also be saved.[25] Ju T'ung-tsu, a deified form of Confucius, was counted the ninth patriarch in the line of transmission, next to the Ancestor of True Emptiness.[26]

Taoist teachers and doctrines also played a part in the vision of the millenarian cults. It was T'ai-shang lao-chün (a deified form of Lao-tzu) whom the Venerable Mother asked to make the boats that would ferry the saved to Heaven.[27] Also, the meditative practice of the cults seems to have been a combination of Buddhist and Taoist meditation. In involved circulations of breath within the internal microcosm of the body. There were ten steps in the process, leading eventually to the opening of the heavenly gate and seeing the Actual Self (*tang-jen*), which is the true nature.[28] Taoist alchemical imagery is evident in some of the selections on meditation,[29] but unfortunately the selections included are so fragmentary that it is impossible to reconstruct the system of meditation and the extent of the amalgamation of Buddhist and Taoist methods. In one section the *Liu San-chiao ching* (Classic of Preserving the Three Teachings) is cited as claiming that when the compassion of the Venerable Mother touches people, they will return to the true classics of the Three Teachings, which teach us to sit in meditation and circulate our breath until we have penetrated the true mantra (*chüeh*) and can see the Actual Self. Only when that is accomplished can one escape the justice of hell.[30]

The millenarian sects were equally hospitable to earlier Buddhist practices. The Venerable Mother promised to make good on Amitabha's vow to save those who called upon his name.[31] The mantra of these sects was *Chen-k'ung chia-hsiang wu-sheng lao-mu* (Venerable Mother, Home of the True Emptiness), but those who called on Amitabha's name in the traditional way would also be met by the Venerable Mother and would avoid the sorrow and suffering of rebirth.

The eschatological vision of these sects was simple and unsophisticated, pulling the heart-strings more than it stimulated the intellect. It was a direct, emotional, and earthy religion, a promise of salvation that would appeal to ordinary folk. The movement took shape in the Wan-li period (1573–1619) of late Ming, toward the end of the period of popularizing movements of "elite" religious synthesis, discussed above. However, millenarian Buddhism continued to grow as more elite movements waned. The millenarian sects were popular, "superstitious," and distasteful by the standards of many Confucian scholars. Huang Yü-p'ien was probably not far wrong when he surmised that the authors of sectarian scriptures must have been storytellers, playwrights, or actors. He argued on two grounds: (1) no member of the scholarly class could stomach these doctrines and (2) the style and rhythms of many of the texts closely resembled novels or short stories.[32] The second seems plausible; playwrights and actors could draw on a vast storehouse of literature and religious teaching, but they were not always sufficiently versed in classical studies to share an orthodox "elite" view. The sectarian vision was most probably articulated by and appealed to those with middling literacy. The unitary visions of Ming "elite" movements and millenarian Buddhism arose out of a situation in which people were seeking religious answers to a bewildering, chaotic, and discomforting situation. Especially in the south, economic factors, population growth, and sociopolitical changes during the Ming had created a situation in which people sought religious answers to the instability of their lives or adjustment to a new but rather confusing and threatening prosperity. The eschatological vision of the millenarian sects and traditional "elite" synthetic visions were compatible with the sense of instability of confusing prosperity.

While Ming elite unitary movements waned, the world view of the millenarian sects found fertile ground in certain elements in the Ch'ing. One example of this is the growth and context of the White Lotus sect in the Hupeh-Shensi-Szechuan triangle, in which the 1795 uprising occurred. Suzuki Chūsei's study of the origins of the uprising throws some light on the one possible attraction of this mode of religiosity to one segment of the population. According to Suzuki, the triangle had been designated in the seventeenth century as a resettlement and "homesteading" area in an effort to reclaim arable lands. At first there was no flood of settlers, and those who came could find rich lands. But later, as population pressures began to be more acutely felt in neighboring regions, the sale of these tax-free lands started a land rush. By 1723 the government prohibited further settlement, but the reputation of the place was established, and land at home was not to be had, so the poor but hopeful kept on coming long after the arable lands were gone. The latecomers were forced into barren mountain areas, worse off than in their home provinces, for here they lacked the web of relatives and long-time friends on which to depend in hard times. Many were too poor to return or had nothing to return to. They scrounged and sometimes stole for a living. The lawless element was bolstered and given leadership by stray soldiers who had deserted and wandered to the land mecca.[33]

It was in these mountain regions where the millenarian White Lotus religion had its strongest base, for the eschatological vision resonated with the experience of the people. They had seen hard times, had acted on hope and faith in the promises of their society, and had been bitterly disappointed. It was not hard for them to believe that these were the last days and that real hope must be in a new world. Their hard luck was proof positive of their bad fate and bad karma; they had done everything they could to better their luck, and things had only gotten worse. They would need a savior who could free them from this fate. Moreover, they were cut off from their extended families and their home regions; what could be more appealing than a mother weeping and calling them home to their real home? Religion offered home for the homeless, and a mother for the abandoned.

Research by Susan Naquin and others on membership in millenarian cults has demonstrated that these groups appealed to a much broader range of people than the destitute and desperate. Prosperous farmers, small businessmen, merchants, and others are included in the ranks of many folk Buddhist religions. If not all adherents had experienced extreme hardship, they shared a sense of general malaise that made the eschatological message of these groups appealing. As the sense of social disintegration continued to plague large segments of the Chinese population in the eighteenth and nineteenth centuries, the appeal of the eschatological sects remained as a powerful religious force. However, this spiritual vision was at odds with the current directions of elite culture. It might have blended well with the Chinese religious economies of the twelfth or sixteenth centuries, but it ran afoul of the more rigid and narrow orthodoxy of the eighteenth century. From the point of view of many Confucians, this vision had gone outside the boundaries of the Way; they responded not with open interest or tolerance, but with polemics.

Confucian Polemics

Huang Yü-p'ien, the editor of these refutations, is a prime example of this response. Huang, perhaps reflecting his position as a local official, zealously denounced these sects in Confucian terms. In his eyes, they were heretical, immoral, rowdy, and in bad taste. Beginning with a recitation of their insurrectionist tendencies, Huang reminded his readers of laws designed to deal with such deviants, while suggesting a few new policies. On the one hand, he wholeheartedly supported severe and swift punishment for all sectarians and their families. On the other, he admitted that some of the blame for uprisings lay with officials for not being zealous enough in their propounding of the truth and, as a remedy, suggested a system of schools designed to inculcate Confucian values and promote classical studies.[34] Unlike earlier, more sympathetic Confucians, he ignored the social conditions that had supported this movement; he wrote as though it were simply a question of wrong-headed thinking.

His refutations of the errors and heresies of the sectarians depicted in graphic terms the intellectual and emotional incompatibility of the Ch'ing Confucian and eschatological Buddhism; he was outraged, condescending, and vitriolic. Although he claimed to have written this book to refute errors, he made almost no attempt to do so on grounds that would have any impact on a Buddhist. He made no attempt to persuade; he simply restated the Confucian position.

His main line of attack was hard-headedly Confucian; the writings of these sects did not base themselves on the Confucian classics and the official histories. The mythical places they described did not appear in the ancient *Shan-hai ching* (Classic of Mountains and Seas), and their stories about sages, teachers, and emperors could not be verified in Confucian histories. Their view of the evolution of history, he said, was based on historical romances and novels.[35]

Judging by the time and energy he gave to refuting it, the single thing that most incensed him was that the sectarians did not accept traditional Chinese cosmology. In his writings, the tenuous reconciliation of the "foreign" Buddhism with native religions became once more a divisive issue. The Buddhists had a different view of time, with eighteen "hours" per day instead of twelve, and they had twelve trigrams and 144 hexagrams in their version of the *Classic of Changes*, rather than eight and sixty-four. He wrote page after page refuting these "outrages" with a detailed explanation of the Confucian cosmology of the Five Phases.[36] He did not defend the Confucian view or explain its superiority for describing reality, nor did he acknowledge the influences of Indian cosmology on Buddhism. For him, Chinese cosmology defined the boundaries of reality; anything that deviated from it was *ipso facto* an error.

Some of his refutations seem to convey a cry of moral outrage. Clearly, Huang was offended by the fact that both men and women were to be ferried to Heaven and assembled without segregating the sexes.[37] He was shocked that they had placed a deity (and a female deity, at that!) above the Jade Emperor, who was the rightful ruler of Heaven. If a goddess were allowed to rule in the highest place, he lamented, yin would prosper and yang would decline.[38] He threatened darkly that the sectarians would be punished by Heaven for their audacity in placing Confucius next to the sectarian avatar Kung Ch'ang in the Venerable Mother's line of transmission.[39]

When he did try to persuade the other side, it was with undisguised disdain. Commenting on their vivid descriptions of hell's punishments for sins in the world, he warned that the sectarians themselves were the prime examples either of each sin in question or of far worse sins. He also argued that if the Venerable Mother had promised to save them from suffering for their sins, they should have been able to escape the arm of the government's law. Their punishment in this life was not only just retribution for their evil deeds but also proof that their promise of salvation was an empty lie. He seemed to relish describing in gory detail the punishments that various sectarian leaders had received.

His most basic refutation was historical. He claimed that the classics or scriptures or histories contained no references to the Venerable Mother; she did not exist before the late Ming. She was, therefore, neither eternal nor the creator. This doctrine was entirely the fabrication of late Ming heretics.[40] Huang had his history straight, but it failed to take into account millenarian faith in revelation. To a sectarian, the fact that the Venerable Mother was not revealed in scriptures until late Ming did not mean that she had not existed eternally; she simply had not made her presence known until her time came.[41] From the Ch'ing Confucian point of view, however, Huang was justified in seeking verification in history and tradition for what purported to be a truth.

Huang Yü-p'ien lived in a different intellectual world from the sectarian Buddhists; because of his world view, he could neither understand nor sympathize with their eschatological vision. Yet his refutations, while hardly subtle, reflected the basic trends of his time: the search for a verifiable definition of the Way in the classics, philology, and history. Within Confucian circles, these emphases produced some dazzling feats of classical scholarship. However, Huang Yü-p'ien's polemics vividly demonstrated the severe strictures this view placed on religious dialogue and unitary religious imagination. The Confucians had moved away from those aspects of their tradition that encouraged a unitary vision and toward those that emphasized difference.

Syncretism and Moral Retribution

If the unitary vision of millenarian Buddhism was irreconcilable with the views of many Ch'ing Confucians, other Buddhists made every effort to prove that Buddhism was more Confucian than Confucianism. In their view, only Buddhism could succeed in bringing Confucian moral values to all Chinese through the teachings of moral retribution in the morality books.

A prime example of this brand of unitary vision can be seen in the commentary to *Yin-chih wen* (Good Deeds Done in Secret) edited by Chou An-shih sometime before 1711.[42] Chou An-shih, a student from K'un-shan, in Kiangsu, was known for his impassioned pleas for the sparing of animal life through strict vegetarianism. He argued that the Buddhist prohibition on killing (*ahimsa, pu-sha*) was the essence of Confucian humaneness.[43]

The *Yin-chih wen* is a morality text dating back to the Sung and attributed to lord Wen Ch'ang, the patron god of literature and Confucian examinations. In this text his role was considerably expanded into a Bodhisattva-like deity, who appeared in a series of incarnations in order to teach people the truths of moral retribution.[44] In his commentary, Chou An-shih used Buddhist arguments to support his view of Confucian morality. However, he was not bashful about exposing certain tensions or deficiencies in the Confucian ethical system. He believed that the higher vision of Buddhism could resolve those tensions.

Chou's justification for writing his commentary for "us scholars" revealed a good deal about his attitudes. He identified himself as a Confucian (*ju*, lit. scholar), but lamented that "we Confucians" denounce the emptiness and quiescence of Buddhism. However, he claimed that, even among Buddhists, only a few attained the emptiness and quiescence of Nirvana; those doctrines served a tiny elite. For the rest, the message of Buddhism lay in its theory of moral retribution, which upheld positive Confucian values.[45] Hence, far from being a vapid and speculative doctrine, Buddhism was the foundation of morality.

One of the most interesting arguments in this book questioned the morality of avenging wrongs to one's parents. According to the dictates of filial piety, one was enjoined to avenge one's father's grievances, "not to live under the same sky" as his enemies. In extreme cases, vengeance extended to the sons of enemies. This extreme filial obligation inflamed the decentralizing and fragmenting influences of clan loyalties; obligations to one's parents took precedence over the voluntary loyalties to political allies or interest groups. Filial claims for vengeance also sowed suspicion and distrust between whole clans. In some areas of late traditional China, these clan rivalries chronically erupted in violent feuds.[46] The arguments against such resentments in the commentary were hybrids of Confucian values and Buddhist logic. First, one should not bear a grudge against the son of one's father's enemy because he might turn out to be a virtuous and loyal official, and it would be wrong to deprive society of a potential talent.[47] The argument is not ethically compelling: what if the son were without talent or prospects as an official, a mere ordinary human being? The question of the son's guilt or innocence is never raised. The argument as stated simply pointed to a possible conflict of values in the Confucian system. The second argument was more clearly Buddhist, resting on the doctrine of reincarnation. The parents have lived for many lives and will have many future lives; in all those lives they have amassed a large number of enemies and have borne grudges against a large number of people. If the son took on the task of repaying all those resentments, he would only create more enemies, which his parents would have to face in future lives. This argument bore a faint resemblance to traditional Buddhist defenses of the filiality of the religious life on the basis that one can earn religious merit for one's parents as well as for oneself. But it was more interesting, for it dealt with a potential and real social problem—the clannish pressures of filiality creating tensions in the larger community.

A second argument raised questions about Mencius' view of human nature.

Mencius said, "A mind without commiseration is not human; a mind without shame and deference is not human." To speak of being human in this way makes being human very difficult.[48]

Chou An-shih argued that people contain all potentialities; they are so noble that they can be emperors or kings, so poor that they are born and die without a penny, and so base that when delicacies enter their mouths they are putrefied in the digestive process. They are slaves of their sexual desires. They are, in short, "mixed bags." In light of this, Mencius' view of human nature put too great a burden on human beings and failed to account for their strengths and weaknesses. The Buddhist view, on the other hand, was more realistic and could motivate people to avoid evil and do good. This line of reasoning turned the tables on Neo-Confucians, who had traditionally argued that Buddhists were selfish and neglected morality; now a Buddhistic Confucian (or Confucian Buddhist) argued that the Confucian ideal was so idealized that it failed to motivate ordinary humans. Chou put his case with an example: if a man were to enter a room where a beauiful woman was offering incense to the gods, which would be more likely to deter him from having his way with her—the thought of the wrath of the Jade Emperor at having his sacrifice disturbed, or the caveat that to molest her is contrary to moral principle?[49] His was an earthy, even a childish, view of human nature, but one with a certain rhetorical appeal.

Although predominantly Buddhist, the commentary incorporates elements from the broader religious heritage of China. In a section called "Broadly Practice the Three Teachings" Chou stated that all teachings were necessary in order to save all people. Chou made an analogy to internal and external medicine; they are different but complementary approaches to healing; and both are needed to heal all ills. In the same way, the sages of the Three Teachings each taught from a different perspective, but the teachings came from and led to the same moral truths.[50]

Chou An-shih's unifying vision was both complex and limited. Although he claimed to be upholding Confucian moral values, his praise of the Buddhist reverence for life and his Buddhist criticism of filial piety and moral principle seemed to suggest that Buddhism could correct certain weaknesses in the Confucian moral system. On the other hand, he showed little interest in Buddhist doctrines and dismissed their "empty discussions" of samadhi. His interest in both Buddhism and Confucianism was intensely pragmatic; he sought to identify doctrines and stories that would inculcate belief in moral retribution and thus motivate ethical behavior. Perhaps one might say that

Chou An-shih saw in moral *praxis* the firm and substantial basis for the Way that many of his contemporaries sought in the classics and history. The emphasis on moral *praxis* rather than the evidential basis for tradition opened him to a more unitary vision, but one focused squarely on his distinctive view of the Way. His evaluations of means and of traditions in terms of the *telos* of moral practice tied him to his Ming predecessors, but his definition of the *telos* in terms of concrete behavior rather than inner spiritual transformation rooted him in the Ch'ing.

The openness of the vision of the commentary also had definite limitations. Although their stated intent was to reconcile Buddhist and Confucian moral practice, his arguments included not a little criticism of Confucian values and society. Second, despite the general statements on the harmony of the Three Teachings, there is little evidence of any significant synthesis of doctrines or practices into a coherent world view. At no point did he develop a rationale for the compatibility of views of human nature, the mind, or meditation in the two schools. His argument was essentially strategic — namely, that Buddhism was the means to Confucian ends, but that those ends were limited to the sphere of ethics. He never developed a firm theory of the nature of the process of ethical cultivation.

Unitary Vision

Although the pressures of Ch'ing society worked against unitary visions, some Confucians broke out of the strictures to a larger view of the Way. However, given the conditions of the intellectual milieu, these scholars turned to Buddhism and wrote about their views from a Buddhist perspective.

The leading voice for a Confucian unitary vision was P'eng Shao-sheng (1740–1796), a native of Ch'ang-chou, Kiangsu. Shao-sheng's father and brothers were "literary officials" (*wen-hsüeh kuan*) at the imperial court.[51] P'eng's education groomed him for the government examinations and an official career. He earned a reputation as an interpreter of the classics and was granted his *chin-shih* degree in 1769. After that, he continued to write on the classics and Confucian philosophy, but he declined all official posts and never took up an official career. Instead, he took the vows of a lay Buddhist and lived as a celibate and vegetarian. After his father's death in 1784, he retired to a temple to live out his days in silent contemplation.[52] P'eng Shao-sheng had a Confucian persona and a Buddhist persona. His synthesis of these two sides was not as thoroughgoing as that of some Ming figures, but he stood head and shoulders above his eighteenth-century contemporaries in terms of his unitary vision.

What caused P'eng Shao-sheng to turn from an official career to Pure Land Buddhism? Like many of his predecessors in the Sung and Ming, he was profoundly dissatisfied with the way in which scholarship was being pursued at this time. He lamented that scholars had forgotten the meaning of the word *wen*. In his opinion, too many saw *wen* simply in its narrow meaning of literature and learning; they saw it as a matter of literary style, knowledge of the classics, and skillful formal scholarship. They had, however, forgotten that *wen* had a broader, more fundamental meaning of culture or refinement; it was meant to be an aspect of self-cultivation. It was not something external to be mastered, but a means of internal spiritual transformation with no meaning unless it was attained or realized in the self (*tzu-te*).[53] He praised one scholar for turning away from mere external studies of the classics and histories:

> Looking within himself, he minutely followed this to the point of realizing it in the self. In discussions of study, he took examining the faults and self-reform to be the foundation and quiet-sitting and observing the mind [*kuan-hsin*] to be the primary step. I take this to mean that one must practice quiet-sitting to recognize one's faults; in recognizing one's faults, one can repent them; in repenting them, one can reform them.[54]

Real learning had to transform the self: real literature took the substance (*shih*) one attained in the self and expressed it in words.[55]

It was not unusual for young and idealistic scholars to become disillusioned with what seemed to them the pointless pedantry of examination studies; what was unusual, at least in the eighteenth century, was to turn to Buddhism for an answer. In P'eng's case, this move was inspired by the friendship he formed at a pivotal period of his life with Lo Yu-kao (1733–1778) and Wang Chin (1725–1792), two prominent members of the lay Buddhist movement.[56] Some years before, Wang Chin, after he failed his examinations, had become deeply troubled and turned to Pure Land Buddhism.[57] In Lo Yu-kao and Wang Chin, P'eng Shao-sheng found kindred spirits; they became not only fast friends but fellow seekers of the Way.

It was not that P'eng and his friends felt that the Confucian Way lacked a spiritual path. It was only that scholars of their day were so narrow-minded that they had neglected an essential part of their spiritual heritage, namely the insights of the School of the Mind, as taught by the founders of that school, Lu

Hsiang-shan (1139–1193) and Wang Yang-ming. Wang Chin scored the narrow views of his contemporaries, who sneered at Wang Yang-ming as pro-Buddhist; he felt that Wang Yang-ming was the giant among recent scholars.[58] P'eng Shao-sheng defended Lu Hsiang-shan's theory of honoring the moral nature, claiming that its purpose was simply to lead people to the highest good.[59] Moreover, in honoring the moral nature, Lu could not be said to have abandoned scholarship, since true learning was nothing other than restoring the moral nature; Lu's doctrine, he claimed, was fully in accord with "The Doctrine of the Mean."[60] In P'eng's view the Confucians of the day were only harming themselves and impoverishing the Way of Chu Hsi (1130–1200) by denying the importance of honoring the moral nature.[61]

Although he defended the School of the Mind, P'eng was not completely at odds with Ch'ing criticisms of the excesses of the school. P'eng conceded that Chu Hsi had quite rightly stressed that only after serious and extended study did the Way become simple and easy.[62] In contrast, the extreme left-wing followers of Wang Yang-ming had argued that the sagely mind was already present in all persons and could be activated simply by dynamic moral action. P'eng criticized those "Confucians who were Buddhists" for "alarming everyone" with such views[63] and cautioned, "If innate good knowledge [*liang-chih*] is not extended, it is not authentic."[64] P'eng Shao-sheng attacked the errors of the School of the Mind in order to salvage for his time what he saw as the authentic insights of that school. He sought a balance between these two sides of Confucianism and an openness to the truths and contributions of all who have sought the Way, regardless of their philosophical school. His friend Wang Chin shared this hope; he wrote to P'eng, "It has been my goal to harmonize the Three Teachings and Chu Hsi and Wang Yang-ming."[65] Thus we see that the thought of P'eng Shao-sheng and Wang Chin entailed an internal reconciliation of the differences within Confucianism.

P'eng Shao-sheng and his friends held to a unitary vision of the Three Teachings, but a vision colored by contemporary Buddhist views. First, like Chou An-shih, they saw morality books as a major means by which Buddhism supported the Confucian Way. P'eng wrote prefaces to both the *Yin-chih wen* (Retribution for Deeds Done in Secret) and the even more famous *T'ai-shang kan-ying p'ien* (Treatise on the Moral Retribution of the Most High).[66] His biographies lauded scholars like Yüan Huang who were responsible for the spread of this mode of spirituality, and he wrote one of the few extant biographies of Chou An-shih.[67] P'eng had especially high praise for the *Yin-chih wen*. In it the god Wen Ch'ang, the patron of literature and of the Confucian examinations, was incarnated in over forty separate avatars to uphold the justice of moral retribution. P'eng Shao-sheng saw Wen Ch'ang as the champion of the Three Teachings.[68] Indeed, Wen Ch'ang's historical connection with Confucianism made this morality book a particularly rich source on the traditions of the unity of Chinese religions. While he conceded that it, like all morality books, exploited popular superstition, such as fear of ghosts, spirits, and the retributions of hell, to motivate morality in people, he defended the practice as an effective teaching device.[69] In other words, he basically agreed with Chou An-shih that, strategically speaking, morality books strengthened the Confucian moral fabric even if they occasionally overstepped orthodox bounds to do so. P'eng Shao-sheng, however, went much further than Chou to give the book a Confucian base. Rather than follow Chou's position that Buddhist moral retribution could serve as the handmaiden of Confucian values, he saw the moral basis of the book in the homology of Heaven and the human, a close interrelationship in which they responded to and interacted with each other in an intricate web of moral responsibility that not even Buddhists and Taoists could escape.[70]

P'eng Shao-sheng also had high praise for the lay Buddhist movement that had been reinvigorated by Chu-hung. His biography of Chu-hung was long and enthusiastic, and in the rest of his Buddhist writings he cited Chu-hung as the model and inspiration of Ch'ing lay Buddhists. According to P'eng, Chu-hung favored Pure Land Buddhism and railed against the abuses of "wild Ch'an";[71] he thus saw Chu-hung as attempting to revive Buddhism by correcting "left-wing" abuses, much as he sought to reinvigorate the School of the Mind by divesting the left wing of its most objectionable excesses. Chu-hung claimed that the Pure Land sutras exhausted the entire Buddhist canon. He wrote, "If a man knows the mind, then the Great Land [i.e., the Pure Land] will have not a speck of soil. The mind is the ground; rebirth in the Pure Land is the doctrine of no-birth."[72] Chu-hung's version of Pure Land teaching purged it of reifying tendencies and united doctrines of all Buddhist schools under this rubric. Thus P'eng Shao-sheng's unitary vision also unified various strands of Buddhist tradition.

However, P'eng's vision of the "rightness" of Buddhism went beyond the doctrines of moral retribution and reverence for life. In his view, most of the charges made against Buddhists by zealous Confucians were unwarranted. For instance, a traditional criticism held that Buddhism was selfish (*ssu*) because it urged people to retire from the world and abdicate their social and public (*kung*) responsibilities. On the contrary, P'eng argued, since the self was the source of selfishness, the Buddhists, who denied the existence of the self, could not be guilty of selfishness.[73] This went beyond the traditional

Buddhist defense that in saving oneself one would transfer spiritual merit to family and descendants, thus fulfilling filial obligations. In a sense, it struck at the heart of the issue. While it did not resolve the problem of social responsibility, it raised a serious doctrinal question about the meaning of selfishness.

P'eng Shao-sheng also took on critics who had traditionally charged Buddhism with placing Nonbeing over Being, and Emptiness over practical reality. In an essay on the "Doctrine of the Mean," he wrote,

> As the world speaks about the Way, [it assumes that] if one follows Being, then one obstructs Nonbeing, and if one embodies Nonbeing, then one harms Being. There are also those who take the Confucian Way to be Being, and the Buddhist Way to be Nonbeing. Both are incorrect.[74]

He tried to show that the Way embraced both by using an analogy with the sky. One could not say that the sky was not empty, since it is through this empty void that we see and move and walk; nor could one say that it was purely empty, since it contained the sun and moon and stars. Likewise one could neither say that it had substance (*t'i*) nor that it lacked it. In the beginning there was simply emptiness. In the beginning of the Confucian Way there was not yet Being; in the beginning of the Buddhist Way, there was not yet Nonbeing. Both emerged from emptiness, from the Mean, in which the one and the boundless were the same and in which big and little contained each other.[75]

The argument was a fascinating attempt to resolve a basic issue between Buddhism and Confucianism by using the Mean as a harmonizing concept parallel to Buddhist Emptiness (*śunyatā*). Emptiness, being beyond or behind all categories, was both Being and Nonbeing; if one understood emptiness, one would know that Samsara is Nirvana.[76] The strategy in moving to the time before either had emerged also recalled an argument by the Taoist philosopher Chuang Tzu.[77] Thus all Three Teachings were brought to bear in this argument.

In the same vein, P'eng argued that the Three Teachings all teach that the cultivation of goodness leads to emptiness as the denial of the moral dimensions of the mind. For P'eng, emptiness represented the highest good, based on the clear, pure, and empty mind, the mind in the harmonious state of the Mean.[78] Again, the argument was essentially Buddhist. Emptiness was not the opposite of any quality; it was neither morality nor amorality. Emptiness represented the original and ultimate state of the realization of enlighten-ment; it was the state associated with the sagely mind. Seen in that way, it did not contradict the Confucian Way; it was in this state of harmonious and pure balance that proper moral judgments could be made.

P'eng Shao-sheng's Buddhism was an ethical path stressing reverence for life, charity,[79] and a spiritual path teaching cultivation of the mind. P'eng believed that Buddhism enriched and elaborated Confucian doctrine because it stressed the boundlessness and vastness of the enlightened mind; it de-scribed the sagely mind, the mind of Heaven and Earth, the state in which one forms one body with all things.[80] Buddhism also provided a path through which one could realize the enlightened mind. In a letter to his fellow students P'eng encouraged them to be zealous in the Pure Land practice of reciting the Buddha's name (*nien-fo*), for recitation of the name of Amitabha was the extension of innate good knowing and the preservation (in the mind) of heavenly principle.[81] Elsewhere, he wrote: "The mind is like the Great Void; originally it had neither life nor death. As the mind becomes pure, so the Buddha Land is pure [i.e., it becomes the Pure Land]."[82] The Confucians of this day had so effectively purged Confucianism of its "Buddhistic" ele-ments that a Confucian feeling the need for this form of spirituality had to reclaim it directly from Buddhism. For him, Buddhism not only supported the Confucian Way; it gave the spiritual path of cultivation form and defini-tion. Herein lay the crux of P'eng's unitary vision. To arrive at the point where Buddhism could fill the spiritual gap he felt in his Confucian studies, without fundamentally challenging his commitment to the Confucian Way of the sages, he had to "purify" his vision of Buddhism, leaving behind doubts and misunderstandings and focusing clearly on those essential truths that he felt were compatible with the Way. He described this process in a letter to Wang Chin:

> In days gone by, I suffered a thousand ailments and ten thousand pains, but these were simply due to my seeing the Buddha outside the mind, without realizing that I had wandered into Mount T'ieh-wei[83] and lost my way. Recently I have resolved my doubts; I believe that the words "seek the lost mind"[84] are simply the fitting and proper effort [of cultivation] and the gate to the essential place of Confucianism and Buddhism.[85]

Thus P'eng Shao-sheng, like his friend Wang Chin, held a vision that to some extent united Confucianism and Buddhism. An admirer wrote that, although the latter-day traces of Buddhism and Confucianism seemed to go in opposite directions, their origin was the same, and P'eng went directly between the two.[86]

P'eng wrote to a colleague:

> I have received your selections of Yang-ming's sayings on the Three Teachings, and they are most penetrating. This is not something that previous Confucians had attained. But the dividing and separating of schools into center and left and right according to their teachings is not the basis of the Way. The Way is simply One; in Confucianism, it takes the form of Confucianism; in Buddhism it takes the form of Buddhism; in Taoism it takes the form of Taoism. There are Three Teachings, but the basis of the Way cannot be divided into Three.[87]

Despite such statements, there were very real limitations on the unitary vision of P'eng Shao-sheng. First, the vast majority of his writings did not reveal that P'eng advocated a unitary view. His Confucian writings tended to be strictly Confucian, and his Buddhist writings were often purely Buddhist. The different "forms" he referred to in the quotation above seemed in his writings to have clear and distinct boundaries; he did not articulate any overlap. He discussed reconciliation of differences within Confucianism and within Buddhism, reconciling Ch'eng-Chu with Lu-Wang and Pure Land with Ch'an, T'ien-t'ai, and Hua-yen. By and large, however, each of his writings reflected only one side of his spiritual and philosophical life. We can surmise that this compartmentalization reflected the constraints of eighteenth-century society, as discussed above. His most striking statements about the unity of the Three Teachings were made in letters to his close friends, the small circle who shared his views. But he had only a small audience for his more unitary views, and he did not parade them in his published essays.

Second, P'eng Shao-sheng's vision, despite his emphasis on the lay Buddhist movement, was highly intellectual; his defenses of Buddhism presupposed a sound understanding of the logic of emptiness, a grasp of Buddhist metaphysics, and familiarity with the metaphysical and cosmological bases of the sagely mind. There is no evidence that he was interested in making the Way more accessible through the simple and concrete practices of Pure Land Buddhism. His interest in the morality books showed a sensitivity to the need for a concrete and practicable Way, but his unitary thought stressed a philosophical dialogue geared, I propose, to revitalizing the insights of the School of the Mind, the interior spiritual side of Confucianism, at a time when the emphasis of many contemporaries was on the scholarly and external aspects of the Way. In this sense his vision, while continuing much of the legacy of the Ming movement, had a different trajectory than the impetus of Ming "elite" Three Teachings movements, which sought to broaden the Way and make it more accessible by teaching elite truths in simple terms. The intellectual milieu of the eighteenth century was simply not congenial to this earlier vision, and to espouse it would have been futile and dangerous. Even the most open and inspired thinker of the day could not revive a vision of the Great Way that would encompass all, regardless of class divisions or education.

In several ways, then, the religious foundation for a unified vision that could unite "all under Heaven" was lost in eighteenth-century China. Even those with the broadest, most open visions were limited both in outlook and in the audiences to which they appealed. This is perhaps symptomatic of a fragmentation or disintegration of traditional culture. By the time of the cultural crisis of the mid-nineteenth century, there was nowhere to turn for a grand religio-cultural vision that could inspire and unite the whole of the Chinese people.

NOTES

1. The social-cultural changes of late traditional China stimulated movement and trade across wide regions and had two opposite effects: (1) the movement and regular interactions of persons across broader geographic spaces and regional and linguistic boundaries were a force for cultural unity; (2) paradoxically, these encounters with others from different regions, in the context of trade and commerce, led to hostilities and intense competition. Not unlike the current experience of a global economy, the Chinese experience of regional and national economies created both unprecedented alliances and deep mutual hostilities.

2. Shigematsu Shunshō, "Shina sankyōshijō no jakan no mondai" (Problems in the History of the Three Teachings in China), *Shien* (1939), 21:125–52.

3. Sakai Tadao, *Chūgoku zensho no kenkyū* (Studies of Chinese Morality Books) (Tokyo: Kokusho kankōkai, 1960), ch. 5, pp. 356–404, esp. 373–78.

4. See Kristin Yü Greenblatt (Yü Chün-fang), "Chu-hung and Lay Buddhism in the Late Ming," in Wm. Theodore de Bary, ed., *The Unfolding of Neo-Confucianism* (New York: Columbia University Press, 1975), 93–140.

5. *Wang Wen-ch'eng kung ch'üan-shu* (The Collected Works of Master Wang Wench'eng) (Hong Kong: Kuang-chih shu-chü, 1959) 3:603, *Shan-tung hsiang-shih lu* (Record of Provincial Examinations in Shantung), trans. and cited in Araki Kengo, "Confucianism and Buddhism in the Late Ming," in de Bary, *The Unfolding of Neo-Confucianism*, 44.

6. *Pai Su-chai lei chi* (Categorized Collection of Pai Su-chai) (Ming edition), 17:1, trans. and cited in Araki, "Confucianism and Buddhism," 53.

232 • The Collapse of the Unitary Vision of Chinese Religion

7. Araki, "Confucianism and Buddhism," 46.

8. See Ronald Dimberg, *The Sage and Society: The Life and Thought of Ho Hsin-yin* (Honolulu: University of Hawaii Press, 1974).

9. See Wm. Theodore de Bary, "Individualism and Humanitarianism in Late Ming Thought," in *Self and Society in Ming Thought* (New York: Columbia University Press, 1970), esp. pp. 157–78.

10. See the author's book, *The Syncretic Religion of Lin Chao-Lin* (New York: Columbia University Press, 1980), esp. ch. 7.

11. The Confucian not only strove to be morally cultivated and learned; he also felt a commitment to put his moral principles into action in official service. This is how we often identify Confucians and scholar-officials. However, some dedicated Confucians chose not to become officials in order to practice personal moral and spiritual cultivation; among such men the spiritual side of Confucianism was often viewed as primary.

12. It was Daniel Overmyer who coined the term *folk intellectuals* to describe this group of people with intermediate literacy. See *Folk Buddhist Religion: Dissenting Sects in Late Traditional China* (Cambridge: Harvard University Press, 1976), 64. David Johnson has developed a sophisticated schema to represent the strata of education and social position in late imperial China. The term *folk intellectual* as used in this paper would correspond to Johnson's "literate" level and corresponds most closely to the "literate/self-sufficient" group, in the middle of his chart. This group is a "middle" class in two senses: (a) in education, it sits between the poles of classical education and illiteracy; (b) in terms of social position, it sits between the legally privileged and dependent. See his "Communication, Class, and Consciousness," in David Johnson, Andrew J. Nathan, and Evelyn S. Rawski, ed., *Popular Culture in Late Imperial China* (Berkeley: University of California Press, 1985), 34–74, esp. the chart on p. 56. It is also noteworthy that Evelyn Rawski's book, *Education and Popular Literacy in Ch'ing China* (Ann Arbor: University of Michigan Press, 1979), argues that the mass of "folk intellectuals" who had a command of vernacular literature is larger than previously estimated. The modest number of extant books geared to this audience, she argues, reflects the prejudice of libraries dominated by elite culture rather than social realities. Lin Chao-en's writings contain at least one work manifestly written for this moderately literate audience. The book is written in a language close to the vernacular, and the introduction clearly states that it was written for those "who have very few characters and words." *I-chieh li-yü* (Plain and Simple Explanations), from a collection of Lin Chao-en's writings called *San-chiao cheng-tsung t'ung-lun* (Discussions on the Combination of Correct Principles of the Three Teachings), Lu Wen-hui, ed. (1597).

13. See, for instance, the author's essays on "Ku Yen-wu" and "Tai Chen," in Mircea Eliade, ed., *Encyclopedia of Religion* (New York: Macmillan, 1987). Also, for an excellent introduction to eighteenth-century Chinese society, see Susan Naquin and Evelyn S. Rawski, *Chinese Society in the Eighteenth Century* (New Haven: Yale University Press, 1987), esp. chs. 3 and 4.

14. The Three Bonds were the relationships between ruler and subject, parent and child, and husband and wife, hence the most basic of human relationships. The Five Constant Virtues were humanity or benevolence, rightness, decorum, wisdom, and trustworthiness. Respectful observance of moral duties defined by these relationships and virtues was the absolute minimum not only for the Confucian but for any Chinese.

15. See *Ta-Ch'ing li-ch'ao shih-lu* (Veritable Records of the Ch'ing) (Taipei: Hua-lien ch'u-pan-she, 1964 photocopy of 1934–40 edition), 218:18a.

16. Sawada Mizuho, *Kōchu Haja shōben* (An Annotated Edition of Detailed Refutation of Heresies) (Tokyo: Dōkyō kankōkai, 1972), 15–33.

17. Overmyer, *Folk Buddhist Religion*, 12–52. There has been a wealth of scholarship on millenarian Buddhism since Overmyer's ground-breaking work, most particularly by Susan Naquin. However, Overmyer's point on religious primacy stands and has been confirmed by both his subsequent scholarship and that of his colleagues.

18. The use of the term *millenarian* to describe these sects is somewhat misleading, since it suggests the clean symmetry of thousand-year cycles. "Eschatological" might be more accurate; it suggests the call to salvation in the face of an impending day of judgment and the establishment of a new era of religious rule. However, since scholars in the field have used the term *millenarian*, I will in general follow them. For the purposes of this essay, "millenarian" is virtually synonymous with "eschatological."

19. Amitabha Buddha, in a previous incarnation as a Bodhisattva, vowed to defer his entry into Buddhahood until he could establish a Pure Land where the faithful might go at death, after calling in faith on his name. In that land, they would be able to hear and practice the teachings of Buddhism without the distractions and temptations of the ordinary world, and thus their long journey toward Nirvana would be greatly shortened. See Wm. Theodore de Bary, ed., *Sources of Chinese Tradition* (New York and London: Columbia University Press, 1960), vol. 1, pp. 334–36, for a translation of the key vow. Maitreya was the Buddha of the future, of the end of the age. As this kalpa drew to an end, Maitreya would come to save those who put their faith in him from the terrors and suffering of the end of the age. Maitreya is thus closely identified with the Buddhist eschatological tradition.

20. The exact translation of the title would be Unborn Venerable Mother; "unborn" indicates that she is eternal or, more accurately, beyond time and Samsara.

21. The secret name is a pun on the actual name. Written together, the elements form the character Chang; written separately, they are read Kung Ch'ang. The secret name was ostensibly used to avoid the watchful eyes of the authorities, althought it does not seem a very effective alias.

22. It was precisely this legend that led the Confucian polemicist Huang Yü-p'ien to charge that the Venerable Mother was invented by Ming Buddhists. See below.

23. *Kōchu Haja shōben*, 1.7b.

24. Ibid., 1.19a.

25. Ibid., 1.32a.

26. Ibid., 1.12a.

27. Ibid., 1.15a.

28. Ibid., 1.19a.

29. See ibid., e.g., 1.7a, which refers to the "bubbling spring" and the "elixir field," both technical names for loci in the internal microcosm of Taoist meditation.

30. Ibid., 1.19a.

31. Ibid., 2.4a.

32. Ibid., 3.27b.

33. Suzuki Chūsei, *Shinchō chūki shi kenkyū* (Studies in Mid-Ch'ing History) (Tokyo: Ryūgen shobō, 1952), 20–26. On the range of causes of millenarian rebellions, also see Susan Naquin, *Millenarian Rebellion in China* (New Haven: Yale University Press, 1976).

34. *Kōchu Haja shōben*, pref., 12a.

35. Ibid., 4.16a.

36. On traditional Chinese cosmology, see Fung Yu-lan, *History of Chinese Philosophy*,

2 vols., trans. Derk Bodde (Princeton: Princeton University Press, 1952), vol. 1, ch. 15; vol. 2. ch. 2. *Kōchu Haja shōben*, 3.11a–26a.

37. Ibid., 1.13a.

38. Ibid., 1.4a.

39. Ibid., 1.15a.

40. Ibid., 4.3bff. He calls the leaders *yao*, meaning "witches" or "demon-sprites."

41. Such a notion is firmly rooted in Mahayana Buddhist doctrine about the transmission of the Buddhist truth. The historical Buddha, they believed, had followed the principle of skillful means (*upaya*) and geared his teaching to the capabilities of his audience. He did not reveal the highest truths (Mahayana truths) during his lifetime because his followers were not ready. However, Buddhas in ages past had preached these doctrines to myriads of worlds of sentient beings. When they were needed, these truths were revealed in the *Lotus Sutra, Heart Sutra, Diamond Sutra*, and others.

42. See Sakai Tadao, *Chūgoku zensho no kenkyū*, 409.

43. P'eng Shao-sheng, *Chü-shih chuan* (Biographies of Lay Buddhists) (comp. 1746; publ., 1878), no. 55.

44. *Yin-chih wen kuang-i* (Commentary to Good Deeds Done in Secret), preface.

45. Ibid., vol. 1, p. 3.

46. See Harry J. Lamley, "Hsieh-tou: The Pathology of Violence in Southeastern China," *Ch'ing-shih wen-t'i* 3:7 (Nov. 1977) 1–39; and "Subethnic Rivalry in the Ch'ing Period," in Emily Martin Ahern and Hill Gates, eds., *The Anthropology of Taiwanese Society* (Stanford: Stanford University Press, 1981).

47. *Yin-chih wen kuang-i*, vol. 1, pp. 27–28.

48. Ibid., vol. 1, p. 37. The reference is to *Mencius* 2A:6, but it is not an exact quotation.

49. Ibid., vol. 1, p. 33.

50. Ibid., vol. 1, pp. 100–107.

51. *Chü-shih chuan*, no. 56, 1a.

52. Arthur W. Hummel, ed., *Eminent Chinese of the Ch'ing Period* (Washington: United States Government Printing Office, 1943), 614–15.

53. P'eng Shao-sheng, *Erh-lin chü chi* (Collection of Lay Buddhists of the Two Groves) (col. 1880; publ. 1881), 9:8a–9a.

54. Ibid., 19:5b–6a.

55. Ibid., 3:11b.

56. Biographical information on Wang Chin and Lo Yu-kao may be found in Hummel, *Eminent Chinese*, pp. 616–17 and 824–26, respectively.

57. Wang Chin, *Wang-tzu wen-lu* (Record of the Writings of Master Wang) (col. 1823, 1881; publ. 1882), 2:3b.

58. Ibid., 5:6a.

59. *Erh-lin chü chi*, 2:2b.

60. Ibid., 3:4b.

61. Ibid., 5:4b.

62. Ibid., 19:8a.

63. *Chü-shih chuan*, no. 44, 20b–21a.

64. *Erh-lin chü chi*, 19:2a.

65. *Wang-tzu wen-lu*, 5:3b.

66. See, e.g., *Erh-lin chü chi*, 5:1aff; 5:14aff.

67. *Chü-shih chuan*, 55.

68. *Erh-lin chü chi*, 5:2a.

69. Ibid., 5:14a.

70. Ibid.

71. *Ching-t'u sheng-hsien lu* (Record of Pure Land Sages and Worthies) (pref., 1783; Kuang-hsü ed.), 5:13b.

72. Ibid., 5:19a.

73. *I-hsing chü chi* (Collection of Lay Buddhists of Singleminded Practice) (ed. for publication 1795; originally published 1824; reprint ed. of 1958), 3:1b–2a.

74. Ibid., 2:21a.

75. Ibid., 2:21a–21b.

76. This is a basic Mahayana Buddhist doctrine, first formulated by Nagarjuna. For a succinct discussion of the Doctrine of Emptiness and its implications, see Richard Robinson, *The Buddhist Religion* (Encino, Cal.: Dickenson Press, 1977; 2d ed.), pp. 88ff.

77. *Chuang Tzu*, "Ch'i-wu lun" (The Sorting Which Evens Things Out). For a translation, see A. C. Graham, trans., *Chuang Tzu: The Inner Chapters* (London: George Allen and Unwin, 1981), 48–61.

78. *Erh-lin chü chi*, 10:9a–9b.

79. For reverence for life, see, e.g., ibid., 6:1a; for a discussion of charity, see ibid., 5:12b.

80. *I-hsing chü chi*, 2:21aff.

81. Ibid., 4:1a.

82. *Erh-lin chü chi*, 3:2a.

83. Mount T'ieh-wei: *Cakravada-parvata*. The outermost mountain range ringing the Buddhist cosmic mountain Sumeru.

84. *Mencius* 6A:11.

85. *I-hsing chü chi*, 4:4a.

86. *Chü-shih chuan*, colophon to no. 56.

87. *I-hsing chü chi*, 4:16a.

GLOSSARY

Araki Kengo　荒木見悟

Chang　張

Chen-k'ung chia-hsiang wu-sheng lao-mu　真空家鄉無生老母

Chen-k'ung lao-tsu　真空老祖

"Ch'i-wu lun"　齊物論

chin-shih　進士

Ching-t'u sheng-hsien lu　淨土聖賢錄

Chou An-shih　周安士

Chu Hsi　朱熹

Chu-hung　株宏

Chūgoku zensho no kenkyū　中國善書の研究

chüeh　訣

Chü-shih chuan　居士傳

Erh-lin chü chi　二林居集

Ho Hsin-yin　何心隱

Huang Yü-p'ien　黃育楩

I-chieh li-yü　易解俚語

I-hsing chü chi　一行居集

ju　儒

Ju T'ung-tsu　儒童祖

Kōchu Haja shōben　校註破邪詳辨

kuan-hsin　觀心

kung　公

Kung Ch'ang　弓長

kung-kuo ko　功過格

liang-chih　良知

Lin Chao-en　林兆恩

Liu San-chiao ching　留三教經

Lo Yu-kao　羅有高

Lu Hsiang-shan　陸象山

Lu Wen-hui　盧文輝

Lung-hua　龍華

nien-fo　念佛

Pai Su-chai lei chi　白蘇齋類集

P'eng Shao-sheng　彭紹升

P'o-hsieh hsiang-p'ien　破邪詳辨

pu-sha　不殺

Sakai Tadao　酒井忠夫

San-chiao cheng-tsung t'ung-lun　三教正宗統論

Sawada Mizuho　澤田瑞穗

Shan-hai ching　山海經

Shan-tung hsiang-shih lu　山東鄉試錄

Shien　史淵

Shigematsu Shunshō　種松俊章

shih　實

"Shina sankyōshijō no jakan no mondai"　支那三教史上の若干の問題

Shinchō chūki shi kenkyū　清朝中期史研究

ssu　私

Suzuki Chūsei　鈴木中正

Ta-Ch'ing li-ch'ao shih-lu　大清歷朝實錄

Ta-kuan　達觀

T'ai-shang kan-ying p'ien　太上感應篇

T'ai-shang lao-chün　太上老君

tang-jen　當人

Te-ch'ing　德清

t'i　體

tzu-te　自得

Wang Chin　王縉

Wang Ken　王艮

Wang-tzu wen-lu　汪子文錄

Wang Wen-ch'eng kung ch'üan-shu　王文成公全書

Wang Yang-ming　王陽明

wen　文

Wen Ch'ang　文昌

wen-hsüeh kuan　文學官

Wu-sheng lao-mu　無生老母

yao　妖

Yin-chih wen　陰隲文

Yin-chih wen kuang-i　陰隲文廣義

Yüan Huang　袁黃

Yüan Tsung-tao　袁宗道

Chapter Eight

THE ACCEPTANCE OF CHINESE NEO-CONFUCIANISM IN JAPAN IN THE EARLY TOKUGAWA PERIOD

MINAMOTO RYŌEN

translated by Joshua A. Fogel

The Character of Neo-Confucianism in the Early Tokugawa Period: What Is the Learning of the Mind-and-Heart (Shingaku)?

The subject of this chapter, the acceptance of Chinese Neo-Confucian teachings in the early Tokugawa period in Japan, is but one extremely small topic in the much broader history of the acceptance of Chinese Confucianism in Japan. The issue addressed, "the learning of the mind-and-heart" (*shingaku*) and "the message of the mind" or "the method of disciplining the mind" (*shinpō*),[1] however, has a depth in the history of Japanese thought that goes beyond what one might expect. Therefore, the discussion begins with an analysis of the problem based in its historical setting and ends with a discussion of the significance of *shingaku* in Japan's modernization process.

Chinese Neo-Confucianism was received in Japan at the beginning of the early modern period as *shingaku* and *shinpō no gaku* (the learning of *shinpō*). What is the significance of this fact? The beginning of the early modern period refers here to the period from the founding of the Tokugawa bakufu in 1603 until the third and fourth years of the Kanbun reign period (1663–1664), roughly sixty years.[2] This chapter investigates the manner in which Neo-Confucianism was accepted in Japan at this time, which I believe requires greater general understanding.

The predominant theory in Japan to this point is that of Maruyama Masao. Professor Maruyama argues that Shushigaku (the learning of the Chu Hsi school) was accepted in Japan by Hayashi Razan (1583–1657) at the beginning of the early modern period, and when his speculative mode of thought dissolved of its own accord, the Ancient Learning school (*kogaku*) formed.[3] A different but nonetheless influential point of view has been elaborated by Ishida Ichirō. Professor Ishida argues that the political establishment and social structures of the Tokugawa regime were themselves imbued with Shushigaku, and he tries to explain Tokugawa Neo-Confucianism in a comprehensive manner from this Shushigaku perspective.[4] Nor does Ishida deny the predominant position held by Shushigaku at the beginning of the early modern period.

A pioneering study that criticized, indeed contradicted, these earlier views was Professor Bitō Masahide's *Nihon hōken shisō shi kenkyū* (Studies in the History of Japanese Feudal Thought).[5] In my 1972 work, *Tokugawa gōri shisō no keifu* (Lineages of Rationalist Thought in the Tokugawa Period), I wrote:

> Professor Maruyama argues in his *Nihon seiji shisō shi kenkyū* [Studies in the History of Japanese Political Thought] that there is a linkage between the establishment of the Ancient Learning school and the decline of the Chu Hsi school. Professor Bitō has already noted, by way of criticism, that there are problems with this thesis. At that time, the Chu Hsi school [in Japan] was not at an intellectual level sufficiently high to withstand the critiques of Itō Jinsai and Ogyū Sorai. However, put in another way, when discussing the formative process of Kogaku in relation to the theoretical decline of the Chu Hsi school, including the Chu Hsi schools of China and Korea which exerted overwhelming influences on the spiritual climate of early seventeenth-century Japan, Maruyama's hypothesis does have some validity. Jinsai and Sorai both created their systems of scholarship and thought principally focused on Ch'eng-Chu learning itself, and their concern for Japanese Chu Hsi school scholars, such as Hayashi Razan, was secondary. It would seem that, of all Chu Hsi school thinkers of the time, they were most strongly conscious of Yamazaki Ansai.[6]

At the time that I wrote this, I saw the problem as one of emphasis but lacked concrete evidence about the nature of early modern Japanese Neo-

Confucianism before Kaibara Ekken (1630–1714). Later, I turned my attention to an analysis of the two polar schools concerning the Chu Hsi school's view of *ri*, or principle: those who stressed the experiential nature of *ri* (the *ki* school) and those who stressed the a priori character of *ri* (the *ri* school).[7] At the time I was able to pursue my research to a certain extent into the history of thought before Ekken, but I had yet to attain a genuine understanding of the issue.

In fact, beginning in the medieval period it was Zen monks who brought Chu Hsi learning to Japan together with Zen Buddhism.[8] Thus, for the problem under analysis here — namely, the beginning of the early modern period — it would be easy to have the impression that the Chu Hsi school predominated from this period if we limit our vision to Hayashi Razan and the Tosanangaku, or the Tosanan School. However, let us expand our vision to include such Neo-Confucian scholars of the time as Fujiwara Seika (1561–1615), Oze Hoan (1564–1640), Matsunaga Sekigo (1590–1655, or 1592–1657), Nawa Kassho (1595–1648), Nakae Tōju (1608–1648), and Kumazawa Banzan (1619–1691); men who were Zen monks but who were deeply concerned with Neo-Confucianism, such as Takuan (1573–1645); and texts of uncertain authorship, such as the *Shingaku gorin no sho* (On the Five Relationships of the School of the Mind-and-Heart), *Honsaroku* (Chronicle of Honda Masanobu [traditionally attributed to Honda]), and *Kana shōri* (On Human Nature [written] in Japanese; also known by the title *Chiyo moto kusa* [often attributed to Fujiwara Seika]). Once we have done this, we will have no choice but to discard the view that Japan at the beginning of the early modern period was overwhelmed by the Chu Hsi school and that the latter was fixed to the foundations of Tokugawa society at that time.

Among the conclusions drawn from this perspective are that Neo-Confucianism of this period in Japan was a mixture of the Chu Hsi school, Yōmeigaku (the Wang Yang-ming school), and syncretism (which found unifying themes in the three religions of Confucianism, Buddhism, and Taoism), as well as schools of thought that coexisted with Neo-Confucianism, such as strategic military science and Zen.[9] If we look for the nature of what was shared by these different schools, then the most appropriate response is *shingaku* or *shinpō no gaku*.[10]

Professor Bitō's study, which attacked the Maruyama thesis by criticizing its ideological component, did not approach Japanese Neo-Confucianism of the early seventeenth century as *shingaku* or *shinpō no gaku*. I was completely unaware of this issue when I was writing the final chapter of my *Kinsei shoki jitsugaku shisō no kenkyū* (Studies in Practical Learning at the Beginning of the Early Modern Period).[11] Even after the publication of my book, the identification of Neo-Confucianism in this period with *shingaku* was still not a generally accepted view. Nonetheless, this formulation of the issue is an extremely important point to emphasize both for our understanding of Neo-Confucian thought in the first half of the seventeenth century, as a transition from medieval to early modern times, and for the understanding it affords us of the *Zeitgeist* underlying this development. This chapter centers on the issue of *shingaku* and *shinpō no gaku* and reanalyzes the points I made in *Kinsei shoki jitsugaku shisō no kenkyū* on the problem of "the acceptance of Chinese Neo-Confucianism in the early Tokugawa period." This discussion responds to the very question prefigured in the work cited above. Still, without the inclusion of Yamazaki Ansai (1618–1682), the resolution would remain incomplete.

What, then, is *shingaku* or *shinpō no gaku*? What elements are to be found in the formation of *shingaku*? Simply put, *shingaku* and *shinpō no gaku* may be defined as "the learning that trains the mind-and-heart so as to heighten and deepen the condition of the mind-and-heart as we actually have it and make it what it ought to be." From this statement, however, it is not clear how Buddhist *shinpō* differs from Neo-Confucian. Thus, I would like to offer the following, more detailed definition. By *shingaku* or *shinpō no gaku*, I refer to the "Neo-Confucian doctrine founded on the belief that, by placing the highest value on the internal condition of the mind-and-heart, and, given its proper training, taking one's own mind-and-heart as a standard," it will be possible either immediately or gradually to resolve not only one's own personal problems but problems of family, society, and the governance of the state. Here "Neo-Confucian" includes the syncretic idea of "the unity of the Three Teachings" in which Confucianism was the central core.

This *shingaku* differs in two respects from Buddhism. First, there is not merely the question of the existence of the self, because, with it, questions of family, society, and the state can be resolved. Second, it does not merely look at the way in which the mind-and-heart should be apart from all else, but examines the question of the proper functioning of the "mind-and-heart" in its relationship to the transcendent position of "Heaven." Thus, Neo-Confucian *shingaku* "sees human existence from the perspective of the mind-and-heart, and yet, in spite of this, it never seeks to escape from this world but focuses on the human relationships within the world which lie at the basis of a relationship with a transcendent heaven."

242 • *Japan and Neo-Confucianism*

The Formation of Shingaku in the Early Tokugawa Period

What then were the principal factors that brought about the formation of *shingaku* at the beginning of the early modern period in Japan? There were domestic causes as well as intellectual influences from abroad, particularly Chinese and Korean Neo-Confucianism.

DOMESTIC FACTORS

Causes indigenous to Japan were of two kinds: societal factors and the spiritual tradition at work within Japanese society at that time. In terms of societal factors, one can point to the interior experience of the people who lived at the start of the early modern period, an age of warfare and, even after the cessation of the fighting, an era in which social and political instability continued. Institutions one could rely upon and value systems in which one could invest trust had not yet taken firm root in the society of the early seventeenth century. The standard that people living in an uncertain age used to reach judgments and to make decisions, when they had to respond to the social turmoil about them, was simply the individual "mind-and-heart."

The spiritual tradition that remained vibrant among the people at that time assumed an attitude toward human life emphasizing the training of the mind. Since the Heian period, Japan had had a tradition honoring the *refinement* of the mind. However, with the rise of the military class in the middle ages and their acceptance of Zen, the more active attitude of *training* the mind was added to this picture. This attitude came to permeate not only the world of Zen priests diligent in the disciplining of their minds but also the realm of the civil and military arts, which stressed both physical and technical training.[12] Cultivation of the human heart (or mind-and-heart) so as to respond to a complex set of circumstances was the trend of the times.

THE INFLUENCE OF CHINESE NEO-CONFUCIANISM

The discipline of *shinpō* involved in Zen and the Japanese civil arts, even assuming the resolution of an individual's problems, did not extend so far that it bore on the questions raised by society and the state. The psychological experiences — the exercise of their minds — of people who lived through the tumultuous period at the beginning of early modern Japan were rich, but these psychological experiences, even if they had provided the motive force to impel people to action, did not constitute a conscious ideology. What gave shape to people's minds-and-hearts in Japan at this time was the acceptance of

Neo-Confucianism from China and Korea. The influence and impetus for Japanese *shingaku* in the early seventeenth century was provided by the following intellectual sources.

THE INFLUENCE OF CHU HSI AND THE CHU HSI SCHOOL

Among the sources of Chinese Neo-Confucian influence in Japan at this time, the Chu Hsi school was by far the strongest. Yet actual study of the immense body of writings by Chu Hsi was still incomplete in Japan, so long wracked by warfare and only now just having concluded a peace. The *Ssu-shu chi-chu* (Collected Commentaries on the Four Books) and the *Ssu-shu huo-wen* (Questions and Answers on the Four Books) were the only works by Chu Hsi that had been read in Japan, and most Japanese gained their understanding of Chu's work through a reading of the *Chu Tzu ta-ch'üan* (Complete Literary Works of Chu Hsi), an edition of Chu's writings edited during the Ming period.[13]

Hayashi Razan himself wrote a critique of Lu Hsiang-shan (Lu Chiu-yüan, 1139–93) and Wang Yang-ming (Wang Shou-jen, 1472–1529) on the basis of Chu Hsi learning at this time; it was based on such works of Chinese scholars of the Chu Hsi school of the Ming period as the *Hsüeh-p'u t'ung-pien* (General Critique of Obscurations to Learning) by Ch'en Chien (Ch'en Ch'ing-lan, 1497–1567) and the *I-tuan pien-cheng* (The Rectification of Heresy) by Chan Ling (early sixteenth century).[14] The genuine acceptance of Chu Hsi's thought did not begin until the emergence of Yamazaki Ansai.

At the start of the early modern era, Chu Hsi's thought was understood through the writings of the Chu Hsi school of the Ming and early Ch'ing. Therefore, Japanese scholars of the Chu Hsi school in this era could simultaneously claim affiliation with the Chu Hsi school and take a *shingaku* position as well. Although the details concerning the influences on their thought still remain unclear to us, there are clear signs that Fujiwara Seika read and was familiar with the *Lu-chai hsin-fa* ([Hsü] Lu-chai's Message of the Mind), by Hsü Heng (Hsü Lu-chai, 1209–1281) of the Yüan period. In his youth Itō Jinsai (1627–1705) adopted a *shingaku* stance and loved to read Hsü's work. (I should point out that the "Jinsai School" took shape on the basis of a denial of *shingaku*.)

Furthermore, the *Hsin-ching fu-chu* (Commentary on the Classic of the Mind-and-Heart) by Ch'eng Min-cheng (Ch'eng Huang-tun, *chin-shih* of 1466) of the Ming, which was an annotated commentary to the *Hsin-ching* (Classic of the Mind-and-Heart) by Chen Te-hsiu (Chen Hsi-shan, 1178–1235)[15] of the late Sung, exerted an influence on both Oze Hoan and Takuan;

and, through its reprinting by Yi T'oegye (1501–1570) of the Yi dynasty in Korea, it exerted an influence on Yamazaki Ansai and his school of thought. In addition, Fujiwara Seika encouraged Hayashi Razan to read both Chen's *Ta-hsüeh yen-i* (The Extended Meaning of the *Great Learning*) as well as the supplement to it by Ch'iu Chün, the *Ta-hsüeh yen-i pu* (Supplement to the *Extended Meaning of the Great Learning*).

It would also be incorrect to say that neither Chu Hsi nor his followers in the Sung period contributed anything to the formation of *shingaku* (Ch. *hsin-hsüeh*) in early seventeenth-century Japan. The *hsin-hsüeh* tendency in Chu Hsi's thought, as developed in his *Ta-hsüeh huo-wen* (Questions and Answers on the *Great Learning*), makes the possibility of this influence on Japanese Neo-Confucians enormous. Seika also strongly recommended to the young Razan that he read the *Yen-p'ing ta-wen* ([Li] Yen-p'ing's Replies to Queries), which is the recorded conversations between Chu Hsi's teacher Li T'ung (Li Yen-p'ing, 1093–1163) and the young Chu Hsi; Seika said it was the "message of the mind of [Li] Yen-p'ing's disciplined effort (*kufū*; Ch. *kung-fu*) and the way into learning the teachings of Tzu-yang [Chu Hsi]."[16] Furthermore, Hayashi Razan provided a colloquial explanation of the *Hsing-li tzu-i* (Meaning of Terms on Human Nature and Principle) by Chu Hsi's disciple, Ch'en Ch'un (Ch'en Pei-hsi, 1159–1223); this made it possible for Razan to take a position on the inseparability of *ri* (Ch. *li*, principle) and *ki* (Ch. *ch'i*, material force) from the perspective of *hsin* or the "mind-and-heart."[17]

THE INFLUENCE OF THE LU-WANG SCHOOL

The influence of Lu Hsiang-shan in this period was comparatively small; Lu was mentioned only to a certain degree by Fujiwara Seika. However, the influence of Wang Yang-ming was considerably greater. Seika and, especially, Nakae Tōju and Kumazawa Banzan were much influenced by Wang's ideas. The influence on Nakae of Wang Chi (Wang Lung-hsi, 1498–1583, a disciple of Yang-ming's) was particularly marked.

Of these three Chinese thinkers, Wang Yang-ming calls for a closer look. Although Seika was not a follower of Wang's teachings, he inherited some of Wang's manner of conceptualizing problems. For example, of the three terms (taken from Wang's reading of the *Great Learning*) — *ming-te* (Jap. *meitoku*, bright or illumined virtue), *ch'in-min* (Jap. *shinmin*, cherish or love the people), and *chih-shan* (Jap. *shizen*, supreme goodness) — Seika laid greatest emphasis on *shizen*. One may see this as his acceptance of Wang Yang-ming's understanding of the issue, which Wang delineated in his *Ta-hsüeh wen* (Inquiry on the *Great Learning*). When we look at Seika's *Daigaku yōryaku*

(Outline of the Essentials of the *Great Learning*), we can see that he did not necessarily fully accept the ancient text of the *Great Learning* (as it initially appeared in the *Li-chi* or Book of Rites) as the definitive text of the *Great Learning* (as Wang Yang-ming and his school did); and, in explaining the work, Seika did not completely follow Wang's ideas. He did go so far as to argue, as Wang did not, that *shinmin* "meant to nourish the people" (*tami o yashinau no gi*); and on the term *ko-wu* (Jap. *kakubutsu*, investigation of things [also from the *Great Learning*]), he followed the explanation given by Lin Chao-en (1517–1598).[18]

In Seika's case, the acceptance of ideas from Wang Yang-ming was selective, but in the case of Nakae Tōju it was far more basic. Nakae was extremely pleased to obtain a set of the complete writings of Wang Yang-ming; he considered it "a blessing bestowed by the Way of Heaven." He even indicated in a letter to one of his disciples (by the name of Ikeda) that, had he not been so blessed, his whole life would have been empty.[19]

Nakae considered the distinctiveness of Wang's learning and thought to lie in two basic points: belief in the ancient text version of the *Great Learning*; and understanding of the term "knowledge" (Ch. *chih*; Jap. *chi*) in the phrase "extending knowledge" (Ch. *chih-chih*; Jap. *chichi*) to mean "innate knowledge" (Ch. *liang-chih*; Jap. *ryōchi*). Yet, if we make a more detailed examination of Nakae's thought, we should note that, while subjectively sympathizing with Wang's views to a profound extent, Nakae differed from Wang in the structure of his mode of thought. The difference between the two men appears especially starkly in Nakae's explanation of Wang's idea of *chih liang-chih* (extending innate knowledge). Wang Yang-ming's *chih liang-chih* had an activist orientation geared toward the realization of innate knowledge in each and every case. For Nakae, when the "five entities" (*goji*, by which he meant "appearance, speech, vision, hearing, and thought")[20] were activated, one should then examine by means of "the mirror (reflection) of innate knowledge" whether or not willful thoughts (*i'nen*) remained. The conditions under which willful thoughts disappeared were for him the "extension of innate knowledge."

At the root of the difference in understanding of the meaning of *chih liang-chih* lay a difference in their perceptions of the meaning of *i* (intentionality, will). Wang saw both good and bad in the activation of *i* and sought to control the evil thoughts in the circumstances in which *i* operated. By contrast, Nakae argued in his "Daigaku kō" (Study of the *Great Learning*) that "intentionality is the root of all desires and evils."[21] Although the mind-and-heart must give rise solely to supreme good, he claimed, the ordinary [man's] mind-and-heart contains both good and evil because of the "intentionality" that lies concealed within it. In this way, Nakae argued in his "Keikai" (Explanation of the Classics) that what eradicates the evil root of intentionality is *ch'eng-i* (honest will, sincere intentions);[22] in his "Kohon Daigaku zenkai" (Complete Explanation of the Ancient Text of the *Great Learning*), he even referred to *ch'eng-i* as that which "eradicates intentionality."[23]

Nakae's idea was that, when intentionality is eliminated, bright virtue can on its own become enlightened. Although he used the vocabulary of Neo-Confucianism, his idea closely resembled the Buddhist intellectual construct in which Buddha-nature becomes enlightened when evil passions are eliminated. This is because, unlike Wang Yang-ming, who removed Buddhism from his way of thinking, Nakae Tōju in his later years assumed a stance that allowed for Buddhism.[24] The twists and turns in his acceptance of Wang's ideas in this context weighed heavily on his own disposition. They surely were based largely on the fact that Nakae had read the works of Wang Chi before encountering the thought of Wang Yang-ming, so that his understanding of Yang-ming's ideas was mediated by those of Wang Chi.[25]

THE INFLUENCE OF THE IDEA OF THE UNITY OF THE THREE TEACHINGS

The third of the Chinese systems of thought that exerted an influence on the formation of *shingaku* at the beginning of the early modern period in Japan was the school that believed that the Three Teachings were united as a single whole. Lin Chao-en's influence as a thinker of this sort was overwhelmingly the greatest. This was particularly true in the case of the thought of Seika in his later years. Similarly, Takuan had studied the significance of the term *i-tuan* (Jap. *itan*, heterodox) from Lin Chao-en's *Ssu-shu cheng-i k'ao* (A Study of the Correct Meaning of the Four Books), on the basis of which Takuan then came to the defense of Buddhism.[26] Nakae also accepted critically Lin Chao-en's *Ken-pei hsin-fa* (The Method of the Mind in Stilling the Back).[27]

The idea of the unity of the Three Teachings was found in the *Hsing-li ta-ch'üan hui-t'ung* (Thorough Elucidation of the Great Compendium on Human Nature and Principle), a collection representing a wide variety of late Ming intellectual trends. In this collection was the *Li-yen sheng-yü* (Further Words on Ritual and Language) by T'ang Shu (1497–1574), which provided an intellectual basis for Nakae's belief in "T'ai-i shen" (the God of Creation).[28] Although not the works of intellectuals, influence from *shan-shu* (morality books), books used in the education of commoners, can be detected in the writings of Oze Hoan and Nakae Tōju.[29]

Let us now focus more closely on the issue of Seika's acceptance of the thought of Lin Chao-en. The concepts of "the unity of the self and others," "the unity of inner and outer,"and "the clear manifestation of the Way" in Seika's *Daigaku yōryaku* are all indebted to Lin's *Ta-hsüeh cheng-i tsuan* (Compendium on the Correct Meaning of the *Great Learning*).[30] Lin's influence was also pronounced in the area of the concept of the "investigation of things," which occupied the most important place within Seika's idea of "the learning of the method of the mind." Seika studied Lin's conceptualization of *ko-wu* (Jap. *kakubutsu*) and from that position moved on to attack the views on *ko-wu* held by Cheng Hsüan (127–200), Ssu-ma Kuang (1019–1086), Chu Hsi, and Wang Yang-ming. Seika argued that the *ko* (Jap. *kaku*) of *ko-wu* carried the meaning of remove or eliminate; and *wu* (Jap. *mono*) did not imply objective "things" but "men transformed into things." He said further of *mono* that they "are desires within the mind-and-heart and shrewd chance-taking by the mind-and-heart," "the dust" (i.e., evil desires of the mind-and-heart).

Thus, what Seika meant by *kakubutsu* was that we should eliminate all conscious phenomena (all thoughts) from our minds and "drive away the evil mind." This perspective he learned from Lin Chao-en.[31] As Seika put it in his *Daigaku yōryaku*:

> *Mono* is dust.[32] Once we wipe every speck of dust away and make the mirror clear and bright, our vision will instantly become bright. This place of clarity and brightness in the mirror, we call empty. It has spirit within it. Perhaps this may be "supreme goodness" as well.

If this is true, then how do we achieve a purity and clarity in our hearts? Seika continued:

> If we strive through disciplined effort to eliminate evil desires [*mono*], this very disciplined effort itself will be an evil desire. If there is so much as a single point of darkness or filth, there will be all manner of considered thought. If these considered thoughts do not exist, then naturally it will have a purity and spirituality and give rise to illumined knowledge. Thus, "it hits the mark without making an effort" in responding to the myriad things [of the world]. To think without considering is [genuine] thought; this does not mean we should despise thinking [itself]. It simply means that we clarify our thinking naturally. That is what is called the complete substance and the great functioning [of the mind].[33]

Although this passage describes the essence of Seika's views on the learning of the mind-and-heart, Seika learned the fundamental core of his way of thinking here in his later years from Lin Chao-en's work.

"LEARNING OF THE MIND-AND-HEART" AND THE LIU-T'AO AND SAN-LÜEH

Finally, I would like to touch on the role played in the formation of *shingaku* thought of the early Tokugawa period by two texts of military strategy, the *Liu-t'ao* (Six Scabbards, a work in six *chüan*, traditionally attributed to T'ai-kung-wang of the early Chou) and the *San-lüeh* (Three Strategies, a work in three *chüan*, traditionally attributed to Huang-shih-kung, ca. 200 BCE). The early seventeenth century in Japan witnessed the emergence of two forms of *shingaku*: the views of those we have examined to this point who considered that "if one purifies the truth of one's own mind-and-heart, then problems of welfare and public in the wider world order will be resolved on their own through contacts between the self and others," and those who concentrated on the efforts of the mind-and-heart with the understanding that, "without ceasing contacts with others, it is necessary to discipline one's own mind-and-heart toward the realization of the goal of resolving in a practical manner problems to which one sets one's mind." The influence of the *Liu-t'ao* and the *San-lüeh* can be seen in the latter case, concretely in the works of Hayashi Razan and in the *Honsaroku*.

Razan argued, following the *San-lüeh*, that one must wholeheartedly (single-mindedly) combine the four qualities of being unyielding (*kang*), pliant (*jou*), powerful (*ch'iang*), and weak (*jo*) in a state that abides with principle.[34] He advocated a "strategy of preserving the mind" (*kokoromochi no heihō*),[35] by which he sought control based not on brute force but on the mind-and-heart. In this way he was devising an interface between *shingaku* of the Chu Hsi school sort and the *San-lüeh*.

Second, while fundamentally following the Chu Hsi school's position on the idea of Heaven, Razan also accepted the idea expressed in the *Liu-t'ao* that "all under Heaven" (*tenka*) was the (real) realm of all that existed under Heaven. He thus opened the way to a realistic political ideology that expected the submission of the populace for the benefit of the entire realm.[36]

Third, on the idea of *kei* (reverence or seriousness), Razan had the following to say: "The substance of the mind-and-heart is originally empty [i.e., pure] and leaves no traces in its interactions with external things. If we lack reverence, then the original mind-and-heart will perish."[37] He spoke of the need to respond to the external world by adopting the standpoint of reverence, as understood in the manner of the Chu Hsi school, as concentrating on one's own interior being. At the same time, he was also attracted to a utilitarian understanding of reverence as concern for others, citing the *Tan-shu* as quoted by the *Liu-t'ao:* "It is auspicious when reverence overcomes indolence [*tai*]; it is inauspicious when disrespect wins out over reverence."[38] For a long time, Razan was confused over how to mediate between these two views, but in his later years he ultimately devised a reconciliation from a Chu Hsi school stance.

Fourth, he also accepted the understanding of "benefit" (profit, *li*; Jap. *ri*) of the *Liu-t'ao:* "That which makes the benefits of the realm common to all is good for the realm, while that which seeks arbitrarily to privatize the benefits of the realm is bad for it."[39] By the same token, Razan also denied this very position elsewhere in his writings: "The mind-and-heart of the Sage is self-possessed. For what reason would it have to seek benefit from the realm? This would not be good."[40] Clearly, Razan's own mind was wavering, though he later resolved this dilemma by fixing on the concept of the "benefit of moral obligation" (*giri no ri*); namely, one benefited by benefiting the people and hence benefited what was good in the external things of the world.

As can be seen here, Razan had acquired a wide variety of experience working for the Tokugawa *bakufu*. Although he had begun his career as an intense scholar of Chu Hsi learning, his touching on such military texts as the *Liu-t'ao* and the *San-lüeh* indicates a different path from those *shingaku* adherents who had earnestly sought an internal, personal purification and from there expanded naturally toward societal and state reforms. Razan was drawn to a kind of realism of thought in which he remained conscious of other people and highly attentive to his connection to others, and in which he sought to win over people's minds-and-hearts by planning in the popular interest. Furthermore, he called his own position *shingaku*, and, ultimately, he found a compromise for the two positions in terms of the conception of *kokoro* (mind-and-heart) found in the Chu Hsi school.

The *Liu-t'ao* and the *San-lüeh*, which exerted an influence on this final type of *shingaku*, bore no particular relationship to Sung or Ming thought. Probably this sort of *shingaku*, which accepted ideas from military texts, was a Japanese innovation, an aspect of *shingaku* as it entered a warrior society. Nonetheless, what lay at the basis of *shingaku* remained the sources from the Sung and the Ming.

We have now looked at four ways in which Chinese Neo-Confucianism was accepted into Japan in the early Tokugawa period. Whatever perspective we take, it appears clear that the influence and stimulation of Sung and Ming thought, especially the latter, played a huge role in the formation of Japanese *shingaku* at the start of the early modern era. From the perspective of Neo-Confucianism, Japan of the early seventeenth century was an intellectually backward nation, and, like surging waves, Sung and Ming thought came flooding into Japan at the same time. Of course, from medieval times, Zen monks, especially those from the Five Mountain temples, had been introducing Chu Hsi learning to Japan together with Zen, and they had even influenced the scholarship of the Kiyowaras, which was based in Chinese learning (*Kangaku*). This development, however, had not permeated society to any considerable extent.

When the long period of war ceased and peace and order were attained, Japanese intellectuals of the time studied the various schools of learning voraciously, and all of these schools were mixed together. This is an important difference from the orderly manner in which Korean scholars of the Yi dynasty received Chinese culture, preserving the specific order in which it was bequeathed by Chinese Neo-Confucians. Japanese intellectuals of the early seventeenth century did not have at their disposal the broad perspective on the entirety of Chinese Neo-Confucian thought. From the places at which they lived and worked, they understood the Chinese and Korean Neo-Confucians with which they came into contact on the basis of their own experiences, and they chose selectively. The scholarly learning and thought that emerged under these circumstances can generally be called *shingaku* or *shinpō no gaku*, but, as we have seen, *shingaku* or *shinpō no gaku* had a variety of guises. At the same time, these systems of Japanese thought reveal, though naively, a Japanese character unlike what we find in the cases of China and Korea. This will become more important in understanding the later development of Japanese Neo-Confucianism. Let me now touch on a few points in this connection.

The Character and Various Forms of Shingaku in the Early Tokugawa Period

Many different kinds of thought in the early Tokugawa era are subsumed under the conceptual rubric of *shingaku*. Unlike the question of *shinpō* in the medieval period, though concern in the later period was not focused solely on the preserving a quiet state in the mind-and-heart. Indeed, one characteristic of *shingaku* in the early seventeenth century was a tremendous concern for the activist potential of the mind-and-heart, its functions, and its movements.

One thing we can say about the Neo-Confucianism of this period is that scarcely anyone dealt with the problems of "human nature" (Jap. *sei*; Ch. *hsing*) or "human nature and principle" (Jap. *seiri*; Ch. *hsing-li*) in terms of a principle that dwelt in the mind-and-heart. Hardly anyone even used the expression "the learning of human nature" (Jap. *seigaku*; Ch. *hsing-hsüeh*). Of course, those who adopted the positions of the Wang Yang-ming school or the syncretist vision of the unity of the Three Teachings did employ terms such as *shin* (Ch. *hsin*), *shinri* (Ch. *hsin-li*, mind-and-heart and principle), and *shingaku* (Ch. *hsin-hsüeh*).[41] This fact demonstrates that these people were also more concerned with the activist functions of the mind-and-heart than they were with the structure of its quiescence.

This issue is intricately tied to the structure of the debate over *ri* (Ch. *li*, principle) and *ki* (Ch. *ch'i*, material force) raised by advocates of *shingaku* at the time. They were not calling for a stress on *ri* over *ki* or vice versa, but shared a position that stressed the inseparability of *ri* and *ki*. I see their views on the "*ri-ki* debate" as constructed on the model of the debate over *shin* and *sei*. That is, my supposition is that the marked tendency to persist in the advocacy of *ri-ki* inseparability — "neither two nor one" — is probably due to a major concern for the functional, activist aspect of the mind-and-heart.[42] The reason they adopted this stance on the *ri-ki* issue was not to clarify philosophically the positions of those stressing one over the other, but to emphasize practicality as a response to the real world from a position based upon the mind-and-heart. This was the aspect of the issue to which they could most readily assent.

Thus, I generalize by characterizing Japanese Neo-Confucianism at the start of the early modern period as "*shingaku*," but, in terms of its content, this *shingaku* is not colored with a single hue. At the beginning of the period under study, *shingaku* was founded with a vitality that brought an end to the lingering strains of the Warring States period (as with Oze Hoan). Among the *shingaku* scholars at the end of this period, it had become purified, transformed into something that had lost its sociality (as with the late Nakae Tōju). From an epistemological point of view, the strength of the transcendental rationalism in the *shingaku* of this period forms a basic undertone, but (in the works of Fujiwara Seika, Matsunaga Sekigo, Nawa Kassho, Nakae Tōju, and Yamazaki Ansai, as well as the *Shingaku gorin no sho* and the *Kana shōri*) it was not playing at speculative metaphysics; it had a profound ethical and practical nature.[43]

By the same token, there was a strong empirical strain, as in the case of Hayashi Razan. He was not an out-and-out empiricist, as was Kaibara Ekken later, for he had a transcendental side that can be seen in his "Hai Yaso" (Attack on Christ[ianity]) and *Shintō denju* (Initiation into Shintō).[44] However, at the end of this period, the *Zeitgeist* was one of a basic transcendentalism that had to include an empirical side to it, as in the case of Kumazawa Banzan.[45]

Following the scholars of the Sung and Ming, some scholars dealt with the question of *ri*, and developed a concept of *ri* as an aspect of social thought without concern for a meeting between Neo-Confucianism and Western learning (*Yōgaku*)[46] and without assuming a position of empirical rationalism like certain later Japanese Neo-Confucians. Among them, Fujiwara Seika tried to forge a basis for equality in international society through *ri*,[47] but Hayashi Razan sought a foundation based on *ri* upon which to fix the distinctions between social superiors and social inferiors.[48]

As we have seen, *shingaku* was varied in its content. Two opposing currents are most important here. According to one point of view, if one could purify the state in which one found one's own mind-and-heart through its relations with others (including problems of society and the state), then the larger issue of helping the people and governing the realm would be resolved on its own. This was a trend of thought that tried to resolve problems idealistically by considering the purification of the mind-and-heart in numerous ways: by illumining the "bright virtue" inherent in the self (Nakae Tōju); by trying to reach the state of "no-mind" or *mushin* (Takuan); by attaining "supreme goodness" naturally through "the investigation of things" (*kakubutsu*) where this phrase is understood as ridding the mind-and-heart of "dust" (Fujiwara Seika); by disciplining the self with a "method of disciplining the mind for centrality [equilibrium] and harmony." The second current was, as with Hayashi Razan and the *Honsaroku*, to preserve the mind-and-heart without imprudence, keeping the relationship between the self and the other always in the forefront of one's consciousness. This was a way of thought inclined to resolve issues realistically.

Of these two currents, the former was the stronger one in this period, but inevitably there arose some extremely important issues with respect to how to form bonds with the real world from this stance. First was the issue of "mind-and-heart and physical form" (Jap. *kei*; Ch. *hsing*). In concrete terms, "physical form" involved the issue of "ritual" (Jap. *rei*; Ch. *li*). Ritual and "humaneness" (Jap. *jin*; Ch. *jen*) formed the two main pillars of the teachings of Confucius, and, in China, knowledge of ritual or lack thereof distinguished the cultured from the barbarian. In the Sung period, Chu Hsi had written *I-li ching-chuan t'ung-chieh* (Comprehensive Exegesis of the Text of the *I-li*

[Book of Rituals] and its Commentaries) and *Wen-kung chia-li* (The Family Rituals of Chu Hsi). The latter in particular was adopted in Yi dynasty Korea and exerted a major influence on culture and society there.

In the case of Japan in the early part of the seventeenth century, Nonaka Kenzan (1615–1663), principal retainer in Tosa domain and an ardent advocate of the Chu Hsi school, had occasion to perform a funeral service for his mother, following the text of the *Wen-kung chia-li*.[49] In general, though, this text was not as widely received as it had been in Korea. One reason for this difference was that a wide variety of ritual methods covering such things as the public funerals of court figures and the members of military houses were well established as a part of daily life in Japanese society. There was little room to accept into Japan a codification of ritual, such as was represented in a text born of the society and culture of China where the customs in daily life were different.

Even the Kimon school (of Yamazaki Ansai), which was rather enthusiastic about accepting the *Wen-kung chia-li*, limited its support for the adoption of the precepts in this text to rituals concerned with funerals and festivals (ceremonies involving offerings to ancestors) over which Buddhist monks, their designated enemies, had supervision.[50] Among the advocates of *shingaku* during this period, Nakae Tōju made a distinction between mind-and-heart and "traces" (Jap. *seki* or *ato*; Ch. *chi*). Rituals were the traces of the external expression of the minds-and-hearts of the Sages. Thus, one did not study these "traces" with the restrictions imposed by time periods, society, or culture, but through it one could grasp the "mind-and-heart" of the Sage and restore it to life in one's own actions.[51] Nakae's disciple, Kumazawa Banzan, expressed the view that Japan should revise the rituals of China in such a way that they would conform to the natural environment of Japan.[52] These views were generally acknowledged, and the rituals that formed an important part of the Chu Hsi school did not penetrate the customs and practices of the Japanese, as they did in Korea during the Yi period.

The second issue, which is closely bound up with the first, involves the problem of universalism and particularism. Supporters of *shingaku* in this period undoubtedly believed in the universality of the teachings of the Sages, but they also felt the need for these teachings to fit the national conditions of Japan. Both Nakae Tōju and Kumazawa Banzan took a hint from the concepts of Heaven, earth, and man to create the concepts of "time" (*ji*, *toki*), "place" (*sho*, *tokoro*), and "rank" (*i*, *kurai*). Furthermore, in an effort to resolve the difficulties inherent in this issue, Kumazawa offered the concepts of "human feelings" (*ninjō*) and "temporal change" (*jihen*). The theoretical basis for these concepts was the "distinction between mind-and-heart and traces," as described above.

The third issue concerns the fact that, although the teachings of *shingaku* supporters of this type were idealistic and optimistic — in the sense that they believed that, if statesmen purified their own minds-and-hearts, government would be reformed — doubt obviously arises as to how in the world real government would ever be effected on this basis alone. In confronting this issue, Fujiwara Seika offered the concept of "complete talent" (*zensai*),[33] and Kumazawa Banzan offered the concept of "basic talent" (*honsai*);[34] they both saw the need for training and appointing men of talent and capability as advisory retainers in government.

The fourth issue involves the following problem: if minds-and-hearts can be purified and human character unified, then this means experience will be subjective; and, with objective knowledge of reality impossible, how in practice can these doctrines be successful? The Zen monk Takuan, who was a believer in the unity of the Three Teachings, recognized the transcendent existence of principle (*ri*), but the nature of this principle did not have the metaphysical essence that is to be found in "the Ultimate of Nonbeing and yet the Great Ultimate" (Jap. *mukyoku ni shite taikyoku*; Ch. *wu-chi erh t'ai-chi*; the Infinite and yet the Supreme Ultimate), as argued by the Chu Hsi school. Takuan was using it in the sense of "nothingness" or "emptiness" as put forward by Mahayana Buddhism. As with the Confucian interpretation of principle based on the idea of "investigating things and extending knowledge," Takuan's interpretation based on the Mahayana Buddhist perspective of "true emptiness and mysterious reality" (Jap. *shinkū myōu*; Ch. *chen-k'ung miao-yu*), created the potential for the objective perception of things and events.[55] While learning from Wang Yang-ming a basic orientation aimed at the inner self, the Neo-Confucian Kumazawa Banzan tried to resolve this issue by learning from Chu Hsi that one clarifies the logic of the wider universe by combining inner and outer.[56] His effort was, however, theoretically unsuccessful.

After Shingaku

There was a period in his youth when Itō Jinsai was fascinated by *shingaku* and loved to read Hsü Heng's *Lu-chai hsin-fa*; he even went so far as to compose an essay entitled "Shingaku genron" (Basic Principles of the School of the Mind-and-Heart). As a result of passionate discipline in *shingaku*, however, he came to the realization that the direction in which he had been striving was wrong and adopted a vital, activist stance.[57] Later, Ogyū Sorai (1666–1728) would fundamentally repudiate *shingaku* by arguing that the individual who tries to control his own mind-and-heart is comparable to the insane man who tries to cure his own insanity.[58] From the middle of the Tokugawa period on, *shingaku* for the most part disappeared from center stage in Japanese intellectual history.

What replaced *shingaku* on the intellectual stage? A wide variety of Neo-Confucian systems of thought were formed with such names as the Chu Hsi school, the Ancient Learning school (*Kogaku*), the Syncretist school (Setchūgaku), and the Textual Critical school (*Kōshōgaku*), as well as independent schools. The emergence of so many and varied schools is closely tied to the fact that Japan did not have a civil service examination system.[59] If we are to examine the content of the ideas expressed by the schools, and not the differentiation of cliques per se, then, aside from the *a priori* rationalism of the Kimon school, with its basis in Chu Hsi learning, a wider tripartite division can be made: (1) empirical rationalism; (2) philological positivism; and (3) teleological rationalist political thought.

The first of these, empirical rationalism, would include the Chu Hsi school (excluding the Kimon school), independent schools, and a part of the Ancient Learning school. This filiation of thought is closely related to the formation of natural scientific thought in the Tokugawa period, and a union of Neo-Confucianism and Western Learning was to come about here. The second of these, philological positivism, included a portion of the Ancient Learning school and the school of Textual Criticism. It made possible documentary scholarship on the ancient classics and provided a major stimulus to the nativist (or National Learning, *Kokugaku*) research of Motoori Norinaga (1730–1801) and others. This also provided the foundation for the development, from the Meiji period forward, of the humanistic sciences in Japan. The third, the political ideology of teleological rationalism, applies to a portion of the Ancient Learning school. It encouraged the formation of an understanding of politics from an institutionalist perspective and the realistic ideology associated with "ordering the realm and aiding the populace." (We should note in addition the reevaluation by Tominaga Nakamoto [1715–1746] of both Buddhism and Neo-Confucianism based on an intellectual historical methodology and the utopian thought of Andō Shōeki [b. 1701?].) These three, it is important to point out, are in a broad sense Neo-Confucian schools of thought in the Tokugawa period that prepared the Japan of the Meiji period and thereafter for modernization.

What happened to *shingaku* after the first half of the seventeenth century? The learning of the method of disciplining the mind, with its long tradition since the medieval period, could not simply be erased from Japanese society. It managed to preserve its lifeline in the middle and late years of the Tokugawa period as a subterranean stream of thought. Buddhist discipline (revolving around Zen) as well as training in the military and civil arts were all concerned in one way or another with the "method of the mind." One item of proof for this in the realm of Neo-Confucianism would be the fact that the *Shingaku gorin no sho*, first published in the early part of the seventeenth century, was republished many times in the middle and later years of the Tokugawa period.[60]

In the eighteenth century, the townsman thinker Ishida Baigan (1685–1744) formed a school of thought known as Sekimon *shingaku*. Numerous scholars have already noted that it was to become one of the sources in the formation of capitalism in Japan.[61] An attitude emphasizing the method of the mind, though without the appellation *shingaku* attached, permeated the concerns of many who were fond of various of Japan's civil and military arts. Many Zen monks surrounding Hakuin (1686–1769) were engaged in a fierce training regimen. At the end of the Tokugawa period, too, ordinary folk (unlike intellectuals) continued to live in the realm of *shingaku* and *shinpō*. Perhaps Japanese intellectual history and culture at the end of the early modern period should be divided into two social strata.

Within Neo-Confucianism of the late Tokugawa period, the three strains of thought—empirical rationalism, philological positivism, and the political ideology of teleological rationalism—provided major thrusts in preparing Japan for the modernization process. Changing our perspective slightly, these systems of thought were concerned with "objective things" (*mono*). Nature, the classics, and institutions, in their view, were all "objective things." By contrast, excluding Sekimon *shingaku*, what sort of role in Japan's modernization did *shingaku*, the system of thought of the mind-and-heart, play?

It is generally believed that the system of thought surrounding the mind-and-heart had no relationship whatsoever to modernization. I believe, to the contrary, that there was a link to the modernizing process, albeit dissimilar in form from systems of thought concerned with "objective things." The first item to be noted is that *shingaku* taught Japanese to have a spiritually independent mind-and-heart. Kumazawa Banzan had the following to say after he described the disciplined effort involved in "watching oneself when alone" (Jap. *shindoku*; Ch. *shen-tu*): "one may imagine that one lives all alone in the realm between Heaven and earth. With Heaven as one's teacher and the clear wisdom of the divine as one's friend, one lacks the mind that relies on other people externally. In this way, one becomes internally fortified against deprivation. At peace with the outside world, one is unassailable."[62] Japanese trained in *shingaku* and *shinpō* are thus liberated from the consciousness of shame that Ruth Benedict pointed out in *The Chrysanthemum and the Sword.*

The second item to be noted is that the training inherent in the learning of the mind-and-heart and its method of the mind cultivated a "spirituality" (*reisei*)[63] among the Japanese. The term *spirituality* was frequently used in Japan by Suzuki Daisetsu, but it was not solely Buddhism that contributed to the nurturing of Japanese spirituality. Neo-Confucianism, by assuming a position on the mind-and-heart, also played its part. Oddly, this point may have been overlooked by scholars until recently. Fujiwara Seika, for example, likened the mind-and-heart to a "mirror" (*kagami*) when he wrote: "There is boundless spirit [*kyorei*] where the mirror is pure and glistening."[64] His use of *kyo* in the expression *kyorei* (Ch. *hsü*, ordinarily meaning empty or vacuous) does not convey the negative sense of "vacuous learning." It has a positive, affirmative sense here, indicating an activity of the mind-and-heart that, by virtue of its quality of *kyo*, possesses limitless spirituality.

These two forces did not work together to propel the modernization process in Japan, but they may have served the function of purifying the minds-and-hearts of the Japanese people, which could easily have been corrupted by modernization.

The third issue that I take up here is not directly related to the question of modernization, although it does have a direct connection to the question of the form of cultural receptivity and thus is ultimately linked to modernization. This concerns the close bonds between *shingaku* and the issue of eclectic cultural receptivity. *Shingaku* was the system of thought that in the early Tokugawa period advocated the unity of the Three Teachings. The same trend of thought can be seen in *Sekimon shingaku*. The system of thought underlying the mind-and-heart made possible the coexistence of numerous schools of thought. This applies to cultural issues as well. Indeed, we cannot deny that *shingaku* gave to Japanese thought and culture an incomplete syncretism, while by the same token creating, when supported by a transcendent force, the possibility for the unification of the diversity within the great richness of Japanese thought and culture. Japanese modernization proceeded smoothly not because Japan had a single, solitary culture, but because that culture was a unity amid diversity.

Finally, I would like to return to the issue of "the thought of the mind-and-heart" (*kokoro* thought) in the *bakumatsu* era and at the time of Meiji Restoration (1868). Although toward the end of the early modern period systems of thought encompassing both *kokoro* and *mono* existed side by side in Japan, men who represented the intellectual realm at the time took the position associated with *mono*. Within this dominant position occupied by *mono* thought at that time, there were two types forming strata. In the *bakumatsu*-Restoration era, *kokoro* thought coexisted on an equal plane with *mono* thought. *Mono* thought was represented by the Chu Hsi advocate Sakuma Zōzan (or Shōzan, 1811–1864) and many scholars of Western Learning; *kokoro* thought was represented by Yokoi Shōnan (1809–1869), Nakamura Keiu (1832–1891), and numerous followers of the Wang Yang-ming school. It would probably be more appropriate to say that, from the perspective of the trend of the times, *kokoro* thought had risen to a superior position. In any event, this was an age of political practice in which action was in the ascendant. In such an age, men often reflected upon the manner in which the individual's mind-and-heart was best tied to action.

During this period some adopted a stance of *kokoro* thought and tried actively to advance modernization while introducing Western civilization into Japan. Yokoi and Nakamura were representative of this brand. They took on this doubly difficult task by seeking simultaneously to introduce Western civilization and push modernization, while purifying the corruption that accompanied the foreign elements. I hope to write about them at a later date.[65] When one looks at the conditions in the *bakumatsu* and Restoration period, what I have dealt with here are problems of the extremely short period of the early Tokugawa years; but, if we consider this within the intellectual context of Japanese *kokoro* thought, then we may have an important question approaching the nature of Japanese speculative thought itself.

NOTES

1. For the translation of these terms, I have followed Wm. Theodore de Bary, *The Message of the Mind in Neo-Confucianism* (New York: Columbia University Press, 1989), esp. pp. xi–xii. For the other technical Neo-Confucian (and the few Buddhist) terms used in this chapter, I have relied on several works, in addition to the one just cited: Wm. Theodore de Bary and Irene Bloom, eds., *Principle and Practicality: Essays in Neo-Confucianism and Practical Learning* (New York: Columbia University Press, 1979), esp. chapters by de Bary, Okada Takehiko, Yamashita Ryūji, Ian James McMullen, and Minamoto

Ryōen; Wing-tsit Chan, ed., *Chu Hsi and Neo-Confucianism* (Honolulu: University of Hawaii Press, 1986); de Bary, *Neo-Confucian Orthodoxy and the Learning of the Mind-and-Heart* (New York: Columbia University Press, 1981); Judith A. Berling, *The Syncretic Religion of Lin Chao-en* (New York: Columbia University Press, 1980); Ch'en Ch'un, *Neo-Confucian Terms Explained*, trans. and ed. Wing-tsit Chan (New York: Columbia University Press, 1986); and Lo Ch'in-shun, *Knowledge Painfully Acquired: The Kun chih chi*, trans. and ed. Irene Bloom (New York: Columbia University Press, 1987). — trans.

2. An epoch-making event in the history of Japanese Neo-Confucian thought occurred in 1663–64 (Kanbun 3–4) when Yamaga Sokō (1622–1685) and Itō Jinsai founded the Ancient Learning school. This event marked the start of the relative independence of Japanese Neo-Confucianism from the orb of Sung and Ming studies to which Neo-Confucianism of the Edo period to that point had completely adhered. From social and political perspectives, the Kanbun reign period (1661–1673) marked the period in which the ruling structure of the *bakufu* and the domains were for all intents and purposes established. In the political realm, the Chu Hsi school clearly occupied a position of dominance from about this time. In other words, just when the early modern Chu Hsi school secured its preeminent position over the Wang Yang-ming school in the political sphere, it met its new rival in the intellectual arena: the Ancient Learning school.

3. Maruyama Masao, *Nihon seiji shisō shi kenkyū* (Studies in the History of Japanese Political Thought) (Tokyo: Tokyo University Press, 1952), translated by Mikiso Hane as *Studies in the Intellectual History of Tokugawa Japan* (Tokyo: University of Tokyo Press, 1974).

4. Ishida Ichirō, "Tokugawa hōken shakai to Shushigakuha" (Tokugawa Feudal Society and the Chu Hsi School), *Tōhoku daigaku bungakubu kenkyū nenpō* 13(1963):72–138.

5. (Tokyo: Aoki shoten, 1961).

6. (Tokyo: Chūō kōron sha, 1972), 21.

7. Minamoto Ryōen, "Shushigaku no futatsu no keifu" (Two Lineages of the Chu Hsi school), *Kan* (1976), 5(5–6):28–54; and Ryōen Minamoto, "'Jitsugaku' and Empirical Rationalism in the First Half of the Tokugawa Period," in *Principle and Practicality*, 375–469.

8. On this question, see the detailed discussion in Ashikaga Enjutsu, *Kamakura Muromachi jidai no Jukyō* (Neo-Confucianism in the Kamakura and Muromachi Periods) (Tokyo: Nihon koten zenshū kankōkai, 1932).

9. The "three teachings," for advocates of the unity of Three Teachings in China, were Confucianism, Buddhism, and Taoism; but in Japan, Shintō often replaced Taoism.

10. Two works that see *shingaku* as the nature of Neo-Confucianism in the beginning of the early modern period: Minamoto Ryōen, *Kinsei shoki jitsugaku shisō no kenkyū* (Studies in Practical Learning at the Beginning of the Early Modern Period) (Tokyo: Sōbunsha, 1980); and de Bary, *Neo-Confucian Orthodoxy*. Professor de Bary has come to this conclusion after many years of research into the intellectual history of the Ming period in China. We may have a few minor differences of opinion with respect to Japan, but I want to express my heartfelt respect for the breadth of Professor de Bary's research covering China, Korea, and Japan; it is otherwise unexplored terrain.

11. (Tokyo: Sōbunsha, 1980).

12. On this issue, see Minamoto Ryōen, "Kinsei zenki no kenpōron ni okeru *shinpō* no mondai" (The Issue of "the Method of the Mind" in the Debate over Fencing in the First Half of the Early Modern Period), *Tōhoku daigaku Nihon bunka kenkyūjo kenkyū hōkoku*

(1982), 18:51–80; and Minamoto Ryōen, *Bunka to ningen keisei* (Culture and Human Formation), ch. 3, "Bunbu no gei o tsūjite no Nihonjin no jiko shūren" (The Self-Discipline of Japanese Through the Civil and Military Arts) (Tokyo: Daiichi Hōki Publishing Company, 1982).

13. The *Chu-tzu ta-ch'üan* was a dogmatic work aimed at preserving and strengthening the establishment, which ignored the reformist elements in the writings of Chu Hsi.

14. Both the *I-tuan pien-cheng* and the *Hsüeh-p'u t'ung-pien* were written in the Ming as attacks on heterodoxy. They can now be found in the Naikaku Bunko together with some Korean texts from the library of Hayashi Razan. Fujiwara Seika lent the copy in his possession of the *Hsüeh-p'u t'ung-pien* to Razan, and, when Razan returned it, Seika wrote him a somewhat sarcastic letter: "Upon the return of the *Hsüeh-p'u t'ung-pien*, it would seem as though [Ch'en] Ch'ing-lan wrote this text for you? In the spots where you itched, you could not wait to be scratched with the divine fingernails of Ma-ku. Why? How amusing." See Abe Yoshio, *Nihon Shushigaku to Chōsen* (The Chu Hsi school in Japan and [Its Relation to] Korea) (Tokyo: Tokyo University Press, 1965), 186–89. These two works can be found on a reading list that dates to a time when Razan was twenty-two (1604) (Japanese style). In that year, Razan had hoped to get Seika to read his work, and he wrote a letter to this effect to Seika's disciple Yoshida Genshi ("Den Genshi ni yosu" [Letter to Yoshida Genshi]). When Razan criticized Lu Hsiang-shan, Seika noted: "Your points of argument are the remnants of the works of predecessors of the Ming and Ch'ing dynasties. I also have read them already." He mildly reproached Razan's work for being a rehash of the works of Ch'en Chien and Chan Ling. For more on this, see Minamoto Ryōen, *Kinsei shoki jitsugaku shisō no kenkyū*, 193–94.

15. As for Chen Te-hsiu, Seika encouraged Razan to read both Chen's *Ta-hsüeh yen-i* and Ch'iu Chün's supplement to it.

16. *Seika sensei gyōjō* (Biographical Account of Teacher Seika), in *Fujiwara Seika, Hayashi Razan, Nihon shisō taikei* (Fujiwara Seika and Hayashi Razan, Compendium of Japanese Thought) (Tokyo: Iwanami shoten, 1975), vol. 28, p. 194.

17. From the period when he emerged as a supporter of the Chu Hsi school, Razan was an advocate of the inseparability of principle (*ri*) and material force (*ki*), as opposed to Chu Hsi's belief in a *li-ch'i* dualism. As he wrote in the letter to Yoshida Genshi (cited in note 14 above): "Although I was aware of having gone against the ideas of Chu Hsi, I still had to speak out." Razan took this view because of a temporary attraction to the work of of Lo Ch'in-shun (Lo Cheng-an, 1465–1547); for a long time thereafter, he was attracted to the view of Lo's opponent, Wang Yang-ming, that "Principle is the regularity of material force, and material force is the functioning of principle." (In my view, Professors Abe Yoshio and Wm. Theodore de Bary, who was much influenced by Abe, overestimate Lo's influence on Razan. Razan was also concerned with the metaphysical aspect of Chu Hsi's conception of principle, although this was not as impressive in his eyes as Lo's stress on material force. Lo's influence on Razan was not fundamental.) However, Razan was undoubtedly troubled by the fact that Wang Yang-ming was opposed to the Chu Hsi school. In this situation, Razan cited the words of Ch'en Pei-hsi (Ch'en Ch'un): "The mind-and-heart . . . involves both principle and material force. . . . The mind-and-heart is an active thing. . . . Its intelligence [spirituality] is the combination of principle and material force. That is why it is intelligent [spiritual]." See Ch'en Ch'un, *Neo-Confucian Terms Explained*, 58. [For the sake of consistency, I have made one slight modification to Professor Chan's translation,

replacing his "mind" with "mind-and-heart" for *hsin*.—trans.] Razan thus believed that one could achieve a stability of mind-and-heart through realizing the possibility inherent in the Chu Hsi school for a doctrine of the inseparability of principle and material force. Razan wrote his *Seiri jigi genkai* (Colloquial Explanation of [Ch'en Ch'un's] *Hsing-li tzu-i* [The Meaning of the Terms of Human Nature and Principle]) in order to introduce Ch'en's ideas to Japan. In his work *Santoku shō* (Outlines of the Three Moral Virtues), Razan advocated the inseparability of principle and material force: "With principle alone, movement is difficult. If the mind-and-heart is in accord with principle and material force, then its movement is easy. . . . However, although principle and material force are two entities, if there is material force, principle will necessarily be present. Without material force, principle has no place to reside because principle lacks form. Principle and material force are inseparable." *Nihon shisō taikei*, vol. 28, p. 164. We should probably note that Razan's construction of the issue of the inseparability of principle and material force is based on the "mind-and-heart."

18. For Lin Chao-en's view of *ko-wu*, see below, note 31.

19. In *Tōju sensei zenshū* (Collected Works of [Nakae] Tōju) (Tokyo: Iwanami shoten, 1940), vol. 2, pp. 440–41.

20. Chu Hsi explained the character *wu* (Jap. *mono*) in *ko-wu* (J. *kakubutsu*) as "*wu* are things" (*shih*; Jap. *ji*), *Ta-hsüeh chang-chü* (The *Great Learning* Divided in Chapters and Sentences). Wang Yang-ming followed this interpretation in the *Ch'uan-hsi lu* (Instructions for Practical Living): "The character *wu* in the expression *ko-wu* is the same as *shih*." Nakae Tōju criticized this point of view: "As for explaining the meaning of the character *wu*, Chu Hsi says it is the same as *shih*. Although most have followed this explanation, it has yet to be closely examined. No one has conclusively established the five *shih*. Thus, successes in *ko-wu* will not urgently be flooding in." *Tōju sensei zenshū*, vol. 2, p. 16. Nakae's explanation of *shih* clearly shows the subjective bent to his thought.

21. *Tōju sensei zenshū*, vol. 2, p. 14.

22. Ibid., vol. 1, p. 13.

23. Ibid., vol. 1, p. 509.

24. When he was a young man, Nakae attacked Buddhism from the position of Neo-Confucianism, but in his later years he identified "bright virtue" with "Buddha-nature" and used the concept of "the Buddha-nature of bright virtue" (*meitoku Busshō*). It was his *shingaku* position that thus compelled him to include Buddhism within the Neo-Confucianism to which he adhered in his later years.

25. Kimura Mitsunori has pointed out that Nakae's idea (in his "Daigaku kō") that "intentionality is the root of all desires and evils" originated in the following citations from the writings of Wang Chi: "The myriad errors and evils are all born of intentionality" (in *Wang Lung-hsi ch'üan-chi* [Collected Works of Wang Lung-hsi] [Ts'ung-shu hui-pien reprint of the 1822 ed.], *chüan* 5); "All ills arise from intentionality" (in ibid., *chüan* 14); and "Intentionality is born from that which is diseased" (ibid.). See Kimura Mitsunori, *Tōjugaku no seiritsu ni kansuru kenkyū* (Studies in the Formation of the Learning of [Nakae] Tōju) (Tokyo: Kazama shobō, 1971), 174.

26. In the edition of the *Lin-tzu ch'üan-chi* (Collected Works of Master Lin [Chao-en]) held in the Naikaku Bunko, there is a section on "Heterodoxy" (*i-tuan*) in the *Lin-tzu ssu-shu piao-chai cheng-i hsü* (Correct Interpretations by Master Lin of the Four Books, by Topic, Continued). Lin argued that Confucius's idea of "timeliness" (*shih-chung*), the

Yellow Emperor's and Lao-tzu's idea of *ch'ing-ching* (purity), and the Buddha's idea of *chi-ching* (quietude) all were based completely in the mind-and-heart, and this Lin dubbed *tuan* (proper); by contrast, those who were ignorant of the need to look into the mind-and-heart to find *tuan* were dubbed *i-tuan* (heterodox). After offering this explanation, Lin raised the query why men of the world called Taoism and Buddhism heterodoxies, and he responded to this query as follows: "As for the doctrine of heterodoxy, when the learning of Taoism and Buddhism arose, Confucianists did not always consider them different teachings and only later did they call them heterodox. To study Confucianism and not to understand the need to plumb the intellectual nature of the mind-and-heart, this is Confucian heterodoxy. To study the Tao and not to understand the need to discipline the refined nature of the mind-and-heart, this is Taoist heterodoxy. To study Buddhism and not to understand the need to illuminate the clarity of the mind-and-heart, this is Buddhist heterodoxy." In his "Sennan gūkyo ki" (Record from the Temporary Residence South of the Spring), the monk Takuan wrote in opposition to the general Neo-Confucian attack on Buddhism as heterodoxy and adopted Lin Chao-en's thesis on heterodoxy in his rebuttal. *Takuan oshō zenshū* (Collected Works of Head Priest Takuan) (Tokyo: Kōgeisha, 1929), vol. 2, pp. 39–40.

27. Nakae Tōju was much interested in the idea of "stilling in the back and responding to contraries" (*ken-pei ti-ying*), which originates in the *I ching* (Classic of Changes, hexagram 52), and he based his critique of Buddhism in the *Okina mondō* (Dialogues with an Old Man) on this idea. In "Keikai," which he wrote in his later years, Nakae strengthened his explanation of "stilling in the back and responding to contraries" from a *shingaku* perspective. Here, it was no longer primarily an attack on Buddhism, but a criticism of the incompleteness of "the method of the mind in the stilling in the back," concerning which Lin Chao-en had said that the "back" (*pei*) was the "water that purified the mind." As Nakae put it: "Water can be transformed into frozen ice. It corresponds to fire's capacity to burn. This shows that his theory is not yet fully refined." *Tōju sensei zenshū*, vol. 1, p. 20.

28. Concerning the influence of T'ang Shu's *Li-yen sheng-yü* on Nakae's belief in T'ai-i shen, see Kimura Mitsunori, *Tōjugaku no seiritsu ni kansuru kenkyū*, and Tamagake Hiroyuki, "Nakae Tōju no 'chūki' no shisō" (Nakae Tōju's Thought During His "Middle Years"), *Bunka* (1972), 35(4):93–126. T'ang Shu's work can be found in the *Hsing-li ta-ch'üan hui-pien* (*chüan* 31), held in the library of Tōhoku University.

29. Using as the core of his work the Ming morality book *Ming-hsin pao-chien cheng-wen* (Main Text of the Precious Mirror for the Enlightenment of the Mind-and-Heart), Oze Hoan compiled several moral instructional texts, including the *Meii hōkan* (Precious Mirror for the Enlightenment of the Will) and the *Seiyō shō* (Extracts on the Essentials of Government). These are included in *Kinsei bungaku shiryō ruijū, kanazōshi hen* (Classification of Materials in Early Modern Literature, Texts Written in the Japanese Syllabary), vol. 18 (Tokyo: Benseisha, 1974). On this issue, see Tamagake Hiroyuki, "Matsunaga Sekigo no shisō to Oze Hoan no shisō" (The Thought of Matsunaga Sekigo and the Thought of Oze Hoan), explanatory text in *Nihon shisō taikei*, vol. 28, pp. 505–20. For a comparative analysis of the process by which the *Ming-hsin pao-chien* spread to China, Korea, Japan, Vietnam, Spain, and Germany, see Fritz Foss, "Meishin hōkan ni tsuite" (On the *Ming-hsin pao-chien*), *Tōhoku daigaku Nihon bunka kenkyūjo kenkyū hōkoku* (March 1985), 21:1–15. There is a detailed description of Nakae's Tōju response to Chinese morality books in Kimura Mitsunori's book, *Tōjugaku no seiritsu*.

30. With respect to the view that regarded "the clear manifestation of the Way" as "the unity of the self and others," "the unity of inner and outer," and "bright virtue" in the *Daigaku yōryaku*, the portion of Seika's writings that relied on Lin Chao-en in this context comes from the *Ta-hsüeh cheng-i tsuan* (held in the Archives and Mausolea Department of the Imperial Household Agency): "'To illumine bright virtue and cherish the people' is the knowledge gained by unifying the self with others. 'To illumine bright virtue and cherish the people until reaching supreme goodness' is the knowledge gained by unifying the inner and the outer. If there is no one else, there is no self. If there is no inner, there is no outer. Thus, it is said that the Way of the Great Learning lies in illumining bright virtue, and this is the manifestation of the Way."

31. On this point, see Lin Chao-en's *Ta-hsüeh cheng-i tsuan*: "That which we call *wu* does not denote the *wu* in the sense of things and affairs [*shih-wu*]. It is the *wu* [as recorded in the *Li-chi*, or *Book of Rites*] denoting the fact that man transforms himself into things. That which we call *ko* does not denote the *ko* in the sense of obstacle [*han-ko*]. It is the *ko* denoting the eradication of that which is inimical to the mind-and-heart. The mind-and-heart is transformed by *wu*. What else can we call this but 'an evil mind'? Thus, *ko-wu* means to eradicate the evil mind, and *ko* carries the meaning of eradicating."

32. Seika derived the important idea here that "*mono* is dust" (i.e., evil desires) from Lin Chao-en as well. As Lin put it in the *Ta-hsüeh cheng-i tsuan*: "Wu is dust. Thus, when the dust is gotten rid of, the mirror will shine brightly."

33. In *Nihon shisō taikei*, vol. 28, p. 55.

34. The *San-lüeh* gives the following explanation for *kang, jou, ch'iang,* and *jo*: "The *Chün-chang* says, 'The pliant can control the unyielding, and the weak can control the powerful. The pliant have potency, while the unyielding are bandits. The weak are helped by others. The powerful are conquered by [the people's] resentment. . . . The pliant have the means to create; the unyielding have the means for a triumphal return; the weak have the means to be useful; and the powerful have the means to be increased. Take these four together, and regulate them appropriately.'"

35. On the subject of *kokoromochi no heihō*, Razan took the position that "to defeat others by force is not as good as doing it with the mind-and-heart." At the same time, Razan went on to say: "If you protect the mind-and-heart well, then the state will be safe, and the people are not harmed. It is the Sage who does not lose this mind-and-heart. Although this mind-and-heart is profoundly faint, if we can preserve and protect it well, the state will never be in confusion because the mind-and-heart will penetrate all the myriad things of the world. Although it is in our breast, if we proclaim its vastness, it spreads throughout the four seas; and if it is put away, it exists in our bosom. . . . Whether large or small only concerns the use made of the mind-and-heart. This is the strategy of preserving the mind." *Sanryaku genkai* (Colloquial Explanation of the *San-lüeh*), 8–9, copy held in the Naikaku Bunko.

36. There are commonalities between the idea of *tenka* (the world, the realm, all-under-Heaven) in Razan's *Rikutō genkai* (Colloquial Explanation of the *Liu-t'ao*) and the idea of *tenka* in the *Honsaroku*. Although authorship of the *Honsaroku* remains unclear, I believe it was written by someone influenced by the *Rikutō genkai*.

37. "Kei setsu" (A Theory of Reverence), in *Razan sensei bunshū*, vol. 1, pp. 310–11.

38. Razan wrote: "T'ai-kung-wang used the expression 'it is auspicious when reverence overcomes indolence' in an announcement to King Wu. Reverence creates a moral power

that compels that reverence be revered." *Razan sensei bunshū*, vol. 1, p. 188. The meaning of this last sentence, "reverence creates a moral power that compels that reverence be revered," is this: the word *kei* (Ch. *ching*) is explained in utilitarian terms as a power one possesses, while maintaining an attitude of reverence, which requires the other to honor oneself. Furthermore, this "reverence" is not the moral virtue of inner refinement such as is found in the idea advocated by the Chu Hsi school of "concentrating oneself chiefly on one thing [the inner self] and not allowing for deviation to another," but is always alert to the other. This formulation of "reverence" is such that it emphasizes concern with the other.

39. *Rikutō genkai*, 8.

40. *Razan sensei bunshū*, vol. 2, p. 431.

41. Of a small number of works from this era that discuss thought from a position of "human nature and principle" (*seiri*), there is the *Kana shōri* of uncertain authorship. Although he was a fervent advocate of the Chu Hsi school, Hayashi Razan used the expression *seiri* extremely rarely. Narrowly speaking, he only used the expression "human nature is principle" in "Tenmei zusetsu batsu" (Epilogue to the Diagram of Heaven's Mandate, Explained) and "Gimon rokujō" (Responses to Six Questions). Otherwise, he almost always used the expression the "principle of the mind-and-heart" (*shinri*). In his "Shisho batsu" (Epilogue to the Four Books), Razan noted: "Principle is the nature of the mind-and-heart. The mind-and-heart and human nature are originally one" (*Razan sensei bunshū*, vol. 2, p. 172). Here, he identified the mind-and-heart with principle. We see a similar case in Razan's "Zuihitsu daijūichi" (Eleventh Random Note): "Ah! The Six Classics are all *shingaku*" (*Razan sensei bunshū*, vol. 2, p. 499). Razan's orientation toward *shinri* and *shingaku* cannot be neglected as a key to understanding the structure of his speculative thought.

42. On Razan's idea on the inseparability of principle and material force, see note 17 above. Nakae Tōju, who took a position within *shingaku* thought diametrically opposed to Razan, nonetheless agreed with Razan on principle and material force. In his *Okina mondō*, for example, Nakae wrote: "The Sage is someone who can elucidate the simultaneous duality of nonduality and the oneness of nonidentity of spiritual principle and vacuous material force, and he possesses a divine quality of purity one level higher. He possesses a mysterious spiritual power and stands at a rank of unimpeded clarity." Unlike Chang Tsai (1020–1077) who identified material force with the Supreme Vacuity (*t'ai-hsü*), Kumazawa Banzan also argued that the Supreme Vacuity was "principle and material force." The predominance among Neo-Confucian scholars of the early Tokugawa period of the view that regarded principle and material force as indivisible demonstrates well the nature of Neo-Confucianism at this time.

43. Professor Kanaya Osamu has made the following observation with regard to Fujiwara Seika's idea of principle (*ri*): "When Seika spoke of *ri*, more than a concept in metaphysical philosophy, this *ri* contained a stronger sense of practical, immediate truth or moral obligation." See his "Fujiwara Seika no Jugaku shisō" (Fujiwara Seika's Confucian Thought), in *Nihon shisō taikei*, vol. 28, p. 462.

44. The aspect of "transcendentalism" in Razan's thought is particularly manifest in his *Hai Yaso* of 1606, a record of his dialogue with the Christian Fabian, and in his *Shintō denju* (composed in 1644–1647) in which he systematically elucidated Shintō thought. In other

words, Razan stressed the metaphysical aspect of the Chu Hsi school's idea of principle in its links to religion.

45. Banzan's idea of principle was fundamentally metaphysical as well as moral by nature, but we must also include various experiential aspects to it, among them: the exhaustive exploration of the principles (*kyūri*) of the mountains, rivers, and topography; the exhaustive exploration of the principles governing how things grow; and the exhaustive exploration of music. As an administrator, he had had to respond to a variety of real situations in society. See Minamoto Ryōen, *Kinsei shoki jitsugaku shisō no kenkyū*, 454–58.

[See also Ian James McMullen, "Kumazawa Banzan and 'Jitsugaku': Toward Pragmatic Action," in *Principle and Practicality*, 337–73, esp. 354–55.—trans.]

46. On the interface between Western Learning and empirical rationalist Neo-Confucianism in the history of early modern Japanese thought, see Minamoto Ryōen, *Tokugawa gōri shisō no keifu*.

47. In the second item under "Shūchū kiyaku" (Compact Aboard Ship), which Seika wrote on behalf of his own disciple Yoshida Genshi (Yoshida Soan), the son of Suminokura Ryōi, Seika wrote: "Although the customs and languages of alien areas within our own country are different [from our own], the principle bestowed by Heaven has always been the same." *Fujiwara Seika shū*, vol. 1, p. 126. In his "Seika tōmon" (Dialogues with Seika), Razan [reported Seika to have] said: "The existence of principle [*ri*] is like heaven covering over everything and earth supporting everything. It is true in this land. It is also true in Korea, in Annam, and in China. To the east of the Eastern Sea and to the west of the Western Sea, these words pertain, and so, too, does principle. It is the same to the north and south. How can it not be the most open, the greatest, the most correct, and the most enlightened? Were it something that we alone possessed, I would not believe in it." *Razan sensei bunshū*, vol. 1, p. 348.

48. On the question of the principle underlying the distinction made between superiors and inferiors, Razan wrote as follows: "The black-eared kite flies, the fish swims, and the Way lies in this. There is a distinction between superiors and inferiors. Rulers have a Way for rulers, and fathers have a Way for fathers. For the former there are faithful ministers, and for the latter there are filial sons. The rankings of high and low, honored and base, are as unshakable now as they were in the distant past. This is called the difference between superior and inferior. In the tiniest of birds and fishes, the principle of the myriad things of Heaven and Earth is altogether present." *Razan sensei bunshū*, vol. 2, p. 402.

49. At the time of his mother's death, Nonaka Kenzan, a believer in the *Hsiao-hsüeh* (Elementary Learning), carried out a Confucian funeral following "the *Wen-kung chia-li* in every detail of clothing, food, and proper coffin." See *Nonaka iji ryaku* (Summaries of Reminiscences of Nonaka [Kenzan]). The story goes that this Confucian funeral gave rise to the rumor that Nonaka was a Christian, incurring the displeasure of the Tokugawa shogunate and causing his situation to be highly uncertain for a period of time. Ultimately, with the support of Hayashi Razan, the issues were resolved. See Yokogawa Suekichi, *Nonaka Kenzan* (Tokyo: Yoshikawa kōbunkan, 1962), 59–60.

50. On this issue, see the extremely interesting essay by Tajiri Yūichirō, "Keisai Kyōsai to *Bunkō karei*" ([Asami] Keisai, [Wakabayashi] Kyōsai, and the *Wen-kung chia-li*), *Nihon shisōshi kenkyū* (1983), 15:14–30. He shows in this article that the *Wen-kung chia-li* set up a

structure of general ritual, cap ritual, marriage ritual, funeral ritual, and festival ritual. However, the *Karei shisetsu* ([My] Teacher's Theory on the Family Ritual [of Chu Hsi]), the recorded notes kept by Wakabayashi Kyōsai (1679–1732) of lectures by Asami Keisai (1652–1711), and Wakabayashi's own *Karei kunmō so* (Notes on Instructions Concerning the Family Ritual [of Chu Hsi]) both omit discussion of the cap and marriage rituals. They restricted their discussion to the funeral and festival rituals which were in the charge of Buddhist monks at that time. For details, see Tajiri's essay, "Keisai Kyōsai to *Bun Kō karei.*"

51. In his *Okina mondō*, Nakae Tōju expands on his view of the distinction between the mind-and-heart and traces: "There is a distinction in regulations as well between the mind-and-heart and traces [i.e., objective manifestations]. What is recorded in the *Chou-li* (Rites of Chou) are the traces of regulations that were established by the Sages, having measured the supreme goodness of the seasons of heaven, the advantages of the earth, and human feelings. We call the basic intent of that which is inherent in these traces the mind-and-heart. We comprehend the basic intent of drawing up the regulations by these traces; we see the regulations of an era as a fixed mirror. We do not adhere completely to the traces of such events, but we see that which accords well with the mind-and-heart of the Sage as the active rules [*kappō*, defined earlier as "good regulations"] of supreme goodness. Not to discriminate the mind-and-heart and to take only the traces as a model to copy, this we call the dead laws [*shihō*] of applying glue to the stops [on a zither, i.e., adherence so strict that there is no adaptability]. They are thoroughly useless." See *Nihon shisō taikei*, vol. 29, p. 70.

[See also the modern Japanese translation of the *Okina mondō*, prepared by Yamamoto Takeo, in *Nihon no meicho* 11: *Nakae Tōju Kumazawa Banzan* (Major Works of Japan, 11: Nakae Tōju Kumazawa Banzan) (Tokyo: Chūō kōron sha, 1976), 85–86, 510. — trans.]

52. Banzan's ideas with respect to the natural environment are elaborated in detail in his "Suido kai" (Explanation of the Natural Environment), ch. 16 of *Shūgi gaisho* (Accumulated Rightness, External Writings), in *Nihon no meicho*, 476–94.

53. In his *Daigaku yōryaku*, Fujiwara Seika discussed the issue of "complete talent" (*zensai*) as follows: "A scholar combines both sagacity and ability. Combining the two is a complete talent that is very hard to attain." *Nihon shisō taikei*, vol. 28, p. 42.

54. Kumazawa Banzan defined his concept of "true talent" (*honsai*) as follows: "True talent is the talent to order the state and bring peace to the realm. To bring order to the disorder perpetuating instability is enormously difficult, requiring the kind of talent and wisdom to which few men can lay claim. If entrusted with a matter, they have made a great achievement." *Kōkyō gaiden wakumon* (Questions on the Outer Sections of the *Classic of Filial Piety*), in *Banzan zenshū* (The Complete Works of [Kumazawa] Banzan) (Tokyo: Banzan zenshū kankōkai, 1940–43), vol. 3, pp. 69–70. However, what Kumazawa meant by a person of "true talent" was not an ingenious or clever person; "true talent in general refers to someone not well skilled in little matters but capable at major affairs." (Ibid., vol. 3, p. 71.) As these words indicate, the man of basic talent might well be inept on an ordinary basis, but when it came to great tasks of state, he would demonstrate his true value. Although "true talent" and virtue are not necessarily synonymous, in the realm of politics, he argued, true talent and morality reinforce each other. True talent is acquired by studying how to increase the abilities with which one is born. Thus, he claimed, it can easily emerge from within the poor samurai class.

55. Takuan took the position that "true emptiness is rarely to be found," criticizing the

Neo-Confucians for mistaking the Buddhist "emptiness" for a relative emptiness — what he called "obstinate emptiness" (*gankū*). The Mahayana idea of emptiness was "true emptiness," in his view: "The mind-and-heart is true emptiness. It is used every day. Therefore, it is called 'true emptiness and mysterious reality.' It is empty but has limitless use — it is thus called "mysterious." *Takuan oshō zenshū*, vol. 2, p. 39. He also wrote: "If emptiness is lacking in substance, there is nothing to be used. Truth, although empty, will always be used" (ibid.). He was arguing that the emptiness of truth, though empty, can serve major functions. One of these functions is "extending knowledge and the investigation of things." See also Minamoto Ryōen, *Kinsei shoki jitsugaku shisō no kenkyū*, 312–13, 288–89.

56. On the relationship between Chu Hsi and Wang Yang-ming in his own thought, Kumazawa Banzan wrote: "By adopting [Wang] Yang-ming's proposition that knowledge is innate, I have trained myself so that the accomplishments of self-reflection and watching over oneself when alone are directed inward. Using Chu Hsi's wisdom concerning the plumbing of principle, I have been able to discern delusons." *Shūgi Washo* (Accumulated Rightness, Japanese Writings), in *Nihon shisō taikei*, vol. 3, p. 141.

57. On this issue, see Minamoto Ryōen, "Itō Jinsai no jitsugaku kan to sono shisō" (Itō Jinsai's Views on Practical Learning and His Thought), *Tōhoku daigaku bungakubu kenkyū nenpō* (1976), 26, esp. part 1: "Wakaki hi no Jinsai no kunō to sono shisō keisei" (The Sufferings of Jinsai in His Youth and the Formation of His Thought), 102–5. The main point I try to make here is that, based on the thoroughgoing idealism in his work "Shingaku genron" (Basic Principles of the School of the Mind-and-Heart), Jinsai wrote: "The learning of the Sage is the method of disciplining the mind-and-heart." Exclusively through his own mind-and-heart, he tried to grasp *a priori* the principle through which the Six Classics were found prior to their formation. To that end he focused on what he termed *chū* or equilibrium (balance, centrality). His use of the term *chū* carried the connotation of a metaphysical entity that he dubbed *chūtai* (substance as equilibrium) and, by fully realizing this *chūtai*, one could rid the "mind-and-heart of men" of complexities and know the truth of "the mind of the Way." This, he argued, came about only through "exhausting one's own mind-and-heart." However, Jinsai also wrote: "The Way lies in exhausting the mind-and-heart, [but] one must not do violence to material force as one holds firmly to one's will." Thus, if one does not exhaust the mind-and-heart in this manner, "this is drawing squares and circles before one has a ruler or a compass; this is drawing a straight line before there is any marking line [from which to judge]. . . . To understand squares and circles without a ruler or a compass and to comprehend a straight line without a marking line," Jinsai argued, made it impossible to dispense with the mind-and-heart of man and to know the mind of the Way. He then raised the issue of going beyond the bounds of Confucian rationalism based on reason. Thus he broke with Neo-Confucianism and turned to Taoism. During this period, he seems to have fallen ill with some sort of nervous disorder, though he ultimately arrived at the Zen view of bleached white bones. At this point, he realized the errors in his own thought; he renounced both Zen and the Chu Hsi school, which, according to him, had taken shape by criticizing but secretly accepting Zen, and took the stance of *kogigaku* (study of the original meaning of Confucian texts), which was based on a vitalism and affirming of the Way of human relations.

58. In his *Bendō* (Distinguishing the Way), Ogyū Sorai has the following to say: "To use one's own mind-and-heart to regulate the mind-and-heart is like a madman trying to cure his own illness. How will he ever be able to cure it?" In Inoue Tetsujirō and Kanie

Yoshimaru, eds., *Nihon rinri ihen* (Compendium on Japanese Ethics) (Tokyo: Kaneo bun'endō, 1911), vol. 6, p. 22.

59. The fact that Japan never had the civil service examination system [that China did have] was a major defect from the perspective of employing talented men from society, but the fact that there was not a standardized study curriculum for passing the examinations meant that [Japan] produced many different schools of scholarship and thought.

60. See Yamamoto Shinkō, *Shingaku gorin no sho no kenkyū* (A Study of the Essay on the Five Relations of *Shingaku*) (Tokyo: Daiichi Hōki Publishing Company, 1985).

61. The most representative study in this area is Takenaka Seiichi, *Sekimon shingaku no keizai shisō* (The Economic Thought of Ishida Baigan's School of Shingaku) (Tokyo: Minerva shobō, 1962). See also Robert N. Bellah, *Tokugawa Religion* (New York: Free Press, 1957).

62. *Shūgi Washo*, in *Nihon shisō taikei*, vol. 30, p. 157.

63. Professor Minamoto uses both the Japanese and the English terms here. — trans.

64. *Daigaku yōryaku*, in *Nihon shisō taikei*, vol. 29, pp. 55–56.

65. As concerns the case of Nakamura Keiu in the late Tokugawa and Restoration periods, see Minamoto Ryōen, "Bakumatsu ishin ki ni okeru Nakamura Keiu no Jukyō shisō" (Nakamura Keiu's Neo-Confucian Thought in the *Bakumatsu* and [Meiji] Restoration Era), *Kikan Nihon shisō shi* (1986), 26:69–97.

GLOSSARY

Abe Yoshio　阿部吉雄

Andō Shōeki　安藤昌益

Asami Keisai　淺見絅齋

Ashikaga Enjutsu　足利衍述

bakufu　幕府

bakumatsu　幕末

"Bakumatsu ishin ki ni okeru Nakamura Keiu no Jukyō shisō"　幕末·維新期に
　　おける中村敬宇の儒教思想

Banzan zenshū　蕃山全集

Bendō　辨道

Bitō Masahide　尾藤正英

"Bunbu no gei o tsūjite no Nihonjin no jiko shūren"　文武の芸を通じての日
　　本人の自己修練

Bunka　文化

Bunka to ningen keisei　文化と人間形成

Chan Ling　詹陵

Chang Tsai　張載

Ch'en Chien (Ch'en Ch'ing-lan)　陳建　陳清瀾

Ch'en Ch'un (Ch'en Pei-hsi)　陳淳　陳北溪

Chen Te-hsiu (Chen Hsi-shan)　真德秀　真西山

Cheng Hsüan　鄭玄

Ch'eng-Chu　程朱

ch'eng-i　誠意

Ch'eng Min-cheng (Ch'eng Huang-tun)　程敏政　程篁墩

chi-ching　寂靜

ch'iang　強

chih (Jap. *chi*)　知

chih-chih (Jap. *chichi*)　致知

chih liang-chih　致良知

chih-shan (Jap. *shizen*)　至善

ch'in-min (Jap. *shinmin*)　親民

ch'ing-ching　清淨

Ch'iu Chün　丘濬

Chiyo moto kusa　千代もと草

Chou-li　周禮

chū　中

chūtai　中體

Chu Hsi　朱熹

Chu-tzu ta-ch'üan　朱子大全

Ch'uan-hsi lu　傳習錄

Chūn-chang　軍讖

"Daigaku kō"　大學考

Daigaku yōryaku　大學要略

"Den Genshi ni yosu"　寄田玄之

Fujiwara Seika　藤原惺窩

Fujiwara Seika, Hayashi Razan　藤原惺窩林羅山

"Fujiwara Seika no Jugaku shisō"　藤原惺窩の儒學思想

Fujiwara Seika shū　藤原惺窩集

gankū　頑空

"Gimon rokujō"　擬問六條

giri no ri　義理の利

goji　五事

Hai Yaso　排耶蘇

han-ko　扞格

Hayashi Razan　林羅山

Heian　平安

Honda Masanobu　本多正信

honsai　本才

Honsaroku　本佐錄

Hsiao-hsüeh　小學

hsin　心

Hsin-ching　心經

Hsin-ching fu-chu　心經附註

Hsing-li ta-ch'üan hui-t'ung　性理大全會通

Hsing-li tzu-i　性理字義

Hsü Heng (Hsü Lu-chai)　許衡　許魯齋

Hsüeh-p'u t'ung-pien　學蔀通辨

Huang-shih-kung　黃石公

i (kurai)　位

i (will)　意

I ching　易經

Ikeda　池田

I-li ching-chuan t'ung-chieh　儀禮經傳通解

i'nen　意念

Inoue Tetsujirō　井上哲次郎

Ishida Baigan　石田梅岸

Ishida Ichirō　石田一郎

Itō Jinsai　伊藤仁齋

"Itō Jinsai no jitsugaku kan to sono shisō"　伊藤仁齋の實學觀とその思想

i-tuan (Jap. *itan*)　異端

I-tuan pien-cheng　異端辨正

ji (toki)　時

jihen　時變

jin (Ch. jen)　仁

jo　弱

jou　柔

kagami　鏡

Kaibara Ekken　貝原益軒

kakubutsu　格物

Kamakura Muromachi jidai no Jukyō　鎌倉室町時代之儒教

Kan　韓

Kana shōri　假名性理

Kanaya Osamu　金谷治

kang　剛

Kangaku　漢學

Kanie Yoshimaru　蟹江義丸

kappō　活法

Karei kunmō so　家禮訓蒙疏

Karei shisetsu　家禮師説

kei (Ch. *hsing*, physical form)　形

kei (Ch. *ching*, reverence)　敬

"Keikai"　經解

"Kei setsu"　敬説

"Keisai Kyōsai to *Bunkō karei*"　絅齋・強齋と「文公家禮」

"Ken-pei hsin-fa"　艮背心法

ken-pei ti-ying　艮背敵應

ki (Ch. *ch'i*)　氣

Kikan Nihon shisō shi　季刊日本思想史

Kimon　崎門

Kimura Mitsunori　木村光德

Kinsei bungaku shiryō ruijū, kanazōshi hen　近世文學資料類徒、假名草紙編

Kinsei shoki jitsugaku shisō no kenkyū　近世初期實學思想の研究

"Kinsei zenki no kenpōron ni okeru *shinpō* no mondai,"　近世前期の劍法論
　　における「心法」の問題

Kiyowara　清原

ko (Jap. *kaku*)　格

Kogaku　古學

Kogigaku　古義學

"Kohon Daigaku zenkai"　古本大學全解

kokoro　心

kokoromochi no heihō　心モチノ兵法

Kokugaku　國學

Kōkyō gaiden wakumon　孝經外傳或問

Kōshōgaku　考證學

ko-wu (Jap. *kakubutsu*)　格物

kufū (Ch. *kung-fu*)　工夫

Kumazawa Banzan　熊澤蕃山

kyo (Ch. *hsü*)　虛

kyorei　虛靈

kyūri　窮理

Lao-tzu　老子

li (Jap. *ri*, benefit)　利

Li-chi　禮記

Li Yen-p'ing (Li T'ung)　李延平　李侗

Li-yen sheng-yü　禮言剩語

liang-chih (Jap. *ryōchi*)　良知

Lin Chao-en　林兆恩

Lin-tzu ch'üan-chi　林子全集

Lin-tzu ssu-shu piao-chai cheng-i hsü　林子四書標摘正義續

Liu-t'ao　六韜

Lo Ch'in-shun (Lo Cheng-an)　羅欽順　羅整庵

Lu-chai hsin-fa　魯齋心法

Lu Hsiang-shan (Lu Chiu-yüan)　陸象山　陸九淵

Lu-Wang　陸王

Maruyama Masao　丸山真男

Matsunaga Sekigo　松永尺五

"Matsunaga Sekigo no shisō to Oze Hoan no shisō"　松永尺五の思想と小瀬
　甫庵の思想

Meii hōkan 明意寶鑑

"Meishin hōkan ni tsuite" 『明心寶鑑』について

meitoku Busshō 明德佛性

Minamoto Ryōen 源了圓

Ming-hsin pao-chien cheng-wen 明心寶鑑正文

ming-te (Jap. *meitoku*) 明德

mono 物

Motoori Norinaga 本居宣長

mukyoku ni shite taikyoku (Ch. *wu-chi erh t'ai-chi*) 無極而太極

mushin 無心

Naikaku Bunko 內閣文庫

Nakae Tōju 中江藤樹

Nakae Tōju no "chūki" no shisō 中江藤樹の「中期」の思想

Nakamura Keiu 中村敬宇

Nawa Kassho 那波活所

Nihon hōken shisō shi kenkyū 日本封建思想史研究

Nihon no meicho 11: *Nakae Tōju Kumazawa Banzan* 日本の名著11: 中江藤樹熊沢蕃山

Nihon rinri ihen 日本倫理彙編

Nihon seiji shisō shi kenkyū 日本政治思想史研究

Nihon shisō shi kenkyū 日本思想史研究

Nihon shisō taikei 日本思想大系

Nihon Shushigaku to Chōsen 日本朱子學と朝鮮

ninjō 人情

Nonaka iji ryaku 野中遺事略

Nonaka Kenzan 野中兼山

Ogyū Sorai 荻生徂徠

Okada Takehiko 岡田武彦

Okina mondō 翁問答

Oze Hoan 小瀬甫庵

pei 背

Razan sensei bunshū 羅山先生文集

rei (Ch. *li*, ritual) 禮

reisei　靈性

ri (Ch. *li*, principle)　理

Rikutō genkai　六韜諺解

Sakuma Zōzan (Shōzan)　佐久間象山

San-lüeh　三略

Sanryaku genkai　三略諺解

Santoku shō　三德抄

sei (Ch. *hsing*)　性

seigaku (Ch. *hsing-hsüeh*)　性學

Seika sensei gyōjō　惺窩先生行狀

"Seika tōmon"　惺窩答問

seiri (Ch. *hsing-li*)　性理

Seiri jigi genkai　性理字義諺解

Seiyō shō　政要抄

seki (*ato*, Ch. *chi*)　跡

Sekimon *shingaku*　石門心學

Sekimon shingaku no keizai shisō　石門心學の經濟思想

"Sennan gūkyo ki"　泉南寓居記

Setchūgaku　折衷學

shan-shu　善書

shih (Jap. *ji*)　事

shih-chung　時中

shih-wu　事物

shihō　死法

shindoku (Ch. *shen-tu*)　慎獨

shingaku (Ch. *hsin-hsüeh*)　心學

"Shingaku genron"　心學原論

Shingaku gorin no sho　心學五倫の書

Shingaku gorin no sho no kenkyū　心學五倫の書の研究

shinkū myōu (Ch. *chen-k'ung miao-yu*)　真空妙有

shinpō (Ch. *hsin-fa*)　心法

shinpō no gaku　心法の學

shinri (Ch. *hsin-li*)　心理

Shintō denju　神道傳授

"Shisho batsu"　四書跋

sho (tokoro)　所

"Shūchū kiyaku"　舟中規約

Shūgi gaisho　集義外書

Shūgi Washo　集義和書

Shushigaku　朱子學

"Shushigaku no futatsu no keifu"　朱子學の二つの系譜、

Ssu-ma Kuang　司馬光

Ssu-shu cheng-i k'ao　四書正義考

Ssu-shu chi-chu　四書集註

Ssu-shu huo-wen　四書或問

"Suido kai"　水土解

Suminokura Ryōi　角倉了以

Suzuki Daisetsu　鈴木大拙

Ta-hsüeh chang-chü　大學章句

Ta-hsüeh cheng-i tsuan　大學正義纂

Ta-hsüeh huo-wen　大學或問

Ta-hsüeh wen　大學問

Ta-hsüeh yen-i　大學衍義

Ta-hsüeh yen-i pu　大學衍義補

tai　怠

t'ai-hsü　太虛

T'ai-i shen　太乙神

T'ai-kung-wang　太公望

Tajiri Yūichirō　田尻祐一郎

Takenaka Seiichi　竹中靖一

Takuan　澤庵

Takuan oshō zenshū　澤庵和尚全集

Tamakake Hiroyuki　玉懸博之

tami o yashinau no gi　民ヲ養フノ義

Tan-shu　丹書

T'ang Shu　唐樞

"Tenmei zusetsu batsu"　天命圖説跋

tenka　天下

Tōhoku daigaku Nihon bunka kenkyūjo kenkyū hōkoku　東北大學日本文化研究所研究報告

Tōhoku daigaku bungakubu kenkyū nenpō　東北大學文學部研究年報

Tōjugaku no seiritsu ni kansuru kenkyū　藤樹學の成立に關する研究

Tōju sensei zenshū　藤樹先生全集

Tokugawa gōri shisō no keifu　德川合理思想の系譜

"Tokugawa hōken shakai to Shushigakuha"　德川封建社會と朱子學派

Tominaga Nakamoto　富永仲基

Tosa　土佐

Tosanangaku　土佐南學

Tzu-yang　紫陽

tuan　端

Wakabayashi Kyōsai　若林強齋

"Wakaki hi no Jinsai no kunō to sono shisō keisei"　若き日の仁齋の苦惱とその思想形成

Wang Chi (Wang Lung-hsi)　王畿　王龍溪

Wang Lung-hsi ch'üan-chi　王龍溪全集

Wang Yang-ming (Wang Shou-jen)　王陽明　王守仁

Wen-kung chia-li　文公家禮

Wing-tsit Chan (Ch'en Jung-chieh)　陳榮捷

wu (Jap. *mono*)　物

Wu (King)　武

Yamaga Sokō　山鹿素行

Yamamoto Shinkō　山本真功

Yamamoto Takeo　山本武夫

Yamashita Ryūji　山下龍二

Yamazaki Ansai　山崎闇齋

Yen-p'ing ta-wen　延平答問

Yi T'oegye　李退溪

Yōgaku　洋學

Yokogawa Suekichi　横川末吉

Yokoi Shōnan　横井小楠

Yōmeigaku　陽明學

Yoshida Genshi　吉田玄之

Yoshida Soan　吉田素庵

Zen　禪

zensai　全才

"Zuihitsu daijūichi"　隨筆第十一

Chapter Nine

CONFUCIANISM AND NATIVISM IN TOKUGAWA JAPAN

PETER NOSCO

For intellectual historians of Japan's Tokugawa period (1600–1867), Confucianism and nativism (*Kokugaku*) — understood here to refer to forms of scholarship that took elements from Japan's own narrow heritage as their primary areas of inquiry, as opposed to the study of a significant cultural "other," represented in the case of Japan by the study of China (*Kangaku*) — have long been major subjects of scholarly research.[1] Within most studies of these subjects, one finds a remarkable degree of consensus on the following points: first, that during the seventeenth century Confucians were largely responsible for delineating the contours and defining the terms of intellectual discourse during the Tokugawa period; second, that nativists then appeared, seemingly *ex nihilo*, and both challenged those terms and reconstituted the parameters of this rationalist Confucian discourse during the eighteenth century, with the nativists' teachings emerging at that time as the principal intellectual alternative to Confucianism; and third, that during the nineteenth century activist intellectuals, most of whom had affiliations with the Mito domain, drew inspiration and justification for their goals from both Confucian and nativist sources and erected a new ideological structure that contributed to the end of the Tokugawa polity and laid a foundation for the new ideology of the early Meiji period.

This chapter is not, properly speaking, about either Confucianism or nativism during the Tokugawa period but rather about the relationship between the two; and its intention is not so much to challenge but, rather, to reappraise the "common wisdom" concerning this relationship as outlined above. For, while these assumptions per se retain considerable merit, I find questionable their shared underlying premise, namely, that Confucianism and nativism represent separate and competing discourses throughout the Tokugawa period in particular and more generally throughout Japanese history. Through a brief examination of the intellectual careers of several figures regarded as prominent within the so-called Confucian and nativist traditions of Tokugawa Japan, this chapter seeks to demonstrate the following three points.

The first is that Confucianism and nativism were components of an essentially singular scholarly discourse during most of the Tokugawa period (as well as Japanese history), much as they had been and were in China, and hence that their adversarial relationship during the eighteenth century was actually somewhat anomalous. It is understood here that the positing of a Chinese form of nativism is problematic, since nativism by its very nature requires the presence of a significant cultural "other," largely absent in the intellectual history of China until the advent of European astronomy.[2] Nonetheless, it is hoped that the comparisons with China will prove useful, both for an understanding of the issues raised herein and in terms of the larger themes of this volume.

The second major contention is that the eighteenth-century bifurcation of this scholarship into competing Confucian and nativist discourses was, on the one hand, a reflection of certain tendencies that emerge during the late seventeenth century among scholars like Yamazaki Ansai who are traditionally identified as Confucian and, on the other, a deliberate construction on the part of would-be nativist scholars as a response to opportunities presented during the last decades of the seventeenth and early decades of the eighteenth centuries. These opportunities include: (1) the rise of the popular academy, which marketed scholarship to willing consumers who derived personal enrichment or professional advancement through their training; (2) certain new opportunities for soliciting central government (*bakufu*) and domainal support of various forms of scholarship; and (3) what is styled below as the "domestication" of the nostalgic impulse.

The third major point is that the reconvergence of the Confucian and nativist discourses during the last decades of the Tokugawa period represents not only a heretofore unobserved symmetry in the history of Tokugawa thought but also a reversion to an enduring, more traditional pattern in the intellectual history of Japan. It is argued that this reconvergence was an outgrowth of the attempt by leading ideologues to justify and thereby popularize their agendas for reform by drawing on a vast array of assumptions, irrespective of those assumptions' pedigree or lineage.

If one examines the intellectual history of China from the late Chou dynasty until early-modern times, one finds no meaningful distinction between the study of native subject matter and Confucian concerns. The evidence of Shang oracle bone inscriptions indicates that historical mindedness in China is far older than Confucianism per se, but because of the emphasis Confucius placed upon the mastery of such works as the *Shu ching* (Classic of Documents), the *Li chi* (Record of Rites), and the *Shih ching* (Classic of Poetry), training in Chinese history, verse, and antiquarian ritual and practices came to be intrinsic from the Han dynasties onward to the training of those who aspired to official service and those who styled themselves Confucian scholars. To be a Confucian in China meant that one had acquired a measure of mastery over the poetic and historical classics of one's native tradition, and the canonization of this curriculum into the so-called Confucian Classics was further responsible for what has been identified as a propensity for ethnocentrism within the Confucian tradition itself.[3] Such tendencies are, of course, characteristic of nativist pursuits. Thus, within China at least, Confucian discourse successfully assimilated and appropriated unto itself such diverse pursuits as the study of Chinese verse, poetics, historiography, and antiquarian studies.

The formal introduction of Confucianism to Japan is dated from A.D. 285 during the reign of Emperor Ōjin, though Korean (and perhaps Chinese) Confucians had immigrated to Japan even earlier. The impact of Confucian teachings upon the intellectual life of early Japan remains uncertain thanks to two particular factors. First, Confucianism entered Japan at a time when its doctrines were largely overshadowed on continental East Asia by the teachings of Buddhism,[4] and on the archipelago as well, Buddhist assumptions remained dominant within scholarly discourse through the sixteenth century. Second, the ethical and political nucleus of Confucian thought was perceived to be of little relevance by a society that placed a premium on pedigree and military prowess, as opposed to performance, for political advancement within an aristocratic imperial bureaucracy. Nonetheless, by the eighth century Confucian assumptions concerning appropriate areas for scholarly inquiry had already become integral to Chinese civilization as it was apprehended in early Japan, and it is for our purposes significant that the earliest extant examples of nativist scholarship in Japan—the *Kojiki* (Record of Ancient Matters) (712) and *Nihon shoki* (Chronicles of Japan) (720) histories, and the *Man'yōshū* poetry anthology—owed their compilation at least in part to the fact that they were intended to correspond to works of central importance within the Chinese world of letters. In these works, compiled during the height of Chinese civilizational influence upon Japan, one encounters the first examples of the convergence of nativist and continental Confucian scholarly goals in Japan.

Japan's disenchantment with China as a civilizational model following the decline of the T'ang dynasty (618–907) meant that Japan had little contact with China at precisely the moment when figures like Han Yü (768–824) and Li Ao (fl. 798) were reasserting the relevance of Confucian teachings and later when the Confucian tradition was refashioned into those doctrines known in the West as Neo-Confucianism. Emperors Hanazono (r. 1308–1318) and Godaigo (r. 1318–1339) in the fourteenth century were among the few Japanese sovereigns to take an active interest in Confucianism, though in the case of Godaigo, his motives were probably more political than intellectual since he sought in Confucianism certain ideals of imperial rule that he hoped to apply to the Japanese state for the advancement of his own political aims. Here again one may observe a certain convergence between Confucian and nativist ideals since Godaigo's principal adviser, Kitabatake Chikafusa (1293–1354), was the author of Japan's most important piece of fourteenth-century historical writing, the *Jinnō shōtōki* (Chronicle of Gods and Sovereigns), a work known for its assertion that Japan's polity is distinguished by its rule by divine sovereigns descended without dynastic disruption from the sun goddess Amaterasu.

Though one might scour the ensuing centuries in Japan for additional evidence of this convergence, it is clear that, in terms of its social ethics, Confucianism in Japan before the seventeenth century played only a minor role in and, aside from its cosmology, exerted little influence upon an intellectual life dominated by Buddhism. So-called "Confucian" diviners were routinely consulted for matters such as the selection of auspicious dates for major undertakings or the correct manner in which to situate a dwelling, but Confucian counsel on how to order either oneself or the polity was little in evidence. Occasional exceptions like Emperors Hanazono and Godaigo notwithstanding, it is not until the seventeenth century and the start of the Tokugawa period that "Confucianism" as a social and ethical discourse began to make its place in Japanese intellectual arenas.

The researches of such scholars as Herman Ooms,[5] Hori Isao,[6] Ishida

Ichirō[7] and Wajima Yoshio[8] have laid to rest a host of widely held misconceptions concerning the Tokugawa *bakufu*'s interest in Confucianism as an ideological instrument, but the tendency among intellectual historians to distinguish seventeenth-century Confucians from nativists on the basis of an alleged Sinophilia has persisted with remarkable vigor. Though Confucian scholars in Japan were certainly perceived at times to be authorities on things Chinese — as when in 1593 Tokugawa Ieyasu (1542–1616) summoned Fujiwara Seika (1561–1617) to lecture on the *Chen-kuan cheng-yao* (Essentials of Government of the Chen-kuan [627–649] Era) — the fact is that *every* major seventeenth-century Confucian scholar in Japan before the Genroku period devoted significant attention to nativist concerns, and in this sense Confucian teachings in Japan's early Tokugawa period may well have been less in need of domestication than has heretofore been suggested.[9]

The question of who is a "major" seventeenth-century Confucian in Japan before the Genroku is, of course, one that might be debated endlessly. This chapter adopts the expedient of simply examining all those figures identified as Confucian (or Neo-Confucian) and discussed as such in *Sources of Japanese Tradition*, an anthology whose selections conform closely to most comparable works in Japanese: Hayashi Razan (1583–1657), Hayashi Gahō (1618–1680), Yamazaki Ansai (1618–1682), Nakae Tōju (1608–1648), Kumazawa Banzan (1619–1691), and Yamaga Sokō (1622–1685), as well as the patrons of scholarship Hoshina Masayuki (1611–1672) and Tokugawa Mitsukuni (1628–1701).

What one observes in the careers of these apparent "paragons" of Confucianism and their patrons may be surprising. Hayashi Razan founded his own school of Shinto (*Ritō shinchi Shintō* [Shinto Where Principle Corresponds to the Heart]), wrote a major work on the history of Shinto shrines (*Honchō jinja kō* [On Japanese Shrines]), and initiated work on a history of Japan modeled after the writings of Ssu-ma Kuang. Hayashi Gahō brought his father's work to completion in the 310-*kan* work, *Honchō tsugan* (Comprehensive Mirror of this Court), and also authored the shorter history of Japanese reigns, *Nihon ōdai ichiran* (Overview of Japanese Reigns). Yamazaki Ansai, frustrated in his ambitions to write a work on Japanese history, which was to have been titled *Yamato kagami* (Mirror of Japan), instead formulated his own school of Shinto called Suika. Nakae Tōju lectured to his students on Japanese history and poetry in addition to the Confucian classics. Kumazawa Banzan used the Confucian classic, the *Great Learning*, to expound upon the *bakufu*'s social, political and economic policies, with a particular focus on what he perceived to be the enervation of the samurai class. Finally, Yamaga Sokō, who asserted the priority of Japanese civilization over that of China, was also the author of a history of the military houses titled *Buke jiki* (Chronicle of the Miitary Houses), as well as a codification of the samurai tradition known as *bushidō*. For their part, the premier patrons of pre-Genroku seventeenth-century scholarship, Hoshina Masayuki and Tokugawa Mitsukuni, likewise appear to have been no less interested in nativist concerns than they were in Confucian principles. Hoshina Masayuki studied Yoshida Shintō under Yoshikawa Koretaru (1616–1694) and influenced Yamazaki Ansai's interest in Shinto theology; and Tokugawa Mitsukuni was responsible not just for initiating the mammoth *Dai Nihon shi* (The Great Japan History) enterprise but also for sponsoring Keichū's (1640–1701) commentaries on the *Man'yōshū*.

In other areas as well one finds persuasive evidence that Confucianism and nativism were components of a singular scholarly discourse during the early Tokugawa. For example, the major Shinto theologians of the seventeenth century — Yoshikawa Koretaru and Watarai Nobuyoshi (1615–1690), as well as Razan and Ansai — were thoroughly versed in the Neo-Confucian teachings of the Ch'eng-Chu tradition and sought to reconcile faith in the native creed with the metaphysical and ontological assumptions of orthodox Neo-Confucianism. Even the long-standing debate between traditional moralistic and avant-garde artistic literary criticism and poetics was refashioned during the seventeenth century in Confucian rather than Buddhist terms. This last tendency was so marked that the *Kokka hachiron* (Eight Essays on Japanese Poetry) controversy of the 1740s — regarded by many as the most significant debate on the nature of *waka* verse during the Tokugawa period — represents essentially a transposition of various Confucian assumptions onto a discussion of native poetics.[10]

It is nonetheless clear that beginning in the 1680s and continuing through the eighteenth century, there was a rupture in what has here been described as a singular scholarly discourse, and a division of this discourse into competing nativist and Confucian discourses that increasingly articulated themselves in opposition to each other. Further, this rupture is evident in precisely those areas of scholarly activity — historiography, poetics, and Shinto theology — that had formed the nucleus of seventeenth-century scholarly inquiry.

Among the earliest traces of this rupture is the dissatisfaction expressed by the students of Yamazaki Ansai over Ansai's involvement with Shinto. Some of his students facetiously suggested that since Ansai had begun his training as a Buddhist, "converted" to Neo-Confucianism, and then turned to Shinto, his only remaining step was to become a Christian.[11] This hostility on the part of Confucian "purists" to Ansai's involvement with Shinto was sufficient following his death in 1682 to provoke a division in his school between those who identified with his Confucian teachings and those who regarded themselves as followers of Suika Shintō.

A similar bifurcation is evident among literary critics. While poets at the imperial court known as the Dōjō school continued to argue that poetry is the great Way of Japan in contrast to the Confucian Way of China, other critics like Toda Mosui (1629–1706) adopted a more radical stance. Mosui argued that Shinto was actually the great Way of Japan, representing the "roots" of Japanese civilization by contrast with Confucianism, which represented only the branches and leaves.[12] According to his analysis, Confucianism was, in fact, no more than a derivative teaching of Shinto.

The writings of the Shingon priest Keichū (1640–1701) likewise reflect an understanding of Japan's past according to which nativist and Confucian concerns were separate and not wholly compatible. Writing in his magnum opus, a commentary on the *Man'yōshū* titled *Man'yō daishōki* (A Stand-in's Chronicle of the *Man'yōshū*), Keichū depicted ancient pre-Confucian and pre-Buddhist Japan as a naive and unlettered age in which the simple truths of Shinto answered all social and political needs.[13] Regarded by many scholars as a forerunner of the ideological nativism of the eighteenth century, Keichū's work suggests the first traces of a nativist distancing from Confucianism, a fact made all the more remarkable because Keichū's work on the *Man'yōshū* was sponsored by Tokugawa Mitsukuni.

Among those identified with early eighteenth-century Shinto, one finds ever more vigorous denunciations of Confucianism. Masuho Zankō (1655–1742), whose intentions were to popularize Shinto by disentangling it from the theological accretions of a century of Confucian-Shinto syncretism, described Confucians as "stinking half-wits" who know nothing of the native tradition.[14] Similarly Kada no Azumamaro (1669–1736), a scion of the family that had served for centuries as hereditary wardens of the Inari Shrine in Fushimi, warned in his 1728 petition to the shogun, Tokugawa Yoshimune, of the dire consequences that might befall Japan if the native tradition were neglected as a result of the seductive appeal of Confucian deluders.[15]

By the middle of the eighteenth century, Confucianism and nativism came to represent competing discourses that articulated mutually antagonistic postures. Four factors that help to account for this rupture within what had previously been a virtually seamless scholarly discourse incorporating both Confucian and nativist elements are: (1) the introduction of "passion" in seventeenth-century scholarly discourse; (2) the successful "marketing" of continuing adult education as one aspect of the nascent popular culture; (3)

evidence of *bakufu* and domainal interest in the sponsoring of certain scholarly endeavors; and (4) the domestication of the nostalgic impulse. Let us examine these in greater detail, beginning with the introduction of passion.

During the early years of the Tokugawa, leading scholars engaged in the study of Confucianism — figures like Fujiwara Seika and Hayashi Razan — had generally been trained in Buddhist settings and understood that if Confucian teachings were to attract a broader scholarly audience, it would be necessary to disentangle Confucianism from the institutional support it had received from Zen monasteries. Indeed, scholars like Seika and Razan approached the study and advocacy of Confucianism seriously. Razan's distaste with being ordered by Ieyasu to wear the very Buddhist robes that he had earlier proudly abandoned as part of his "conversion" to Confucianism is just one example of the intensity with which Confucianism was embraced by its early followers, and it is understandable that early Tokugawa Confucians most often articulated their doctrines in juxtaposition with those of Buddhism.

Nonetheless, no seventeenth-century Confucian in Japan was more passionate in this regard than Yamazaki Ansai. It might be argued that Ansai himself had acquired this "passion" from his exposure to the writings of prominent Korean Neo-Confucians like Yi T'oegye, whose zeal for the creed exceeded anything found in China. Whatever its origin — Ansai appears, by all accounts, to have been an unusually "intense" fellow to start with — it resulted in certain new extremes. For example, Ansai forbade his students to read works of poetry or history — even those within the Confucian canon — that, in his opinion, did not direct one toward the goal of moral perfection. His students complained of the stern and humorless atmosphere in his school, the Kimon, and Ansai was often severely critical of both his predecessors in the study of Confucianism (like Hayashi Razan) and his contemporaries (like Hayashi Gahō). It was said of Ansai that when asked what course to follow if China were to attack Japan with Confucius and Mencius leading the invasion, he counseled capturing them alive — a response the more moderate Itō Tōgai is said to have ridiculed with the comment, "I guarantee that it will never happen."[16]

In the intellectual history of mid-Tokugawa Japan, it was Ansai's passion that drove the wedge between nativism and Confucianism. It will be recalled that Ansai formulated a new school of Shinto and aspired to write a history of Japan, goals that are emblematic of the convergence of nativist and Confucian scholarly ideals characteristic of Tokugawa thought before the 1680s. It was Ansai's students, however, who, having acquired their teacher's passion but not his breadth, belonged to the first generation of Tokugawa thinkers to choose between nativism and Confucianism. After Ansai's death in 1682 the Kimon in fact split into those who followed Ansai's Confucian teachings and those who followed his Shinto theology, with considerable antagonism between the two branches.

A second factor in this division into nativism and Confucianism as separate fields of study is related to opportunities presented by the rise of private academies in the late seventeenth century. The earliest financially successful private academies in Tokugawa Japan were those of the poetry markers, who were paid by their students to critique the students' attempts at versification. Their proliferation was so swift and their quality so uneven that Ihara Saikaku, the celebrated author and wry observer of the follies of his age, referred to them as "crooks."[17] The opportunities for marketing Confucian wisdom were apparently likewise obvious, for the unknown author of a work titled *Gion monogatari* (Tales of Gion) complained of the ease with which a Buddhist monk with a smattering of knowledge of Confucian texts might establish himself as an authority.[18] Further, knowledge of Confucianism had also become fashionable by the late seventeenth century, for in a list of the accomplishments of a dandyish young man, Saikaku included having heard Utsunomiya Ton'an, a well-known scholar, lecture on Confucianism alongside such other cultural training as instruction in both tea ceremony and flower arrangement.[19]

During the Genroku years Itō Jinsai's (1627–1705) Kogidō demonstrated the potential for success of an academy providing instruction in Confucian texts. Later, during the eighteenth century, Masuho Zankō showed that public lectures on Shinto theology might be just as attractive, but in general nativist private academies lagged behind their Confucian counterparts in numbers of students until the nineteenth century. The significance, however, lay in the fact that the successful private academies of the eighteenth century were all either nativist academies or Confucian academies, but not both, and their competition in the marketplace of ideas exacerbated the tension between these now separate discourses.

Yet another factor in the competition between nativism and Confucianism may have been the new opportunities for government support that arose during the late seventeenth and early eighteenth centuries at a time when scholarship in general was in the process of becoming increasingly specialized. Tsunayoshi (r. 1680–1709), the fifth Tokugawa shogun, fancied himself to be something of an authority on Confucianism, lecturing frequently on the Confucian classics to assemblies of daimyo and other notables: in 1691 he conferred the title of *Daigaku no kami* (head of the university) on Hayashi

Hōkō (1644–1732), relocated the Hayashi school in Yushima, and established the Hayashi family as hereditary custodians of Confucian instruction within the *bakufu* establishment. The paradigmatic Confucian scholar-statesman Arai Hakuseki (1657–1725) was both tutor and adviser to the sixth Tokugawa shogun, Ienobu, and also served his successor, Tokugawa Ietsugu. Tokugawa Yoshimune (1684–1751), the eighth shogun (r. 1716–1745), was virtually besieged with unsolicited counsel from a variety of largely Confucian but also Shinto sources. Though he is well known for having relaxed the prohibition on European studies, he was formally advised in Confucian matters by Muro Kyūsō; Ogyū Sorai wrote his *Seidan* (Discourses on Government) for Yoshimune and might have replaced Muro had Sorai not died in 1728; and in 1726 Yoshimune conferred a formal charter upon the Kaitokudō merchant academy in Osaka. This in turn may help to explain Kada no Azumamaro's hopeful 1728 petition to Yoshimune to found a school for nativism in Fushimi. Though the petition was never acknowledged by the *bakufu*, Azumamaro's vituperative attacks on Confucianism and its proponents herald the adversarial relationship between nativism and Confucianism for the rest of the eighteenth century. When regarded in this context, his comments seem reminiscent of the kind of scholarly hyperbole characteristic of grant applications in modern academe.

Another factor that helps to explain this separation of nativism and Confucianism might be styled the "domestication" of the nostalgic impulse. Nostalgia — that idealization of the past in response to dissatisfaction with the present — was, of course, nothing new either within the Japanese tradition or the human personality. From the verses of Kakinomoto Hitomaro in the *Man'yōshū* to the grumblings of Yoshida Kenkō in *Tsurezuregusa* (Essays in Idleness), expressions of nostalgic longing for times even then long past were virtually a literary conceit in the Japanese tradition before the Tokugawa period. What changed in the eighteenth century, however, was, first, that the idealized depiction of the archaic past became an only thinly veiled critique of the present, and second, that the nostalgic fantasy was transformed into an exhortation either to escape the present by reentering the past spiritually (as advocated by Kamo no Mabuchi, 1697–1769) or to reanimate the numinous qualities of the past within the fallen present (as prescribed by Motoori Norinaga, 1730–1801).[20] These specifically normative forms of nostalgic expression had traditionally been identified with Confucianism, but during the eighteenth century major nativists appropriated them into their newly ideological nativist constructions.

Not only was this new in terms of the long-standing tradition of nostalgia within the Japanese tradition, but it was new in terms of the manner in which nativism and Confucianism articulated themselves vis-à-vis each other. For example, in his *Bendō sho* (On Distinguishing the Way), Dazai Shundai (1680–1747), a student of Ogyū Sorai, asserted that "the fact that there were no [native] Japanese words for humaneness, rightness, propriety, music, filial piety, and so on proved that the Way had not existed in Japan prior to the introduction of Chinese learning."[21] Kamo no Mabuchi attempted to refute this assertion and, in the process, to reclaim the Way from the Confucians for the nativists, by insisting that the so-called Confucian virtues mentioned by Shundai existed "throughout the world like the movement of the four seasons,"[22] and that the proof that Japan had the Way in its perfected all-pervading state lay precisely in the fact that Japan had no need for terminology to describe it. Mabuchi's *Kokui kō* (On the Concept of the Country) was, in fact, one of not fewer than thirty attacks on the Sorai school written between 1750 and 1790,[23] and the *Kokui kō* in turn itself became a subject of both attacks and defenses well into the early nineteenth century.[24]

Considering the antipathy of the major nativist writers toward Confucianism, the reconvergence of these discourses in the early decades of the nineteenth century is all the more remarkable, and an examination of the writings of Hirata Atsutane (1776–1843) — probably the most xenophobic of all nativists in Japan — sheds light on how this came about. Unlike his nativist predecessors, Kamo no Mabuchi and Motoori Norinaga, Atsutane was neither a classicist nor a fundamentalist but, rather, an exceptionally successful popularist. For example, when his critics charged that one should not lend credence to matters not discussed in the ancient classics, Atsutane countered, "If you refuse to believe in things not mentioned in the ancient classics, you cannot very well believe what we know about man's internal organs, for they are not mentioned in the classics, but will you deny that they exist?"[25] Among texts from the native tradition, Atsutane gave priority neither to the *Kojiki* nor the *Nihon shoki*, and in what might be called his "universalization" of "truths" that he attributed to the native tradition, Atsutane was prepared to support his views with arguments gleaned from a variety of traditions. For example, in his maiden work, *Kamōsho* (Rebuke of Error) (1803), Atsutane relied largely on arguments developed by Norinaga; in his *Shin kishin ron* (New Discussion of Spirits and Deities) (1805), however, Atsutane attempted to refute certain claims by Arai Hakuseki by drawing on largely the same Confucian classics that Hakuseki had used. Furthermore, in Atsutane's *Honkyō gaihen* (Outer Chapters of Our Teachings) (1806), he attempted to verify Shinto "truths" by using reasoning drawn from Roman Catholicism;

and in his *Zoku Shintō taii* (Popular Shinto Outline) (1811), Atsutane personalized these claims by asserting that Japanese men are "endowed at birth with a host of qualities ranging from revering our deities, lords, and parents, cherishing our wives and children, to the Way which Confucians call the Five Relationships and the Five Virtues."[26]

Atsutane's intention was to popularize his teachings by drawing on a variety of sources for verification and by removing his nativist scholarship from a preoccupation with philological method that had, by the nature of its scholarly demands, limited the appeal of ideological nativism to a broader audience during the eighteenth century. What he accomplished in the process, however, was a reaffirmation of the compatibility of Confucian and nativist social goals — goals like respect for authority (whether parental or political) and social stability. That this, in turn, was made possible by the successful penetration of a host of eighteenth-century nativist assumptions into the broader scholarly discourse is attested to by the fact that Confucians during the early nineteenth century were themselves arriving at altogether similar formulations and conclusions.

Nowhere was this more evident than among those scholars identified with Mito learning. During the late eighteenth and early nineteenth centuries, when numerous religious and political figures in Japan were seeking ways to "rectify" what they perceived to be the shortcomings of their world (*yonanoshi*), Mito historians like Fujita Yūkoku (1774–1826) and his son Tōko (1806–1855) sought to apply the "lessons" gleaned from their historical scholarship to contemporary problems. For example, Ogyū Sorai's historicist understanding of the "Way" as ancient practices with only relative value in the changed present had diluted the strongly restorationist character of more orthodox Confucian thought. The response of Mito writers like Fujita Tōko and Aizawa Seishisai (1781–1863), however, was to reassert this traditional restorationist theme, and thereby to renew the present with what they believed to be the unchanging and time-tested Way of the past. Since their studies included an examination of Japan's mythological past as if it were history, their conclusions were rooted as much in the principles of the Confucians as in the rhetoric of the nativists.

Another enveloping strategy that enabled the scholars of Mito to draw from both Confucian and nativist arguments derived from the strongly xenophobic character of both traditions. Among nativists during the eighteenth century the antiforeignism of figures like Mabuchi and Norinaga was fundamentally an anti-Chinese sentiment, but as Japan's intellectual horizons were broadened, on the one hand, through European studies and, on the other, by the seemingly ineluctable encroachment of the major Western powers, the xeno-phobic expressions of a figure like Hirata Atsutane were likewise expanded to include vitriolic comments on Europeans as well as other Asians. In other words, as their sense of a cultural "other" was broadened, nineteenth-century nativists found ever more to despise.

It was here, curiously, that nineteenth-century Confucians found common ground with their nativist colleagues. The old Sinocentric world view had by this time long since lost whatever limited hold it once commanded in Japan,[27] but the challenges that China faced in the nineteenth century were in some respects similar to those confronting Japan. This conjunction of world views vis-à-vis the European powers, in turn, contributed to an intellectual climate in which the traditional xenophobia of Confucianism converged in a compel-ling manner with the more recent xenophobia of the nativists.

The other element that bound nativist and Confucian ideals for the early-nineteenth century Mito scholars was the fact that, in their minds, learning (*gakumon*) and politics (*matsurigoto*) had become a singular concern.[28] In the involuted realm of Mito political thought during the Tokugawa period's last decades, when even the most activist thinkers were more concerned with sustaining the crumbling Tokugawa order than displacing it with another system, ideologues did not hesitate to buttress their analyses and arguments with material drawn from a variety of sources. Further, since their research into early Japanese mytho-history had led them to replicate numerous asser-tions of the major eighteenth-century nativists — particularly those concerning the relationship among the sun goddess Amaterasu, the imperial institution, its delegates, and the populace at large within the political hierophany of the Japanese polity — their differences with the nativists became largely a matter of the nativists' discarding their earlier overtly anti-Confucian stance. In fact, once the nativists were prepared to dispense with their anti-Confucian dia-tribes — a shift that occurred not later than the early 1840s with the death of Atsutane and perhaps as much as two decades earlier — the convergence of nativist and Confucian ideals marked the reversion to what was actually an earlier pattern of considerable antiquity within the Japanese tradition. This, in turn, may help to account for the anti-Buddhist tone of much early Meiji rhetoric and ideology, since with Japan's new myths grounded within the reassembled singular discourse of Confucianism and nativism, the exclusion of and attendant aversion to Japan's other major intellectual and religious tradition become all the more understandable.

By way of conclusion, it is important to note one qualification to this chapter's premises concerning the relationship between Confucianism and nativism during the Tokugawa period. Throughout this interpretive analysis, the focus has been on major figures generally regarded as paradigmatic within the historiography of Confucianism and nativism in Tokugawa Japan. The adversarial relationship described above, the eighteenth-century rupture in the seemingly seamless web of seventeenth-century scholarship in Japan, was a fissure that existed primarily at the level of the major teachers and leaders of the respective modes of thought and was much less a factor either among their students or the "second tier" of Confucian and nativist scholars. In fact, the evidence suggests that for the majority of students in Confucian and nativist academies, and among the majority of scholars whose celebrity was lesser than the figures discussed above, the tensions between nativism and Confucianism were not a compelling intellectual concern. This, in turn, suggests that throughout the Tokugawa period, and indeed throughout Japanese history, there remained an enduring and significant measure of scholarly consensus concerning the appropriate areas for scholarly inquiry and the rationale for such inquiry. It is, finally, hoped that this qualification to this chapter's thesis may also contribute to our understanding of the parameters and contours of the intellectual terrain of Japan during later eras as well.

NOTES

1. I wish to thank the members of Harvard's Japan Forum and Columbia's University Seminar in Neo-Confucian Studies for the opportunity to "test" earlier drafts of this chapter before exceptionally distinguished and helpful groups. I also wish to thank the following colleagues for their helpful suggestions: Gordon Berger, Hosea Hirata, John Wills, Jr., Samuel Yamashita, and Eri Yasuhara. As always, however, the remaining culpa are entirely mea.

2. Indian Buddhism is only an apparent exception to this interpretation. China's embrace of Buddhism never translated into a heritage of respect for India as a civilizational source.

3. See Wm. Theodore de Bary, "Some Common Tendencies in Neo-Confucianism," in David S. Nivison and Arthur Wright, eds., *Confucianism in Action*, 25–49 (Stanford: Stanford University Press, 1959).

4. "Indeed, it may be said that during this period, while there were Confucian scholars, there were virtually no Confucianists; that is, persons who adhered to the teachings of Confucius as a distinct creed which set them apart from others" (in Wm. Theodore de Bary, Wing-tsit Chan, and Burton Watson, comps., *Sources of Chinese Tradition* [New York and London: Columbia University Press, 1960], vol. 1, p. 369).

5. Herman Ooms, *Tokugawa Ideology: Early Constructs, 1570–1680* (Princeton: Princeton University Press, 1985).

6. Hori Isao, *Hayashi Razan*, Jinbutsu sōsho no. 118 (Tokyo: Yoshikawa kōbunkan, 1964).

7. Ishida Ichirō, "Zenki bakuhan taisei no ideorogii to Shushigaku no shisō" (Chu Hsi Learning and the Ideology of the Early Tokugawa State), in Ishida Ichirō and Kanaya Osamu, eds., 411–48, *Fujiwara Seika, Hayashi Razan*, Nihon shisō taikei no. 28 (Tokyo: Iwanami shoten, 1975).

8. Wajima Yoshio, *Chūsei no Jugaku* (Confucian Thought in the Medieval Period), Nihon rekishi sōsho no. 11 (Tokyo: Yoshikawa kōbunkan, 1965).

9. As, for example, by Kate Wildman Nakai in "The Naturalization of Confucianism in Tokugawa Japan," *Harvard Journal of Asiatic Studies* (June 1980), 40(1):157–99.

10. See my "Nature, Invention, and National Learning: The *Kokka hachiron* Controversy, 1742–46," *Harvard Journal of Asiatic Studies* (June 1981), 41(1):75–91.

11. Taira Shigemichi, "Kinsei no Shintō shisō" (Shinto Thought in the Modern Period), in Taira Shigemichi and Abe Akio, eds., *Kinsei Shintō ron zenki kokugaku* (Early Modern Shinto and Early Nativism), Nihon shisō taikei no. 39 (Tokyo: Iwanami shoten, 1972), 543.

12. Donald Keene, *World Within Walls* (New York: Holt, Rinehart and Winston, 1976), 310; Toda Mosui, *Nashimoto no sho*, in *Kinsei Shintō ron zenki kokugaku*, 275.

13. *Kinsei Shintō ron zenki kokugaku*, 310.

14. From his *Shinro no tebikigusa* (Grasses Picked along the Divine Path), in ibid., 222.

15. Ryusaku Tsunoda, W. T. de Bary, and Donald Keene, comps., *Sources of Japanese Tradition* (New York: Columbia University Press, 1964), vol. 2, p. 9.

16. Tsunoda, de Bary, and Keene, *Sources of Japanese Tradition*, vol. 1, pp. 360–61.

17. See my translation of Saikaku's *Some Final Words of Advice* (Rutland, Vt., and Tokyo: Charles E. Tuttle, 1980), 132.

18. In *Tenri toshokanzō kinsei bungaku mikanbon sōsho* (Archives in the Modern Literature of the Tenri Library) (Kyoto: Yūtokusha, 1949), 61.

19. *Some Final Words of Advice*, 41.

20. On eighteenth-century nostalgia, see my *Remembering Paradise: Nostalgia and Nativism in Eighteenth-Century Japan* (Cambridge: Council on East Asian Studies, Harvard University, 1990).

21. Quoted in Saigusa Yasutaka, *Kamo no Mabuchi*, Jinbutsu sōsho no. 93 (Tokyo: Yoshikawa kōbunkan, 1962), 288.

22. In Yamamoto Yutaka, comp., *Kōhon Kamo no Mabuchi zenshū: shisō hen* (The Collected Works of Kamo no Mabuchi: Thought) (Tokyo: Kōbundō, 1942), vol. 2, p. 1095.

23. Masao Maruyama, *Studies in the Intellectual History of Tokugawa Japan* (Tokyo: University of Tokyo Press, 1974), 136–37.

24. Saigusa, *Kamo no Mabuchi*, 290–91.

25. From his *Tensetsu benben* (A Rejoinder on Cosmology) (1817), quoted in Donald Keene, *The Japanese Discovery of Europe, 1720–1830*, rev. ed. (Stanford: Stanford University Press, 1969), 159.

26. Muromatsu Iwao et al., comps., *Hirata Atsutane zenshū* (The Collected Works of Hirata Atsutane) (Tokyo: Itchido shoten, 1911–18), vol. 1, ch. 2, p. 3.

27. See Bob Tadashi Wakabayashi, *Anti-Foreignism and Western Learning in Early-*

Modern Japan: The New Theses of 1825 (Cambridge: Council on East Asian Studies, Harvard University, 1986).

28. A formulation first articulated in Mito by Fujita Yūkoku. See J. Victor Koschmann, *The Mito Ideology: Discourse, Reform, and Insurrection in Late Tokugawa Japan, 1790–1864* (Berkeley, Los Angeles, and London: University of California Press, 1987), 4.

GLOSSARY

Abe Akio　阿部秋生

Aizawa Seishisai　會沢正志齊

Amaterasu　天照

Arai Hakuseki　新井白石

bakufu　幕府

Bendō sho　辨道書

Buke jiki　武家事記

bushidō　武士道

Chen-kuan cheng-yao　貞觀政要

Ch'eng-Chu　程朱

Chou　周

Chūsei no Jugaku　中世の儒學

Dai Nihon shi　大日本史

daigaku no kami　大學頭

daimyō　大名

Dazai Shundai　太宰春台

Dōjō　堂上

Fujita Tōko　藤田東湖

Fujita Yūkoku　藤田幽谷

Fujiwara Seika　藤原惺窩

Fushimi　伏見

gakumon　學問

Genroku　元祿

Gion monogatari　祇園物語

Godaigo　後醍醐

Han　漢

Han Yü　韓愈

Hanazono　花園

Hayashi Gahō　林鵞峰

Hayashi Hōkō　林鳳岡

Hayashi Razan　林羅山

Hirata Atsutane　平田篤胤

Honchō jinja kō　本朝神社考

Honchō tsugan　本朝通鑑

Honkyō gaihen　本教外篇

Hori Isao　堀勇雄

Hoshina Masayuki　保科正之

Ihara Saikaku　井原西鶴

Inari　稲荷

Ishida Ichirō　石田一郎

Itō Jinsai　伊藤仁齊

Itō Tōgai　伊藤東涯

Jinnō shōtōki　神皇正統記

Kada no Azumamaro　荷田春満

Kaitokudō　懐德堂

Kakinomoto Hitomaro　柿本人麻呂

Kamo no Mabuchi　賀茂真淵

Kamōsho　呵妄書

Kangaku　漢學

Keichū　契沖

Kimon　崎門

"Kinsei no Shintō shisō"　近世の神道思想

Kinsei Shintō ron zenki kokugaku　近世神道論前期國學

Kitabatake Chikafusa　北畠親房

Kogidō　古義堂

Kojiki　古事記

Kokka hachiron　國歌八論

Kokugaku　國學

Kokugakusha　國學者

Kokui kō　國意考

Kumazawa Banzan　熊沢蕃山

Li Ao　李翶

Li chi　禮記

Man'yōshū　万葉集

Man'yō daishōki　万葉代匠記

Maruyama Masao　丸山真男

Masuho Zankō　増穂残口

matsurigoto　政

Meiji　明治

Mito　水戸

Motoori Norinaga　本居宣長

Muramatsu Iwao　室松岩雄

Muro Kyūsō　室鳩巣

Nakae Tōju　中江藤樹

Nashimoto no sho　梨本の書

Nihon ōdai ichiran　日本王代一覧

Nihon shisō taikei　日本思想大系

Nihon shoki　日本書紀

Ogyū Sorai　荻生徂徠

Ōjin　應神

Ritō shinchi Shintō　理當心地神道

Saigusa Yasutake　三枝康高

Seidan　政談

Shang　商

Shih ching　詩經

Shin kishin ron　新鬼神論

Shingon　真言

Shinro no tebikigusa　神路の手引草

Shu ching　書經

Ssu-ma Kuang　司馬光

Suika Shintō　垂加神道

Taira Shigemichi　平重道

T'ang　唐

Toda Mosui　戸田茂睡

Tokugawa　徳川

Tokugawa Ienobu　徳川家宣

Tokugawa Ietsugu　徳川家繼

Tokugawa Ieyasu　徳川家康

Tokugawa Mitsukuni　徳川光圀

Tokugawa Tsunayoshi　徳川綱吉

Tokugawa Yoshimune　徳川吉宗

Tsurezuregusa　徒然草

Utsunomiya Ton'an　宇都宮遯菴

Wajima Yoshio　和島芳男

waka　和歌

Watarai Nobuyoshi　度會延佳

Yamaga Sokō　山鹿素行

Yamamoto Yutaka　山本饒

Yamato kagami　大和鏡

Yamazaki Ansai　山崎闇齋

Yi T'oegye　李退溪

yonaoshi　世直し

Yoshida Kenkō　吉田兼好

Yoshida Shintō　吉田神道

Yoshikawa Koretaru　吉川惟足

Yushima　湯島

Zen　禪

"Zenki bakuhan taisei no ideorogii to Shushigaku no shisō"　前期幕藩體政
　のイヂオロギーと朱子學の思想

Zoku Shintō taii　俗神道大意

Chapter Ten

MASTERY AND THE MIND

OKADA TAKEHIKO

Translated by Martin Amster

In reading *Chuang Tzu* we at times encounter anecdotes describing the subtle exercise (Ch. *miao-yung*; Jap. *myōyō*) of know-how,[1] the extraordinary mastery (Ch. *shen-chi*; Jap. *shingi*) of everyday skills rooted in practice inherent in the heart/mind (*shin no kufū*), that is, skills embodied in the workings of the mind (Ch. *hsin-shu*; Jap. *shinjutsu*) or in a method of the mind (Ch. *hsin-fa*; Jap. *shinpō*). Examples would be Cook Ting's cutting up the ox,[2] the hunchback catching cicadas, the ferryman poling his boat, Chi Hsing-tzu training his gamecocks, the swimmer at Lü-liang, Woodworker Ch'ing and his bell stands, Artisan Ch'ui's freehand drawing, Lieh Yü-k'ou's archery, and the grand marshal's buckle maker.[3] But these stories do not have as a goal the direct explanation of such skills. Although they rely on allegory to give material shape to the exercise of skill, through them we can see that even by ancient times the fundamental reality of skill was a phenomenon to be sought within the mind.

Since skill is an inherent element of human experience, it is naturally inseparable from the mind and obviously a method of the mind is necessary for the mastery of skill. If we pursue such an empirically logical approach, even if this method of the mind is regarded as a necessity, then mastery is likely to be regarded as something that can be achieved merely through the refinement of skill itself. To put it another way, skill would necessarily be regarded as nothing more than a technique to be applied in the phenomenal world rather than something that goes beyond it. Yet, in later times, particularly in Japan, such a view was clearly held to be erroneous because of renewed inquiry into the fundamental nature of skill: skill was decidedly not limited to technique but ultimately seen as a spiritual phenomenon. Thus, if the refinement of skill was not regarded solely as the exercise of technique, and since it embodied something overwhelmingly spiritual, through that it began to assume the status of an absolute — something clearly regarded as the *raison d'être* for an extraordinary kind of mastery that lay beyond conscious choice. As a result, skill was even thought identical to study (Ch. *hsüeh*; Jap. *gaku*) as something with which to grasp the fundamental principles of life in the world: considered as human activity, skill by itself could realize the mission of learning. In other words, the absolute principles that the learning process sought were embodied in skill, and thus skill was also something that led to a self-awareness penetrating the very core of one's life in the world. Put briefly, in East Asia ideas concerned with study were ideas concerned with experience (*jissen*) — doctrines realized through practice (*jissenteki kufū*). The exercise of skill is one form of practice. Although, considered as experience, some aspects of it differ from study, it ultimately becomes apparent that skill is a form of human activity by virtue of the fact that the mental effort it entails is similar to that involved in the learning process. Such a conception asserts the indivisibility of study and the arts ("arts" means "skill")[4] and is the basic reason that we become aware of the fact that the goal of skill is realization of basic concepts concerning life in the world. Such activities thus made a great imprint on the spiritual history of the East Asian world. Among these, the military arts (*bushidō*) of Japan were the most representative. Although referring to skill in *bushidō* as a "Way" (Ch. *Tao*; Jap. *Dō*) and not as technique (Ch. *shu*; Jap. *jutsu*) is quite recent, if we really examine the reasons for attributing spiritual qualities to skill, we see that the phenomenon of elevating it to a "Way" had already come into existence in early modern times.

The idea of the "Way" is a basic spiritual concept in East Asia. Why does a technique become a Way? Techniques are the processes by which humankind controls nature. The movements of the natural world are a matter of law (Ch. *fa*; Jap. *hō*). The Way is that with which such laws act in accordance, and it is therefore the Way that delimits nature.[5] Originally, the Way could not be possessed merely through knowledge or discursive thought but had to be gained through experience. The Chinese character for "Way" represents the road or path upon which one travels. It is the Way that humanity ought to follow and that ought to be understood through personally traveling it — one must take possession of it through practice. Characterized intellectually, concepts founded on experience ought to be referred to as "rules without rules" (*mukiteiteki kitei*). By extension, that could be termed "nonbeing" (Ch. *wu*; Jap. *mu*), another fundamental idea in East Asian thought. It is basically within such a concept that the phenomenon of skill is to be sought.

Since "nonbeing" is predicated on practice, one can say that it is also an experientially based concept, that is, one not rooted in discursive or rule-based thinking. If this is so, then what kind of phenomenon is this nonbeing? Although by calling it "nonbeing" we make it the opposite of "being" (Ch. *yu*; Jap. *u*), "nonbeing" as discussed here is not its opposite. If it were made opposite to "being," then that would make it something already qualified by "being," so even if we called it "*non*being" it would not be at all different in kind from the "being" we opposed it to — when qualified by something else it is nothing more than a thing that exists in a mutually contradictory relation with that other thing. Therefore "nonbeing" as referred to here must be without qualification and without contradiction — it ought to be "absolute nonbeing" (Ch. *chüeh-tui wu*; Jap. *zettai mu*). Therefore it would be something that straightforwardly and absolutely "exists" (is in a state of being). If it really exists, we cannot then say that what we call "being" is really something "existing" because each of the myriad things of which it consists are always qualified by some other thing, always in contradiction to something else. Therefore one might say that it is precisely "absolute nonbeing" that is genuine being, that is, "absolute being." So that state of nonbeing, which is at first thought of as a negative concept, is in fact a positive one. But that positivity is something wherein the negative — the absence of distinctions, "nonbeing" — is directly positive in character: it is a positivity wherein negative and positive are identical.

If we put that sort of dialectic into play, this "nonbeing" would clearly become something that perhaps really existed. But such a rule-bound method does not at all go beyond the scope of the intellectually based strictures of Western philosophy. These are Western rules and not East Asian ones.

The main current of modern Western philosophy, based on what I call "intellectualism" (*shuchishugi*), has been an attempt to understand basic concepts of human life and the world and to establish a rational view of them. Indeed, in recent times it would seem that the main issues have been how to overcome the opposition between subject and object and the opposition between "being" and "nonbeing." But are the ideas resulting from such speculation absolute ones? If we follow experientially based notions that refute such intellectualism, we become aware that it is erroneous to try to impose experience-based ideas on a framework of logical concepts. Although one can attempt to seek out some ideas based in experience, unless we are able to contemplate experience itself, the resulting concepts (in many instances) will be no more than things rooted in speculative thought. If we think of it as a thing to be observed or gained as an object of knowledge, it is not the result of action; if it is the result of action, it is basically different in terms of its "knowability" even if we contemplate it or think about it.

But since East Asian concepts are wholly grasped through action, they are different from Western ones. Therefore the ways in which Western philosophy is practiced (if looked at from an Asian perspective) do not in the end go beyond the bounds of ratiocination. One might say that they objectify and dichotomize knowledge rather than possess holistic or absolute insight. (If knowledge is the basic purpose of study, then action is its opposite. But in East Asia we regard study as indistinguishable from action—action is even thought of as the basis of study.) Consequently, if we define "nonbeing" in the dialectical way set down above, from the perspective of Eastern peoples it is like capturing a ghost, or "toying with things and losing one's purpose" (Ch. *wan-wu sang-chih*; Jap. *ganbutsu sōshi*).[6]

Of course, I am certain that this way of defining "nonbeing" is, from a Western point of view, childish in the extreme, but, methodologically speaking, it cannot be denied that Western and Eastern thought are fundamentally different no matter how sharp or detailed the analysis.

Nevertheless, what kind of phenomenon is action? It is something consonant with the unconditioned experience embodied in practice (*jissenteki junsui keiken*), which does not rely on abstract thought of the kind we refer to as knowledge or speculation. Effecting such action can be defined as mystical experience because it tries to seek the rational through actual experience without bringing conscious knowledge or speculation into play in a search for rationality. Since "nonbeing" can first be concretely realized only through such experience, one would have to say that it too is a practical concept. Consequently it is not subject to the realm of knowing but, being subject to the realm of awareness (Ch. *chüeh*; Jap. *kaku* [*satori*]), is established on a mystical basis. But even when we speak of it as based in active practice, it is something we can, in general terms, speak of and so one cannot say that knowledge and speculative thought are completely useless. On the whole, however, they are secondary phenomena, no more than conveniences for describing the structure of the world. Since genuine knowledge and insight are to be regarded precisely as being within unconditioned experience embodied in practice, abstract thought alone is something that exists at a remove from that. While we tentatively acknowledge the value of knowledge and speculative thought, they also breach the realm of awareness only when they become truth-bearing and infused with life through the unconditioned experience embodied in practice.[7] But we should recognize that these thought processes do not of themselves possess an absolute character, nor are they capable of attaining a state of heightened acuity; on the contrary, they are pretexts, acting only to quicken the birth of understanding based on unconditioned experience embodied in practice. Even though necessary, they should not be thought of as something enabling us to realize truth (Ch. *chen-li*; Jap. *shinri*) directly. Truth is something that has to be realized to its fullest through the unconditioned experience embodied in practice. Therefore the important thing is how to go about purifying practical experience. As a result of such purification, knowledge and speculative thought are detached from experience, and the great self-delusion they cause us to embrace is firmly rejected. Thus it could be called to "reverse the thought processes [and not let them gallop about in the outer world]."[8] If we broadly explained practice, it would probably include such reversal.

As discussed above, study in East Asian culture begins and ends with all-inclusive practice. Learning that relies on this methodology is not really philosophy but ought to be characterized as pre-philosophical in nature. According to some Japanese scholars who are students of Western thought, philosophy in Socrates and Plato results in knowledge that has to go beyond the purely theoretical: it is wisdom that truly penetrates to the core of life. But the term *philosophie*, or *philosophy*, transplanted unchanged from the various modern European languages could not from the outset fully and clearly express its inherent meaning, and the word *tetsugaku* (Ch. *che-hsüeh*), with which we in Japan translated *philosophy*, was even more ambiguous.[9] Still, Socrates and Plato were men who had a passion for wisdom—they were possessed by the "Greek passion."[10] It became a paradox that the more passionate they were with respect to wisdom based on knowledge and speculation, the more impassioned they became.

From early times East Asians realized that true wisdom existed within such a paradox. Conversely, just after Socrates and Plato in the West, wisdom involved rejection of such passion in an attempt to establish a universe based in wisdom itself. But in Asia (and during any period one cares to mention), that paradox, radiating passionate energy, continued to preserve its truth and, because of the prestige of such concepts, the lives of East Asians were for a long time guided by phenomena that we might refer to as extraphilosophical.

At this juncture, yet another point must be made. In Asia this passion was preserved by practice and was in fact inner-directed and tranquil. When I said that true wisdom lay in paradox, that really goes no further than regarding practice as inner-directed and tranquil. Even if faith and love are elements of practice, they too are inner-directed and tranquil. In Asia, passionate faith and love (as well as wisdom) taken in isolation are generally denigrated for being dependent on man-made opposites. Thus in practice a mystical union with nature is sought by means of inner-directed and tranquil unconditioned experience. Such experience admits of neither human attempts to control nature nor the intent of the human mind to analyze it; rather it is a union with the natural world and a uniquely tranquil passion that attempts a return to nature. Therefore the doctrine of practice in East Asian culture can be characterized as based on naturalism (Ch. *tzu-jan chu-i*; Jap. *shizenshugi*).

I have attempted here a general explanation of the significance and special character of the East Asian notion of practice. Yet with respect to how we speak of the experience-based idea of "nonbeing" possessed through such means, from the point of view of the nature of practice described above, it is something that becomes clear by itself through experience. Whether we rely on dialectic or even utilize the intuition or unconditioned awareness upon which nonbeing is predicated, if in the end — beyond the inescapable fact of its still being objective, contemplative, and direct — it is seen from the point of view of practice, it is not simply a method whereby one gains access to an experiential concept of "nonbeing." Rather, one's subjectivity itself experientially "becomes nonbeing." (Regarding the "sageliness" of the sage [Ch. *sheng-jen*; Jap. *seijin*] and the "Buddhahood" of the Buddha in conceptual terms speaks most clearly to this fact.) The reason why we in East Asia deny the efficacy of mere knowledge and speculative thought also seems to lie in this. Therefore the essential thing is precisely one's possession of this unconditioned experience by means of practice — the conscious knowledge one comes to have of the experiential is secondary and that which one endeavors to explain or construct with such knowledge is flimsy in the extreme.[11]

Practice involves being in a state of awareness that, by its very nature, entails exclusion of discursive thought. As described above, in discursive thought the opposition between "being" and "nonbeing" and between "things" and "ourselves" is inescapable. In East Asia extraordinary effort has been expended on the denial of such oppositions. Many different texts attest to the difficulties involved in that denial; one example is the chapter in *Chuang Tzu* entitled "Ch'i-wu lun" (Discussion on Making All Things Equal).[12]

First, the "Ch'i-wu lun" tentatively defines "absolute nonbeing" according to the dialectic of the opposition between "being" and "nonbeing." Then, in the instant it takes to utter the word *wu* (Jap. *mu*, "nonbeing"), this definition is negated; since "nonbeing" is made into the opposite of something when it is characterized in words, its absolute nature is lost, having collapsed into the realm of opposites. Perhaps it can be expressed without speech, or perhaps it can be expressed by repeatedly replying that one doesn't know — "Discussion on Making All Things Equal" describes the effort that goes into trying to establish concepts through paradox.

In Zen Buddhism the practice of shouting or of disciples being beaten with a stick by their teachers demonstrates the difficulty involved in going beyond concepts and words. In such behavior there is paradox but no logic; it is something that has to be regarded as entirely mystical in nature.

Awareness excludes discursive thought; therefore the self (Ch. *wo*; Jap. *ware*) is excluded because the self is conscious subjectivity (*shiki no shutai*). Awareness is without self; therefore self is forgotten or perhaps a realm where both other things and the self are forgotten (Ch. *wu-wo liang-wang*; Jap. *butsuga ryōbō*) is established. If what is referred to as the "mind" is the establishment of self and the opposition between things and the self, awareness can indeed be called a phenomenon established in the realm of "no-mind" (Ch. *wu-hsin*; Jap. *mushin*). But "no-mind" does not mean the vacuity of the mind but in general means doing away with the opposites inherent in the conscious mind and the effort that brings about its return to an original absolute state. From that perspective one can say that "no-mind" is being in possession of "a mind that is not mind" (*mushin no shin*). This is what is referred to as the "original mind" (Ch. *pen-hsin*; Jap. *honshin*), and this is the absolute mind. Nonbeing is that which is established in the absolute mind. If we go a step further, the absolute mind is nonbeing. To think thus is to probably regard nonbeing as an ideal concept. But, conceptually speaking, what is referred to here as being "idealistic" (Ch. *wei-hsin*; Jap. *yuishin* [literally; "mind only"]) does not have that meaning because it is different in character from what the West calls idealism.

In the main there are three categories involved in seeking out the concept of nonbeing through what has been described above as practice. Divided into categories along with their representative kinds of know-how, they can be shown as follows.

I. In the Mind:
  A. Lao-Chuang Thought and Buddhism (particularly Zen)
  B. Confucianism (particularly Sung-Ming Confucianism)
  These are characterized by learning
II. In Things:
  A. The Tea Ceremony
III. In the Human Body:
  A. Nō Drama
  B. The Martial Arts
  These (II and III) are arts

The goals of practice are realized directly through use in human life and activity once we have grasped the necessary practice-based concepts. These are classified according to use as follows.

I. The Comprehensive — Self-Realization (*gugen*) as the Goal
  A. The World-at-Large — Lao-Chuang Thought
  B. The Religious Realm — Buddhism
  C. The Ethical World — Confucianisn
II. The Specialized
  A. Expression as the Goal — The World of Art
    1. Nō Drama
    2. The Tea Ceremony
  B. Confrontation as the Goal — The World of Conflict
    1. In Groups: Strategy (Ch. *ping-fa*; Jap. *heihō*)
    2. Individually: The Martial Arts (Ch. *wu-tao*; Jap. *budō*)

The classification given above is not a strict one, each category being mutually related to the others — in some instances the first (I) also includes the others. Yet I think it makes clear at a glance what kind of position skill occupies in the spiritual history of East Asia.

If explained broadly as in the first outline, II and III include examples of the arts, Nō and the tea ceremony, while IIIB explains skill in the narrower compass of the martial arts.

The divisions between IIA, IIIA, and IIIB can be understood from the second outline. The tea ceremony, Nō drama, and the martial arts all broadly involve skill, but the first two have artistic expression as their goal while the last concerns the outcome of combat. It is immediately clear that the first two directly express skill as spiritual in intent while the martial arts show it as no more than skill.

The question we should advance at this point is the following: how can skill in the martial arts, thought of as technique, be a spiritual phenomenon? Furthermore, how do we attempt to explain the way in which attainment of the state of "nonbeing" is perfected? Before going into this, I would say that both the art of tea and Nō theater, which have artistic expression as their aim, also embody the experiential concept of nonbeing and that the potential for realizing utmost mastery in these arts lies in restoring that concept in skill.

> In the tea ceremony desolate beauty is auspicious,
> Feigned desolation is odious.[13]
> Genuine refinement is precisely that which is refined in its naturalness.[14]

It is also said: "That the forgotten mind can be squared-up to five or six sides is quite mysterious!"[15]

In addition, such expressions as "tea with neither guest nor host" and "tea ceremony without tea" point to extraordinary mastery as the expression of nonbeing and describe the attainment of "unassertiveness" ("doing nothing contrary to the Way" [Ch. *wu-wei*; Jap. *bui*]), "naturalness" (Ch. *tzu-jan*; Jap. *shizen*), "forgetting the self" (Ch. *wang-wo*; Jap. *bōga*), and "forgetting both things and self." The same can also be said for Nō. Zeami (1363–1443) speaks of the "Nō of no-mind" (*mushin no nō*) by saying, "Particularly within the lonely beauty of Nō-that-is-not-Nō, what stirring of the mind exists?" It was not something that attached the greatest importance to entertainment but was the Nō of great actors who communicated a sense of profundity to their audiences through a theater of "no-mind" and the "absence of surface elegance."

No one can deny that the Way of Tea and Nō are highly valued in the spiritual history of Japan, but we must not forget to recognize the martial arts as well. The martial arts achieve a state of absolute nonbeing through physically oriented practice, but we could say that in later times they were again reduced to skills whose goal was to decide the outcome of combat by complete victory. Thought of in such terms, in their ultimate form the martial arts can probably be called spiritualized skill. The reason they came to be looked on as such in Japan was not due to the necessity of battlefield use, since it was only in the modern period that they came to be used as combat skills, although perhaps in archery that kind of awareness had existed from an early time. Since archery was the resolution of confrontation between a "self" and a target or between a person and a thing—in other words, since it was a quiescent display of know-how—self-realization by means of it was unavoidable, and thus it was easy to explain as the resolution of conflict between "self and self," that is to say, conflict *an sich*.

> By archery in the traditional sense, which he esteems as an art and honors as a national heritage, the Japanese does not understand a sport but, strange as this may sound at first, a religious ritual . . . an ability whose origin is to be sought in spiritual exercises and whose aim consists in hitting a spiritual goal, so that fundamentally the marksman aims at himself and may even succeed in hitting himself. . . .
>
> It must, however, be borne in mind that the peculiar spirit of this art, far from having to be infused back into the use of bow and arrow in recent times, was always essentially bound up with them and has emerged all the more forthrightly and convincingly now that it no longer has to prove itself in bloody contests. It is not true to say that the traditional technique of archery, since it is no longer of importance in fighting, has turned into a pleasant pastime and thereby been rendered innocuous. The "Great Doctrine" of archery tells us something very different. According to it, archery is still a matter of life and death to the extent that it is a contest of the archer with himself; and this kind of contest is not a paltry substitute but the foundation of all contests outwardly directed—for instance with a bodily opponent. In this contest of the archer with himself is revealed the secret essence of this art.[16]

The reason why the martial arts began to occupy an important place in early modern times in terms of spiritual history was that in an era of peace (with Japan unified under Tokugawa rule) leisure time allowing for tranquil introspection into the basic nature of skill now existed, and it thus assumed a markedly spiritual identity. We also cannot discount the tremendous influence of early modern thought with respect to this self-awareness in the martial arts—that being the spirit of *bushidō* combined with Zen Buddhism and the "Learning of the Way" (Sung-Ming Neo-Confucianism [Ch. *Tao-hsüeh*; Jap. *Dōgaku*]). If we compare the spirit of *bushidō* with Zen and Neo-Confucianism, rather than their having a direct influence on skill itself, they were a force endowing the martial arts with self-awareness of the world-historical significance of skill. For example, the master swordsman who served Tokugawa Ieyasu, Yagyū Munenori (1571–1646) said, "Ten thousand may suffer due to the evil of one man, but destroy the evil of one man and you will give life to ten thousand. Truly the sword that kills should be the sword that brings life to people."[17] He also said: "Thinking that the martial arts [*heihō*] are simply a matter of cutting people up is a mistake. One does not cut people up but destroys evil; it is simply destroying the evil of one man and giving life to ten thousand."[18]

In his classic *Gorinsho* ("The Five Wheels"), another master swordsman, Miyamoto Musashi (1584–1645), stated:

Only by diligently pursuing the Way will you be able to strike and conquer with your [sword] arm as well as overcome others in affairs visible to the eye. Furthermore, if by training one gains complete physical freedom, one will vanquish others with one's body—what is more, if one vanquishes others by means of the mind imbued with the Way, how can one be beaten after attaining such a level of skill?[19]

. . . Furthermore, by cultivating the martial arts to the greatest extent, one will succeed in maintaining the allegiance of worthy men, in dealing with subordinates, in the correct way of conducting himself, in governing the nation, in nourishing the people, and in putting into effect the various laws of the realm. No matter what path one finds oneself on, one will know how not to be defeated, how to help oneself and gain honor—this is the way of the martial arts.[20]

Such remarks are for the most part the result of a self-awareness of the significance of the martial arts based in the spirit of *bushidō*. But since martial arts skills were ultimately thought of in terms of a method of the mind, the influence of cultivation of the martial arts spirit on the practicing of skill itself is undeniable.[21] For example, it is said that "*bushidō* discovered dying."[22]

By day and by night, from the morning when he takes up his chopsticks to eat his New Year's breakfast to Old Year's night when he pays his yearly bills, one who is a samurai must before all things keep constantly in mind the fact that he has to die—that is his chief business.[23]

The cultivation of the *bushidō* spirit is a smashing of the bonds of life and death[24] directly connected to the realization and practice of the warrior's skills; that is, it enables one to cultivate a realm of the heart/mind that transcends life and death. In the words of Miyamoto Musashi: "When active or at rest, at all times those who would be warriors never forget the potential for victory and defeat, regarding it as essential by keeping it squarely in mind."[25]

This can be regarded as the dynamic for directly realizing the kind of cultivation characteristic of the martial arts[26] and may even be seen as describing the statement that "*bushidō* is the basis for the study of swordsmanship."[27] When explaining the state of emptiness that was the foundation of his concept of the martial arts, Miyamoto spoke of how the accomplishments of the warrior, or rather the spiritual cultivation of the warrior, were predicated on developing skill to the highest degree.

> In practicing the warrior's way, the things about the way that are not known are not to be regarded as emptiness. . . . The warrior must certainly be knowledgeable in strategy (*heihō*) and be able to exert himself in the other martial skills, not in the least deviating from the conduct of the warrior's way. . . . When not the slightest haze remains and the clouds of confusion dissipate, this ought to be understood as true emptiness.
>
> When you don't know true emptiness, whether in terms of Buddhist Law or the ways of the everyday world, you may well be under the impression that "I'm the only one that's right," but when looked at objectively from the point of view of the direct way (Ch. *chih tao*; Jap. *jikidō*) of the heart/mind, such views are based on the partiality of each individual's mind and the distortions of visual sense-perception. This is something that turns its back on the True Way. Deny that mind and take that which is unconditioned [Ch. *chih*; Jap. *jiki*] as the root and broadly put strategy into practice with the true mind as the Way. To really think clearly about that which is great, one ought to regard emptiness as the Way and the Way as emptiness.[28]

Zen Buddhism and Neo-Confucianism had the greatest influence on the concept of skill in the martial arts and, by extension, on its world-historical awareness. In the words of Yamaoka Tesshū (1836–1888), a swordsman active at the time of the Meiji Restoration (1868):

> My sword-method does not place high value solely on skill. It desires only that the practitioner attempt to realize to the utmost its principles of the mind. In other words, one develops the source of the Way of Heaven to the greatest degree and, at the same time, wishes to discern the method by which it functions. Even more briefly, it is only to see one's nature and realize the Way. Of anything more than that one cannot speak.[29]

Also, Mori Keichin notes that "Although swordsmanship is technique, when one cultivates its essentials one ought to understand the principle which was born before Heaven and Earth and which will not perish with Heaven and Earth."[30]

For Yamaoka the martial arts have a goal similar to that of Zen: "to see one's nature and realize the Way" (Ch. *chien-hsing wu-tao*; Jap. *kenshō godō*). For Mori their goal is similar to the Neo-Confucian one of inquiring into the "spontaneous character of heavenly principle" (*tenri no shizen*). In short, skill in the martial arts is the instantaneous functioning of the spontaneity inherent in the mind's substance (*shintai shizen no myōyō*) and the expression of heavenly principle. The martial arts were regarded as something that investigated these things through the exercise of skill.

The influence of Zen on the martial arts, particularly swordsmanship, was extremely great. The master swordsman Yagyū Munemori, a major figure of the early modern era, cultivated a method of the mind for swordsmanship through Zen. When the Zen priest Takuan gave him a text that explained swordsmanship by means of the Zen method of the mind, it became the impetus for his own method of realization.[31] Consequently, among swordsmen in recent times, there have been many who gave the greatest expression to their ideas on swordsmanship by means of Zen cultivation. Yamaoka Tesshū (mentioned previously) was another such person.

It would not be an exaggeration to say that this kind of influence on the martial arts was decisive. Just as it is said that "the art of tea and Zen have the same flavor," it could be said that swordsmanship and Zen have the same flavor. That being the case, why is the study of Zen a necessity in the martial arts? The *Tengu geijutsuron* (On the Skill of the *Tengu*) has the following to say.

When well-practiced in this art, there is neither doubt nor apprehension; when there are no fears, *ch'i* is in motion, yet one's inner state [Ch. *shen*; Jap. *shin*] is at rest, and changes and transformations take place in response to function, and one is unobstructed and quiescent. Until now, however, the refinement of *ch'i* is by nature a matter of conscious knowledge and thus is something one depends on. It ought, therefore, to be discussed in words. As to its being of no-mind, its being in accord with that-which-is-so-of-itself [Ch. *tzu-jan*; Jap. *shizen*], its going without physical form and its coming without leaving any trace, or its subtle working and unfathomability—such neither reside in the affect and response embodied in the mind's substance [*shintai*] as it thinks nor by what may be known through what one hears. It is only spontaneously possessed by means of what is achieved through self-cultivation.[32]

The text holds that the height of mastery cannot be achieved only by refining the *ch'i* that goes into cultivating a skill: ultimately, mastery is impossible unless one enters a state of mindlessness. Moreover, possession of spontaneous mastery of a state of no-mind is something in which one must, in short, be enlightened to an infinitude of phenomena that go through changes that occur only in the mind. Zen is really the learning of the mind that takes such enlightenment as its main concern. Therefore practitioners of the martial arts may exercise their skills to the utmost, but only after enlightening the mind with Zen meditation will they attain the desired mastery at the highest level.

The Learning of the Way influenced the martial arts along with Zen. The Learning of the Way sought

to develop to the utmost the source of the Way of Heaven within,
and also to discern the ways in which it functions.

There were swordsmen who, in cultivating the Neo-Confucian method of the mind, could attain mastery without relying on Zen. In the process, the martial arts emerged as the servitor of Neo-Confucianism.[33]

Although Neo-Confucianism (along with Zen) is a learning of the mind, Neo-Confucians reviled Zen. According to them, Zen sought "empty principles" (Ch. *k'ung-li*; Jap. *kūri*) without "investigating things and exhausting Principle" (Ch. *ko-wu ch'iung-li*; Jap. *kakubutsu kyūri*); it desired to reach on high without studying that which lay below; by toying with the superficially dazzling, it lacked any practical use. Also, in not relying on the "way open to all" (Ch. *kung-tao*; Jap. *kōdō*), Zen depended on a path of selfish benefit and thought that sought to escape mortality. Thus, it was said that if one was not in accord with heavenly principle wherein "substance and function have a single source and the subtle and the obvious are indivisible,"[34] one merely sought empty substance and cast away real function.

Looking at Neo-Confucian ethics from the swordsmen's point of view, contrary to victory and annihilation of the enemy—that being regarded as improper—it seemed that the ideal was realized by striking and being struck simultaneously.[35] In that case, with respect to the main principles of Neo-Confucianism with which the swordsmen were in sympathy, would there not be instances when substance (Ch. *t'i*; Jap. *tai*) and function (Ch. *yung*; Jap. *yō*) interpenetrated in terms of the Way wherein "substance and function have a single source and the subtle and the obvious are indivisible"? In other words, it was probably because the main thing concerning substance and function considered together was the practice involved in seeking function within substance and apprehending substance in conformity to function. That the martial arts hold "affairs (Ch. *shih*; Jap. *ji*) and principles (Ch. *li*; Jap. *ri*) as indivisible"[36] is because (like Neo-Confucianism) they stress a Way wherein substance and function have a similar source. (Here "affairs" refers to skill and "principles" to the heart/mind. The mind is referred to as principle because within the mind "myriad phenomena become a single principle" [Ch. *wan-fa i-li*; Jap. *banpō ichiri*].)[37] Consequently, the martial arts consider the goals sought by study to be the things sought in the exercise of skill and thus the unity of study and the arts came to be emphasized. Study assists the arts and the arts assist study, and they both attempt to seek mastery rooted in the mind's substance and heavenly principle (Ch. *t'ien-li*; Jap. *tenri*); that is:

> In principle (Ch. *li*; Jap. *ri*) there is neither large nor small. The ultimate standard in skill with the sword is also nothing more than this. Therefore look within yourself when engaged in the tasks whereby you cultivate its techniques. If the workings of the mind (Ch. *hsin-shu*; Jap. *shinjutsu*) are borne out in day-to-day use and in the way you normally conduct yourself, technique will also permeate your inner being and, by their assisting and nourishing each other, the advantages will certainly be great.[38]
>
> The firm (Ch. *kang*; Jap. *gō*) and the yielding (Ch. *jou*; Jap. *jū*) change and transform [into one another], and the person who is at ease responds to their functioning and is unobstructed. This is true not only of swordsmanship but of learning and the arts: if one can cultivate the whys and wherefores of the changes and transformations of *ch'i*, the subtle working (*myōyō*) of the heart/mind becomes apparent. The subtle workings of the heart/ mind's substance are without trace and cannot be spoken of; therefore, if one cultivates swordsmanship through *ch'i*, one will be aware of the place wherein the substance of the heart/mind is revealed.
>
> If learning is cultivated through the heart/mind, one will be aware of the subtle working of *ch'i's* changes and transformations. When one is unable to cultivate one's person and knows things in conscious terms only through reason, it is not the functioning [of the heart/mind and *ch'i* that you are comprehending but only the knowing of] the heart/mind and *ch'i* through gossip or rumour about them.
>
> Although those who practice swordsmanship cultivate their *ch'i*, since

they cultivate only those aspects of it corresponding to its use with respect to sword technique, it is indeed something that penetrates only one facet of the heart/mind's numinous consciousness, not extending to daily usage or to the way one normally conducts himself. The heart/mind and *ch'i* are a single substance. If you can get hold of the vastness of its meaning through your own efforts, even though the accomplishment has not yet matured, it ought to be beneficial in terms of your individual capacity.[39]

These two passages from the *Tengu geijutsuron* can tell us the reasons why the unity of study and the arts was emphasized and at the same time make us aware of the differences between them. This point, I think, also becomes clear by means of the first outline discussed above which equates study (or learning) and the arts: both study and the arts are predicated on experience based solely in the heart/mind. To put it in a different way, both involve purposive action. Particularly with respect to study, Zen completely rejects knowledge in its devotion to action-oriented practice. The martial arts are identical as far as this point is concerned. But in contrast to Zen practice, which lies in the mind, the martial arts are seated in the body. Thus they mutually differ yet have in common their devotion to practice. I think this is the basic reason for the tremendous influence Zen had on the martial arts.

I will attempt now to describe how skill in the martial arts reverts to the mind or, to put it differently, in what sense it can be described as a method of the mind.

In archery it is taught that in shooting at a target, one should not aim at it. If one aims, the target and the self (the archer) become opposites and thus skill cannot become absolute. One must be selfless (Ch. *wu-wo*; Jap. *muga*), because only in a state where "things and self are both forgotten" will mastery emerge. In that instance the realm of genuine selflessness is one where thinking of being in a state of selflessness and even the fact of thinking about being in that state must both be denied. If it is genuine selflessness then target and self are one: I do not hit the target; it is mastery where the target itself hits the target.

A teaching in archery similar to this concerns the movement involved in drawing the bow: one is instructed to draw the bow with the mind without using one's arm. By bringing up this question of "drawing the bow with the mind" and submitting it to scrutiny, we touch on the fundamental relationship between mind and skill. Moreover, by asking how skill became a method of the mind I will try to explain how the concept of nonbeing is attained through it.

How can "drawing the bow with the mind" be taught? In terms of rational judgment and knowledge, when we draw the bow it is fitting to regard it as predicated upon "drawing the bow with one's arm." That is, it is difficult to place "drawing the bow with the mind" in the realm of rational knowledge — it evidently lies opposite the notion of "drawing the bow with one's arm."

Why does such a paradoxical concept become acceptable? It is remarkable that among the really experienced this kind of paradox became acknowledged as an absolute. For them, using the mind to draw the bow embodies something that makes skill all the more genuine and decisive compared to drawing the bow with the arm. If we accept "drawing the bow with the arm," archery would as a result be recognized as little more than skill. On the contrary, if we accept "drawing the bow with the mind," that is skill beyond skill, art without art, something recognized as spiritual mastery. The reason that practiced archers accept the latter premise and reject the former is that drawing the bow with one's arm is only a question of using sight and conscious thought and not one of performance and action. Rejecting the arm and accepting the use of the mind in drawing the bow signifies the rejection of knowing and the acceptance of acting; in other words, this indicates that things grasped through knowing are not genuine while things grasped through action are.

That being the case, why is skill predicated on action referred to as a spiritual phenomenon? It is because such action is predicated upon the rejection of knowing [based on the division between the knowing subject and the known object], while absolutely maintaining its rational nature [as performance]. That is, because the "action that is knowledge" (*chi no ko*) is rational [because based on the division between the knowing subject and the known object], while the "knowledge which is action" (*ko no chi*) is rational [because no division exists between performer and performance], the rationality of the realm of knowledge is denied and only the rationality of the realm of action is acknowledged, due to its absolute nature. Such rationality is founded completely on mystical experience. Moreover, it is only this mystical experience that can apprehend reality — such experience should also be referred to as "unconditioned experience realized in the course of practice" (*jissenteki junsui keiken*).

Why is knowing to be thus rejected? Because the result of such knowing only grasps skill as an object and is unable to apprehend genuine mastery. Such objectified knowledge is abstract, idealized, and partial, and in the final analysis unable to free itself from its own relativity. In such an instance, no matter how one rationally explains the reasons for skill being the thing that it is, clearly it is not a spiritual phenomenon, nor is the mastery thereby gained something based on mystical experience. Even if we make earnest progress in refining such skill, the harsh fact of our defeated efforts is aptly proved by what I have described above.[40]

Skill as a spiritual phenomenon becomes clearer if we analyze it by means of the expression "drawing the bow with the mind." The most significant part is the phrase "with the mind," a refutation of "[drawing the bow] with the arm." In fact, for the archer to concentrate physical effort in his arm is forbidden. Consequently one is always taught to eliminate such effort. But drawing the bow has to be accomplished with physical effort. What is referred to as eliminating physical effort in the arm is not to seek the locus of strength in one's arm. But where should it be sought? If, in considering that, we say "with the mind," then we might be thought to mean that strength resides in "the power of thought." Yet the power of thinking itself is incapable of directly exerting the effort necessary to draw the bow. But if we take "with the power of thought" to mean "[drawing the bow] with the mind" and try to explain rationally the expression "with the mind," we would have to say "singlemindedly concentrating one's strength and drawing the bow with the arm." But that way of putting it ends up affirming the expression "[drawing the bow] with one's arm" and making it identical to "[drawing the bow] with the mind." It goes without saying that this is irrational, so we have to pay attention to the fact that the "mind" referred to in "[drawing the bow] with the mind" is not the kind of mind involved in our general thought processes.

What kind of mind is it? To answer this question, we once again have to scrutinize the reasons for the denial of the notion that one "draws the bow with the arm." If we draw with the arm, the focus of effort is placed in the arm and, in that case, pain accompanies physical exertion. This kind of strength is partial and incomplete, consequently lacking in wholeness. Therefore movement based on it cannot be considered truly decisive. But if one draws the bow by concentrating the whole strength of one's body in the arm, although it is still partial, it is one part consonant with the whole body. By repeating it over and over, the pain of physical exertion and the sense of effort will indeed dissipate by themselves; the strength thus exerted will be genuinely decisive and the motion of drawing the bow will probably be performed in a completely natural manner. From a rational viewpoint, all of this seems appropriate. But if it were appropriate, archery could, as a result, be said to be confined to the realm of skill. But experienced practitioners would deny that. If physical effort is centered in the arm, then of course the arm possesses its strength by virtue of muscular contraction. But to those who practice archery, that kind of strength is curiously nonexistent, yet the drawing of the bow is easily and flawlessly accomplished. This must be completely mystical in nature because those who do it draw the bow with their minds without using the arm. By using the mind, an effortless yet quite all-encompassing physical effort emerges. That is because it is centered in the mind rather than in the arm. This is the reason they deny "drawing the bow with the arm."

"Drawing the bow with the mind" is not a matter of the power of thought but means drawing the bow with the center of effort located in the mind. But obviously the mind that has this physical effort located within it from the outset is not something defined in terms of thought, for if it was, it would remain a matter of "using the arm [to draw the bow]." So what kind of thing is that mind? To know that we have first to understand directly what strength as subjectivity consists of.

When effort is exerted in the course of performing some skill, it becomes that skill. Therefore its subjective aspect is also the same as the subjectivity inherent in the skill being performed. Considered as a holistic phenomenon, what is the subjective nature of physical effort and skill? It is *ch'i* (Jap. *ki*). *Ch'i* is the basis of the life force in human beings and the vital force of the cosmos. All phenomena in the universe consist of changes and transformations in this *ch'i* — it is the living element in the universe that permeates people as well as living and inanimate things. This was something understood early on in the East Asian cultural sphere. In ancient Chinese medicine, for example, the human body is seen as a microcosm because all physical processes are regarded as changes in this *ch'i*.[41]

Ch'i is really the root of East Asian spirituality. The reason why this spirituality can be characterized as experiential is that *ch'i* is really the basis of any attempt to seek out concepts that underlie human life and the cosmos. Moreover, the reason for the tremendous impression the martial arts came to have on the history of East Asian spirituality consists in the fact that the main elements that comprise its skills are made manifest in the workings of *ch'i*. This *ch'i* is really the genuine substance of the universe felt throughout the human body and constitutes the subjective element of strength and mastery in the martial arts. Therefore the martial arts channel the greatest effort into cultivation of *ch'i*, and it would be appropriate to regard it as the reason why the martial arts are in fact the martial arts.[42] Because *"ch'i* carries the mind and moves physical form"[43] we can know that *ch'i* is the seat of the heart/mind and of the energy that constitutes the basis of both physical strength and the know-how with which the human body is endowed.

The emergence of real strength to draw the bow naturally, that is, strength that is not strength (something unaccompanied by pain or a sense of effort) and decisiveness in drawing the bow through the nurturing of this *ch'i* is a genuine truth archers experience with their own bodies. In their own words:

> Press your breath down gently after breathing in, so that the abdominal wall is tightly stretched, and hold it there for a while. Then breath out as slowly and evenly as possible, and, after a short pause, draw a quick breath of air again — out and in continually, in a rhythm that will gradually settle itself. If it is done properly, you will feel the shooting becoming easier each day.[44]

Thus we can all the more clearly comprehend the reasons why they deny "drawing with the arm"; when they say "drawing with the mind" they really mean "drawing the bow by means of *ch'i*." But the breathing referred to here is called "breathing from the 'cinnabar field'" (Ch. *tan-t'ien*; Jap. *tanden*) [lower abdomen] and was a purposeful method of breathing, something already utilized by Taoists, Buddhists, and Confucians. Perhaps this too can be regarded as a type of skill. However, one has to emphasize that it is not merely something that seeks to modulate breathing but is also an inner-directed and tranquil kind of practice. (Such breathing is esteemed not only in archery but also in swordsmanship.)

If the *ch'i* is nourished in this manner then one's strength is total rather than partial. As *ch'i* becomes more and more refined, it becomes increasingly harmonious and completely fills the body. As a result, strength expands from being partial to total and, in response, strenuous effort gradually diminishes as mastery becomes decisive. Conversely, the more skill advances, the more the refinement of one's *ch'i* increases. That is because *ch'i* and skill are insepara-ble: if *ch'i* is substance (Ch. *t'i*; Jap. *tai*), then skill is function (Ch. *yung*; Jap. *yō*). Substance does not exist apart from function, and function does not exist apart from substance — they are not two different things. Therefore, although cultivating *ch'i* is to be regarded as the most important practice in the martial arts, obviously it is something that should basically be exercised in terms of skill. Thus, if we only refine our *ch'i*, it does not directly determine skill. (This is the same with respect to the practice of mind cultivation that I discuss below.) Therefore, among practitioners of the martial arts some held that *ch'i* and the mind in the martial arts differed from the Sung Neo-Confucian "method of the mind" and the Buddhist "path of enlightenment" and warned against getting aimlessly caught up in Confucian or Buddhist doctrine when cultivating them.[45]

As stated above, the notion of "drawing the bow with the mind" is directly interchangeable with "drawing the bow by means of *ch'i*." But is the concept of "drawing the bow with the mind" something really explained by this? Although the fact of *ch'i* being contained within the mind of "drawing the bow with the mind" is certainly clarified by the above explanation, when we venture to say "with the mind" without saying "with one's *ch'i*," elements of considerable significance are still left lying dormant. So, at the same time we look at the subjective nature of strength, we still have to scrutinize the subjective character of *ch'i*. Thus it is necessary for us to consider again the idea that "*ch'i* carries the mind and moves physical form."

According to this, *ch'i* is the agent that sets the body (skill) in motion. At the same time it serves as "carrier" of the mind, that is, the "seat" (*za*) of the mind. Furthermore, "The body moves by means of *ch'i* and *ch'i* goes where the mind goes. Therefore when the mind changes, *ch'i* changes. And when *ch'i* changes, the body changes."[46]

Therefore, since mind is the ruler of *ch'i*, we can then understand that skill is subjectively constituted. Thus when we refer to "the drawing of the bow with the mind," we mean performing the motion of drawing the bow through the mind's intuitive mastery of that movement brought to its highest pitch. Needless to say, as described previously, that mind is in fact not mind. If that is so, then in what sense is it to be considered as mind?

First of all, to consider the mind that we generally take to be the mind (the mind that performs the function of thought) in relation to the power necessary to draw the bow is not to explain "the drawing of the bow with the mind" as meaning that the bow is drawn by the power of thought. Is it not, rather, more suitable to attempt to consider "drawing the bow with the mind" in terms of what we now discern as that mind's relation to *ch'i*, the subjective manifestation of physical effort and skill?

If the mind is the master of *ch'i*, then, when the mind changes, *ch'i* also changes. If, from the very beginning, the mind and *ch'i* are a single entity, then it goes without saying that if *ch'i* changes, then the mind also will change. Therefore, in learning, the practice of settling the mind through quiet-sitting (Ch. *ching-tso*; Jap. *seiza*) is utilized since if one's *ch'i* is at rest, one's inner state (Ch. *shen*; Jap. *shin*) will also be at ease. Thus when *ch'i* is at rest, the mind must also be at rest because mind and *ch'i* are one: when the mind is settled, *ch'i* is also settled.

Therefore, if in this instance we attach importance to mind practice, then practice with respect to the cultivation of *ch'i* unavoidably emerges. The distinction between the two comes about through the polarities inherent in a world in which we revert to thinking of things in terms of ideas and concepts. If we go by what practitioners of the martial arts maintain, the martial arts place emphasis on practice relating to *ch'i*, whereas learning emphasizes practice with respect to the heart/mind. (But obviously the cultivation of *ch'i* in the martial arts, as stated before, has to involve skill being exercised.) In any event, the things achieved through this are the same: the embodiment within oneself of both the substance of the heart/mind's subtle functioning and the heavenly principle inherent in the natural world.

In addition to the martial arts regarding refined *ch'i* as central and the mind's being taken as the ruler of *ch'i*, mind practice itself cannot be disregarded. That is, over and above its place as the subjective constituent of *ch'i* and skill, unless the mind becomes something absolute, *ch'i* and skill cannot also reach an absolute state.

Just as in study, the achievement of absolute mind is sought by mind practice in the martial arts as well. Moreover, in this absolute mind absolute nonbeing is realized. As described above, the absolute mind is mind-without-mind — a mind that has done away with discursive thought. The discursive mind is a mind of opposites — in it "things" and "self" as well as "being" and "nonbeing" are opposed to one another. For example, if one thinks while drawing the bow, the bow and the "I" drawing it are opposed. The mind that exists in such a state of opposition with respect to something else cannot avoid being relative in nature. If the mind becomes relative then the circulation of *ch'i* will of itself be obstructed and, doubtless, the strength and skill issuing from such obstructed *ch'i* cannot be absolute. Therefore, in order for strength and skill and the harmonious circulation of *ch'i* to become absolute, the relative mind must become the absolute mind. In terms of drawing the bow, since the subject's mind-in-thought-trying-to-draw-the-bow is the "self," by its thoughts becoming absolute the self is discarded and must become "without-self." If without-self, the dichotomy between self and other vanishes — self and other become one. In that instance desiring to become selfless as described above is unacceptable because to think of oneself as becoming selfless or to be able to consider being selfless is already using thought in a relative way. From that we can see that the absolute mind is mind-without-mind. In this mind-without-mind bow and self are one: I do not draw the bow but an intuitive and imperceptible mastery (Ch. *shen-chi*; Jap. *shingi*) is let loose whereby the bow itself draws the bow.

"Intuitive and imperceptible" means the functioning of absolute *ch'i* in the mind-without-mind. The mind-without-mind where self and other are one is also the unattached mind. If the mind is unattached, then the entire body becomes the mind — the mind is not stopped up in a single place within the body. Thus *ch'i* also expands throughout the body and its harmonious state becomes complete. In other words, it becomes absolute. Thus when, spiritlike, it lets loose, both physical effort and skill become truly decisive in nature. They are boldly borne by the spontaneous life-force developing within, without recourse to discursive thought—that is, intuitive and imperceptible mastery. Obviously it is absolute nonbeing revealed in its totality.

The mind that is part of the concept of "the bow drawn with the mind" is really mind-without-mind, that is, it signifies absolute mind. Thus this seemingly paradoxical concept—"drawing the bow with the mind"—is predicated on something genuine. Through this, skill is properly returned to the mind; that is, in the end it becomes evident that skill is a method of the mind.

Above I have mainly explained the fact that skill in archery is a method of the mind and its highest state of development is "mind-without-mind." This is also the same with respect to swordsmanship.

The method of the mind in swordsmanship is not, as in archery, a simple matter. (By "simple" I do not mean lacking in profundity—both archery and swordsmanship are equally profound.) Archery is a skill where an arrow hits a target—a skill that entails confrontation between a person and a thing. Since swordsmanship is a skill where one kills another person with the blade, its skill is not, as in archery, static, but multifaceted in its changeability. Consequently, its attendant elements are complex and variegated. Put briefly, archery is a skill characterized by quiescence (*jōteki*) and swordsmanship is a skill characterized by movement (*dōteki*). The former is simple while the latter is richly complex and changeable. Thus, although both seek to develop the Way to its utmost through attainment of absolute nonbeing, in archery it is nonbeing where "being is nonbeing" (Ch. *yu chi wu*; Jap. *yū soku mu*) and in swordsmanship it is nonbeing where "nonbeing is being" (Ch. *wu chi yu*; Jap. *mu soku yū*). In other words, the former is quiescent nonbeing while the latter is dynamic nonbeing. The concept of absolute nonbeing that was sought—for swordsmen, the result of great effort whereby they gained extraordinary mastery which remained unobstucted and free on the field of conflict—served to strengthen a self-awareness that was a basic principle of the world and of human life. That way is a Way one cultivates by oneself and, at the same time, one that strengthens the consciousness one has of a way by which to order the world.

Swordsmanship (*kendō*) as a dynamic skill that sought face-to-face confrontation naturally has elements similar to strategy (Ch. *ping-fa*; Jap. *heihō*). Therefore in early modern times swordsmanship was called *heihō*[47]—what was referred to as "strategy" was warfare practiced on a large scale, and what was called "swordsmanship" was warfare practiced on a small scale. (Accord-

ing to the *Gorinsho*, swordsmanship utilized out in the world is also referred
to as warfare on a large scale.)[48]

Strategy is a Way by which conflict between opposed groups — "them" and
"us," "enemy" and "ally" — returns to a unitary state through combat. As seen
in thinkers of the Warring States (403–221 B.C.) period such as Sun-tzu, from
early on strategy was something where the opposition between "being" and
"being" was sublated into the opposition between "nonbeing" and "being."
The apotheosis of that Way was sought in controlling the inevitability of
victory. For example, in discussing the disposition of troops, Sun-tzu says:

> The ultimate skill in taking up a strategic position [Ch. *hsing*; Jap. *gyō*] is to
> have no form [Ch. *hsing*; Jap. *kei*]. If your position is formless [Ch. *wu-hsing*;
> Jap. *mukei*], the most carefully concealed spies will not be able to get a look
> at it, and the wisest counsellors will not be able to lay plans against it.[49]

Also, with respect to strategic advantage:

> For gaining strategic advantage [Ch. *shih*; Jap. *sei*] in battle, there are no
> more than "surprise" and "straightforward" operations, yet in combination,
> they produce inexhaustible possibilities. "Surprise" and "straightforward"
> operations give rise to each other endlessly just as a ring is without a
> beginning or an end. And who can exhaust their possibilities?[50]

Or about attack and defense:

> . . . the expert on the attack strikes from out of the highest reaches of the
> heavens.[51] . . . The expert at defense conceals himself in the deepest
> recesses of the earth.[52]

In other parts of the text, similar examples, such as the way to use spies, are
also described.

The dichotomy between "being" and "nonbeing" is actually one between
"weak points" (Ch. *hsü*; Jap. *kyo*) and "strong points" (Ch. *shih*; Jap. *jitsu*).[53] In
strategy it is regarded as the way "we," by means of strength, attack "them" in
their weakness. When I attack "them" by relying on their weak points, it is an
attempt to succeed at the "law of weakness and strength" whereby the enemy
is guided by weakness and I am guided by strength. Leading the enemy on by
means of weakness is the method of deception about which *Sun Tzu* says: "in
warfare rely on deceptive maneuvers to establish your ground."[54] The method

of being guided by strength is a miraculous one that contrives victory when one is on "terrain with no way out" (Ch. *ssu-ti*; Jap. *shichi*),[55] that is, a way that seeks life in the face of death.[56]

When developed to the utmost, all the above involve phenomena where "Everyone knows the position (Ch. *hsing*; Jap. *kei*) that has won me victory, yet none fathom how I came to settle on this winning position,"[57] as well as something wherein "I present the rank and file with victories gained through (Ch. *yin*; Jap. *in*) strategic positioning (Ch. *hsing*; Jap. *gyō*), yet they are not able to understand them,"[58] certainly that which ought to be called "strategy based in nonbeing." The workings of that state of nonbeing are called "*shen*" ([Jap. *shin*] "the imperceptible").[59]

Such principles of warfare also permeate swordsmanship because both seek means to resolve person-to-person confrontation. However, the difference lies in the fact that conflict in one is between individuals and in the other between groups of people. Furthermore, in contrast to warfare, which is to be pondered by the talented strategist/general; swordsmanship seeks to endow conflict with ultimate form by the refinement of an individual's mind and *ch'i* through individual mastery. One could say that swordsmanship embodies the principles of warfare within the body and mind of the individual.

Mind, *ch'i*, and the mastery of swordsmanship, seeking resolution of person-to-person confrontation, as stated before, differ in their multifaceted character from archery, which involves people and things. Moreover, since swordsmanship undertakes to resolve confrontation between mind and mind, between *ch'i* and *ch'i*—not limiting itself merely to a contest between the skills of the combatants—its method of the mind is something mysterious and marvelous. But in the end, this kind of confrontation does not differ from archery in that its absolute principle is sought in the mind-without-mind. It is not possible here to explain each of the reasons why swordsmanship places its absolute principles in a method of the mind but I will attempt to explain this by citing two or three examples divided according to physical form (*hsing*; *gyō*), *ch'i*, and the mind.

With respect to physical form in swordsmanship, there is the matter of position or posture (*kamae*). The swordsman regards posture at its ultimate point of development as being without form. This results in the advocacy of "having-a-posture-in-no-posture." Why must "having-a-posture" involve "having-no-posture"? Musashi says the following.

Both the long sword and one's body are things that position themselves in space dependent on the existence of a mind-that-determines-posture. When they follow the thing on which they rely, it is not a mind that thinks "there is the long sword" or "there is a posture being taken."

When the long sword responds to the enemy, within the posture where it is held above one's head (*jōdan*) there are three aspects; also, within the posture where it is at the ready (*chūdan*), and where it is held below the waist with point toward the floor (*gedan*) there are also three minds. Even in the posture where it is held horizontally at the right side with the point facing back (*wakigama*) there are, of necessity, multiple elements. Looked at from this point of view, it is a mind of no-posture (*kamae naki kokoro*).[60]

True posture must be one where every posture has to include each of the other two. If that does not happen then it is fixed and becomes useless. When it does happen, it is because the mind is placed within the posture and thus the mind becomes *not* placed in the posture; that is, posture becomes a phenomenon of "no-mind." But referring to it in that way does not mean that we have done away with it; it means that we take a particular position but it is not attached to the mind. Since when we do that the posture is not fixed, it can change in response to the moment in time, to particular events, and to one's position in space. Therefore "having-no-posture" is something that issues forth from the absolute no-mind by means of the position one assumes. Since it is always in a state of flux, other postures are contained within the one, and the harmonious identity of being and nonbeing is maintained. Therefore that posture naturally comes to possess the force of life itself. If posture is regarded as function, the absolute nonmind is substance. Within substance there is function and within function there is substance: therefore the swordsman's posture exists but is in a state of nonbeing, and the mind is nonexistent but is in a state of being. This, in other words, is the idea of "having-a-posture-in-no-posture." This may be regarded as similar to the beat marking rhythm in music, which, as it were, "fills in an empty space" in alternation with the music itself, which is "without" the beat that marks time.[61] Perhaps if being and nonbeing are spoken of in terms of the sword, they can be called "without the blade."[62] This is nothing more than referring to the being and nonbeing of the swordsman's posture from the perspective of the opposition between "him" (the opponent) and "me." In short, it all comes back to the absolute nonmind.

The method whereby the long sword and the body are suspended (*kentai*) is where we can most easily apprehend how the absolute nonmind is a necessity in the mastery of swordsmanship. In principle it involves awaiting the thrust of the long sword by holding the body in abeyance. But trying to adhere to this method is impossible unless we spontaneously overcome thoughts of living and dying. This transcendence of life and death is one of the important aspects of the method of the mind in both Confucianism and Buddhism. Particularly in Buddhism, breaking the hold of life and death can be seen as the highest truth—"seeing one's nature and realizing the Way." One has to say that this is also the essential method of the mind in the martial arts where the "mind-without-mind" is fundamental. Such expressions as "when skin gets cut, flesh is cut" or "when flesh gets cut, bone is cut" are in general to be thought of as common explanations of that method of the mind in the martial arts. Also, as some verses that come down to us as the highest expression of the martial arts say:

> In mountain streams there are fish-traps fashioned by the wind,
> Discarding the body is how one floats free.
> Under the clash of swords delusion does not exist,
> In discarding the body lies the way to conduct one's life.[63]

If when facing the enemy one has truly transcended thoughts of living or dying, then body, long sword, and mind are all in a state of emptiness. If that is the case, then mind and *ch'i* are unimpeded and one's mastery becomes free and without obstacle. Through this we understand that the fundamental substance (Ch. *pen-t'i*; Jap. *hontai*) of skill lies in the mind and that skill and the mind are indivisible. Therefore cultivation of the mind influences skill and the refinement of skill also influences the progress of mind cultivation. Then, when cultivation of the mind deepens, not only does a particular skill become more subtle but a subtlety of skill responsive to that mind also comes into being. Such skill is the secret within the secret—needless to say it is hard to comprehend unless to a large extent one attains mastery of the mind, *ch'i*, and skill all together. That which brought into being such a concept of skill and made a great contribution to the Way of the Sword was the method of the Yagyū school founded by Yagyū Munenori's father, Muneyoshi (1527–1606).

In the Yagyū school, for example, there is the [secretly transmitted method called] *Shuji shuri ken* [which, since it cannot itself be written down, is written using different *kanji* having the same sound], the "Miraculous Sword" (*Shinmyō ken*), the "Heart/Mind That Counters Blows" (*Geibō shin*), and the "Waters of the River to the West (*Seikō sui*).[64] These were names for types of skill corresponding to the level attained by the practitioner's mind and were characterized as mind-skills (*kokoro no waza*) in accordance with their names. Moreover, the "Waters of the River to the West" was the highest in status and a multitude of sword techniques culminated in it. From *Shuji shuri ken* to the "Heart/Mind That Counters Blows" we are still concerned with a skill that has not transcended the realm of having-a-mind. But "Waters of the River to the West" is mastery that comes forth completely from mindlessness. In the *Unjūryū kenjutsu yōryō*[65] it is explained as follows.

> These are all modes of cultivating skill characterized by "discarding" (*suteru*). Although we speak of "discarding," it is not a question of reverting to emptiness (Ch. *wu*; Jap. *mu*). The *Shuji shuri ken*, the "Miraculous Sword," and the "Heart/Mind That Counters Blows" are all results of a heart/mind that is responsible for their inception at every level. There are also aspects of them characterized by artifice (Ch. *wei*; Jap. *gi*). But when we come to the "Waters of the River to the West," there is no heart/mind responsible for its inception or to present a sticking-point (*jiso*) that ensnares it. . . . It [is skill] spontaneously responding to each and every thing from a center devoid of even a single thing.[66]

Furthermore, in the same text it also states,

> If I am empty, so too is the enemy. When I abide in emptiness, the ills pertaining to feelings of joy and anger, sorrow and happiness, do not exist. How much more is this so in swordsmanship when, unless in the presence of an enemy, one is also unobstructed and at ease. "Waters of the River to the West" is a name for something as broad and boundless as the sea to the west. By comparing it to crossing to the farthest reach of the heavenly canopy, one can see the limitlessness of emptiness — this is called "Waters of the River to the West."[67]

In addition to skill's being the expression of the dynamics of *ch'i*, one might say that confrontation in which it is involved is also confrontation between the *ch'i* of the two combatants and, as such, is both subtle and mysterious in nature. Within that, for example, there can exist a state of "union between the two *ch'i*" (*ch'i-ho*; *kiai*). This is skill whereby, in a single swordstroke, the weak and strong points of both parties are governed by *ch'i*. Complete victory in that confrontation must from the outset rely on the absolute nature of *ch'i*'s imperceptible functioning. Through that, the subtle workings of the combatants' each and every weak and strong point become manifest and one of them is guided to an advantageous position by a single stroke of the blade. This is completely impossible unless that state lies within the mind-without-mind with its intuited subtlety of affect and response, that is, within the absolute mind.[68] If the mind is absolute then *ch'i* becomes absolute and displays the instantaneity (Ch. *miao-yung*; Jap. *myōyō*) of ten thousand hands. Such absolute *ch'i* is called the "The Great Inward Spring of Movement" (Ch. *ta-chi*; Jap. *daiki*).[69] When activated, the ten thousand hands are called "The Great Functioning" (Ch. *ta-yung*; Jap. *daiyō*). The reason why *ch'i* is also called a "Spring of Movement" (Ch. *chi*; Jap. *ki*) is because it is the direct source of skill. In nurturing it various methods such as "inhaling and exhaling from the lower abdomen," "repeated breaths," and "regulated breathing" are used. But in swordsmanship, which is based on the mastery of movement, it is in particular regarded as something that fills the watchful mind (*yudan naki kokoro*). Therefore, Yagyū Munenori said, "'Spring of Movement' means that within [Ch. *nei*; Jap. *nai*] one is neglectful of nothing and reflects on each and every thing."[70]

Obviously mastery resulting from the "union of the two *ch'i*" is also possessed through such a watchful mind. Nevertheless, while one's mind is still in a state of confusion, this "Inward Spring of Movement" cannot also be regarded as "The Great Inward Spring of Movement" because it cannot avoid being blocked up. When such *ch'i* becomes ripened, the blockage will naturally dissipate and "The Great Functioning" will freely emerge. This is "The Great Inward Spring of Movement" and "The Great Functioning" of which Munenori says the following.

> That *ch'i* which is the product of intense thinking is congealed, and, in turn, being tangled up in the Inward Spring of Movement, is unfree. It is because the Inward Spring of Movement has not yet matured. When that task is achieved and it matures, it suffuses the entire body and works freely. This is called "The Great Functioning."[71]

It thus becomes clear through this that "The Great Inward Spring of Movement" also comes into one's possession from the "mind-without-mind" and within that the "union of the two *ch'i*" also becomes effective and attains formal beauty in its display of the subtle workings of affect and expression (*kannō no myōyō*). This mechanism, with respect to its being put into play in combat, must from the outset also be nourished by the events of everyday life through the watchful mind. This is referred to as "making the device visible." The importance of this is made clear in Munenori's *Heihō kadensho*.

This "Inward Spring of Movement" can also be called "unaroused [Ch. *wei-fa*; Jap. *mihatsu*] skill." When a move is made in swordsmanship, presumably striking at an opponent in response to a skill that is "already aroused" (Ch. *i-fa*; Jap. *ihatsu*), a blow is also given in response to "unaroused skill." This must be done freely. Consequently, when Munemori discusses being and nonbeing with respect to the sword, being strikes in response to being and nonbeing strikes in response to nonbeing.[72]

This kind of "unaroused" and "aroused" skill, that is, striking one's opponent in response to skill's "nonbeing" or "being," is impossible unless one is a great swordsman whose cultivation of mind and *ch'i* is mature. Obviously the free and unobstructed display of skill in response to being or nonbeing is a matter of mind-without-mind. Thus the unleashing of skill when unaroused is called the "unaroused strike" or, also, "unleashing emptiness." It is a precious skill, to be regarded as "nonpurposive warfare" [literally; "warfare before the Inward Spring of Movement"]. In addition, skill issuing from "The Great Inward Spring of Movement" is free and unobstructed in its changes and transformations, its instantaneous character not allowing a hair's breadth of hesitation. That is also most highly esteemed, being called the "Spring of Movement that Sparks Like a Struck Flint" (*Sekka no ki*).

As stated above, the mind is the thing that directs *ch'i*. Therefore, refining the *ch'i* that cultivates skill is obviously at the same time a process that must cultivate the mind. Moreover, since swordsmanship involves skill that seeks resolution of person-to-person conflict, it is natural that the mind-practice that conforms to that is wide-ranging. I cannot clarify each and every element of the mind-practice discussed here, but shall attempt, using one or two examples, to explain how it is both a subtle and complex phenomenon.

The most important element of the mind-method in swordsmanship is the notion of "staying the mind" (Ch. *tsan-hsin*; Jap. *zanshin*). The opposite of that is "letting the mind loose" (Ch. *fang-hsin*; Jap. *hōshin*). Musashi explains them as follows.

> The staying mind and the mind let loose are dependent on events and time. When I take up the long sword, the volitional mind (*i no kokoro*) is always something let loose and the ideative mind (*shin no kokoro*) something stayed. Yet when I strike an adversary, the ideative mind is let loose and the volitional mind stayed—it is the manifestation of the character of staying the mind and letting the mind loose.[73]

Accordingly, "staying the mind" and "letting the mind loose" are practices related to substance and function in the mind. Although the two are identical with respect to the mutual indivisibility of substance and function, they are diametrically opposed as far as the positions they take with respect to subjectivity and the world outside. Substance is the mind of ideation [= "the stayed mind"] and function is the mind of volition [= "the mind let loose"].

What are ideation and volition? Musashi, for instance, says to "Polish the two minds of ideation (*shin* [*no kokoro*]) and volition (*i* [*no kokoro*]). Sharpen the two eyes of passive (Ch. *kuan*; Jap. *kan*) and purposive [Ch. *chien*; Jap. *ken*] sight."[74] Although explaining "the volitional mind" and "the eye of purposive sight" is easy, explaining "ideation" and "passive sight" is difficult. I think they probably mean the kind of ideation that remains unattached to intentionality when thinking and the kind of eye that remains unattached to the involuntary (in)flow of sense data when seeing. If that is the case, then practice involving "staying the mind" and "letting the mind loose" is to be examined in terms of what kind of subtleties they manifest with respect to mind-method.

These practices succeed in harmonizing substance and function, subjectivity and the external world, and yin and yang with the human mind. Obviously this kind of harmony must also not be neglected in the relationship between *ch'i* and skill or among the mind, *ch'i*, and skill. It is precisely by possession of this harmony that skill can realize its inner vitality — if not, it decays into lifeless method.

Since the method-of-the-mind in swordsmanship is so diverse, explaining it involves a considerable degree of detail, and, as a result, a detailed explanation of the mind-without-mind would also have to be added. First, it would be advantageous to say that being in a true state of mindlessness must do away with the dichotomies occasioned by discursive thought; on the other hand, if the mind is *not* in a state of vacuity and we refer to it as something returning to what it was originally, what might this mean? If we consider the very earliest step in the practice of attaining mindlessness, it is the process of concentrating the mind. That is the same as the practice the Sung Neo-Confucians called seriousness (Ch. *ching*; Jap. *kei*)[75] that "abides in the One without deviation."[76] (What Mencius calls "seeking the lost mind" [Ch. *ch'iu fang-hsin*; Jap. *kyū hōshin*][77] can also be seen as corresponding to this.) Takuan Sōhō explained seriousness in swordsmanship as follows:

Concentrate the mind in one place and it will not scatter elsewhere. In exercising any skill, grasp it single-mindedly, not letting your concentration stray. Seriousness refers to the fact that afterward, although one has drawn his sword and cut, the mind does not go off in the direction toward which one has cut.[78]

According to him, the mind using discursive thought is the "mind-in-the-state-of-being-mind" (*yūshin no shin*). In other words, it is mind that "gives rise to thinking divided between a point of concentration exerted [outward] in a single direction and a mental event existing [within]."[79]

If the mind remains fixed on a single place, it gives rise to attachment. If there are attachments in the mind, skill becomes immobile. Therefore he warns against it:

> When mind is applied to the exercise of a skill, the hands do not as a result move. When, in doing something, the mind becomes active, it becomes fixed on the thing being done. If there is no point to be fixed upon [in the thing being done], the mind does not become active. When active, it becomes fixed at the place where it became active.
>
> When the mind is not active, the hands do not as a result move. When the hands move, the mind fixes on them. Those who, when mind is active, are without a point to fix on in the course of doing something are called "Masters of the Various Paths" (*Shodō no meijin*).[80]

The mind attached to things arises from this "fixed mind." Such a mind is fettered by life and death. He explains that even in seeing spring flowers or autumn leaves, while a mind that sees the flowers and leaves emerges, it is vital that within it there is a mind that does not persist.[81] Thus he speaks of the mind of swordsmanship through Zen phrases such as "giving birth to a mind that in response [to things] fixes on nothing" or "before and after — all causal connections joining one thought to another are sundered" or "the unabiding mind." (Such explanations of the method of the mind in swordsmanship based in Zen can be seen in great detail in the text Zen master Takuan presented to Yagyū Munemori, the *Fudōchishinmyōroku* [Mysteries of the Unmoved *Prajñā*]). The "fixed mind" is probably what the Sung Neo-Confucians called the "mind that gallops abroad" (Ch. *wai-ch'ih hsin*; Jap. *gaijishin*). "Galloping abroad" is an illness of the mind, and, obviously, seriousness (Ch. *ching*; Jap. *kei*) that "emphasizes oneness without deviation" is a practice that aims to rid one of that. Nevertheless, the mind that tries to do away with this sickness still cannot escape attachments, so Yagyū describes the "emptiness of the mind" by speaking of the "initial level" and the "later level" of illness.[82] He thus considers the practice of seriousness as still functioning on the initial level of the mind. One will be unable to attain emptiness of the mind unless one advances beyond seriousness; thus one must not stop at seriousness. Zen master Takuan also makes the following remarks to Munemori.

In Buddhist law the word *seriousness* does not occupy the most exalted place. It is similar to practices performed to grasp hold of the mind and not disorder it. If such training accumulates over months and years, no matter in what direction the mind is pressed or propelled, it remains free. . . . I think that in being restrained in its going off to other places, the mind characterized by the word *seriousness*, when it does move, is in disorder and ultimately to be placed on the level of a mind that is restrained and not unwatchful. This is an instance of the mind temporarily not being scattered. If it remains like this, it means that the mind becomes unfree. . . . In your tactical method . . . one completely forgets one's adversary and strikes, cuts people but does not lodge one's mind in people. Understand that people are empty and I am empty also, that both the hand that strikes and the long sword that strikes are also both empty.[83]

At the very end he says that "there is no fixing of the mind in emptiness." This, in other words, is mind as described by Zen Master Wu-hsüeh tsu-yüan (Mugaku Sogen),[84] mind that within "shadow cast by lightning stroke cuts down the spring breeze." All is emptiness within:

There is no mind in the long sword that strikes; there is no "I" in my body and no mind in the "I" being cut. The other person struck is also empty and "I" who strike am empty. There is no person in the other person who strikes. There is no long sword in the long sword that strikes and there is also no "I" in the "I" that strikes.[85]

This, in other words, is the "mind-without-mind." That is the mind that does away with the attached mind trying to achieve no-mind, mind where everything is assumed in terms of being. Munenori refers to it as the "original mind" (Ch. *pen-hsin*; Jap. *honshin*) and warns that the original mind should not be mistaken for the "false mind" (Ch. *wang-hsin*; Jap. *mōjin*). He cites a poem that speaks of the false mind and the original mind:

The very mind itself is the mind that casts the mind into confusion,
The mind in the mind is the mind not allowed.[86]

From the outset, the mind-without-mind as described above is embodied by the concept of nonbeing. Moreover, when that state becomes the source of skill, it inevitably results in mastery. What we ought to emphasize is that just as set forth in the doctrine of the unity of things and principles or the unity of heart/mind, *ch'i*, and physical form, the obvious fact with respect to the heart/mind is that anywhere skill is cultivated success is something only attained through the cultivation of mind and *ch'i*. Therefore Munenori says that

> When one has done all the types of routines and accumulated repeated experience in a variety of practices, what one has accomplished is in the hands, feet, and body, not in the mind. Liberated from these routines but not diverging from them, one's skill becomes free no matter what one does. At such a time we do not know where our mind is and harmful doctrines are also unable to spy it out. As to practice done, if one has attained such a level — once achieved, it is a state of completion where [the need for] further practice is nonexistent. This is advancement in the highest sense. When you utterly discard the heart/mind that has forgotten practice and have in earnest attained a state where the "I" is also not known — that is the ultimate achievement.[87]

Also, in the words of Musashi:

> Beyond that expressed as "emptiness," what might one call profound, what might one say? When one grasps the Way in its rightness, one has gone beyond the Way in its rightness. The Art of Warfare (*Heihō*) is of itself free and performs extraordinary deeds. . . . All of this is the Way of Emptiness.[88]

How is the concept of absolute nonbeing in swordsmanship able to attain a state of refinement through the broader realm defined by physical form, *ch'i*, and the mind? Moreover, how is it grasped as reality without reliance on Confucianism or Buddhism? The answers become clear by themselves when we take a look at the "Chapter on Emptiness" in Musashi's *Gorinsho*, which embodies an ideal in that it solely advocates cultivation of the martial arts.

> The mind referred to as "empty" is adjudged as empty in that nothing exists and in that it [is a mind which] cannot know [things].
> Emptiness, of course, does not exist.
> Knowing that things exist, you can then know that things do not exist — this is emptiness.
> From the vulgar perspective of those who live in the world, emptiness is

understood as not being able to discriminate among things, but this is not genuine emptiness—their minds are all deluded.

In practicing the Way as a warrior with respect to strategy [*heihō*], he is not empty who does not know the Way of a warrior.

Although everything in the phenomenal world is delusion, and he who is method-less with respect to that is called empty, this is not genuine emptiness: when the warrior positively gains awareness of the Way, ably exerts himself in the other martial skills, is not in the least ignorant or confused in mind with respect to a warrior's conduct, from morning to morning is not idle, and polishes the minds of ideation and volition and sharpens the eyes of passive and purposive sight—just as clouds of confusion clear and not the slightest blur remains, he ought to know true emptiness.

Although you do not know the True Way, you are convinced that each individual is correct whether in terms of Buddhism or in terms of common sense [*sehō*]. When you rely on the important standards that prevail in the world looked at through the mind's unmediated way, [you see that] the True Way is violated by the leanings of each person's mind and the distortions imposed by each and every eye.

When you know that mind and then take the unmediated as the root, you will broadly put strategy into practice with the truth of the mind as the Way. When you really consider the totality of things clearly, you ought to see the Way as Empty[89] rather than regard it as the Way of Emptiness.

Emptiness is good and devoid of evil.

To know[90] is something that exists and to benefit from things is something that exists. The Way is something that exists but the mind is Empty.[91]

If we read those words carefully, we realize that this has a great deal more to it with respect to the basic character of the martial arts we have hitherto described. If we look at the verse written by Musashi in his *Inkahiden*:

In a spring breeze on the day when peach and plum open,
    autumnal rain and the leaves of the plane tree fall.[92]

we can understand how the martial arts penetrate the innermost recesses of the East Asian sense of the natural world. Also, in reading a line of verse that Musashi took pleasure in setting down:

The moon floats in the cold stream, spotless and still as a mirror image,[93] we can perceive how that mind-mirror is something permeated by quiescence. These things flow within the deepest recesses of East Asian spiritual history.

NOTES

This essay was first published in *Tetsugaku nenpō* (1952), no. 13. It was later reprinted in a collection of Professor Okada's work titled *Chūgoku shisō ni okeru risō to genjitsu* (Ideal and Reality in Chinese Thought) (Tokyo: Mokujisha, 1983). The translator wishes to thank Miss Miwa Kai and Professor Philip Yampolsky for their kind help in answering his many questions.

1. The Japanese term *waza* (Ch. *chi*) is rendered as "mastery" (in the title of this essay, for instance), "know-how," and (in the majority of cases) "skill." — trans.

2. The story of Cook Ting is probably the most famous of these anecdotes. For English versions see: A. C. Graham, trans., *Chuang Tzu* (London: Allen and Unwin, 1981), 63–64; and Burton Watson, trans., *The Complete Works of Chuang Tzu* (New York: Columbia University Press, 1968), 50–51. — trans.

3. English versions appear in Watson, the hunchback, 199–200; the ferryman, 200–201; Chi Hsing-tzu, 204; the swimmer at Lü-liang, 204–5; Woodworker Ch'ing, 205–6; Artisan Ch'ui, 206–7; Lieh Yü-k'ou, 230–31; the buckle maker, 244–45. — trans.

4. See Tetsuzai Shūsanshi, *Tengu gakujutsuron*, in *Bujutsu soshō* (Tokyo: Kokusho kankōkai, 1933), 3d ed., p. 323.

5. See Kanahara Shōgo, *Tōyōga gairon* (Tokyo: Kokin shoin, 1925).

6. These are the words of Ch'eng Hao (*Erh-Ch'eng i-shu*, ch. 3; *Wen-yüan ko ssu-k'u ch'üan-shu*, vol. 698, p. 56). Chu Hsi, in his *Chin-ssu lu*, cites this passage: "Master Ming-tao considered memorization, recitation, and acquiring extensive information as 'trifling with things and losing one's purpose.'" (Wing-tsit Chan, trans., *Reflections on Things at Hand — The Neo-Confucian Anthology Compiled by Chu Hsi and Lü Tsu-ch'ien* [New York: Columbia University Press, 1967], 52). — trans.

7. This is the case with respect to Confucianism.

8. *Lu Hsiang-shan chi-yao, chüan* 5 (*Kinsei kanseki sōkan* [*Shisō zokuhen*], vol. 4, p. 369).

9. See Kubo Tsutomu and Abe Jirō, trans., *Kyōen* (*The Symposium*) (Tokyo: Iwanami bunkō, 1986), 155–56.

10. These are Søren Kierkegaard's words.

11. See Eugen Herrigel, *Zen in the Art of Archery* (New York: Vintage Books, 1971), 3–13.

12. Watson, *Chuang Tzu*, 36–49; Graham ("The sorting which evens things out"), *Chuang Tzu*, 48–61.

13. *Sadō zenshū*, vol. 1, p. 731.

14. *Shinshū sadō zenshū* (Tokyo: Shunjūsha, 1956), 355.

15. Ibid., 194.

16. E. Herrigel, *Zen in the Art of Archery*, 5.

17. Yagyū Munenori, *Heihō kadensho*, in *Budō hōkan* (Dai Nihon yūbenkai kōdansha, 1944), 507.

18. Ibid., 509.

19. Miyamoto Musashi, *Gorinsho, Tsuchi no maki*, in *Bujutsu sōsho*, 241.

20. Ibid.

21. We know this from the statement "a thousand swords and ten thousand double-edged swords are found in a single heart/mind." See Furuta Yoshisada, *Ikkensai sensei kenpōsho*, in *Bujutsu sōsho*, 293.

22. Yamamoto Tsunetomo, *Hagakure*, in *Bushidō zensho* (Tokyo: Jidaisha, 1943), 2d ed., vol. 6, p. 30.

23. *Budō shoshinshū*, in *Bushidō zensho*, vol. 2, p. 299.

24. Beneath raised long swords, hell on earth;
    If you advance one step, paradise lies ahead.
    Without enemies, I, too, in a fisherman's boat on the strand,
    row out into the breakers.

This poem of Miyamoto Musashi conveys the idea that smashing the bonds of life and death is attainment of skill in its most highly developed form.

25. *Bushidō zensho*, vol. 2, p. 306.

26. *Bushidō zensho*, vol. 2, p. 299.

27. Kubota Kiyone, *Kenpō ryakuki*, in *Bujutsu sōsho*.

28. Miyamoto, *Gorinsho*, in *Bujutsu sōsho*, 264–65.

29. See *Budō sōsho*.

30. *Kenpō gekishi ron*, in *Bujutsu sōsho*, 547.

31. See Takuan Sōhō, *Fudōchishinmyōroku*, in *Bujutsu sōsho*. Also available in an English translation — William Scott Wilson, trans., *The Unfettered Mind: Writings of the Zen Master to the Sword Master* (Tokyo: Kodansha International, 1986). — trans.

32. See *Tengu geijutsuron*, in *Bujutsu sōsho*, 324–26. *Tengu* were supernatural creatures "half-man and half-hawk, [with a] large beak, long wings and glittering eyes, but a man's body, arms and legs" (Carmen Blacker, *The Catalpa Bow* [London: Allen and Unwin, 1986], p. 182). Among other things, *tengu* were believed to be the guardians of supernatural skills.

33. *Tengu geijutsuron* in *Bujutsu sōsho*, 324–26.

34. Ch'eng I (1033–1107), "I-ch'uan I-chuan hsü" (Preface to Ch'eng I's Commentary on the [*Classic of*] *Changes*) (*Wen-yüan ko ssu-k'u ch'üan-shu*, vol. 9, p. 157).

35. See *Kenpō Sekiun sensei sōden*, in *Bujutsu sōsho*, 279–80.

36. See *Ikkensai sensei kenpōsho*, in *Bujutsu sōsho*, 291.

37. A similar formulation is *li-i fen-shu* (principle is one; its particularizations are diverse).

38. *Tengu geijutsuron*, in *Bujutsu sōsho*, 325.

39. Ibid., 329–30.

40. Herrigel, the author of *Zen and the Art of Archery*, personally experienced this.

41. "The character *ch'i* consists of two distinct segments; a pictogram indicating 'rising vapor' is placed above the pictogram of 'rice' or 'millet.' Hence, the entire character should be read as . . . 'vapors rising from food.' . . . Used in the literature of the third and second centuries in a broader context; its meaning included related ideas or phenomena such as

'that which fills the body,' 'that which means life,' 'breath,' and 'vapors' in general, such as clouds in the sky, or even 'wind.' . . . *Ch'i* was considered to float through the air and, together with blood, through the organism" (Paul U. Unschuld, *Medicine in China—A History of Ideas* [Berkeley: University of California Press, 1985], 72).—trans.

42. See *Tengu geijutsuron*, in *Bujutsu sōsho*, 315.

43. Ibid.

44. Herrigel, *Zen and the Art of Archery*, 22–23.

45. See the afterword in Kubota, *Kenpō ryakuki*, in *Bujutsu sōsho*.

46. *Ikkensai sensei kenpō*, in *Bujutsu sōsho*, 293.

47. Literally, "methods of warfare."

48. See *Gorinsho, Tsuchi no maki*, in *Bujutsu sōsho*, 241.

49. Roger T. Ames, trans., *Sun-Tzu: The Art of Warfare* (New York: Ballantine Books, 1993), 126.

50. Ibid., 119–20.

51. Ibid., 115.

52. Ibid., 115. In the Yin-ch'üeh-shan text used by Ames in his translation of the *Sun Tzu*, these lines appear in the reverse order.

53. "Just as the flow of water avoids high ground and rushes to the lowest point, so on the path to victory avoid the enemy's strong points [*shih*] and strike where he is weak [*hsü*]" (*Sun Tzu*, ch. 6; Ames, *Sun-Tzu*, 127).—trans.

54. Ames, *SunTzu*, 130.

55. "Ground on which you will survive only if you fight with all your might, but will perish if you fail to do so, is terrain with no way out [*ssu-ti*]" (*Sun Tzu*, ch. 11; Ames, *Sun-Tzu*, 55).—trans.

56. "On terrain from which there no is way out, I would show our troops my resolve to fight to the death" (Ames, *Sun-Tzu*, 160).—trans.

57. Ibid., 126.

58. Ibid., 126.

59. See *Sun-Tzu*, ch. 6.

60. Miyamoto Musashi, *Heihō sanjūgokajō*, in *Bujutsu sōsho*, 232.

61. See Miyamoto, *Gorinsho*, in *Bujutsu sōsho*, 240, and Yagyū, *Heihō kadensho*, in *Budō hōkan*, 521–22.

62. Yagyū, *Heihō kadensho*, in *Budō hōkan*, 524, 532.

63. The first line is a variant of a verse in the *Kokinshū* (Bk. 6, no. 303; dated ca. 905). Also, both lines echo poetry by the monk Kūya (903–72).

64. Yagyū, *Heihō kadensho*, in *Budō hōkan*. (For *Shiuji shuri ken*, 521.)

65. Kimura Kubo, *Unjūryū kenjutsu yōryō*, in *Bujutsu sōsho*.

66. Ibid.

67. Ibid.

68. Negishi Shingorō, *Kendō kōwa*, in *Budō hōkan*, 689.

69. In the "No-blade" (*Mutō*) chapter in *Heihō kadensho* (*Budō hōkan*, 533), Yagyū Munenori has the following to say:

"Inward Spring of Movement" [*ki*] is substance. That manifested outward from the Inward Spring of Movement in its various operations is function. Just as the plum has its substance and from such substance its flowers bloom, its color and fragrance appear, and its scent spreads abroad, so the Spring of Movement is within and its functions operate in the outer world. Attaching [to a thing], covering [things], on the outside [of things], on the inside [of things], [or held] in abeyance: all its manifold aspects rely on the Spring of Movement holding itself ready within so as to issue forth in the outer world—this is function. . . . Since it is the "Great Inward Spring of Movement," it is made manifest as the "Great Functioning."

70. *Heihō kadensho* in *Budō hōkan*, 534.

71. Ibid.

72. Ibid., 521–22.

73. Miyamoto Musashi, *Heihō sanjūgokajō*, in *Bujutsu sōsho*, 231.

74. Miyamoto, *Gorinsho*, in *Bujutsu sōsho*, 264–65.

75. "Ching: 'seriousness.' In ancient Confucianism the word *ching* is often interchangeable with *kung* and means 'reverence' but in Neo-Confucianism the two words are sharply different . . . *Kung* has to do with one's appearance and expression in respect for others while *ching* has to do with one's effort; the former is external and the latter internal. The main difference is that reverence implies an object whereas *ching* is a state of mind" (Chan, *Reflections on Things at Hand*, 361).—trans.

76. *Erh-Ch'eng ch'üan-shu* (Chūbun shuppansha ed.), 16:1a.

77. "Mencius said, 'Benevolence is the heart of man, and rightness his road. Sad it is indeed when a man gives up the right road instead of following it and allows his heart to stray without sense to go after it. . . . The sole concern of learning is to go after the strayed heart [*fang-hsin*]" (*Mencius* 6A:11, trans. D. C. Lau [London: Penguin Books, 1970], 167).—trans.

78. Takuan Sōhō, *Fudōchishinmyōroku*, in *Bujutsu sōsho*, 218.

79. Ibid., 216.

80. Ibid.

81. Ibid.

82. For details see Yagyū, *Heihō kadensho, Katsuninken no maki*, in *Budō hōkan*, 517–21.

83. Takuan, *Fudōchishin myōroku*, in *Bujutsu sōsho*, 218.

84. A Chinese monk who came to Japan in 1279 and was founder of the Engaku-ji, one of the "Five Mountains" (Gozan) monasteries. See Heinrich Dumoulin, *Zen Buddhism: A History, vol. 2—Japan* (New York: Macmillan, 1990), 34–35.—trans.

85. Ibid.

86. Yagyū, *Heihō kadensho*, in *Budō hōkan*, 530.

87. Ibid., 510.

88. Miyamoto, *Gorinsho*, in *Bujutsu sōsho*, 238.

89. The character for *emptiness* (*kū*) is given as *principle* (*ri*) in another version of the text.

90. The character for *to know* (*chih*) is given in another edition as *wisdom* (*chih*).

91. Ibid., 264–65.

92. From "Song of Everlasting Sorrow "(*Ch'ang hen ko*) by Po Chü-i (772–846).

93. From "Farewell Banquet on a Pavilion by the Yangtze" (*Chiang lou yen pieh*) by Po Chü-i.

GLOSSARY

Abe Jirō　阿部次郎

Budō Hōkan　武道寶鑑

Budō shoshinshū　武道初心集

Budō soshō　武道叢書

Bujutsu sōsho　武術叢書

bushidō　武士道

Bushidō zensho　武士道全書

Busho sōsho　武書叢書

chen-li, shinri　真理

Ch'eng I (1033–1107)　程頤

chi, ki　機

ch'i, ki　氣

ch'i ho, kiai　氣合

"Ch'i-wu lun"　齊物論

chien, ken　見

chien hsing wu-tao, kenshō godō　見性悟道

chih (to know)　知

chih (wisdom)　智

chih, jiki　直

chih-tao, jikidō　直道

ching, kei　敬

ching-tso, seiza　静坐

ch'iu fang-hsin, kyū hōshin　求放心

chūdan　中段

chüeh, kaku (satori)　覺

chüeh-tui wu, zettai mu　絕對無

Chūgoku shisō ni okeru risō to genjitsu　中國思想における理想と現實

nai, nei　內

dōteki　動的

fa, hō　法

fang-hsin, hōshin　放心

Fudōchishinmyōroku　不動智神妙錄

gai, wai　外

gedan　下段

Geibōshin　迎棒心

Gorinsho　五輪書

gugen　具現

heihō　兵法

Heihō kadensho　兵法家傳書

Heihō sanjūgokajō　兵法三十五ケ條

hsin-fa, shinhō　心法

hsin-shu, shinjutsu　心術

hsing, kei/gyo　形

hsü, kyo　虛

hsūeh, gaku　學

"I-ch'uon I-chuan hsü"　伊川易傳序

i-fa, ihatsu　已發

i no kokoro　意のこころ

Ikkensai sensei kenpō　一刀齊先生劍法

Inkahiden　印可秘傳

jiso　持所

jissen　實踐

jissenteki junsui keiken　實踐的純粹經驗

jissenteki kufū　實踐的工夫

jōdan　上段

jōteki　靜的

jou, jū　柔

kamae　構

kamae naki kokoro　かまへなき心

kang, gō　剛

kannō no myōyō　官能の妙用

kanshin no myōyō　感心の妙用

kendō　劍道

Kendō kōwa　劍道講話

Kenpō ryakki　劍法略記

Kenpō Sekiun sensei soden　劍法夕雲先生相傳

kentai　懸待

Kimura Kubo　木材久甫

kokoro no waza　心の技

ko-wu ch'iung-li, kakubutsu kyūri　格物窮理

kū　空

kuan, kan　観

Kubota Kiyone　窪田清音

Kubo Tsutomo　久保勉

k'ung-li, kūri　空理

kung-tao, kōdō　公道

Kyōen　饗宴

li, ri　理

miao-yung, myōyō　妙用

Miyamoto Musashi　宮本武藏

Mori Keichin　森景鎮

Mugaku Sogen　無學祖元

mukiteiteki kitei　無規定的規定

mushin no shin　無心の心

mushin no Nō　無心の能

myōyō　妙用

Negishi Shingorō　根岸信五郎

nei, nai　內

Nitei zensho　二程全書

Okada Takehiko　岡田武彦

pen-hsin, honshin　本心

pen-t'i, hontai　本體

ping-fa, heihō　兵法

ri　理

sehō　世法

Seikō sui　西江水

Sekka no ki　石火の機

shen, shin　神

shen-chi, shingi　神技

sheng-jen, seijin　聖人

shih, ji 事

shih, jitsu 實

shih, sei 勢

shiki no shutai 識の主體

Shinmyō ken 神妙劍

shin no jikidō 心の直道

shin no kokoro 心のこころ

shin no kufū 心の工夫

shintai 心體

shintai shizen no myōyō 心體自然の妙用

Shuji shuri ken 手字種利劍

Shodō no meijin 諸道の名人

shu, jutsu 術

shuchishugi 主知主義

ssu-ti, shichi 死地

Su wen 素問

Sun-Tzu 孫子

suteru 捨てる

ta-chi, daiki 大機

ta-yung, daiyō 大用

Takuan Sōhō 澤庵宗彭

tan-t'ien, tanden 丹田

Tao, Dō 道

Tao-hsüeh, Dōgaku 道學

Tengu geijutsuron 天狗藝術論

tenri no shizen 天理の自然

tetsugaku, che-hsüeh 哲學

t'i, tai 體

t'ien-li, tenri 天理

tsan-hsin, zanshin 殘心

tzu-jan, shizen 自然

tzu-jan-chu-i, shizenshugi 自然主義

Unjūryū kenjutsu yōryō 運籌流劍術要領

wai-ch'ih hsin, gaijishin 外馳心

wakigama 脇がま

wan-fa i-li, banpō ichiri 萬法一理

wan-wu sang-chih, ganbutsu sōshi 玩物喪志

wang-hsin, mōjin 妄心

wang-wo, bōga 忘我

waza 技

wei, gi 偽

wei-fa, mihatsu 未發

wei-shin, yuishin 唯心

wu, mu 無

wo, ware 我

wu chi yu, mu soku yū 無即有

wu-hsin, mushin 無心

wu-hsing, mukei 無形

Wu-hsüeh Tsu-yüan (Mugaku Sogen) 無學祖元

wu-tao, budō 武道

wu-wei, bui 無為

wu-wo, muga 無我

wu-wo liang-wang, butsuga ryōbō 物我兩忘

Yagyū Munenori 柳生宗矩

Yamaoka Tesshū 山岡鐵舟

yin, in 因

yu, u, yū 有

yu chi wu, yū soku mu 有即無

yudan naki kokoro 油斷なき心

yūshin no shin 有心の心

yung, yō 用

za 座

Zeami 世阿彌

Chapter Eleven

CONFUCIAN PILGRIM: UNO TETSUTO'S TRAVELS IN CHINA

JOSHUA A. FOGEL

In the preface to the account of his travels in China, *Shina bunmei ki* (A Chronicle of Chinese Civilization), written in the same month (January 1912) that the fledgling Republic of China was born, Uno Tetsuto (1875–1974), the renowned Sinologist, wrote:

> The national conditions of China, that country which has maintained intimate contact with our land for well over a thousand years and which is separated from us by only a narrow strait, should already be quite clear to us. But, they are not clear at all.
>
> Those who understand China by reading her revered classics and sagely scriptures of antiquity may think that China is a paradise on Earth with sages and men of virtue wafting about like the clouds. Is China really a paradise?
>
> Based on their own limited experiences, men of the world often scorn the Chinese people and consider them ungrateful, immoral, and incorrigible. Can we really dispense with the Chinese nation with such scorn?
>
> I originally wrote this book in the days of the Ch'ing dynasty [1644–1911] and sent it to my parents back home in Japan; in it I discuss a variety of

matters large and small, such as Chinese customs and practices, social conditions, famous places, and ancient sights. If, on the basis of this book, a glimpse of the national conditions of China is introduced to the world, then the honor is not only mine.[1]

What sort of false impressions or stereotypes of contemporary China was Uno trying to overcome and why? To whom was his lengthy travel account directed? Why had he traveled to China and what did travel to China mean for him?

The Tokugawa *bakufu* lifted its ban on travel abroad in 1862 when the *Senzaimaru*, the first official ship sent on a mission to China in 223 years, set sail for Shanghai to investigate conditions there in the wake of the Opium War (1839–1842). In the years that followed, a number of brave souls and official emissaries journeyed to the mainland for a variety of reasons.[2] Understandably, the first group to travel to China and report on what they found were Japanese scholars of Chinese history and culture, Kangakusha. Strictly speaking, several of those aboard the *Senzaimaru*, such as Takasugi Shinsaku (1839–1867) and Hibino Teruhiro (1838–1912), were Kangakusha; but the genre of a Kangakusha travel account of China only began to take form in the next decade, even though elements of it can be found in their earlier accounts.

Takezoe Shin'ichirō (1842–1917) was one of the first Kangaku scholars to travel to China in the Meiji period. Following a trip of over three months there in 1876, he penned a lengthy account, composed in elegant Kanbun or literary Chinese, which he titled *San'un kyōu nikki* (A Diary of Clouds in the Mountain Pathways and Rain in the Ravines, published 1879). Although Takezoe was attentive to local custom, water conservancy methods, and opium, among the more concrete realities he noted, the greater sense he conveys to readers of his account is of his having finally arrived in China, the motherland of culture as he saw it. He took great pains to make his account a lasting work of poetry and prose, not a mere travel guide; for this reason he wrote it in Chinese. He described contemporary China as a nation that had come down with a cold incorrectly diagnosed by the doctor. With proper treatment—and Takezoe applauded the modernization efforts he witnessed in China during the self-strengthening movement—the patient was sure to recover.[3]

The year 1884 marks the first watershed in changing Japanese attitudes toward China as revealed in this developing genre of travel accounts. The outbreak of the Sino-French War in 1884, the first major confrontation between an East Asian and a European power since the Opium War, prompted many Japanese travelers to publish reports. One of the results of China's apparent defeat by the French and the loss of Annam was a general diminution of the grand image of China. A typical response of the time, although not the work of a Kangaku scholar, was that of Komuro Shinsuke who complained about the wartime exaggerations in the Chinese press, a characteristic he came to associate with the Chinese people generally. He also thought they were greedy, petty people with no sense of shame or integrity, concerned only with their personal advantage—the sort of condescending statement that could have been written by Arthur Smith or Père Huc, two of the more famous European travelers and commentators about China of the previous century.[4]

The most famous Japanese to visit China in 1884 was the Kangaku scholar Oka Senjin (1832–1913), and he remained there for an entire year. He composed his long and detailed account, *Kankō kiyū* (Trip Report), in Kanbun but without the devotion to China and her culture that one finds in the account of his forerunner Takezoe. Oka adopted a straightforward, descriptive style. The critical importance of his work is its place as the first severe critique of China by a Kangaku scholar, and it opened the door for others to follow. Adopting the familiar metaphor of illness, he diagnosed China's disease as twofold: *endoku* (the poison of smoke, or opium) and *keidoku* (the poison of the Chinese classics). The former confronted Oka two days after arriving in Shanghai when he went to meet the famous Chinese reformer Wang T'ao (1828–1897) and was told by his intermediary, Kishida Ginkō (the nefarious mainland adventurer, 1833–1905), that Wang was indisposed, undoubtedly because of his opium addiction. Oka's shock would give birth to a disillusionment with Chinese intellectuals generally. He questioned other Chinese closely about the extent of the opium problem, examined and described opium dens himself, and even witnessed the problem personally after a Chinese banquet. The experience left him thoroughly revolted.

The problem of *keidoku* involved both Oka's sense of a Chinese slavishness to antiquity and an essential and unhealthy Sinocentrism. Throughout his travels, Oka made use of the "brush conversation" (Jap. *hitsudan*; Ch. *pi-t'an*), the primary means by which Chinese and Japanese who shared no spoken language communicated through the medium of written literary Chinese, the lingua franca throughout East Asia. He had many *hitsudan* with a wealthy *chü-jen* (a scholar who had passed the second level of the imperial examinations) by the name of Wang Yen-yün. Oka was horrified by the waste and profligacy of the Wang household. At one point he said to scholar Wang that he felt Li Hung-chang's (1823–1901) efforts to build Chinese industry and encourage commerce would be good for China as they had been for the West. Detecting Wang's anger, Oka gave an example from the classics, something Kangaku scholars were never at a loss for, to demonstrate that the sages had used machines to help the people. Wang responded: "The French and the English are jackals and wolves. They have nothing to say on the subject of human principles." After further, completely fruitless, discussion, Oka concluded: "Yen-yün is a strange man. As a scholar he is a rare talent indeed, but when he talks of foreign affairs, he becomes perverse, runs to extremes, and fails to understand." Oka saw this as a general Chinese problem.[5]

What makes Oka's case so interesting is that it was precisely the depth of his learning in traditional Chinese subjects that enabled him to enter elite Chinese society to a considerable extent and made it nearly impossible for his hosts to ignore him. By the same token, it meant a even starker realization of the depth of perceived decay in China. He was prepared to concede the personal, spiritual realm to Confucius and sons, but the physical realm belonged to modernization on the model of the Meiji reforms. Nothing could have brought the necessity of this dualism closer to home than a meeting he had in Shao-hsing with three Chinese students who explained in a perfectly rational frame of mind that solar eclipses were caused by a bullfrog eating the sun (following a description in the *Ch'un-ch'iu*, or Spring and Autumn Annals).[6] It was sadly ironic that this long trip to China should produce a sustained attack on China from within the Kangaku fold.

Oka queried many Chinese about what they planned to do in the war with France, and no one came up with a satisfactory answer. Sheng Hsüan-huai (1844–1916) threw the question back, asking if Japan would enter the war to assist China. Oka squirmed: "Japan is a small island country, and we are prudent in our intercourse with the West. Why should we cooperate with China and incur the animosity of France for no reason whatsoever?" The best route for Japan to take, Oka ultimately decided, was "secession" (*ridatsu*) from the Chinese cultural world, a view completely consistent with the famous formula of "dissociation from Asia" (*datsu-A*) elaborated the following year (1885) by Fukuzawa Yukichi (1834–1901).[7]

One equally scornful attitude can be found the same year in the trip account of the liberal intellectual Sugita Teiichi (1851–1920). Although earlier he had been favorably disposed to Sino-Japanese cooperation to confront the West, after his 1884 trip Sugita radically reformulated the issues. Either Japan would stand with China and be carved up, he claimed, or it would not only not stand aside but actually join in the carving of China. That year's

Sino-Japanese conflict over Korea, he argued, provided a pretext for just such an attack on China, and he urged immediate imperialist advances.[8]

Over the next two decades, greater access to travel in China by people from many different occupational groups led to a wide variety of responses to contemporary China. From his 1891–1892 trip to the Yangtze delta area, Andō Fujio, a Kangaku scholar and journalist, put together an altogether new kind of travel account. Composed of newspaper articles describing his experiences in China, Andō's *Shina manyū jikki* (True Account of a Voyage to China) was explicitly written to enable the Japanese to expand their commercial and shipping interests. Since no sufficient guides to China's geography existed, he sought to fill the lacunae, adding a wealth of information on Chinese commercial organization, local foods and clothing, and practices in marriage, funerals, and religion. Although he counseled diligence and frugality by Japanese enterprises, he also encouraged unity among like industries so as to demonstrate Japanese resolve to the Chinese. Continuing the metaphor of illness employed earlier by Takezoe and Oka, Andō spoke of China as a "sick old man" (*yameru rōya*) and Japan as a "lively youth" (*katsuratsutaru shōnen*); were China to decline further, Japan could step in and take over, he noted.[9]

This sort of openly instrumental view of China was prevalent but hardly typical of the 1890s. No one, Japanese or Chinese, could deny that China was in serious trouble, but there was no single response to that dilemma in Japan or China. Miyauchi Isaburō confronted the same situation when he went to China in 1892, and his response is perhaps more typical of the confused mixture among Kangakusha of cultural Sinophilia and political Sinophobia:

> Although the cowardice of this people is well known to everyone, no nation opened its doors earlier, has more territory or greater population, gave rise to more wise men and heroic figures, or produced cultural relics earlier than the people of continental China. Men of letters have recited widely all the many sorts of things that we Japanese have copied from them in the past. Thus, we must be careful when we look at contemporary Chinese politics or trade. . . . Three hundred years have passed since then [i.e., the founding of the Ch'ing dynasty], and although the imperial throne has already been handed down consecutively for more than ten generations, the Chinese state has now fallen into decay and has become the laughingstock of the world.[10]

His account features information on seventy-seven items, from public works projects and agriculture to religious practices, military conditions, opium, women, currency, and poisonous snakes.

Okakura Tenshin (1862–1913) spent the latter half of 1893 in China, and he either ignored or simply missed the harsher side of life in China altogether. Sent by the Imperial Household Department to investigate Chinese art, he concentrated on museums and curio shops and traveled about in Chinese dress with his hair in a queue. From his subsequent speeches and writings that mention his travels, we can isolate several conclusions he reached. While holding to his favorite slogan that "Asia was one," Okakura came to believe that there was no one "China" (*Shina ni Shina nashi*), namely, that the cultures of the Yellow and the Yangtze Rivers were sufficiently different to warrant a basic distinction.[11]

As the nineteenth century came to an close, China increasingly began to attract the type of person who fashioned himself rugged. The popular image of China as an age-old country, extremely poor, and much in need of modern conveniences emerged at this time, largely because of the picture of China presented in travel reports. Also, organizations of Japanese adventurers cropped up throughout China beginning in the mid-1890s. When Takase Bintoku arrived in 1902, he insisted on traveling on foot. He noted that Chinese streets were dirty, workers and coolies looked like beggars, and the general populace was filthy and insensate—all images soon to become elemental to any portrait of China then. While a few lived in grand elegance, the lower classes enjoyed an extremely low level of hygiene. And, here was a severe problem for China: Chinese society had no healthy middle ranks (*chūtō shakai*), also a common view over the next few decades. After a lengthy description of life in China, particularly in Peking, Takase came to the conclusion that China was not a "nation" (*kokka*) but had 400 million individuals and four thousand-year-old customs; in the same breath he claimed, apparently unaware of the non sequitur, that the Chinese "nation" was headed for extinction. He called on all foreign (read Japanese) educators, religious leaders, and businessman to pursue their lines of work in China.[12]

Among the more famous and undoubtedly the most obnoxious travel account of the late Meiji period was that of the journalist Tokutomi Sohō (1863–1957). No sooner had he arrived in Manchuria en route to Peking than he wrote home to say that merchants in An-tung expressed what appeared to be genuine thankfulness for the protection to their property and persons now available because of Japanese domination in the region. He arrived in the Chinese capital just when "the rights recovery fever had reached 40°C."

Agreeing with an unnamed English reporter who claimed that the Chinese defiance of the civilized powers derived from this xenophobic fever, he concluded that "'rights recovery' may be the other side of xenophobia." And, revealing his true colors, Tokutomi added: "Where will this . . . movement end? Perhaps it will unite with the antiforeign movement of the lower classes? Is such an apprehension needless anxiety? I hope it is."[13]

He generally concluded that China lacked the concept of nation, a rapidly developing idea about China in Japan. He had looked hard for a Chinese sense of commonality, and all he could find was effeminacy, lack of skill and drive, and a virtual cult of despair. Although clever in planning in their own self-interest and thoroughly opportunistic, he claimed, the Chinese were, in the final analysis, untrustworthy, again virtually the identical superficial conclusions of Père Huc and Arthur Smith, two famous missionary-travelers in China some decades earlier. "In sum," he concluded, "China is in a state of transition at present. . . . But, will she be able . . . to form a national unity and raise a national spirit, while at the same time joining in the life and thought shared by the civilized nations and become a great and powerful state? This is the gravest of my many doubts."[14]

In later years travel accounts of China by Kangaku scholars became the most pedantic subgenre in this entire vast literature. Every sight, every stele, every mountain or village elicited a veritable outpouring of historic and cultural information of interest largely to people who already knew it all. Furthermore, such information was always presented as if the author were gushing forth with quotations from the *Shih chi* (Record of the Grand Historian) or poems by Su Tung-p'o (1037–1101) that hung on the tip of his tongue; in fact, it was perfectly clear that he had packed his account just before publication back in Japan, where he had access to his library. Nonetheless, we would be hard-pressed now to imagine the excitement such men, who had lived Chinese history and the Chinese classics entirely from written texts (many of them memorized just as Chinese scholars had memorized them for centuries), must have felt as they actually came into personal contact with "China."

This revelatory (in many cases, self-congratualatory) style, however, was still novel and fresh in the decade (1897–1906) preceding Uno Tetsuto's travels. During this decade several remarkable Kangaku scholars with formidable credentials in traditional Chinese learning traveled to China for the first time and left marvelous accounts of their experiences. Where earlier Kangaku travelers had been shocked by the reality of a China wholly different from their unrealistic expections, just as Uno expected they might in his introduction, this group had both the advantage of much more information about contemporary China and the opportunity to read the accounts of earlier travelers, including Takezoe and Oka. However, they also were burdened with the developing negative images of China we have seen.

Yamamoto Baigai (1852–1928) devoted his academic life to traditional Chinese scholarship, particularly to the histories and the *Tzu-chih t'ung-chien* (Comprehensive Mirror for Aid in Government) of Ssu-ma Kuang (1019–1089), which he allegedly read six times. He was also an activist in the popular rights movement of the Meiji period and was centrally involved in the Osaka Incident, in which a number of Japanese were arrested for involvement in plotting a coup in Korea. Over a decade later in the fall of 1897, he seized an opportunity to travel through China's major cities for several months. In many ways, his account of that trip is typical of Kangaku travelers — inclusion of capsule histories of every sight, every statue, every hillock visited, and usually with quotations from Chinese texts. Entitled *Enzan sosui kiyū* (Chronicle of a Trip to the Mountains of North China and the Rivers of South China), it was also the last of this subgenre to be written completely in Kanbun.

Yamamoto's extraordinary ability in Kanbun and his journalistic contacts in China enabled him to enjoy considerable contact with Chinese reformers, such as Wang K'ang-nien (1860–1911), Liang Ch'i-ch'ao (1873–1929), and Chang Chien (1853–1926), as well as with the conservative scholar Lo Chen-yü (1866–1940). His discussions in China were all recorded in his account, which expressed general agreement with the reformist movement. Back in Japan he maintained contacts with his Chinese friends for many years, particularly when Liang and his mentor K'ang Yu-wei (1858–1927) were forced to flee there from China at the end of 1898. Yamamoto later organized a Sino-Japanese Cooperative Society, and he offered help to Liang's publishing efforts from Japan. When asked by the Foreign Ministry, in view of his close association with the Chinese reformers, to inform Liang and K'ang that the Japanese government was expelling them, Yamamoto simply refused.[15]

Naitō Konan (1866–1934), a figure of legendary proportions in prewar Japanese Sinology, made his first voyage to China proper in the late summer and fall of 1899. I have dealt with his trip account, *Enzan sosui* (The Mountains of North China and the Rivers of South China) in detail elsewhere[16] and will be brief here. Like Yamamoto's similarly titled work, Naitō embellished his account with countless historical and classical references, as if to remind himself that he was actually visiting the same China that he had so long studied. Among the many prominent Chinese reformers and intellectuals with whom he "conversed" in Kanbun were Yen Fu (1853–1921), Wen T'ing-shih (1856–1904), Chang Yüan-chi (1866–1959), Liu Hsüeh-hsün, and Lo Chen-yü. Their discussions covered many topics but always, perhaps because Naitō was so insistent, returned to the problems of rulership in contemporary China and what role Japan might play in helping China reform itself.[17]

Despite his insistence that Japan play a role, even if only as a model, and despite his negative remarks about the general state of hygiene there, Naitō retained an enormous respect for China and the Chinese, as witnessed by several sketches appended to his trip report. In part, this was because of a frozen image of "China," the motherland of culture itself, in the words of Takezoe Shin'ichirō. Naitō's realization that China had severe problems, from opium addiction and footbinding to the lack of an adequate sewer system in Peking, never led him to reject China, as it had Oka Senjin and Sugita Teiichi fifteen years earlier. In fact, it never led him to the despair of the writer Lu Hsün (1881–1936), who would soon describe the entire history of Chinese culture as that of cannibalism. His understanding of its ills went too deep for such an extreme response. Also, by the turn of the century the times had changed, and to reject China in the manner of Oka and Sugita usually carried pro-Westernization political baggage with it (as in the case of Tokutomi Sohō), anathema to someone of Naitō Konan's education and proclivities.

This background should help explain the many different images Uno Tetsuto was trying to overcome when he set down to write his fascinating *Shina bunmei ki*. Although he allegedly based his report on his eighteen months of study in Peking (1906–1907), his actual travels occupied only a few months of his time on the mainland. As indicated by his title, this was not merely a simple trip report from China, as so many others had written; it was to be a descriptive account of the state of Chinese civilization. Uno had graduated from Tokyo Imperial University in 1900 and would become full professor there in 1918. Although barely thirty years old when he set out, Uno was already extraordinarily learned in classical Chinese traditions, citations from which appear on virtually every page of his work. He had already published several books in his major field of expertise, Chinese philosophy, especially of the Sung period. He returned to Japan for nearly seventy more years of prodigious scholarly productivity.[18]

As Uno's account begins, one is easily led to believe that what follows will be the typical Kangakusha's chronicle of each and every stone (and its history) in China, punctuated only by an occasional statement of irritation with the Chinese. At sea for several days before landing at the port of T'ang-ku in

Hopeh province (near Tientsin), Uno expresses genuine sadness at the horrific sight of people's homes, constructed of mud, built right by the water — "they looked more like pig sties." But he is revived when he sees, fluttering in the wind, a Hinomaru (the Japanese flag), as if reassured that one might find civilized comforts even in T'ang-ku. This is no place, he notes in fairness, to get a first impression of China. Uno's next stop is Tientsin, where life appears much better to his eye, and then on to Peking, which is even better.[19]

Uno makes Peking his headquarters, and from there he begins a series of trips throughout China. His descriptions of people, places, roadside stands and their wares, fruits for sale, theater, local festivals, and the like are all interesting, but they read now like an almanac. In fact, Takeuchi Minoru has suggested that Uno's descriptions are so thick that he may have simply borrowed much of his information from an almanac published at this time in China by Tun Li-ch'en, the *Yen-ching sui-shih-chi* (Almanac of Yen-ching).[20] In other words, the material in the first 125 pages of Uno's nearly four hundred-page travel account provides interesting reading in the way that an encyclopedia provides interesting reading. However, the atmosphere suddenly changes at this point.

On September 4, 1906, shortly after arriving in China, Uno leaves Tientsin by ship, although he does not mention his destination. The next day he arrives at noon in Cheefu (Chih-fu), where the sight of numerous Japanese ships in dock proves especially comforting to him. The next day he boards a German vessel that carries him past the Shantung peninsula south. On the morning of September 7, the ship docks in Tsingtao, and Uno disembarks to check in at, reportedly, the only Japanese inn there. (Several years later, after Japan seized German holdings in Tsingtao during World War I, Tsingtao would be overwhelmed by Japanese businesses, tourists, and traders.) Although Uno is unable to control his penchant for introducing historical tidbits into the sights thus far seen on this side trip, the account takes on an altogether different flavor in Shantung.

From Tsingtao, Uno boards a train bound for Tsinan. On the train, he finds himself uncomfortably surrounded for over twelve hours by Chinese and several Englishmen. The Chinese, he reports, were particularly talkative and "extremely bothersome" (*hanahada urusai*), although he admits that he was not offended by them. An occasional mention of an ancient Chinese text and a reference to Mencius's well-known meeting with King Hsüan of Ch'i (which had allegedly occurred nearby) — still, Uno offers not a hint as to where he is headed.

Upon arrival in Tsinan, Uno hires a rickshaw, his third mode of transport, each one progressively more primitive, to convey him to the home of a local Japanese resident. There he meets several other Japanese for a "circle of unexpected satisfaction." For five days (September 8–12), this Japanese resident shows him the sights of Tsinan and introduces him to Governor Yang Shih-hsiang, with whom he exchanges pleasantries. On the morning of the thirteenth, he departs Tsinan, this time by horse-drawn carriage, which arrives on the afternoon of the fourteenth in T'ai-an-fu. Highly attentive to propriety, Uno pays his respects to the local prefectural magistrate, Yü Kou, immediately upon arrival.[21]

The next morning he rises at dawn to climb Mount T'ai (actually, he is carried up bodily, his fifth and most ancient mode of hired transport). From there he can see all around him, and now it becomes clear what this trip is really all about. He has returned, figuratively, to the fount of civilization itself. He has retraced the steps of progress back to its origins in the homeland of Confucius and Mencius. Just as Confucius climbed the sacred Mount T'ai and saw how small the realm appeared from its summit, so too does Uno Tetsuto some two thousand and five hundred years later. No longer is this travel account a historical almanac. It suddenly is transformed into the record of a Confucian pilgrimage. Now, even when Uno recounts historical and geographical details, they take on added philosophical, virtually religious, meaning. They now enhance his chronicle rather than simply occupy space.

From this point forward, every single sight elicits a profoundly meaningful impression in his "memory," as his classical education comes alive. Leaving the glorious Mount T'ai, he travels for several days by land and river, again not mentioning where he is headed until he arrives. And, then, Ch'ü-fu appears in the distance:

> The yellow roof tiles that I saw high in the city were the those of the Temple of Confucius (*Sheng-miao*). The azure tiles to its left were probably the Temple to Yen Hui [Confucius's disciple]. A forest of cypress densely surround the city to the north and form a wall there — this was, without a doubt, the Chih Sheng [Great Sage] Forest.

Then, continuing in this euphoric vein, Uno reports (without a trace of arrogance): "It was as if we were a band of Crusaders, just arrived in ecstacy, looking at Jerusalem."[22]

Uno's rapture takes on religious fervor when he actually enters Ch'ü-fu and stands before the Temple of Confucius: "I was born in a land of decorum across the Eastern Sea (*Tōen kunshikoku*); separated spatially by several thousand *li* and temporally by over three thousands years, I have revered this place and looked up to it for many years. Today, whatever day it is, I visited the Temple of Confucius and gazed upon the Chih Sheng Forest."[23] Throughout his travel account, Uno is meticulous about recording not only the day of the events but the time as well. At the Temple of Confucius, it is not that he failed to remember the day—"whatever day it is"—but that the actual date had no meaning. The spirit of Confucius had inhabited these environs for ages, and the particular date of Uno's appearance there had no special importance; it was for all time. It was, in fact, September 18, 1906, a date Uno himself supplies several lines later. One can sense at this point Uno's joy as he inhaled the same air as Confucius and prayed at the Confucian Temple: "Unconsciously, I bowed my head as if I were closely approaching the spirit of the Sage. Without looking I saw his spirit; without listening I heard his voice. And my insignificant little body immediately became absorbed in the great spirit of the Sage."[24]

Lest the reader of this account doubt that Uno actually saw what he claims to have seen, four photographs (an important addition to travel writing) from Ch'ü-fu and neighboring Tsou county are inserted in the text at this point, including those of the gravestones of Confucius and Mencius, each with an explanatory caption. Once inside the Temple of Confucius, every single plaque to the disciples of Confucius is described. Not only do the classics come alive for Uno as he walks around these buildings and stelae, but he begins to feel as though he too is walking with the disciples of the Sage. When he visits the Chih Sheng Forest, his concludes his detailed depiction with the words: "The spirit . . . of the great sage Confucius fills the atmosphere [there] with its permanence . . . and brilliantly illuminates public morality."[25]

When he returns to his inn, Uno finds that his view of the religious centrality of Ch'ü-fu to East Asia is corroborated by County Magistrate Liu, albeit for somewhat different reasons. "Our Ch'ü-fu," complains Liu, "is comparable to the West's Jerusalem, although Confucianism [*K'ung-chiao*] and Christianity [*Ye-chiao*] cannot be mentioned in the same breath. . . . In the Book of Genesis it states that the omnipotent God created Heaven, earth, and all creatures and that, on the seventh day, he rested. This is a most irrational, laughable matter. There has yet to be a Christian believer in Ch'ü-fu."[26] Liu's evocation of Jerusalem is nationalistic and antiforeign; he was angry about foreign concessions in nearby Liao-chou-wan. This was not

Uno's concern in the least, and he quickly diverts his discussion to another topic.

"Does the legacy of Confucius and Mencius," asks Uno for the second time, "still exist in the land of Lu?" "No," answers Liu, "our scholars prattle about Confucius and Mencius, but it's all just chatter." Uno offers his reader not a clue as to his reaction to this stark response, unless we read something into the absence of a comment. But Uno is only learning, slowly, what he will later include in his introduction (cited at the outset): that China of the classics is not the China of today. He has elicited his image of China not from newspapers or current events but from late Chou dynasty texts. As he leaves Shantung province on his way toward Kaifeng, he sadly notes: "Because [the state of] Lu was the site of the graves of the sages, I expected to find their legacies in as pure and simple form as in antiquity. I was greatly disappointed."[27]

The rest of this side trip, to Kaifeng and elsewhere in Honan before returning to Peking, is all epilogue. In fact the next 175 pages, which include seven side trips, revert to the earlier tone of this travel account. His style becomes that of a diary; the dates are no longer incidental to his experiences and so integrated into the account (let alone unimportant as on that one day in Ch'ü-fu), but they become the organizers of the events described. The result is considerably less of Uno's personal and immediate responses to China and considerably more detail, history, poetry, stone inscriptions — and, less exciting reading, to be sure. The trip to Shantung was obviously the centerpiece of his entire stay in China; it was his first substantial sidetrip from his base in Peking, and he never returned there.

The final 150 pages of the text are topical essays in which Uno assesses aspects of life in China and thirteen qualities he associates with the Chinese "national character" (*kokuminsei*). These essays represent his effort to sort out what he observed and to enter that information coherently back into his mind in such a way that his world view would not be destroyed. In other words, he came to China with the classics in his head; he confronted Chinese realities that seemed to conflict with the purity and perfection of those classics; and then he returned to Japan with a vision of two radically distinct Chinas. In no way did contemporary China injure his mental picture of antiquity; the latter remained completely frozen and idealized. But he was at least able to separate the two and see the need to reintegrate them.

Uno's travel account shares certain elements both with earlier Japanese travel and pilgrimage literature and with the pilgrimage literature of medieval Europe, and reference to those bodies of material may help explain some of the seeming disjunctures in style and presentation of Uno's record. One of the earliest Japanese accounts of foreign travel was the diary of the monk Ennin (793–864), *Nit-Tō guhō junrei gyōki* (The Record of a Pilgrimage to China in Search of the Buddhist Law). But, if one reads through this long account with any expectation of gaining an insight into the mind of Ennin, then one reads in vain. This was his account of a religious quest, and he allowed little of himself to intrude. When the priest Shunjō wrote his account of pilgrimage to Zenkōji in 1225, he similarly says virtually nothing of the scenery along the way, undoubtedly because it was superfluous to his intent in writing and, indeed, in traveling.[28]

As became clearer with subsequent travel and pilgrimage literature in Japan, the reason for such travel was not pleasure, not even of the beauty of a given temple; the idea was to commune directly with the spirit of a divine place. One could pray anywhere, and there were temples and shrines through-out Japan for that purpose, but to go to the source was also seen as the best. Matsuo Bashō (1644–1694) put it succinctly and much more poetically, if in a more secular vein:

> Mountains crumble, rivers flow away, roads are changed, stones are buried and hide in the earth, trees grow old and give way to saplings, times passes and the world changes. Everything is uncertain, but coming here and seeing an inscription that without doubt was a thousand years old, I felt I was now seeing before me the minds of the men of old.[29]

The literature on accounts of European pilgrimages is even richer. Pil-grimage was an extremely important institution in late medieval times. Al-though the Church made allowances for pilgrimage to secondary holy places, such as Rome or Canterbury, the Jerusalem pilgrimage was in a class by itself, necessitating for the truly pious a long voyage (much as travel from Japan all the way to China must have been in Ennin's day). There are hundreds of pilgrimage accounts; and it is this genre that was most responsible for making the metaphor of travel for life itself elemental to early European fiction, from Chaucer's *Canterbury Tales*, to Thomas More's *Utopia*, to Jonathan Swift's *Gulliver's Travels*, and numerous works by Daniel Defoe.[30]

Christian pilgrims had a unilinear sense of history. Getting to the Holy Land was the essential, indeed the only, reason for travel (and travel writing). The return trip home was altogether less important. In fact, this may be why Chaucer never had his pilgrims recount their promised second tales on the return voyage. The process of getting to the Holy Land and the experiences there were all that mattered; thus, every step along the way was worthy of mention. Once there, the Holy Land set off countless images from the past, as recorded in the Bible and associated apocrypha. This was where Jesus had walked and preached and died. Time collapsed. Every sight and sound deserved translation into written form. And, when it was over, there was no purpose, save sinful egotism, in telling the story of the trip home.[31]

There was always an uneasy balance between the Church's willingness to allow pilgrimages and the sin of curiosity (travel and observation for its own intrinsic sake). In a study of fourteenth-century British pilgrimage literature, Christian Zacher notes: "Pilgrimage was a theological idea and a cultural phenomenon—but above all it was a religious institution, a devotional practice which let pious Christians travel through the physical world only because their destinations were places sanctified by spiritual, otherworldly associations." By the end of the Middle Ages, however, the "pilgrimage" had become a thinly veiled excuse to see the outside world itself.[32]

At the end of the fifteenth century, a change transpired in the writing of pilgrim accounts, which Donald Howard associates with a transition from medieval to modern times. Now, pilgrims do include sections in their records that concern the trip home, and the return trip becomes an essential element of the trip itself. It is still not a record of the experiences of that return; rather, it involves the lessons learned, the fresh smells of home, and security from the perils of the journey. It becomes a time for summing up the experience of the pilgrimage, and it allows the author a personal voice beyond that of mere observer. By the sixteenth and seventeenth centuries, curiosity is no longer a sin, but an intellectual strength. The betterment of the self through travel and the return of the pilgrim from the Holy Land to his point of departure are now far more important to the traveler than communing with some relic in Jerusalem.[33]

The travel account of Uno Tetsuto similarly centers entirely on the experiences of getting to and absorbing Ch'ü-fu (the Jerusalem of East Asia) and its surroundings; the rest of his account by comparison pales in vibrancy. In fact, the rest of the account could easily have been written without ever having been in China. Travel to China was not like going to the South Pole or the far side of the moon; as a Kangaku scholar, Uno "knew" China thoroughly before he ever left Japan, just as pilgrims to the Holy Land "knew" the Land of Israel. Both relied exclusively on ancient texts.

Uno's excitement as he sees Chinese soil from aboard his approaching ship, just as had been the case with Naitō Konan several years earlier, parallels European pilgrimage literature. For example, the longest and most thoroughly detailed pilgrim account of the fifteenth century was that of Felix Fabri, a Franciscan monk. Brother Felix describes the great joy (weeping, singing, and the like) of his group of pilgrims when they saw the Holy Land for the first time from sea.[34]

Every sight in the Holy Land, and every problem encountered aboard ship on the way there, was recorded by Brother Felix, because everything became important. Nor was his merely a detailed listing of what passed before his eyes. As we have seen, Uno too had a penchant for descriptive detail, but the cataloguing of sights and sounds in Peking before his trip to Shantung and his many side trips after returning to Peking is qualitatively different from the ecstacy with which he presented the innumerable sights of Shantung.

Felix Fabri's account was also the first pilgrimage chronicle that contained a detailed record of the return voyage. There he laid out the lessons learned as he reentered his life back home. One rarely made a second pilgrimage, so this event was to have inspirational meaning for the rest of one's mortal existence. Although Uno does not describe his return to Japan, he does append several lengthy essays about "the Chinese" in which he tries to explain the source of all their problems in an effort to introduce the contemporary bearers of a once-great civilization to his fellow Japanese.

In part this represents an attempt to domesticate "the Chinese" for the Japanese readership. Uno knew well how culturally indebted Japan was to China, and sorting out what that implied for the contemporary era — the lessons for the present following his trip to China — was highly important. Japan owed its greatness in many regards to its inheritance of mainland traditions, but Japan could only learn by negative example from contemporary China. In part these appended essays represent as well Uno's own effort to make sense out of what he had experienced in China, an attempt to merge the China of the classics with the real China of his day. Because this effort was largely futile and indeed occasioned by a series of experiences external to China, the result is often bizarre, even confusing; although some pearls of wisdom are strewn throughout these essays, ultimately they inform us much more about Japan and Japanese concerns than about China. Many would argue this applies to all travel literature.

The four essays about "the Chinese" all aim to explain customs, institutions, and behavioral patterns. Their topics are: the Chinese family system, social welfare enterprises, the concept of "revolution" (Jap. *kakumei*; Ch. *ko-ming*), and the national character of "the Chinese." Lest there be any doubt about the principal intent of these essays, Uno begins the first of them: "Because China was the wellspring of our Japanese culture, we must study the

Chinese family system to speak intelligently about the Japanese family, ancient and modern." He then moves immediately to make an important distinction, one he shared with other Kangakusha of the time. It is wrong, he contends, to ridicule China for the present decline in political authority of the Chinese state; the government may have no power, but "the Chinese people" indeed remain an influential "ethnic group" (*minzoku*). This point leads Uno to the central theme of these four essays: "My feeling is that as a state China's lack of prosperity has been due to an age-old democracy [*minshushugi*], the changes of dynastic control [Jap. *ekisei kakumei*; Ch. *i-hsing ko-ming*], and the lack of a unifying authority under a fixed sovereign."[35] Japanese readers, for whom this account was of course written, would immediately recognize the implicit comparison Uno has drawn here between China (with its seemingly endless string of changing dynasties) and Japan (with its one, unbroken line still sitting on the throne, descended from the Sun Goddess).

He goes on to say that one reason there is still an entity known as "China," despite countless changes of dynasties, lies in the strength of the Chinese family as the moral fabric of society. This would have been an interesting point to investigate; but, rather than proceed to examine the contemporary Chinese family, or even to make a series of observations, Uno immediately begins citing ancient texts, such as the *Hsiao-ching* (Classic of Filial Piety), and speaking in stereotypical generalities about such personal qualities as "filiality." While we may expect too much if we look for modern sociological analyses in Uno's account, by the same token we should note that one need not go to China to quote from the *Hsiao-ching*, as Japanese had done for centuries. In order to make sense of the distinctive qualities of the Chinese family, Uno does what many of us would probably do: draw on our knowledge of our own culture and note the comparison with the case in China.

> In Japan the imperial family embodies the principle of a large family uniting the entire nation into a single group. Thus, the thorough consistency of loyalty (*chū*) and filial piety (*kō*) exists as an absolute truth (*zettai no shinri*) in Japan. But China is different. There, because of centuries of changing dynastic control, this concept of the family writ large has not taken root, and the unity of loyalty and filiality has not fully developed among the populace. This, I believe, is the greatest cause for China's weakness as a state.[36]

The second essay on China's social welfare institutions begins on the same note of the sad fate that China's "national polity" (*kokutai*) has long been highly democratic, understood as meaning the unstable state structure always subject to rebellion by the people. The very idea of the changeability of Heaven's will that one finds in the Chinese classics speaks directly to the essential "democratic" nature of Chinese civilization. Again, this thesis requires a state-society bifurcation: "In spite of its also having an autocratic state, China has long been a democracy, and the spirit of autonomy [among the local populace] has remained vibrant." The modern Western reader (indeed, many contemporary Chinese readers as well) are likely to read all their own democratic biases into this sentence and think Uno was celebrating China's democratic heritage. Far from it, for democracy was the root of so many of China's ills, in his estimation.

Real power in China, he continues, lies not with the central authorities but with the local gentry (*kyōshin*), for they are the ones who have contact with the Chinese people. Because of this Chinese democracy and the inattentive rule of the central government, local Chinese society (under the leadership of local gentry families) had taken it upon itself, he notes, to establish social and philanthropic institutions.[37]

After a fascinating list and description of these institutions, Uno finds himself painted into a corner. He has noted several times in his account and will soon repeat that the Chinese are by nature egotistical and individualistic. But, we now see that they have probably the most developed system of social philanthropy in the world. Several platitudes about state and society do not elucidate this contradiction. It reflects his own efforts to understand, while simultaneously trying to explain, qualities of life in China for which a thorough knowledge of the classics provides little help. The contradictions here are important in and of themselves, for they slowly become the main story.

The third essay repeats all the empty generalizations about national character and "revolution" that Uno has already laid out above. He does interject the caveat that it is difficult to speak of Chinese national traits because of regional differences, something he reiterates constantly in the travelogue section of his account. He even admits that "it may be impossible" to depict a Chinese national character. Then, without so much as a paragraph break, he begins to do the "impossible." After a rather idiosyncratic reading of late imperial Chinese history, the ultimate cause of all China's problems is once again laid at the door of the country's changing dynastic fortunes. Despite three thousand or more years of autocratic government, he claims, the Chinese classics, histories, and poetry are imbued with a thoroughly democratic spirit — and, therein lies China's tragedy.[38]

How, then, if the entire Chinese tradition is to be labeled "democratic," can one speak of the influence of Confucianism in Japan, which decidedly does not share this democratic propensity? This is no easy matter for Uno. He has been citing text after text to prove how different the Chinese and their historical experience are from the Japanese and theirs. Although this democratic form of government fits the Chinese well, indeed is the root of contemporary China's tragedy, he argues, it is qualitatively different from Confucius's key idea of "serving one's king" (*sonnō*). Thus, Uno distinguishes Confucius from his "democratic" epigones, Mencius and Hsün-tzu. In later ages, the prodemocratic, prorevolutionary ideas introduced by Mencius and others of the late Chou period held sway in China, while the teachings of Confucius never fully developed in the Sage's own homeland. Only in Japan did those teachings find a natural home, further proof of the perfection of the Japanese *kokutai*.[39]

This reading of the history of Chinese thought sets the stage for Uno's delineation of the thirteen character traits of the Chinese, the longest, most revealing, and most contorted of his appended essays. Their first characteristic, expectedly, is "democratic." Uno repeats all his major claims about how the followers of Confucius twisted his most brilliant insight (that of fidelity to one's sovereign); as a result, subsequent thinkers and poets in China all developed ideas of self-contained, autonomous villages, and, simultaneously, because the central government was unreliable, the local populace developed self-defense organizations against bandits.[40]

Second, the Chinese were "familistic" (*kazokushugi*) rather than oriented toward a state or central government. Again, this points to their qualitative difference with the Japanese. Third, the Chinese were "selfish" (*rikoteki*) — namely, concerned with personal gain — a product of their individualistic and family-oriented tendencies. Even Uno recognizes the contradiction at this point: How can the Chinese be both devoted to their families and selfishly individualistic at the same time? Chinese families are formed on the basis of individual bonds in symbiotic fashion; thus, the individual finds personal gain only through devotion to a family. The fact remains that Confucius, Mencius, and their followers through the ages consistently spoke out against selfish profit. How can it have become a basic characteristic of the Chinese people? Uno is unable to solve this conundrum, but he does note that this selfish quality has enabled the Chinese to become extraordinary businessmen.[41]

Uno admits that the fourth quality, superstitiousness, is one that the entire world (including Japan) shares with the Chinese. The Chinese also have a "penchant for exaggeration" (*kochōsei*); in this they far outstrip the more naive Japanese. The Chinese also "follow others blindly" (*fuwa raidō*). This quality would seem to pose yet another contradiction: How can the Chinese be both individualistic and selfish, on the one hand, and blind, unthinking followers of others, on the other? One would also, of course, like to know how a people, an entire ethnic group (*minzoku*), can be any *one* way or another. At fault is the blanket fashion by which theories of national character portray entire nations or peoples. The unspoken assumption throughout these essays is that because he has actually been to China, he has gained firsthand, authoritative information about the Chinese people.

Uno additionally claims that the Chinese are also extremely "sociable," and he offers a bizarre theory of the spoken Chinese language (which he hardly knew at all) in which the musical quality of Chinese affords it all the strengths of vowel-rich languages (a sense of peace and joy) and of consonant-rich languages (a means of articulating anger) elsewhere in the world.[42] This assessment on his part is simply sophomoric, and best forgotten.

As apparently individualistic as the Chinese are, they are also, according to Uno, masters at assimilating foreign beliefs and customs of the non-Han peoples surrounding them and incorporating these alien elements into Han culture. And, as radically and proudly democratic as the Chinese are, Uno claims that they are also extremely conservative. This quality is responsible for the great difficulty Chinese reformers have had in implementing their programs. But not only are the Chinese stubbornly selfish and resistant to external interference in their lives; they are also, in Uno's estimation, submissive, "a people extraordinarily resigned to their lot in life" (*goku akirame no yoki kokumin*). This quality has much to do with their eleventh trait, their peaceful, antiwar, antimilitaristic nature.[43]

The penultimate characteristic of the Chinese, according to Uno, is their extraordinary orientation toward society. This developed sense of society, he argues, fits well with their democratic, peace-loving, autonomous spirit. Indeed, it does, but it would certainly seem to clash with their alleged traits of selfishness, individualism, and blindly following others.

Their final quality is their "leisureliness" (*yūchō naru koto*). The Chinese seem to Uno always to be composed and never under pressure; this is the one characteristic he suggests, albeit equivocally, that the Japanese might want to examine for themselves.[44]

No reader of this last essay could come away with a clear picture of the national character, if we can even speak of such a thing, of the Chinese people. It is a potpourri of contradictory qualities, some extremely interesting, others clearly offensive, all dated. However, it is the confusion itself that should be examined, for we learn nothing by studying Uno's ideas by themselves in an effort to resolve the contradictions. Uno had gone to China for the first time with a preconceived image of China drawn exclusively from classical texts. China was a place he thought he knew. He was making a pilgrimage to the origins of civilization itself. But something—many things—went wrong. The contemporary Chinese were not living up to the great standards set down in the Chou dynasty; actually, it was the Japanese who were doing it, as indicated by his bifurcation of Confucius from the subsequent Confucian tradition. Only the Japanese were still loyal to the original Confucius, while the Chinese had followed a frighteningly democratic road from the time of Mencius.

Uno was too intelligent and too devoted to Chinese (or East Asian) culture to jettison the entire Kangaku tradition, to lose faith in his image of "China." That survived in frozen, still-life form, but contemporary China had to be incorporated somehow into this image of China. However disjointed we may find the two Chinas in reading Uno now, he felt compelled to unify them. His effort was not a rousing success, as his last essay on Chinese character traits indicates. He was still too confused himself. What is ironic is that he commenced this voyage—at least the writing of his account after returning, as noted at the outset—intent on overcoming the plastic images people had been popularizing about China. "Those who understand China," he wrote in his introduction to this travel account, "by reading its revered classics and sagely scriptures of antiquity may think that China is a paradise on Earth with sages and men of virtue wafting about like the clouds." One cannot help but think that this was an autobiographical admission. But what began as an effort to overcome a simplistic and stereotypical view of China ended up providing just that: a stereotypical view with thirteen well-defined national characteristics.

Uno lived nearly another seventy years and reached the pinnacle of his profession at Tokyo University in Japan. His was the last Kangaku travel account of China that, initially at least, entertained an undiluted picture of a pristine China. Kangaku scholars would still travel in China and write about their experiences, but Uno was the last of the great ones in Meiji Japan. It is a telling fact that he completed his account in 1912, just after the final collapse of the imperial system in China and just a few months before the end of the Meiji period. His is also the last travel account of China that truly followed Bashō's credo: "Do not seek to follow in the footsteps of the men of old; seek what they sought."[45]

NOTES

1. Uno Tetsuto, *Shina bunmei ki* (Tokyo: Daidōkan, 1912), 1–2.

2. Take, for example, the case of Sone Toshitora (1847–1910). One of the earliest advocates of genuine Sino-Japanese friendship, Sone was a naval officer who first went to China in 1873 to accompany Foreign Minister Soejima Taneomi on official business. See Kuzuu Yoshihisa, *Tō-A senkaku shishi kiden* (Biographies of Pioneer Men of Spirit in East Asia) (Tokyo: Kokuryūkai shuppanbu, 1933–1936), 316. He made many trips thereafter and enjoyed the friendship of such Chinese intellectuals as Wang T'ao and Feng Tzu-yu (1882–1958). The latter wrote of him: "Among the Japanese, Sone was the most concerned with Chinese affairs." See Feng, *Chung-hua min-kuo k'ai-kuo ch'ien ko-ming shih* (A History of the Revolution Before the Founding of the Republic of China) (Shanghai: Ko-ming shih pien-chi she, 1928), vol. 1, p. 303.

He made another trip to China late in 1874 and transcribed a long and detailed description of the activities of the Taiping rebels from a monk at the Ching-chi Temple. He also copied out a manifesto delivered in 1858 by Hung Hsiu-ch'üan (1813–1864) and his "kings." And, he compiled yet another account when he returned in 1875 and 1876, describing his travels to Chinese and Korean port cities and military installations and his meetings with local officials; he also listed the prices of virtually every product in every place he visited, as well as the temperature and a whole host of other information. See Sone, *Shinkoku manyū shi* (Record of Travels through China) (Tokyo: Sekibunsha, 1883), as cited in *Meiji ikō Nihonjin no Chūgoku ryokōki* (Japanese Travel Accounts of China from the Meiji Period On) (Tokyo: Tōyō bunko, 1980), 1–2.

Sone's true motives remain murky, however, for recent research indicates that he was in fact passing all his information directly to the highest levels of the Japanese government and military. He wrote a report in 1881 that detailed the cargoes at various ports in China. See his *Shinkoku kakkōbin ran* (An Overview of the Ports in China) (n.p., 1881). In 1884, Sone was assigned as Japan's official observer of the Sino-French conflict over Annam, and he criticized the Japanese government for failing to come to the aid of the Chinese. See his *Hō-Etsu kōhei ki* (Record of Conflict Between France and Annam), ed. Wang T'ao (1886; reprinted, Taipei: Wen-hai ch'u-pan she, 1971); and Paul Cohen, *Between Tradition and Modernity: Wang T'ao and Reform in Late Ch'ing China* (Cambridge: Harvard University Press, 1974), 103–4. Yet, in this 1884 trip report, he provided a wealth of intelligence on the port of Yen-t'ai (Shantung), including troop and ship numbers and the speed and variety of the ships. He noted as well that Yen-t'ai would be the crux of a naval victory over the Ch'ing. When Port Arthur fell to the Japanese in 1894, Japanese forces attacked at Weihaiwei, near Yen-t'ai, where the Peiyang naval armada was crushed, just as Sone had hinted would be the case. See Kawamura Kazuo, "Kaigun taii Sone Toshitora no Shinkoku shisatsu ni tsuite" (On Lieutenant Sone Toshitora's Inspections of China), *Gunji shigaku* (December 1978), 39:44–48.

3. Takezoe Shin'ichirō, *San'un kyōu nikki*, translated from Kanbun into classical Japanese by Yonaiyama Tsuneo (Tokyo: Ōsaka yagō shoten, 1944). See also Takeuchi Minoru, "Meiji Kangakusha no Chūgoku kikō" (Travel Accounts of China by Kangaku Scholars of the Meiji Period), in Takeuchi, *Nihonjin ni totte no Chūgoku zō* (Japanese Images of China) (Tokyo: Shunjūsha, 1966), 232–44; and Fuse Chisoku, *Yūki ni arewaretaru Meiji jidai no Nis-Shi ōrai* (Sino-Japanese Intercourse in the Meiji Era as Seen in Travel Accounts) (Tokyo: Tō-A kenkyūkai, 1938), 34–44.

4. Komuro Shinsuke, *Daiichi yū-Shin ki* (Record of a First Trip to China), in *Meiji ikō Nihonjin no Chūgoku ryokōki*, 2–3. See also the marvelous piece on Huc by Simon Leys, "Peregrinations and Perplexities of Père Huc," in Leys, *The Burning Forest: Essays on Chinese Culture and Politics* (New York: Holt, Rinehart and Winston, 1986), 47–94.

5. Oka Senjin, *Kankō kiyū* (self-published, 1892), entry for July 25, 1884. See also Takeuchi, "Meiji Kangakusha no Chūgoku kikō," 249–55; and Fuse, *Yūki ni arewaretaru Meiji jidai no Nis-Shi ōrai*, 44–58.

6. See Takeuchi, "Meiji Kangakusha no Chūgoku kikō," 258.

7. Ibid., 250, 262.

8. Sugita Tei'ichi, "Yū-Shin yokan" (Impressions from a Trip to China), included in Saika Hakuai, *Sugita Kakuzan ō* (The Venerable Sugita Kakuzan [Tei'ichi]) (Tokyo: Kakuzankai, 1928), 582–85. See also Hashikawa Bunsō [Bunzō], "Japanese Perspectives on Asia: From Dissociation to Coprosperity," in Akira Iriye, ed., *The Chinese and the Japanese: Essays in Political and Cultural Interactions* (Princeton: Princeton University Press, 1980), 331–33.

9. Andō Fujio, *Shina manyū jikki* (Tokyo: Hakubutsukan, 1892). See also *Meiji ikō Nihonjin no Chūgoku ryokōki*, 5; and Takeuchi Minoru, "Sandai no Chūgoku kenbun" (Travelers to China of Three Eras), in Takeuchi, *Nihonjin ni totte no Chūgoku zō*, 222.

10. Miyauchi Isaburō, *Shinkoku jijō tanken roku* (Record of a Factual Investigation of China) (Tokyo: Shinkoku jijō henshū kyoku, 1894), 1a.

11. Okakura Tenshin, "Shina nanboku no kubun' (The Difference Between North and South China), *Kokka* (March 1894), 54, reprinted in *Okakura Tenshin zenshū* (The Collected Works of Okakura Tenshin) (Tokyo: Seibunkaku, 1939), 191–98; Saitō Ryūzō, *Okakura Tenshin* (Tokyo: Yoshikawa kōbunkan, 1960), 73–78; Kiyomi Rikurō, *Okakura Tenshin* (Tokyo: Heibonsha, 1934), 70–87; Okakura Kazuo, *Chichi Okakura Tenshin* (My Father, Okakura Tenshin) (Tokyo: Chūō kōron sha, 1971), 84–104; Hashikawa Bunzō, "Fukuzawa Yukichi to Okakura Tenshin" (Fukuzawa Yukichi and Okakura Tenshin), in Takeuchi Yoshimi and Hashikawa Bunzō, eds., *Kindai Nihon to Chūgoku* (Modern Japan and China) (Tokyo: Asahi shinbun sha, 1974), vol. 1, pp. 27, 29–32; and Takeuchi Minoru, "Ajia wa hitotsu nari: Okakura Tenshin to Izuru" (Asia Is One: Okakura Tenshin and Izuru), in Takeuchi, *Kikō Nihon no naka no Chūgoku* (China in Travel Accounts of Japan) (Tokyo: Asahi shinbun sha, 1976), 65–85.

12. Takase Bintoku, *Hoku-Shin kenbunroku* (Record of a Trip to North China), in *Meiji ikō Nihonjin no Chūgoku ryokōki*, 12.

13. Tokutomi Iichirō [Sohō], *Nanajūyōka yūki* (Record of a Trip of Seventy-Eight Days) (Tokyo: Min'yūsha, 1906), included in *Sekai kikō bungaku zenshū* (Collection of International Travel Literature) (Tokyo: Shūdō sha, 1959), vol. 11, pp. 64, 73.

14. In *Sekai kikō bungaku zenshū*, vol. 11, p. 74. See also *Meiji ikō Nihonjin no Chūgoku ryokōki*, 14–15.

15. Masuda Wataru, "Yamamoto Ken (Baigai)," in Masuda, *Seigaku tōzen to Chūgoku jijō* (The Spread of Western Learning to the East and Conditions in China), 322–25, 330–33, 337–42 (Tokyo: Iwanami shoten, 1979); and Fuse, *Yūki ni arewaretaru Meiji jidai no Nis-Shi ōrai*, 58–64.

16. Joshua Fogel, *Politics and Sinology: The Case of Naitō Konan (1866–1934)* (Cambridge: Council on East Asian Studies, Harvard University, 1984), 91–109. *Enzan sosui* can be found in Naitō Kenkichi and Kanda Kiichiro, eds., *Naitō Konan zenshū* (The Collected Works of Naitō Konan) (Tokyo: Chikuma shobō, 1971), vol. 2, pp. 1–178; reading it, which

is very difficult, can be greatly facilitated by the annotations in the appropriate sections of Ogawa Tamaki, *Nihon no meicho: Naitō Konan* (Masterpieces of Japan: Naitō Konan) (Tokyo: Chūō kōron sha, 1971).

17. This concern of Naitō's account prompted Ojima Sukema to refer to it as a work of statecraft (*keisei*), "Konan sensei to *Enzan sosui*" (The *Enzan sosui* and Professor [Naitō] Konan), *Shinagaku* (July 1934), 7(3):533–34.

18. Before his appointment at Tokyo Imperial University, Uno taught Kanbun for a time at the high-school level, where among his pupils was a young Morohashi Tetsuji (1883–1983). For nearly two decades, he and Hattori Unokichi (1867–1939) were the two pillars of learning in Chinese philosophy at Tokyo University. In 1931 he became dean of the Faculty of Letters; in 1936 he retired and became professor emeritus. From 1939 to 1944 he traveled to Peking annually to give lectures on Chinese philosophy, and he was named a professor emeritus of Peking University in 1939. His publications and annotated translations are numerous; and two *Festschriften* were published in his honor, one on his eighty-eighth birthday and one on his ninety-ninth. See Yen Shao-tang, *Jih-pen ti Chung-kuo-hsüeh-chia* (Japanese Sinologists) (Peking: Hsin-hua shu-chü, 1980), 580–81; Morohashi Tetsuji, "Uno sensei no omoide" (Memories of Professor Uno), *Tōhōgaku* (1974), 48:148–49; Katō Jōken, "Tsuitōbun" (Eulogy), *Tōhōgaku* (1974), 48:152; Abe Yoshio, "Daidō o ayumareta Uno Tetsuto" (Uno Tetsuto Who Traveled the Great Way of Morality), *Tōhōgaku* (1974), 48:154, 156; and Akatsuka Kiyoshi, "Uno sensei no *Jugaku shi*" (Professor Uno's *History of Confucianism*), *Tōhōgaku* (1974), 48:160–63.

19. Uno, *Shina bunmei ki*, 2–10.

20. Takeuchi Minoru, "Aru Kangakusha no Chūgoku kikō" (One Kangakusha's Travel Account of China), in Takeuchi, *Nihonjin ni totte no Chūgoku zō*, 274. Tun Li-ch'en was the Chinese name adopted by Tun-ch'ung, a Manchu by birth. This work by him has been translated into English by Derk Bodde as *Annual Customs and Festivals in Peking* (Peiping: H. Vetch, 1936; reprinted, Hong Kong: Hong Kong University Press, 1965). Thanks to Susan Naquin for bringing the translation to my attention.

21. Uno, *Shina bunmei ki*, 125–38, citations on pp. 130, 132, respectively.

22. Ibid., 139, 142–46, citation on p. 146.

23. Ibid., 146.

24. Ibid., 148–49.

25. Ibid., 149–53, photographs between p. 146 and p. 147, citation on pp. 152–53.

26. Ibid., 154.

27. Ibid., 155, 163.

28. Donald Keene, *Travelers of a Hundred Ages* (New York: Henry Holt, 1989), 17–20, 121, 203. Some years ago, Edwin O. Reischauer translated Ennin's diary into English as *Ennin: The Record of a Pilgrimage to China in Search of the Law* (New York: Ronald Press Company, 1955).

29. As cited in Keene, *Travelers of a Hundred Ages*, 225. See also pp. 30, 34–35.

30. Donald R. Howard, *Writers and Pilgrims: Medieval Pilgrimage Narratives and Their Posterity* (Berkeley: University of California Press, 1980), 11–12; Percy G. Adams, *Travel Literature and the Evolution of the Novel* (Lexington: University Press of Kentucky, 1983), 38, 60, 112–13, 254, 259–60, 275; and Percy G. Adams, *Travelers and Travel Liars, 1660–1800* (Berkeley: University of California Press, 1962), 78–79, 90, 229, *passim*.

31. Howard, *Writers and Pilgrims*, 50–51, 69, 77–78, 86–87, 97, 117.

32. Christian K. Zacher, *Curiosity and Pilgrimage: The Literature of Discovery in Fourteenth-Century England* (Baltimore: Johns Hopkins University Press, 1976), 4–5, citation on p. 4.

33. Howard, *Writers and Pilgrims*, 42–43, 45, 48, 106–7.

34. Uno. *Shina bunmei ki*, 2; Howard, *Writers and Pilgrims*, 36–44.

35. Uno, *Shina bunmei ki*, 343–44.

36. Ibid., 344–46, 348, citation on p. 350.

37. Ibid., 353–56, citation on p. 354. Naitō Konan was coming to similar conclusions at precisely the same time.

38. Ibid., 362–68, citation on p. 363.

39. Ibid., 369–70.

40. Ibid., 370–73. Again Naitō Konan was developing virtually identical ideas at this time; see especially his *Shinaron* (On China), translated in part by Joshua A. Fogel, in *Naitō Konan and the Development of the Conception of Modernity in Chinese History* (Armonk, NY: M. E. Sharpe, 1984).

41. Uno, *Shina bunmei ki*, 373–79.

42. Ibid., 379–86.

43. Ibid., 386–91, citation on p. 389.

44. Ibid., 391–92.

45. As cited in Keene, *Travelers of a Hundred Ages*, 220.

GLOSSARY

Abe Yoshio　　阿部吉雄

"Ajia wa hitotsu nari: Okakura Tenshin to Izuru"　　亞細亞は一つなり: 岡倉天
心と玉浦

Akatsuka Kiyoshi　　赤塚忠

Andō Fujio　　安東不二雄

An-tung　　安東

"Aru Kangakusha no Chūgoku kikō"　　ある漢學者の中國紀行

bakufu　　幕府

Chang Chien　　張謇

Chang Yüan-chi　　張元濟

Cheefu (Chih-fu)　　芝罘

Ch'i　　齊

Chichi Okakura Tenshin　　父岡倉天心

Chih Sheng　　至聖

Ch'ing　　清

Ching-chi　淨慈

chū　忠

Ch'un-ch'iu　春秋

Ch'ü-fu　曲阜

Chung-hua min-kuo k'ai-kuo ch'ien ko-ming shih　中華民國開國前革命史

chü-jen　舉人

chūtō shakai　中等社會

Daiichi yū-Shin Ki　第一遊清記

"Daidō o ayumareta Uno Tetsuto"　大道を歩まれた宇野哲人

datsu-A　脱亞

ekisei kakumei (i-hsing ko-ming)　易姓革命

endoku　煙毒

Ennin　圓仁

Enzan sosui　燕山楚水

Enzan sosui kiyū　燕山楚水紀遊

Feng Tzu-yu　馮自由

Fukuzawa Yukichi　福澤諭吉

"Fukuzawa Yukichi to Okakura Tenshin"　福澤諭吉と岡倉天心

Fuse Chisoku　布施知足

fuwa raidō　附和雷同

goku akirame no yoki kokumin　極くアキラメのよき國民

Gunji shigaku　軍事史學

hanahada urusai　甚だうるさい

Hashikawa Bunsō (Bunzō)　橋川文三

Hattori Unokichi　服部宇之吉

Hibino Teruhiro　日比野輝寛

Hinomaru　日の丸

hitsudan (pi-t'an)　筆談

Hō-Etsu kōhei ki　法越交兵記

Hoku-Shin kenbunroku　北清見聞錄

Honan　河南

Hopeh　河北

Hsiao-ching　孝經

Hsüan　宣

Hung Hsiu-ch'üan   洪秀全

Jih-pen ti Chung-kuo-hsüeh-chia   日本的中國學家

Kaifeng   開封

"Kaigun taii Sone Toshitora no Shinkoku shisatsu ni tsuite"   海軍大尉曽根俊
虎の清國視察について

kakumei (ko-ming)   革命

Kanbun   漢文

Kanda Kiichirō   神田喜一郎

Kangakusha   漢學者

K'ang Yu-wei   康有為

Kankō kiyū   觀光紀遊

Katō Jōken   加藤敍賢

katsuratsutaru shōnen   潑剌たる少年

Kawamura Kazuo   河村一雄

kazokushugi   家族主義

keidoku   經毒

keisei   經世

Kikō Nihon no naka no Chūgoku   紀行日本のなかの中國

Kindai Nihon to Chūgoku   近代日本と中國

Kishida Ginkō   岸田吟香

Kiyomi Rikurō   清見陸郎

kō   孝

kochōsei   誇張性

Kokka   國華

kokka (nation)   國家

kokuminsei   國民性

kokutai   國體

Komuro Shinsuke   小室進助

"Konan sensei to *Enzan sosui*"   湖南先生と燕山楚水

K'ung-chiao   孔教

Kuzuu Yoshihisa   葛生良久

kyōshin   鄉紳

Li Hung-chang   李鴻章

Liang Ch'i-ch'ao   梁啟超

Liao-chou-wan　膠州灣

Liu　劉

Liu Hsüeh-hsün　劉學詢

Lo Chen-yü　羅振玉

Lu　魯

Lu Hsün　魯迅

Masuda Wataru　增田涉

Matsuo Bashō　松尾芭蕉

"Meiji Kangakusha no Chūgoku kikō"　明治漢學者の中國紀行

Meiji ikō Nihonjin no Chūgoku ryokōki　明治以降日本人の中國旅行記

minshushugi　民主主義

minzoku　民族

Miyauchi Isaburō　宮內猪三郎

Morohashi Tetsuji　諸橋轍次

Naitō Kenkichi　內藤乾吉

Naitō Konan　內藤湖南

Naitō Konan zenshū　內藤湖南全集

Nanajū yōka yūki　七十四日遊記

Nihonjin ni totte no Chūgoku zō　日本人にとつての中國像

Nihon no meicho: Naitō Konan　日本の名著：內藤湖南

Nit-Tō guhō junrei gyōki　入唐求法巡禮行記

Ogawa Tamaki　小川環樹

Ojima Sukema　小島祐馬

Oka Senjin　岡千仞

Okakura Kazuo　岡倉一雄

Okakura Tenshin　岡倉天心

Okakura Tenshin zenshū　岡倉天心全集

Peiyang　北洋

ridatsu　離脫

rikoteki　利己的

Saika Hakuai　雜賀博愛

Saitō Ryūzō　齊藤隆三

"Sandai no Chūgoku kenbun"　三代の中國見聞

San'un kyōu nikki　棧雲峽雨日記

Seigaku tōzen to Chūgoku jijō　西學東漸と中國事情

Sekai kikō bungaku zenshū　世界紀行文學全集

Senzaimaru　千歲丸

Shao-hsing　紹興

Sheng Hsüan-huai　盛宣懷

Sheng-miao　聖廟

Shih chi　史記

Shina bunmei ki　支那文明記

Shinagaku　支那學

Shina manyū jikki　支那漫遊實記

"Shina nanboku no kubun"　支那南北の區分

Shina ni Shina nashi　支那に支那無し

Shinaron　支那論

Shinkoku jijō tanken roku　清國事情探檢錄

Shinkoku kakkōbin ran　清國各港便覽

Shinkoku manyū shi　清國漫遊誌

Shunjō　俊芿

Soejima Taneomi　副島種臣

Sone Toshitora　曽根俊虎

sonnō　尊王

Ssu-ma Kuang　司馬光

Su Tung-p'o　蘇東坡

Sugita Teiichi　杉田定一

Sugita Kakuzan ō　杉田鶉山翁

T'ai (Mt.)　泰

T'ai-an-fu　泰安府

Taiping　太平

Takase Bintoku　高瀬敏德

Takasugi Shinsaku　高杉晉作

Takeuchi Minoru　竹內實

Takeuchi Yoshimi　竹內好

Takezoe Shin'inchirō　竹添進一郎

T'ang-ku　塘沽

Tientsin　天津

Tō-A senkaku shishi kiden　東亞先覺志士記傳

Toen kunshikoku　東瀛君子國

Tōhōgaku　東方學

Tokutomi Iichirō　德富猪一郎

Tokutomi Sohō　德富蘇峰

Tsinan　濟南

Tsingtao　青島

Tsou　鄒

"Tsuitōbun"　追悼文

Tun-ch'ung　敦崇

Tun Li-ch'en　敦禮臣

Tzu-chih t'ung-chien　資治通鑑

"Uno sensei no *Jugaku shi*"　宇野先生の儒學史

"Uno sensei no omoide"　宇野先生の思い出

Uno Tetsuto　宇野哲人

Wang K'ang-nien　汪康年

Wang T'ao　王韜

Wang Yen-yün　王硯雲

Weihaiwei　威海衛

Wen T'ing-shih　文廷式

Yamamoto Ken　山本憲

Yamamoto Baigai　山本梅崖

yameru rōya　病める老爺

Yang Shih-hsiang　楊土驤

Yeh-chiao　耶教

Yen-ching sui-shih-chi　燕京歲時記

Yen Fu　嚴復

Yen Hui　顏回

Yen Shao-tang　嚴紹璗

Yen-t'ai　沿台

Yonaiyama Tsuneo　米內山庸夫

yūchō naru koto　悠長なること

Yūki ni arawaretaru Meiji jidai no Nis-Shi ōrai　遊記に現はれたる明治時代の日支往來

Yü Kou　玉構
"Yü-Shin yokan"　遊清餘感
Zenkōji　善光寺
zettai no shinri　絕對の真理

CONTRIBUTORS

Martin Amster is a doctoral candidate in the Department of East Asian Languages and Cultures, Columbia University. His interests include the cultural history of the Warring States and early Han periods in China.

Judith A. Berling is Professor of History of Religions at the Graduate Theological Union in Berkeley. Her publications include *The Syncretic Religion of Lin Chao-en* (1980); "Three Teachings Thought in the Mongol-Yüan Period" (co-authored with Liu Ts'un-yüan), in Hok-lam Chan and Wm. Theodore de Bary, eds., *Yüan Thought* (1983); "Religion and Popular Culture: The Management of Moral Capital in the *Romance of the Three Teachings*," in Andrew J. Nathan, Evelyn Rawski, and David Johnson, eds., *Popular Culture in Late Imperial China* (1985); and "Self and Whole in Chuang Tzu," in Donald J. Munro, ed., *Individualism and Holism: Studies in Confucian and Taoist Values* (1985). Her present research deals with the role of ecumenism and religious diversity in theological education and the relationship of theological education to public universities. A book in progress is entitled *Living with Religious Neighbors: Lessons for Us from the Chinese*.

Irene Bloom is Wm. Theodore and Fanny Brett de Bary and Class of 1941 Collegiate Associate Professor of Asian Humanities at Columbia University and chair of the Department of Asian and Middle Eastern Cultures at Barnard College. She is editor, with Wm. Theodore de Bary, of *Principle and Practicality* (1987) and of *Approaches to the Asian Classics* (1990). With J. Paul Martin and Wayne Proudfoot, she is editor of *Religious Diversity and Human Rights* (forthcoming, 1996). She is the editor and translator of *Knowledge Painfully Acquired: The K'un-chin chi of Lo Ch'in-shun* (1989).

Julia Ching is University Professor at the University of Toronto. Among her many books and articles are *To Acquire Wisdom — The Way of Wang Yang-ming* (1976) and *The Records of Ming Scholars by Huang Tsung-hsi* (1987), which was edited in collaboration of Chaoying Fang. Her most recent publications include *Probing China's Soul* (1990) and *Chinese Religions* (1993).

Patricia Buckley Ebrey is Professor of East Asian studies and history and head of the Department of East Asian Languages and Cultures at the University of Illinois at Urbana-Champaign. Among her publications are *Family and Property in Sung China — Yüan Ts'ai's Precepts for Social Life* (1984), *Chu Hsi's Family Rituals — A Twelfth-Century Chinese Manual for the Performance of Cappings, Weddings, Funerals, and Ancestral Rites* (1991), and *Confucianism and Family Rituals in Imperial China — A Social History of Writing about Rites* (1991). For her work *The Inner Quarters — Marriage and the Lives of Chinese Women in the Sung Period*, she was awarded the Joseph Levenson Prize of the Association for Asian Studies for the most outstanding book in traditional Chinese studies published in 1993.

Joshua A. Fogel is Professor of Chinese and comparative East Asian history at the University of California, Santa Barbara, and is editor of the international journal, *Sino-Japanese Studies*. He is author of *Politics and Sinology: The Case of Naitō Konan (1866–1934)* (1984); *Ai Ssu-ch'i's Contribution to the Development of Chinese Marxism* (1987); *Nakae Ushikichi in China: The Mourning of Spirit* (1989); *The Cultural Dimension of Sino-Japanese Relations* (1994); and *The Literature of Travel in the Japanese Rediscovery of China, 1862–1945* (1996). He has also published nine volumes of translation.

Minamoto Ryōen has taught at Japan Women's College and Tōhoku University and is now Professor at the International Christian University. His many publications include *Giri to ninjō* (Duty and Human Emotions, 1972), *Tokugawa gōri shisō no keifu* (Pedigree of Tokugawa Rationalist Thought, 1972), *Tokugawa shisō no shōshi* (A Short History of Tokugawa Thought, 1973), *Kinsei shoki jitsugaku shisō no kenkyū* (Studies in Practical Learning in the Early Part of the Early Modern Era, 1989), and *Edo kōki no hikaku bunka kenkyū* (Studies in Comparative Culture of the Late Edo Period, 1990).

Peter Nosco is Professor of East Asian languages and cultures and of history at the University of Southern California. He is the author of *Remembering Paradise: Nativism and Nostalgia in Eighteenth-Century Japan* (1990), the editor of *Confucianism and Tokugawa Culture* (1984), and the translator of Ihara Saikaku's *Some Final Words of Advice* (1980). He guest-edited a special issue of the *Japanese Journal of Religious Studies* on "The Emperor System and Religion in Japan" (17, nos. 2–3), He is currently doing research on underground religious communities in early modern Japan.

Okada Takehiko is Professor Emeritus of Chinese at Kyūshū University. He has held faculty positions at Kassui Women's College and Seinan-Gakuin University and has been a visiting professor at Columbia University. His many volumes in Japanese include *Zazen to seiza* (Zen Meditation and Quiet-sitting, 1972), *Ō Yōmei to Minmatsu no Jugaku* (Wang Yang-ming and Late Ming Confucianism, 1970), *Sō Min tetsugaku josetsu* (Introduction to the Philosophy of the Sung and Ming Periods, 1977), *Sō Min tetsugaku no honshitsu* (The Essence of the Philosophy of the Sung and Ming Periods, 1984), *Edo ki no Jugaku* (Confucian Learning of the Tokugawa Period, 1982), and *Kinsei kōki Jugaku* (Confucian Writings of the Late Tokugawa Period, 1972). He has been the editor of some of the most important studies of Neo-Confucian thought, including *Shushigaku taikei* (An Outline of the Learning of the Chu Hsi School, 15 vols., 1974) and *Yōmeigaku taikei* (An Outline of the Learning of the Wang Yang-ming School, 12 vols., 1986), as well as *Kusumoto Tanzan Sekisui zenshū* (The Complete Works of Kusumoto Tanzan and Kusumoto Sekisui, 1980) and a fifty-volume series on Japanese thought.

Koichi Shinohara is Professor of religious studies, McMaster University. With Phyllis Granoff, he edited *Monks and Magicians: Religious Biographies in Asia* (1988) and co-authored *Speaking of Monks: Religious Biography in India and China* (1992). With Gregory Schopen, he edited *From Benares to*

Beijing: Essays on Buddhism and Chinese Religion in Honour of Dr. Jan Yün-hua (1991).

Rodney L. Taylor is Professor of religious studies and associate dean of the Graduate School at the University of Colorado at Boulder. His works include *The Cultivation of Sagehood as a Religious Goal in Neo-Confucianism* (1978), (with F. M. Denny) *The Holy Book in Comparative Perspective* (1985), *The Way of Heaven: An Introduction to the Confucian Religious Life* (1986), *The Confucian Way of Contemplation; Okada Takehiko and the Tradition of Quiet-Sitting* (1988), (with J. Watson) *They Shall Not Hurt: Human Suffering and Human Caring* (1989), and *The Religious Dimensions of Neo-Confucianism* (1990).

Chün-fang Yü is Professor of religion at Rutgers, The State University of New Jersey. She specializes in the history of Chinese Buddhism since the T'ang dynasty. Her publications include *The Renewal of Buddhism in China: Chu-hung and the Late Ming Synthesis* (1981) and *Pilgrims and Sacred Sites in China* (co-edited with Susan Naquin, 1992). She is currently writing a book on the cult of Kuan-yin in China.

INDEX

Tao-chiao (Taoist religion), 108
tao-li (meaning), 112
tao-yin (inferior effort), 124
Taoism, 108, 123; and Chu Hsi, 108–132 *passim*; religion, 109; deities, 123; borrowings from Buddhism, 131; Canon, 116; concept of the Three Pure Ones, 131; philosophy, 122; practice of counting, 124
te (moral qualities/virtue), 15, 24, 112
Te-ch'ing (1546–1623), 149, 211
tea ceremony, 304, 305
technique (Ch. *shu*; Jap. *jutsu*), 298
Temple of Confucius, 351–352
temporal change (*jihen*), 254
Tengu geijutsuron (On the Skill of the Tengu), 309, 312
tenka (all under Heaven), 248
tetsugaku (philosophy; Ch. *che-hsüeh*), 301
Text Critical school, 255
that-which-is-so-of-itself (Ch. *tzu-jan*; Jap. *shizen*), 309
thought of the mind-and-heart (*kokoro* thought) in the Bakumatsu era, 258
Three Bonds and Five Constant Virtues, 213
Three Buddhas (Lamplighter, Sakyamuni, and Maitreya), 215
Three Teachings, 209–213, 216, 217, 223, 224, 226, 228, 230, 231, 241, 251, 254, 257
t'i (substance), 191
t'i/yung (substance and function), 25
t'ien-chi (heavenly secrets), 119
t'ien-ming chih hsing (nature ordained by t'ien), 29; *see also* human nature
t'ien-wen (astrology/astronomy), 92
ti-li (geomancy), 83, 87, 89, 92
Ti-li hsin-shu (The New Book of Earth Patterns), 76, 79
Ti-li ching (Classic of Earth Patterns), 78
t'ien-li (principle of nature), 26
T'ien-t'ai (Buddhist sect), 230
Toda Mosui (1629–1706), 284
Tokugawa *bakufu*, 238, 249, 342; and Confucianism, 281–283

Tokugawa gōri shisō no keifu (Lineages of Rationalist Thought in the Tokugawa Period) (Minamoto Ryōen), 239
Tokugawa Ietsugu, 287
Tokugawa Ieyasu, 282, 306
Tokugawa Mitsukuni (1628–1701), 282–284
Tokugawa Tsunayoshi (r. 1680–1709), 286–287
Tokugawa Yoshimune (1684–1751), 284, 287
Tokutomi Sohō (1863–1957), 346, 349
Tominaga Nakamoto (1715–1746), 255
Tosanan School (Tosanangaku/Hayashi Razan), 240
traces (Jap. *seki* or *ato*; Ch. *chi*), 253
Tripiṭaka, 161
True Way, 308
truth (Ch. *chen-li*; Jap. *shinri*), 301
ts'ai (capabilities), 20, 21
Ts'ai Fa, 92
Ts'ai Chi-t'ung: *see* Ts'ai Yüan-ting
Ts'ai Ching (1046–1126), 146
Ts'ai Yüan-ting (Ts'ai Chi-t'ung, 1135–1198), 57, 71, 92–95, 96, 109, 118, 127, 130
Ts'an-t'ung-ch'i, 109, 117–120, 122, 130, 131
Ts'an-t'ung-ch'i k'ao-i (A Study of the Ts'an-t'ung-ch'i), 110, 117–120, 122, 126, 130, 131
Ts'ao-mu shih-i (Corrected Pharmocopeia) (Ch'en Tsang-ch'i), 152
Tsa-hsüeh pien (Essay on Miscellaneous Teachings) (Chu Hsi), 188
Tsai Wo, 14
tsang-shih (burial specialists) Ssu-ma Kuang on, 80
Tsang-shu (Book of Burials), 76
Tseng K'ai, 175–194, *passim*; letter of, 176–177; and Neo-Confucian Learning, profile as statesman, 186–189; *Sung shih* biography of, 181, 186
Tseng-tzu, 12
tso-ch'an (sitting meditation), 56, 64
Tsurezuregusa (Essays in Idleness) (Yoshida Kenkō), 287